ROOSEVELT'S PURGE

ROOSEVELT'S PURGE

How FDR Fought to Change the Democratic Party

SUSAN DUNN

The Belknap Press of Harvard University Press

Cambridge, Massachusetts

London, England

2010

.

Library of Congress Cataloging-in-Publication Data

Dunn, Susan, 1945–

Roosevelt's purge : how FDR fought to change the Democratic Party / Susan
Dunn.

p. cm.

Includes bibliographical references and index.

ISBN 978-0-674-05717-3 (alk. paper)

1. Democratic Party (U.S.)—History—20th century. 2. United States—Politics
and government—1933–1945. 3. Roosevelt, Franklin D. (Franklin Delano),
1882–1945. I. Title.

JK2316.D86 2010

324.273609´043—dc22   2010022411

For my two teams,

    Deborah Davidson

    Naomi Pasachoff

    Jane Howland

    Kit Dobelle

    Phyllis Cutler

    Tela Zasloff

    Carole Siegel

    Suzanne Laloë

    Dori Katz

    Adriana Brown

    Spyros Triantos

    Tammy Winters

    Joan Paradis

Contents

ROOSEVELT'S PURGE

◄ I ►

Getting Ready to Fight

IT WAS PAST MIDNIGHT on March 31, 1938. Franklin Roosevelt was asleep in the Little White House in Warm Springs, Georgia. It was a modest getaway, a one-story cottage with a combination living and dining room, three small bedrooms, and the refrigerator on the back porch.

While the president slept, his appointments secretary, Marvin McIntyre, was still working. A former newspaperman from Kentucky whose friendship with Roosevelt went back twenty years, McIntyre sent out word to the reporters covering the president in Georgia that he had breaking news. Most of the reporters were still awake, playing bridge or ping-pong or attending a carnival in nearby Manchester. When they assembled, McIntyre handed out copies of a statement written by the president himself. "A. I have no inclination to be a dictator," it read. "B. I have none of the qualifications which would make me a successful dictator. C. I have too much historical background and too much knowledge of existing dictatorships to make me desire any form of dictatorship for a democracy like the United States of America."[1]

The reporters looked at one another in astonishment. What had caused this remarkable announcement? Why had the president taken the trouble to officially deny the ludicrous and tired charge that he had dictatorial ambitions? It was extraordinary, mused Senator Edward Burke, a Democrat from Nebraska, that things had gotten to the point where the Roosevelt had to refute such accusations. "If the President says he doesn't want to be a dictator," Republican Senator Arthur Van-denberg of Michigan dryly remarked, "it makes it unanimous as far as I am concerned."[2]

There had been omens. Just a few weeks earlier, FDR's critics in the press and in Congress had railed about his sinister designs. Crying out against "Dictator Roosevelt," they accused him of seeking nothing less than to topple constitutional government.[3] Sparking the firestorm was a bill he had proposed that called for the reorganization and stream-lining of the executive branch of the government. But how could such an innocuous proposal, the product of decades of pressing need and thoughtful suggestions, have set off such a squall of protests? Did it forecast even a bigger battle in the months ahead?

In his first term in office, the president had sailed through relatively smooth waters, able to pass landmark New Deal legislation that helped the nation recover from the abyss of the Great Depression. Americans welcomed the economic emergency measures of 1933, the Agricultural Adjustment Act that increased farmers' incomes by controlling crop production, the Tennessee Valley Authority that provided low-cost power, and the transformational programs of 1935, the Social Security Act and the National Labor Relations Act.

Little by little, an astounding, historic revolution was taking place, turning the traditional role of American government upside down. Coming after decades of inert government and especially after the laissez-faire, passive presidencies of Harding, Coolidge, and Hoover, Roosevelt's administration took the bold step of expanding and har-nessing the power of government for the many, not for the few.

The goal of the New Deal was to increase Americans' prosperity, to set fair labor standards for workers, to provide help for the unemployed—a quarter of the total workforce—and security for the elderly. "Necessi-tous men are not free men," Roosevelt declared at the 1936 Democratic National Convention, explaining that true freedom meant more than political freedom, more than the right to vote, more than the right to express oneself freely, more than the right to practice one's religion. "Liberty," FDR said, "requires opportunity to make a living—a living decent according to the standard of the time, a living which gives man not only enough to live by, but something to live for." To truly secure for citizens the right to life, liberty, and the pursuit of happiness, Roosevelt put the national government to work on their side. No longer would it be small, frugal, and responsive only to the needs of big business and concentrated wealth; no longer would an American president be deaf to the desperate needs of the nation's citizens.[4]

In November 1936, every state in the union—except Maine and Vermont—had joined in a collective vote of confidence in Roosevelt and the New Deal. Only in four states did Landon garner more than 45 percent of the vote.[5] At home in Hyde Park, New York on election night, the president could hear the Associated Press and United Press tickers in the dining room clattering out the returns. To relieve the tension of waiting, Roosevelt kept his own tally as party operatives reported results from across the country. As the astonishing results came in, he leaned back in his chair, blew a ring of cigarette smoke at the ceiling, and exclaimed, "Wow!" He had beaten Republican Alf Landon of Kansas by a vote of 27,752,309 to 16,682,524 and by 523 electoral votes to 8.[6]

In that critical election of 1936, a majority of voters had not merely registered a protest against Hoover's anemic response to the Great Depression, as they had in 1932, but were expressing their wholehearted approval of FDR's economic and social policies and ensuring the durable shift of party strength to the Democrats.[7] Americans gave Franklin Roosevelt a stupendous, unequivocal mandate to fulfill the promises of the New Deal. After all, there remained so much more to be done, as the president acknowledged on a cold, rainy day in January 1937 in his second inaugural address. "I see one-third of a nation ill-housed, ill-clad, ill-nourished." Americans, he said, as the rain poured down, splattering the pages of his speech, "insist that every agency of popular government use every effective instrument to carry out their will." His vision, determination, and leadership, he promised, would ultimately help establish "a morally better world."

Franklin Roosevelt embodied the hopes of tens of millions of people.

Seated around their radios, families listened in rapt attention to the president's reassuring, intimate fireside chats. They felt that he was with them in their homes, confiding in them, talking out their problems with them. He carefully explained his plans, appealing to their understanding as well as to their emotions. This master of the techniques of communication knew how to comfort Americans with his warm voice, his deliberate inflections and slow cadences. People were excited and inspired by his calls for collective action and even by his reminders that sacrifices would have to be made by all. For millions, he was their hero, their savior—they hung his portrait in their living rooms, often next to pictures of Jesus Christ.

But soon after that earthquake election the political winds seemed to change. By the spring of 1937, Roosevelt's long honeymoon with Congress was over, and by 1938 things had fallen apart. Not only had the country slid back into recession, but the Supreme Court had struck down key legislation and Congress was voting down the administration's new bills. The overwhelming mandate Roosevelt received in 1936 proved to be anything but shatterproof. An eighteenth-century, horse-and-buggy Constitution—designed by the Framers to fragment power, pit the branches of government against one another, thwart a popular majority as well as a domestically bred tyrant, and ensure stability (read inertia and deadlock) rather than energy—was effectively preventing the president from making the transformational changes that he had promised and that voters continued to support.

But it was not only checks and balances that frustrated Roosevelt; he also confronted the problem of a serious cleavage within his own party. Political parties had evolved in the 1790s to the consternation of many of the Founders themselves. But parties would prove to be highly effective, allowing an organized majority of citizens to overcome James Madison's constitutional system of majority-pulverizing checks and balances. Only a national party, capable of winning presidential as well as congressional and senatorial elections, could capture the reins of government and mobilize support for a national agenda.

In later life, Madison himself came to believe that his system of checks and balances was hindering majority rule and stalling the wheels of government. "The vital principle of republican government," he wrote in 1833, "is the *lex majoris partis,* the will of the majority."[8] At the age of eighty-two, he demanded from government not fragmentation of power or even, as he had stressed in his *Federalist* essays, protection for minorities, but rather protection for the majority and the assurance of its ability to wield power. But with his constitutional system now written in stone, it was only through political parties that the will of the majority could override checks and balances.

But the party system called for internal unity and discipline among congressional party members. And in 1938, even though the Democrats held staggering majorities of nearly four-fifths of the seats in both chambers of Congress, that huge Democratic majority was deceptive, for a real division in the vast Democratic ranks had existed for several years.[9]

From the beginning of the New Deal, there were five Senate Democrats who wanted nothing better than to maul and cripple FDR's legislation: Carter Glass and Harry Byrd of Virginia, Millard Tydings of Maryland, Thomas Gore of Oklahoma, and Josiah Bailey of North Carolina.[10] Later, more Democrats—men such as Walter George of Georgia, Ellison "Cotton Ed" Smith of South Carolina, Robert Bulkley of Ohio, Bennett Champ Clark of Missouri, Burton Wheeler of Montana, Tom Connally of Texas, Pat McCarran of Nevada, Guy Gillette of Iowa, and others—joined the obstructionist crew. And yet, when FDR ran for reelection in 1936, none of them had the courage to criticize him. On the contrary, they gave lip service to the New Deal—and then, insisting that they were only voting their consciences, proceeded to knife it. Allied with Republicans, they were succeeding in wrecking the New Deal.[11]

Stymied, Roosevelt would fight back—impulsively, haphazardly, emotionally, boldly—by seeking to drive his conservative foes out of the Democratic Party. His plan was to take them on at the ballot box in 1938, by intervening in Democratic primaries and backing liberal challengers to the wayward incumbents. He was determined to pit his popularity and policies against their objections to New Deal programs. It was a highly risky venture that had danger signs written all over it. Reporters branded his tactic a "purge"—and the inflammatory label stuck.

The goal of FDR's attempt to oust conservatives from the party, in fact, made utter sense: he believed that the nation should have two effective and responsible political parties, one liberal, the other conservative, each ideologically consistent and united, each supporting its leaders and offering voters meaningful choices about the direction the nation should take. Roosevelt would spend the summer months of 1938 traveling across the country and campaigning in Democratic primaries against conservative incumbents. But in the end, his effort to "purge" those conservatives from the party would fail, at great political cost to him. It was one of the few glaring political miscalculations in his long career.

"I expected the punishment to be much rougher than it was"—words that might have been pronounced by FDR in the aftermath of the purge—but that were spoken by Douglas Corrigan, the genial, carefree young pilot who gave Depression-weary Americans something to laugh about when he flew across the Atlantic from New York to Dublin that same summer of 1938. "Where am I? I intended to fly to California!" he said to astonished Irish airport workers on landing at Baldonnel Airport without landing papers, passport, radio, instruments, or even a map. "My compass went wrong," he fibbed, wearing his good-natured, ever-present grin. Newspapers—and Hollywood, too—ate up the story.

During the summer of 1938, Roosevelt, like "Wrong Way Corrigan," found himself, if not merrily heading on purpose in the wrong direction, then trying to maneuver through the political skies without adequate instruments, papers, and maps.[12]

And yet the whole episode of the "purge," though dramatic, flawed, and fueled by anger and resentment, was the product of Roosevelt's deep, principled conviction that it was critically important to forge ahead with New Deal programs and create lasting change in the nation; and that to do so, he needed the solid support of the members of his own party.

But the purge represented even more than a scheme to restart the New Deal. It was also the precursor of a historic transformation of American political parties. In the aftermath of the purge, the momentum for the kind of party realignment Roosevelt had sought in 1938 through the eviction of the Democratic Party's conservative wing would gather steam, first with the "Dixiecrat" rebellion of conservative southern Democrats in 1948 and then, over the decades that followed, with Lyndon Johnson's Civil Rights Acts and then with Goldwater, Nixon, and Reagan's appeals to right-leaning Democrats to join the Republicans. By the end of the century, the irreconcilable tensions within the Democratic Party had exploded, transforming the nation's traditional political landscape—and the once solidly Democratic South was solid no more.

Roosevelt's purge was a valiant if premature and mismanaged plan to remedy a complex political dilemma. Unlike Douglas Corrigan, Roosevelt would not be hailed for his feat by a million cheering New Yorkers lining lower Broadway for a ticker-tape parade. But the legacy of the purge colors American politics to this day.

In the spring of 1938, Roosevelt's bill for executive reorganization should reasonably have mustered strong bipartisan support. Not only had

Theodore Roosevelt and Woodrow Wilson called for reorganization of the executive branch, but so had FDR's predecessor Herbert Hoover. In the summer of 1937, FDR had voiced the hope that the Democratic Party would finally answer that call and "accomplish something which so many previous Administrations and Congresses have failed to do at all."[13]

A committee of nonpartisan reformers and political scientists, chaired by Louis Brownlow, an expert in the field of public administration, had crafted Roosevelt's bill. They recommended expanding the White House staff, adding cabinet departments of Social Welfare and Public Works, reorganizing the civil service under one administrator, and introducing a merit system for federal employees. By reducing the clutter and lack of coordination among various agencies, the president explained, the government would become more efficient and businesslike. But not even Hoover's approval of Roosevelt's executive reorganization plan quelled the storm of allegations against the "dictator bill."[14]

In the late 1930s—an epoch infamous for power-driven dictators erecting their miserable totalitarian regimes—some Americans were frightened by the idea of increasing executive power. "I am not willing, in the search for efficient management," cried Nebraska's Senator Burke, "to establish one-man rule in this country!"[15]

Over a hundred protesters, all dressed up as Paul Revere, paraded up Pennsylvania Avenue in April 1938, waving banners that denounced "One Man Rule." Father Charles Coughlin, the demagogic priest who used his radio programs to pummel FDR, chimed in, exhorting his followers to defend their liberties against Roosevelt tyranny.[16] All the wild dictator talk was a bit irrational, admitted Senator Burton Wheeler, a progressive Democrat from Montana and a great White House friend who was evolving into one of Roosevelt's most spirited foes. Still, Congress would be unwise, he added, to strengthen the executive branch of government "at this particular time, when a certain form of *hysteria* is sweeping over the United States." Indeed, a flood of 330,000 telegrams protesting the bill poured into Congress.[17]

And yet, if the government was ever to be modernized and made efficient, some restructuring was necessary. Even Arthur Krock, the chief political correspondent of the *New York Times*, who usually relished his daily exercise of skewering Roosevelt, approved of the bill. Though a week after Roosevelt's inauguration in 1933, Krock was already hammering the new president with an article headlined "Roosevelt Gets Power of Dictator, All Protests Are Stilled," in 1938 the *Times*'s man conceded that the executive branch was full of duplication, waste, and disorder.[18]

For his part, Roosevelt recognized the possibility of an American dictatorship. At the bottom of the Depression in 1932, with so many extremist groups appealing to the underprivileged and unemployed, the United States, FDR later reflected, "might have had a dictator if the New Deal hadn't come along with a sensible program." But he considered the chatter about himself as a potential dictator nothing short of "stupid and ridiculous"—though some of it amused him. "Thank the Lord I have not decided to become a Dictator," he commented tongue-in-cheek when residents of Connecticut besieged him with pleas to halt construction of a power plant that was spoiling the Saugatuck River. He was delighted to pass the buck, he happily added, to Governor Wilbur Cross, the "Sovereign Dictator of the Independent State of Connecticut." When one Englishman wrote to Roosevelt in 1938, asking him to send five hundred airplanes to Great Britain for its defense against Nazi Germany, the president could only laugh. "Almost it makes me feel like a dictator!" he wrote, imagining the stricken, irate faces in Congress if he asked for such authority.[19]

Despite the demonstrations of the Paul Reveres on Pennsylvania Avenue, few Americans shared the fears of a Roosevelt dictatorship. When asked by the pollster George Gallup in April 1938 if the president should have more power or less, 47 percent of those polled answered that he should have the same amount of power, and 18 percent said he should have more. In another Gallup poll, 63 percent of Americans favored a New Deal candidate for the presidency in 1940 over a conservative. And a majority of Democrats polled wanted Franklin Roosevelt to be that candidate—for an unprecedented third term.[20]

When the executive reorganization bill finally came up for a vote in the Senate on March 28, 1938, visitors poured into the galleries above the chamber. It was standing room only. Even the president's daughter-in-law, the wife of James Roosevelt, FDR's eldest son, had to sit on one of the steps in the family gallery. Hundreds more, unable to get in, milled around in the corridors of the Capitol. After two hours of maneuvering and voting on motions to recommit the bill to committee, senators finally called out their votes.[21]

The reorganization bill squeaked through the Senate. Although Democrats held a huge majority with seventy-six seats, the vote was close: 48 to 42. Predictably, some of FDR's conservative Democratic foes—Walter George of Georgia, Harry Byrd and Carter Glass of Virginia, Josiah Bailey of North Carolina, Millard Tydings of Maryland, and others—voted against the legislation. It was more surprising, however, when New York's Senator Robert Wagner, Roosevelt's staunch ally and the author of key New Deal bills, switched sides at the last minute and joined them in voting against the legislation. Still, the unrelenting pressure mounted by the White House had paid off—at least in the Senate.[22]

It had been too close a vote, fretted Jim Farley, the postmaster general and chairman of the Democratic National Committee, who had worked with Roosevelt since 1928. "If this thing doesn't go through the House, you are going to lose control of your party," he warned the president, urging him to join him in some personal arm-twisting. Roosevelt's close advisor, Secretary of the Interior Harold Ickes, agreed; the bill's defeat in the House, the pugnacious and prickly Ickes wrote in his diary, would be a "major catastrophe." Ickes felt that the loss of prestige to the administration would be so devastating that he would have little choice but to pack his bags "and move away from Washington."[23]

* * *

When reporters trooped into the Oval Office on April 5, they saw a gold-handled, seven-inch saber on the president's desk—a *yataghan* presented to him by the sultan of Muscat and Oman. "I can put it in the wall at thirty paces," Roosevelt boasted, waving it above his head. "How far down Pennsylvania Avenue can you throw it?" asked one sly reporter.[24] But the more troubling question was whether members of the House would throw a knife of their own back up the avenue to the White House when it was their turn to vote on the reorganization bill.

The Speaker of the House, William Bankhead of Alabama, should have been in an impregnable position to get the legislation passed: Democrats held 334 seats compared to only 88 Republicans. And yet Bankhead had to struggle to wrest the bill from the powerful Rules Committee, which directed traffic on legislation. The Committee's defiant chairman, a New York City Democrat named John O'Connor— the brother of Roosevelt's old friend and former law partner Basil O'Connor—was determined to bottle up the bill. "The fact is, there hain't goin' to be no dictator in this country," O'Connor barked, "not as long as some of us have a voice and two strong hands."[25]

On April 8, after days of raucous debate, punctuated by boos, laughter, and sarcastic comments, the House was finally ready to vote. Majority leader Sam Rayburn of Texas pleaded for party unity and urged the members of the House not to deliver a "lethal blow" to FDR by sending Americans "the message that tonight Democrats voting with Republicans have said in effect that our President is no longer the leader of his country."[26]

In a dramatically hushed chamber, representatives called out their votes on a motion to recommit the bill to the hostile Rules Committee—the euphemism for legislative burial. When the final tally was announced and they heard that the motion had won by an eight-vote margin—with 108 Democrats and all the House Republicans voting to recommit—the victorious opponents of executive reorganization broke out into a visceral roar of spiteful cheers. One representative from Pennsylvania ran across the floor and raised O'Connor's arm, shouting, "Here's our leader! Here's our leader!"[27]

The next day the *Chicago Daily Tribune* celebrated Roosevelt's stunning defeat with the headline "KILL DICTATOR BILL: 204–196." That same day, the stock market soared, with reporters attributing the rally to the House vote. The real reason for the bill's defeat had nothing to do with fears of dictatorship or concerns about the powers of Congress, judged Representative Lindsay Warren, a Democrat from North Carolina. It had been killed, he said, by Republicans and Democrats who "hate Roosevelt." Louis Brownlow, the architect of reorganization, concurred; the opposition was "just anti-Roosevelt."[28]

The emboldened members of the anti-Roosevelt and anti–New Deal coalition had just dramatically demonstrated their power. Suddenly they were the *real* dictators, Roosevelt's allies maintained, for they had no national support and were acting contrary to the wishes of the American people.

"I was completely surprised," stammered Harold Ickes. He was more than surprised: he was also enraged. And he was exasperated that the president seemed to be taking this loss "lying down."[29] Shortly after the bill's defeat, Ickes walked into the office of Missy LeHand, FDR's devoted secretary, and picked up an unmailed note the president had written to Rayburn. In the note, Roosevelt thanked the Texan for his leadership and stressed that there was "no occasion for personal recrimination." A postscript was addressed to Speaker Bankhead, indicating that the president did not intend to fight any more for the bill. Soon after, Ickes saw the president and greeted him with a verbal blast. "I hit him with words," the abrasive interior secretary boasted in his diary, "telling him that he couldn't accept such a defeat; that if he did this Administration was through."[30]

★   ★   ★

For the president, the fate of the executive reorganization bill was the last straw in his battle against conservative Democrats. That battle had begun in May 1935 when the Supreme Court struck down the National Industrial Recovery Act—the heart of the New Deal—declaring its codes for competition, prices, wages, and work hours were unconstitutional. FDR's reaction? He fought back hard against right-wing conservatives—with the most radical, far-reaching and enduring legislation of the New Deal. He was not going to play dead, he declared, and let the high court turn back the Constitution to the "horse-and-buggy" days. Throughout the summer of 1935, he launched bill after bill—the National Labor Relations Act, the Social Security Act, the Banking Act of 1935, the Revenue Act of 1935, and the Works Progress Administration—all the transformational legislation of the "Second New Deal."[31]

But then in 1936, the Supreme Court struck again, this time judging that the Agricultural Adjustment Act was unconstitutional and that the government had no authority to regulate agricultural production. Out of touch with conditions in the mid-1930s, reactionaries on the high court were second-guessing Congress and substituting their own judgment for that of elected legislators and the president.

Roosevelt considered it an ominous failure in American government that nine unelected, elderly men could thwart the New Deal and block the will of the popular majority. Nowhere in the Constitution did the founders give the Supreme Court the power of judicial review, the power to veto legislation and act as a policy-making body. "Again and again the Constitutional Convention voted down proposals to give Justices of the Court a veto over legislation," the president declared in a scorching Constitution Day speech in the fall of 1937, blasting those who cried "unconstitutional" at every effort he made to improve the condition of the American people.[32]

Roosevelt's remedy for the situation was his court reform bill, immediately dubbed by opponents a "court-packing" scheme. The bill did not tackle the underlying issue of the power of judicial review. Instead, the president proposed adding justices to the Supreme Court when justices declined to retire after reaching the age of seventy, a plan that, in 1937, would have given him six new Supreme Court appointments. The tradition of nine Supreme Court justices, after all, was not written in stone—or even in ink. The Constitution does not specify the number of justices—and the number has varied over the years. The original Court had just six justices. Under President Jefferson, it was increased to seven, under Jackson to nine, during the Civil War to ten, and then reduced back to nine after the war.

Roosevelt's idea of increasing the size of the Court was hence neither unprecedented nor radical. But the normally sure-footed president stumbled politically. He failed to lay the groundwork with Congress and presented the legislation deceptively—as an "efficiency" measure, concealing his real goal of liberalizing the reactionary Supreme Court. Representatives and senators felt blindsided.

"Boys, here's where I cash in," said Hatton Sumners of Texas, chair of the House Judiciary Committee, to Vice President John Nance Garner, William Bankhead, and a few others after FDR had sprung the proposal on them in a private White House meeting just before he announced it to the press. In the Senate lobby, Garner—a Texas conservative who was no political friend of the president or the New Deal—expressed his own opinion of the bill by holding his nose with one hand and making a thumbs-down sign with the other.[33]

Archconservatives blasted the bill. Virginia's Carter Glass, the oldest member of the Senate, pronounced it a "frightful proposition" that was "utterly destitute of moral sensibility" and would destroy the "purity" of the Court. Surmising that a more liberal Court might very well move against racial segregation in the South, he pledged "implacable antagonism to the dangerous and fool things that are being done in

Washington."[34] But even some reliable, loyal, and usually liberal senators like Joseph O'Mahoney of Wyoming, Tom Connally of Texas, George Norris of Nebraska, and more than a dozen others washed their hands of the "court-packing" plan. Montana's Wheeler, who had supported the president up until 1936, organized and orchestrated the battle against the bill on the Senate floor, warning that it represented "the temptation to a President to make himself a dictator." If the court bill was passed, chimed in Senator Josiah Bailey of North Carolina, "the road to an American dictatorship will be cleared of all obstacles."[35]

One of the few supporters of the bill was Roosevelt's friend and confidant Josephus Daniels, the ambassador to Mexico. Daniels had been secretary of the navy and FDR's boss when he served as assistant secretary of the navy under Woodrow Wilson. For Daniels, the president's plan was really one to *un*pack the Court, which had been packed, he sneered, since 1860 with men on the side of privilege.[36]

At the Gridiron Club's semiannual dinner in Washington at the Willard Hotel in April 1937, the Court bill provided juicy material for Roosevelt-roasting. In a musical skit, a tribunal of fifteen timid judges sang—to the tune of Cole Porter's 1935 hit "It's De-lovely":

> You can tell at a glance
> What this Court will decide in advance
> You can hear Brother Franklin murmuring low:
> Let yourself Go! . . .
> It's delib'rate, it's deceptive . . . it's de-lousy!

Then the chief justice called the others to order: "Gentlemen of the court, let us go to work! Get out your rubber stamps!"[37]

On Broadway, too, court-packing made an appearance. In the 1937 Kaufman and Hart play *I'd Rather Be Right,* the Supreme Court justices, made up to look like nine copies of the chief justice, Charles Evans Hughes, emerged from the park shrubbery to shout "No" at the President and declare that everything except the Court itself was unconstitutional.[38]

Month after month, from February through August 1937, Roosevelt spent precious political capital trying to persuade senators and congressmen of the benefits of the legislation—and when that didn't work, he poured on the charm.

Franklin Roosevelt had always prided himself on knowing how to work with friends and adversaries alike. While governor of New York, he had once explained that he had to deal with people he neither liked nor trusted—"but I have worked with them and through them, in order to obtain the ultimate goal." His greatest political strength in obtaining that "ultimate goal" had always been his dexterity in tacking with the wind.[39]

Far from acting the part of a rigid taskmaster who whipped his team into line, during his first term as president he was a flexible, engaging ringmaster, adept at charming, managing, and reining in an unruly circus of Democratic beasts. He lavished his natural and profuse talents for flattery, wheedling, horse-trading—and even his talent for deception—on Senate and House leaders. Almost always finding ways to reconcile opposing interests, he won the support of politicians North and South, East and West.[40]

And so, just days after the Senate Judiciary Committee slammed his court reform bill in June 1937, calling it "an invasion of judicial power such as has never before been attempted in this country," an amiable Roosevelt invited all four hundred Democrats in Congress—well, except for the five women in the House of Representatives and the one woman in the Senate, Hattie Caraway of Arkansas—to be his guests at the Jefferson Islands Club in Chesapeake Bay. Good fellowship and a splendid island picnic, he hoped, would dissipate at least some of the friction in the party and perhaps smooth the way for the passage of the court bill the following month.[41]

Ferried to the island by a flotilla of navy patrol boats, the congress-men found the president seated in a chair near the water's edge; they saw a man with a massive head and torso that dwarfed his shrunken legs and poignantly pristine shoes. Casually dressed in an open shirt, relaxed and welcoming, FDR was a display of nonchalant showman-ship at its best—a most unusual pose for him. "With Roosevelt, you could never forget the majesty of the office and in a sense the majesty of the person," Roosevelt's old friend and chief speechwriter Sam Rosenman later remarked. The president was "always cordial, affable, but he was never really familiar, except on very rare occasions when he'd go on picnics or when he'd be off on the boat."[42]

It was an all-male weekend of nude swimming, skeet shooting, fish-ing, Senate-House softball games, and poker, at which the president usually won. With politics and serious talk banished from the menu, the men lunched on crabs, potato salad, and apple pie and drank iced tea. In the late afternoon, they sat in the shade and enjoyed cold beer. The president had done himself a "world of good," cheered the *New York Times*.[43]

But the *Times* had it wrong. Four weeks later, seventy senators voted to recommit the president's court bill to the hostile Judiciary Commit-tee. They included conservative Democrats like Bailey, George, Smith, Tydings, Wheeler, McCarran, and Gillette. But some liberals, too, voted against court-packing—the majority leader, Alben Barkley of Kentucky, along with Robert Wagner of New York, Claude Pepper of Florida, James Pope of Idaho, and William McAdoo of California. Among the twenty who sided with Roosevelt and against the motion to recommit were some New Deal loyalists: Hugo Black of Alabama, Hat-tie Caraway of Arkansas, and Harry Truman of Missouri.

"The Supreme Court thing," gloated Vice President Garner, was "out the window." Barely eight months after one of the most triumphant electoral victories in the history of the American presidency, the president's court reform plan lay in abject tatters. It was one of the most humiliating defeats a president had suffered since the Senate rejected Woodrow Wilson's League of Nation's covenant in 1920. In late August, an emasculated court bill was finally passed, and the dejected president signed it into law. A few minor administrative reforms had come at an enormous price: his fight for court reform had seriously weakened and fractured his own coalition, leaving his liberal base in Congress in alarming disarray and a bitter taste of defeat in his own mouth.[44]

Suddenly feeling the thrust of their power, the conservative bloc in Congress reveled in its newfound ability to foil the president. Gleefully they banded together to sabotage the rest of the New Deal, voting down Roosevelt's progressive tax measures, abolishing the graduated tax on capital gains, killing his proposal for seven regional agencies patterned after the TVA, tearing apart his executive reorganization plan, and burying in committee his Fair Labor Standards Act. Vaunted presidential power was slipping through the president's fingers. Opposition to his proposals was developing into "blitzkrieg" proportions, wrote Sam Rosenman.[45]

Outwardly, Roosevelt appeared as confident and captivating as ever, but inwardly, Jim Farley noted, he was seething at the swaggering politicians who had double-crossed him. For weeks and months after the court-packing debacle, wrote Farley, "I found him fuming against the members of his own party." Roosevelt had been "completely humiliated," agreed Rosenman. In meetings with congressmen, the president let it be known that those who had opposed him had better be on guard. "I've got them on the run, Jim," he gloated prematurely to Farley. "They have no idea what's going to happen and are beginning to worry. They'll be sorry yet."

"Boss, you're a hard man," Farley replied half in jest and half in earnest. "I hope you never get angry at me."[46]

★   ★   ★

Just one year into his second term, Roosevelt already seemed a lame duck. And it was all the more galling to him that opposition was coming not just from anti–New Deal Republicans, as he could reasonably have expected, but also from members of his own party. Some of them were Roosevelt's old friends, Democrats who had been his supporters and allies during his first term in office, happily running for office on the president's coattails, adroitly milking the magic of the Roosevelt name for all it was worth. And yet, once in office, they veered to the right and found every excuse to block or gut his New Deal legislation. It made his "blood boil," wrote Josephus Daniels to Roosevelt, that legislators who were elected on a pledge to "stand back of the President" were standing so far back "that it would require a telescope to see them!"[47]

Roosevelt felt special animosity toward those who were willing to run with him on a liberal party platform and then vote against the very pledges on which they had been elected. The "shenanigans" of turncoat Democrats disgusted him, for he believed that they were wreaking permanent injury on the nation. The tough-talking Harry Hopkins, one of FDR's closest advisors and the head of the Works Progress Administration, also railed against certain Democrats "who tricked the voters by wearing our insignia, only to turn against us as soon as they got in office."[48]

So this president was not merely frustrated and tired of endlessly compromising with these saboteurs who ran under his banner: he was indignant, outraged, infuriated—and desperate. As Congress debated and buried the executive reorganization bill in the spring of 1938, Roosevelt's "hatred," wrote Jim Farley, "glowed as fierce as ever under the ashes of the past six months." The president "took no pains to hide his anger," remarked George Creel, a newspaper man and Roosevelt critic who had served in the government under Woodrow Wilson. His "resentment crystallized into the desire to crush all who conspired against the throne."[49]

Roosevelt's "Dutch" was up, blared a headline in the *New York Times* in early April 1938, referring to the president's famous temper. He would sorely need, the *Times* reporter concluded, "all the dogged persistence he is supposed to have inherited from that Claes van Rosenvelt who nearly 300 years ago took up residence on Manhattan Island." Dogged persistence—perhaps. But after the defeat of both court-packing and executive reorganization, Roosevelt instinctively felt that the situation required more than that: it demanded some form of retribution—if not revenge.[50]

His head tilted back, his cigarette holder tipped at a jaunty angle, his face lit up by a joyful smile, Roosevelt had given Americans the invaluable gift of his buoyant, energizing, enchanting personality—self-confident, forward-looking, gloriously sunny. That combination of his seductive charm and contagious optimism had restored hope to a broken nation. Was he capable, too, of feelings as dark as hatred, of impulses as destructive as revenge?

Two years earlier, Americans had encountered his fighting side. "We have earned the hatred of entrenched greed," the president exulted in his state of the union speech on January 3, 1936, denouncing the selfish few who "spread fear and discord among the people" and "gang up against the people's liberties." He had told Raymond Moley that he wanted that January 1936 message to be a "fighting speech," and it was that and more.

Later that year, in a rousing, polarizing, climactic campaign speech in Madison Square Garden, FDR had pointed to the nation's domestic enemies—speculators, reckless bankers, and irresponsible financial barons, the selfish plutocrats concerned only with protecting their own wealth and safeguarding their profits. "They are unanimous in their hate for me," he exclaimed to the excited, roaring crowd, his voice rising to a crescendo, "and I welcome their hatred!" And after drawing the battle lines against the saboteurs of the New Deal, he predicted his own victory: "I should like to have it said of my first Administration that in it the forces of selfishness and of lust for power met their match. I should like to have it said of my second Administration that in it these forces met their master!" One reporter who was present at that rally, Thomas Stokes, later remembered a "vengefulness in his voice when he said it."[51]

Roosevelt's aggressiveness was entirely appropriate in Madison Square Garden—the arena that had long been the mecca for whopping prizefights. In that campaign speech, after underscoring each of America's dire needs—increased wages, cheaper electricity and transportation, home mortgages, an end to child labor—Roosevelt repeated the militant refrain: "For all these we have only just begun to fight!" And if there was any doubt about his readiness to fight or his will to dominate, Roosevelt reminded a crowd in Washington, D.C., a few months after his breathtaking election victory in 1936: "we gave warning last November that we had only just begun to fight. Did some people really believe we did not mean it? Well—I meant it!"[52]

The people in Roosevelt's inner circle were already acquainted with his taste for crushing his opponents and enemies. One of his best speechwriters, playwright and liberal Robert Sherwood, found that FDR could oscillate between the Christian spirit and a "capacity for vindictiveness." Frances Perkins, FDR's secretary of labor, who had known him for decades, also allowed that he may have had "a streak of vindictiveness." She recalled that once, after the president did a favor for someone who had been nasty to him, he was told that he had performed a magnanimous gesture. "I'm not magnanimous," FDR replied. "I'm a mean cuss at heart." Jim Farley explained that people who thought Roosevelt was "weak and vacillating" didn't realize that the key to his whole character was his "battling nature." His easygoing air of affability was only a mask. If he wanted something to be accomplished, he was "ready to fight for it without ever letting up." In the depths of the Depression, that willingness—that eagerness—to fight was, for tens of millions of Americans, bracing, inspiring, confidence-restoring, uplifting. The president, Farley concluded, was "not afraid of any man in shoe leather."[53]

A few years earlier, Roosevelt had met briefly with retired Supreme Court justice Oliver Wendell Holmes, who offered him a lesson in battlefield tactics. "When you are losing a battle," Holmes advised the new president, "you must halt the retreat, blow the trumpet, and charge. And that's exactly what you are doing. You are in a war, Mr. President, and in a war there is only one rule, 'Form your battalion and fight!' "[54]

But in the early months of 1938, Roosevelt had no clear battle plan. He randomly flailed about, spewing his anger and frustration against all those who opposed him—especially editorial writers and journalists. At press conferences in the spring of 1938, he upbraided reporters, accusing them—correctly—of giving more coverage to the few rabid enemies of the New Deal than to the vast armies of its supporters.

The headlines and editorials in 85 percent of the nation's newspapers featured conservative opinion, the president complained. He never received "two-fisted support" from editorial writers, only a "yes, but" attitude: "'Oh, yes, we are in favor of flood control, but we do not like this way of doing it . . . Oh yes, we are in favor of maintaining good prices for crops, but this bill is terrible. It is regimentation on the farmer.' Period, end of the paragraph, end of the story!"[55]

He even raged against women's magazines that ran full-page ads designed to whip up opposition to his Fair Labor Standards Act, legislation that would set a minimum wage and abolish child labor. "Housewives beware!" FDR exclaimed, parodying the advertisements. "If the Wages and Hours Bill goes through, you will have to pay your Negro girl eleven dollars a week!" "Of course," the president told the reporters, "no law ever intended a minimum wages and hours bill to apply to domestic help."[56]

But the president saved most of his burning resentment for the Democratic senators and congressmen who were now thwarting him, foiling his efforts to improve education, raise salaries, create purchasing power, and raise the standard of living—especially in the backward, impoverished South. While most southern senators had been among the most dependable Roosevelt supporters on Capitol Hill during the president's first years in office—like majority leader Joseph Robinson of Arkansas, Democratic whip James Byrnes of South Carolina, and Pat Harrison of Mississippi, chairman of the Senate Finance Committee—a small, intransigent old guard remained. Those senators, FDR grumbled during a press conference in late April, "if they lived in the North, would not be Democrats anyway."[57]

On the one hand, those conservatives had not bolted the Democratic Party completely to join the Republicans—as had embittered turncoats like John Jacob Raskob, the former national chairman of the party; John W. Davis, the Democratic candidate for president in 1924; and Al Smith, FDR's political mentor, predecessor as New York governor, and the party's 1928 candidate for the presidency. Indeed, these three and others went on to found the archconservative American Liberty League, seeking to destroy the New Deal in the name of laissez-faire economics. Nor had even the most conservative southern Democrats completely repudiated the New Deal, as had Raymond Moley, a former member of FDR's Brains Trust, his inner circle of policy advisors, and Lewis Douglas, FDR's first budget director.[58]

On the other hand, the Democratic rebels in Congress were causing far greater harm than those ineffectual malcontents. "The Tydings, Smiths, Georges, Byrds," wrote an irate Josephus Daniels to Roosevelt in 1938, "hurt our cause more than the Fishes and Vandenbergs," referring to conservative Republicans in Congress.[59]

How could the president seize the initiative once again and reestablish his leadership? "Roosevelt must either fight as he has never fought before," the *New Republic* editorialized in April 1938, "or let everything slide. There is no other logical choice." But beyond impotent expressions of anger, the softball tactic of withholding patronage appointments, his appointment of Alabama's liberal senator Hugo Black to fill a Supreme Court vacancy, and his insistence that Congress take up the executive reorganization bill again, what concrete plan of action could Roosevelt and his inner circle devise?[60]

On June 18, 1938, the gavel fell in the House and in the Senate, ending the stormy session. The same day, President and Mrs. Roosevelt left Washington for the resort town of Nahant in Massachusetts Bay and the wedding of their youngest son, John. Under radiant sunshine, the president held court, laughing, clasping hands, chatting, joking with scores of old friends as well as his cabinet members.[61]

But back in Washington some of the president's allies believed that the time had come to wage battle, not to beguile. Four days after the president was seen generously dispensing his dazzling charm in Massachusetts, Senator Joshua Lee of Oklahoma exhorted him to change gears, slug it out—and punish. "What would you think about bearing down on those who voted against your program?" he wrote to Roosevelt on June 22, suggesting that the vote that spring on the executive reorganization bill could serve as a litmus test of loyalty.[62]

The same day, June 22, crowds poured into Yankee Stadium to witness the boxing match of the decade. The "Brown Bomber," Joe Louis, the son of an Alabama sharecropper and great-grandson of a slave, would defend his world heavyweight title in a rematch against the German boxer Max Schmeling, whom the *Atlanta Constitution* called the "Nazi contender." "Schmeling is about as unpredictable in the ring as FDR is in the White House," wrote one sports columnist before the fight.[63]

Sitting in the best ringside seats were Hollywood stars—from Cary Grant and Edward G. Robinson to George Burns and Gracie Allen. Political insiders sat next to them—New York governor Herbert Lehman; New York City's mayor, Fiorello LaGuardia; FBI director J. Edgar Hoover; and one of FDR's sons. Also joining them was Jim Farley, the former chairman of the New York Boxing Commission. Thanks to pressure from Farley, Joe Louis had supported Roosevelt in the 1936 election. But four years later, the boxer would come out for FDR's opponent, Wendell Willkie, telling audiences that Willkie "has got punch." "Stick to your boxing, Joe," wrote one reader to the black weekly newspaper, the *Chicago Defender*.[64]

Seventy thousand more, paying a dollar each, passed through the turnstiles and crowded into the grandstands. Not an empty seat in Yankee Stadium. The country seemed suddenly immobilized as millions of Americans—half the nation's population—listened for free on the radios in their kitchens and living rooms. NBC sports announcer Clem McCarthy gave his electrifying blow-by-blow description of Schmeling's first-round collapse under the relentless downpour of Louis's fists: ". . . Schmeling is going down . . . Schmeling is down. The count is 4. It's . . . And he's up. And Louis right and left to the head, a left to the jaw, a right to the head, right to the body, a left up to the jaw—and Schmeling is down. The count is 5. 6. 7. 8. The men are in the ring. The fight is over! Max Schmeling is beaten in the first round!" Two minutes and four seconds—and it was over.[65]

Joyous cheers rang out in the hot Bronx night. At Yankee Stadium and all over America, in taverns, restaurants, night clubs, and homes, people celebrated; motorists honked their horns; in Harlem, thirty blocks were closed to traffic for the party. Everyone was ecstatic. Well, not everyone. "I always feel sorry for the man who is beaten," the contrarian Eleanor Roosevelt wrote plaintively in her newspaper column "My Day" a few days later. After her tortured childhood and her husband's infidelity, she apparently identified with the loser. To the victor,

Joe Louis, she offered condescending advice to "take his money and put it away."[66]

Unlike Eleanor, her husband Franklin, adrenalin surging, loved a fight—and just two days after the historic Louis-Schmeling match, he, too, climbed into the ring.

On June 24, 1938, the president finally announced the plan of action that he and his close advisors had agreed on. Soon to be dubbed in the press the "elimination committee," they were a clever, inventive group: the combative sixty-four-year-old Harold Ickes, a former Bull Moose Republican from Illinois who became FDR's secretary of the interior; forty-eight-year-old Harry Hopkins of Iowa, FDR's most trusted advisor and troubleshooter, whom he appointed Works Progress administrator and then secretary of commerce; Joseph Keenan, a fifty-year-old special assistant to the attorney general who had been assigned the impossible task of lobbying hostile senators to back FDR's court-packing bill; and a closely knit duo, Thomas ("Tommy the Cork") Corcoran, the thirty-eight-year-old master political operator, an engaging, tough Irish lawyer from New England who liked to crack jokes and sing Irish ballads, always ready to undertake any kind of task and completely devoted to the president; and the Brains Truster Ben Cohen, a shy, brilliant legal technician, the son of an immigrant peddler.[67]

This informal inner circle believed that the quickest and most decisive way to remedy the problem of conservative, obstructionist Democrats in Congress was simply to defeat them in the 1938 midterm Democratic primaries. By intervening in the primaries and supporting liberal challengers, Roosevelt hoped to prevent the reelection of at least some anti–New Deal Democrats. And perhaps such hardball tactics might frighten others into falling back in line.[68]

Before it crystallized in June, "purge talk"—ideas for cleaning house and sweeping out Democratic dissidents—had been percolating for over a year. "There has got to be a fight and there has got to be a purge," wrote Roosevelt's loyal friend Treasury Secretary Henry Morgenthau in his diary in 1937. But when an article by a White House insider named Stanley High appeared in the *Saturday Evening Post* in early 1937, confirming rumors of an imminent crackdown, the White House strenuously denied that anything like that was in the works. The influential syndicated columnist Walter Lippmann insisted that the president's inner circle was upset not that High had misrepresented the facts but rather that he had prematurely let the cat out of the bag.[69]

Denials and obfuscations went on for months. In January 1938, Jim Farley issued a statement declaring that the administration would not become involved in primary fights, though the president had insisted that Farley delete the line "nominations are entirely the affair of the states." And as recently as May 1938, the president had announced at a press conference that he would have nothing to say publicly on state primary contests. Thus Roosevelt would choose when and where to strike.[70]

The president decided to use a fireside chat to explain his intentions to the American people. It was the medium in which he excelled—he knew just how to modulate his tone, time his pauses, and create a sense of the dramatic. On the sultry evening of June 24, he descended into the unventilated soundproof studio in the White House basement, made even warmer by the bright lights of a movie cameraman. Leaning over the microphone, wiping away the perspiration from his brow, he could not resist departing from his prepared text. "The American public and American newspapers are certainly creatures of habit," he said. "It is the warmest night I have ever seen in Washington. And yet this talk will be referred to as a 'fireside talk.'" The fireside was the last place where many Americans on that sweltering evening wished to imagine themselves.[71]

Still, the president was in superb form. His voice had the ring of real conviction, a new vibrancy, the columnist Joseph Alsop remarked. Throughout the previous winter, there had been something dull, flat, uncertain in his delivery, but now Alsop heard an aggressive commander. "All the old magic was there without a flaw," agreed the *New York Herald Tribune*.[72] Calmly, reasonably, Roosevelt laid out the facts. He began by reminding his listeners that the Seventy-fifth Congress had left many things undone, especially in its refusal to provide more efficient machinery for the executive branch of government. But then he went on to emphasize the session's achievements, which were so numerous that a few failures, however significant, seemed to pale in comparison. Congress had established a new Civil Aeronautics Authority; it set up the United States Housing Authority to fund large-scale slum clearance and low-rent housing; it had reduced taxes on small businesses and made it easier for the Reconstruction Finance Corporation to make credit available to all businesses; and it had increased funding for the Works Progress Administration, the Public Works Administration, Rural Electrification, the Civilian Conservation Corps, and other agencies.

All of that might have been reason for celebration. But the president looked through a darker glass. More progress had to be made, he insisted, to finally solve business, agricultural, and social problems. "The great majority of you," he told his listeners, "want your own Government to keep on trying to solve them." Then he came to the meat of his talk—his dual role as president and party leader. As president, he would not ask Americans to vote for Democrats or for Republicans. "Nor am I, as *President*, taking part in Democratic primaries," he added.

But as the head of the Democratic Party, he explained, he had a responsibility, too: that of leading his party in a liberal direction and carrying out the 1936 party platform. Thus, he continued, striking a militant note, it was his right and duty, as party head, to speak out in the upcoming Democratic primaries and support liberal candidates who stood by him and the New Deal. "Do not misunderstand me," he said, making it clear that he would not oppose candidates who disagreed with him on any single issue, like court-packing or executive reorganization. He would, however, work to prevent the election of "outspoken reactionaries" and hypocrites—the politicians "who say 'yes' to a progressive objective, but who always find some reason to oppose any specific proposal designed to gain that objective."[73]

Although FDR's confidant Sam Rosenman later said that "the basis of the purge arose out of the determination to get rid of the people who opposed [FDR] during the Court fight," in 1938 the president denied that there was any such link.[74] And to defuse the idea that he was out for revenge after the humiliation of that defeat, he noted that although he had lost the battle on court-packing, he had actually won the war. While the bill was still before Congress, Justice Owen Roberts had switched sides on some crucial judicial decisions; the Court ruled in favor of the National Labor Relations Act and Social Security; and Justice Willis Van Devanter retired and was replaced by Hugo Black of Alabama. Thus he now made the case that his real objectives had been attained. The Court's "recent decisions," FDR stated, "are eloquent testimony of a willingness to collaborate with the two other branches of Government to make democracy work."

And yet the president was hardly as sanguine as he wished to appear, for he personalized his quarrel with conservative Democrats, portraying their conservatism as disloyalty to him. Striking out at them for running on his coattails, he bristled that they had dared to make a "clear misuse of *my own name.*" This was not the first time that he personalized politics, playing up his own role in events. "There's one issue in this campaign," he had told Raymond Moley in 1936, "and people must be either *for me* or *against me.*"[75] A few months later, he again placed himself at the center of the great ideological struggle of the decade in his Madison Square Garden speech, when he declared that the economic royalists "are unanimous in their hate for *me!*" Now, in his fireside chat, rocked once again by his feelings of betrayal and an all-consuming desire to re-taliate, his great talents for compromise, conciliation, and charm aban-doned him, leaving him vulnerable to committing a major blunder.

The message of the fireside chat was clear: the president would break with precedent as well as with his own calculating and cautious behavior. In the face of the conservative congressional revolt, he would intervene in Democratic primaries and appeal directly to voters. Eager to exploit the precious capital of his prestige and the popular New Deal, he was determined to help his friends and whip his foes. Frances Per-kins, his loyal friend and secretary of labor, feared that it was a "reck-less" plan.[76]

Right on cue, editorial writers around the nation slammed the presi-dent's talk, calling his tactic a drastic "purge." Roosevelt himself obvi-ously disliked the term "purge," dismissing it as an "immature" headline word.[77] But those provocative headlines sold newspapers, especially because they reminded readers of recent grim events in the Soviet Union—Stalin's murderous elimination of senior colleagues in the Communist Party leadership. Just that past March, one of the largest of the Moscow "show trials" had ended with the speedy execution of all twenty-one defendants, Stalin's political opponents. If President Roosevelt succeeded in his own purge, the *Chicago Tribune* editorialized, the only people remaining in the Democratic Party would be "Hitler yes-men or Stalin Communists."[78] The malicious columnist Westbrook Pegler judged that Roosevelt, like Hitler, was demanding "absolute per-sonal power" and a "purely nominal legislature."[79]

A few commentators, however, offered more balanced appraisals. "It's too dangerous," cautioned the *Christian Science Monitor.* "Selection of candidates is left to local powers that be; Presidents grin and bear it." Other papers made similar points, suggesting that it was far too risky to challenge local candidates who had their own political machines as well as the support of state officials and local newspapers. But a few undaunted spirits sided with the president. Democratic voters had a right to know if the leader of their party regarded certain candidates "as the friend or the enemy of the New Deal," argued columnist Ernest Lindley in the *Washington Post*.[80]

In the White House, anticipating the thrill of battle and the exhilaration of open conflict, people were energized—especially the president. The purge, Tommy Corcoran later recalled, "was all strong food for [the president's] love of political excitement, his feeling for political power, and his satisfaction in promoting the aims of the New Deal without compromise or apology." In the world of politics, as in ancient Greek theater, nothing is more intoxicating than passion, conflict, and vengeance. And no one loved taking on the starring role in a taut, perilous, high-stakes drama more than Roosevelt himself. The president, wrote Lindley, was "aching for a show down."[81]

But who would get trounced that summer? The rebels in the Democratic Party up for reelection—or the president himself? For their part, conservative Democrats were willing to go all out to defend their turf. "Their attempt to pack the Court failed and their attempt to pack the Senate will fail," predicted Burton Wheeler. "The President's message was a *plain declaration of war*," wrote Josiah Bailey to Harry Byrd, "and whether we wish to or not, we must fight now." Even Roosevelt's friend and ally James Byrnes, whom he would appoint to the Supreme Court in 1941, told the president not only that it was "folly" to purge independent thinkers from the party but that he himself would do everything in his power to prevent his friends from falling "under the ax." Also throwing in with the insurgent Democrats was Walter Lippmann, always eager to deliver a punch of his own. "The purgees must fight!" he wrote in his column. Otherwise, he predicted with a dramatic flourish, the New Dealers would attain dictatorial powers "which no normal political opposition can hope to check." Warning that Roosevelt sought nothing less than "overwhelming and centralized" governmental power, Lippmann cried, "Now is the time for resistance!"[82]

The tall, bald-headed Jim Farley, who towered over most of the other men in FDR's inner circle, was the one White House insider who wanted no part of the purge. As the chair of the Democratic National Party, his job, he wrote, was "not to take sides or to encourage factionalism but to promote harmony, teamwork, and united action in the interests of party success at the November balloting." The Roosevelt administration represented the first time since the Civil War that the Democratic Party was the undisputed dominant party of the United States, Farley wrote—and he was not about to declare war on a winning formula or do anything to undermine party unity. He was determined to keep out of what he called "dirty party-splitting work." It seemed obvious to him that a broadly based party, one that recruited its members from farmers, laborers, businessmen, and the professions, in every region of the country, could not please everybody.[83]

"To Jim Farley, any Democrat is a Democrat," the razor-tongued Harold Ickes sneered. But Farley was a brilliant political technician—a consensus man, not a conflict man—whose job demanded his own neutrality. And he had his own political aspirations, too, and toyed with the idea of running for the presidency in 1940. As far as he was concerned, the bitter cleavage in the Democratic ranks was nothing but "pure politics, nothing but politics and, to my mind, stupid politics."[84]

A president had to be a fighter, Farley granted. The Democratic chairman had no patience for a "spineless jellyfish" who wouldn't try anything and everything to get his policies through Congress. But Farley had also learned that in politics, nothing was ever gained by vindictiveness. "The man who starts out to destroy another man for revenge," he wrote, "usually winds up destroying himself."

Upset that none of his warnings were heeded, he made up his mind that his role in the purge would be "non-participation."

"I prepared to go to Alaska," he wrote in his memoirs, "where I hoped it would be cooler. As I surveyed the coming primaries, certain that the purgers were headed for trouble, I wondered if Alaska was far enough."[85]

◄ 2 ►

The Nonpartisan Leader

"DO YOU WISH TO WIN for yourself the undesirable title of the 4-P's Candidate: Pusillanimously-Pussyfooting-Pious-Platitudinous Roosevelt?" wrote a Harvard friend to Franklin Roosevelt during the presidential campaign of 1932, imploring him to stand up, address the crucial issues of the day forthrightly, and cease straddling. But his friend missed the point. Roosevelt's cautious game of dodgeball was a masterful, surefire strategy for winning elections. His bewildering versatility enabled him to appeal to as broad and diverse a swath of the electorate as possible while showering upon voters his ready charm.[1]

Roosevelt was really a "scrootch owl," said Louisiana senator Huey Long, who understood Roosevelt's game. A hoot owl, like Herbert Hoover, Long explained, simply knocks the hen off the roost and takes her. "But a scrootch owl slips into the roost and scrootches up to the hen and talks softly to her. And the hen falls in love with him. And the first thing you know, there ain't no hen!"[2]

The surprise was not that a cunning Franklin Roosevelt instinctively knew how to beguile, deceive, and subjugate others. The surprise was the abrupt shift he decided to make in June 1938, when he suddenly cast himself as a hardnosed ideological leader, defiantly determined to force all Democrats to toe the New Deal line or be excommunicated from the Democratic Party. That confrontational stance signaled a strange about-face, for there had never had been anything doctrinaire—or unsubtle—about FDR. In 1938, in a fit of pique, however understand-able, he seemed to be throwing away the very keys to his success.

From the beginning of his quest for the presidency in 1931, Roosevelt had chosen a safe game plan, purposefully seeking to be elusive and vague. That way, he could appear to be all things to all people—to Democrats, progressives, Independents, and moderate Republicans. During the 1932 election, Roosevelt resembled "a chameleon on plaid," grumbled his baffled opponent, Herbert Hoover. Chameleon or not, his strategy of appealing simultaneously to the left, right, and center worked brilliantly.[3]

The press, though, dismissed FDR as a mild and affable waffler. An "excessively cautious" candidate, Roosevelt mouthed "two-faced plati-tudes" so that he could hold on to right- and left-wing supporters, charged Walter Lippmann. "FDR is no crusader. He is no tribune of the people. He is no enemy of entrenched privilege," Lippmann wrote. "He is a pleasant man who, without any important qualifications for the office, would very much like to be president." In 1932, Lippmann had endorsed Newton Baker for the Democratic nomination, explain-ing that Baker, an Ohio lawyer who had served as Woodrow Wilson's secretary of war, was the "real first choice of responsible Democrats." Three years later, still failing to grasp Roosevelt's political genius, Lipp-mann confidently predicted that FDR would fail to be reelected in 1936—and endorsed Alf Landon.[4]

But Roosevelt was following the advice of a deeper political thinker than Lippmann. He was instinctively attuned to the centuries-old wis-dom of Niccolò Machiavelli who counseled that a prince must be both a lion and a fox—a lion to terrify the wolves and a fox to discover all the snares. By perfecting the art of dissembling and the skill of tacking with the winds of changing fortune, the prince would be able to preserve and wield his power.[5]

That Machiavellian formula for political survival and success, as historian James MacGregor Burns insightfully demonstrated, came second nature to Roosevelt. While contemplating a run for the presidency in 1931, FDR intuitively strove to be a fox. The lion would bide his time; he would roar with powerful New Deal programs only after winning the election. As FDR began to campaign for his party's nomination, he argued that while it was important to speak out on the issues facing a Depression-stricken nation, it was more important to maintain broad party unity. "Leadership can be successful," he wrote to Bernard Baruch, "only through the greatest amount of party harmony during the coming year." The conclusion? It was safer *not* to speak out forcefully on the issues.[6]

Roosevelt the fox saw the Democratic Party for what it was: an amorphous association representing a wide variety of interests and perspectives. His canny strategy was to hold together all the factions and shades of opinion within the party, somehow alleviating the stress of its ideological and racial fault lines and keeping on board an improbable mix of southern states' rights conservatives, eastern liberals, western progressives, union activists, Wilsonian idealists and internationalists, and Wall Street bankers and financiers.

He could not afford to take polarizing positions. It was a lesson he had learned from the missteps of his two mentors, Theodore Roosevelt and Woodrow Wilson. Teddy Roosevelt had broken with his Republican Party in 1912 and taken too progressive a stance when he ran for the presidency that year on a third-party ticket. Afterward, when he sought to return to the GOP fold in 1916, he found himself exiled in a political wilderness, without a party and without followers. Wilson, on the other hand, had stuck with his party and his ideals, but his position on the League of Nations had been so unyielding that both the League and the Democratic Party went down to defeat in 1920. Neither man had mastered the art of mediating interests, left and right.[7]

The press, always ready to pounce and whack, had also taught Frank-lin Roosevelt to be evasive and prudent. In the mid-1920s, he had at-tended a luncheon in the carved mahogany dining room of the *New York Times,* where, he remarked, the "self-anointed scholars" had made him feel like "an uneducated worm." But FDR quickly learned how to deal with the press. In 1931, the *Times's* Arthur Krock had hammered then-governor Roosevelt for refusing to comment on national and in-ternational affairs. Roosevelt shot back with a tongue-in-cheek fable. Once, when the New York governor "dipped into" national problems, believing that they related to problems facing his own state, Roosevelt wrote, "an All-Wise Press hopped all over him and said that he was ob-viously seeking national honors." When the governor later declined to state his position on a certain international problem, "an All-Wise Press chided the said Governor" for his silence.[8]

In January 1932, a week before his fiftieth birthday, Roosevelt an-nounced his candidacy for the presidency and then proceeded to cobble together a motley crew of advisors. On his team were moderates, pro-gressives, and conservatives. Some were politicians: senators Cordell Hull of Tennessee, Alben Barkley of Kentucky, Thomas Walsh of Mon-tana, and Carter Glass of Virginia. Others were longtime aides, like Jim Farley and Louis Howe. He recruited Harvard friends as well as Co-lumbia University economics professors. There were western radicals, southern Bourbons, and even a few Ku Klux Klanners. They all advo-cated different approaches and different policies. Roosevelt's task was to weave together the contradictory strands of their advice—into an all-purpose, all-weather fabric.

Vying for his party's nomination, Roosevelt carefully clouded the is-sues, often substituting platitudes for convictions. Some of his advisors and a few politicians, like New York senator Robert Wagner, balked at his hazy political message and yearned to see him take bold stands. In the early months of the Great Depression, as the nation was sinking into the fog of despair, Wagner himself had not hesitated to attack the passivity and cruelty of the federal government. He blasted President Hoover for refusing to extend a helping hand to the "forlorn Americans" in every village, town, and city in the United States who had been without wages since 1929. Roosevelt's mild message also disappointed Rexford Tugwell, a young Columbia University economics professor and expert in agricultural economics who was a member of Roosevelt's Brains Trust. And yet Tugwell recognized the political wisdom of FDR's strategy. "Nothing drastic, nothing unexpected," Tugwell wrote.[9]

Only once, during the campaign for the Democratic nomination, did FDR dare to stray from that bland course. In a speech at Oglethorpe University in Georgia, in the spring of 1932, he declared that the country needed and demanded "bold, persistent experimentation." The millions of people who were in desperate need, he pointedly warned, "will not stand silently by forever while the things to satisfy their needs are within easy reach."[10] Was a gutsy Roosevelt raising the explosive specter of mass revolt? Frantically worried by what he considered a major gaffe in a flawless campaign, FDR's close advisor and confidante Louis Howe insisted that his boss tone down his message. And so Roosevelt obediently retreated to his unadventurous tack.

As the Democratic National Convention in Chicago approached, FDR stressed to his soon-to-be campaign manager, Jim Farley, that the strategy would be harmony and inclusivity. Even though most of the industrial states were opposed to him and preferred other candidates, he would not "criticize, cry down, or defame any Democrat from any part of the country." It would be a daunting task to find concord in Chicago in the summer of 1932. But Roosevelt possessed a "sixth sense," remarked his confidant Ed Flynn, that enabled him to perform a singular marriage—between conservatives from the South and liberals from the North and the West.[11]

"We must stake everything on Texas; it's our only chance," whispered Louis Howe, tortured by asthma and gasping for breath, as he lay stretched out on the hotel floor, telephone to his ear.[12] With two other candidates vying for the nomination—Al Smith of New York and Speaker of the House John Nance Garner—Roosevelt decided to offer the vice presidency to Garner. It was an astute olive branch to Texas.

Another concession he made to the South was his decision not to challenge the "two-thirds rule," meaning that two-thirds of the convention delegates had to approve a presidential nominee. That had long given the South a virtual veto on any nomination, but Roosevelt yielded to the southern Democrats, he said, in the name of good "sportsmanship." But it was surely less a question of sportsmanship than careful calculation. The goodwill and support of southern delegates, he knew well, were crucial to win the nomination.

And win he did.

By an old tradition, presidential nominees made their acceptance speeches weeks after the convention, but FDR decided to break with a tradition he labeled "absurd." Along with Eleanor and four of their off-spring, he made a dramatic flight in a small plane from New York to Chicago to address the delegates in person.

His speech that night, in which he promised the American people "a new deal," was extraordinarily audacious and confrontational—a complete about-face from his preconvention game plan. He boldly underscored the political cleavages in the nation—not only between Democrats and Republicans but also between liberal and conservative Democrats. Instead of papering over those cleavages, he emphasized them; and instead of trying to please all Democrats, he suggested that some take a hike.

"Never before in modern history," he declared, "have the *essential differences* between the two major parties stood out in such striking contrast as they do today." The Democrats, he said, comprised a party of "liberal thoughts, of planned action, of enlightened international outlook, and of the greatest good to the greatest number of our citizens." Defining the party in the terms of his own liberal credo, he demanded that conservative Democrats join this mainstream. "I warn those nominal Democrats," he said with a surprising note of hostility, "who squint at the future with their faces turned toward the past, and who feel no responsibility to the demands of the new time, that they are out of step with their Party." Also inviting moderate Republicans "to join hands with us," Roosevelt was making a tacit call for party realignment that foreshadowed his risky political venture of 1938.[13]

That unusually divisive speech—which would have no follow-up for six years—represented a momentary deviation from Roosevelt's centrist strategy, for during the campaign that fall, there was little evidence of an ideological chasm between the two candidates—or between the two party platforms, which were virtually interchangeable.

Though confronted with a numbed, stricken nation, with tens of millions of fearful, angry, and hungry people, the Republican platform of 1932 called not for government action to help the jobless and the needy but instead passed the buck to the people, expressing confidence in their ability to "work out the cure" to the nation's economic hardships. According to the platform, individual initiative—and not reliance on the federal government—would do the trick.

The succinct Democratic platform—only fourteen hundred words long—offered little more. It recognized the need for unemployment and old-age insurance but repeated the Republican line that the states and not the federal government should take the lead in providing these programs. In a campaign speech that October in Atlanta, Roosevelt told the crowd that only after state governments and charitable organizations like Community Chests did everything in their power to help the poor should the federal government step in, as a last resort. Luckily, comedian Will Rogers pitched in. Since the repeal of Prohibition was a major issue, Rogers commented that the Democrats were "going to show the people where to get some bread with the beer."[14]

When the final stretch of the presidential campaign got under way, Roosevelt found it less risky to reject President Hoover's policies than to spell out his own, especially since he had no real program to offer. He had only a collection of proposals—some well-thought-out, others vague and amorphous. But inspired by his own voracious curiosity, he called for "experiments"—"Take a method and try it, if it fails, try another. But above all, try something."[15]

Of course, making Roosevelt's campaign against Hoover easier was none other than Hoover himself, the morose leader of a dazed administration. Although Hoover had been an energetic, competent, and compassionate administrator during and after World War I, providing food relief to war-torn Belgium and also heading the U.S. Food Administration, as president he appeared frozen in conservatism and confusion.

As the United States slid deeper into the Depression, Hoover made things both better and worse. He proposed—and Congress passed—important programs like the Home Owners Loan Corporation and the Farm Mortgage Refinancing Act, which reduced foreclosures and encouraged home construction, and the Reconstruction Finance Corporation, which provided liquidity to banks and helped restore confidence in the banking system. But he also slashed spending and raised taxes, intensifying the economic crisis. The public face of his administration was his own dour one, devoid of any sign of compassion for the agonizing economic distress of his fellow Americans. "If someone could get off a good joke every ten days," he unthinkingly said in 1931 to reporter Raymond Clapper, "I think our troubles would be over." His diagnosis was that the country needed a "good big laugh."[16]

But laughter came hard. Campaigning for the presidency in October 1932, Hoover was jeered and booed by thousands of jobless men in Detroit and had to be protected by scores of police. Only the wealthy applauded his scathing attack on Roosevelt's "frivolous promises" to provide federal jobs to the "ten million unemployed." Hoover's name entered the American lexicon as a synonym for what people perceived as the government's torpid and callous indifference to a distraught nation: encampments full of shacks for the homeless were dubbed "Hoovervilles," and the newspapers with which the homeless covered themselves for warmth were called "Hoover blankets." Roosevelt, said Frances Perkins, considered Hoover a "solemn defeatist," who had no consciousness of people as human beings or of their needs.[17]

But for the millions of battered Americans—25 percent of the country—who were out of work, penniless, embarrassed, immobilized in sheer desperation, standing slumped, hollow-eyed, in long breadlines, begging or selling apples, sleeping under frayed overcoats or under Hoover blankets on streets lined with stark, empty storefronts, the words of Hoover and Roosevelt were often equally irrelevant.

"Let us have the *courage* to stop borrowing to meet continuing deficits": not Hoover's words but Roosevelt's. The campaign speeches of the two candidates, commented Marriner Eccles, a Utah banker who would serve as chair of the Federal Reserve's Board of Governors under Roosevelt, "often read like a giant misprint, in which Roosevelt and Hoover speak each other's lines."[18] In speech after speech, FDR rattled off a laundry list of proposals for curbing deficits, creating a sound currency, and covering expenditures with revenues. And topping it all off, he offered the avuncular advice that the government, like any responsible family, should live within its means. And yet, though their policies were not dramatically different, Roosevelt presented the appealing image of a caring man who was willing and eager to act. He gently defined his own liberalism as essentially a desire to find the middle path. "Say that civilization is a tree which continually produces rot and dead wood," he told an interviewer in the fall of 1932. "The radical says: 'Cut it down.' The conservative says: 'Don't touch it.' The liberal compromises: 'Let's prune.' . . . Compromise is the essential tool of the fine art of politics."[19]

Roosevelt's calls for reductions in government spending and simultaneous promises of expensive relief programs for the nation's unemployed, commented campaign aide Rex Tugwell, were "about as contradictory as it was possible to be." Still, Tugwell knew that despite Roosevelt's cautious words and evasive tactics, both candidates were "the protagonists in an epic struggle of ideas." Fortunately, people found themselves fascinated and seduced by Franklin Roosevelt—captivated by his effervescent smile, energized by his self-confidence, uplifted by the cheering crowds. Roosevelt used his buoyant personality, Tugwell later recalled, "in a lavish way." Tugwell and others who worked with Roosevelt in 1932 sometimes wondered why he bothered to shower his charm on his campaign staff. "We concluded that it was not conscious, but rather something . . . habitual."[20]

Roosevelt's strategy—his calculated vagueness along with the force of his personality—paid off. He swept the nation, winning almost 60 percent of the vote, carrying forty-two states and 472 electoral votes. The GOP lost twelve seats in the Senate and over a hundred seats in the House, giving control of both chambers to the Democrats. A seat change had taken place. After ignominious defeats in 1920, 1924, and especially in 1928, when Democrat Al Smith won only 87 electoral votes compared to 444 for Hoover, the Democrats were back.

"I take my hat off to the greatest political general of our times," Republican senator Hiram Johnson of California wired to Roosevelt. Senator Carter Glass of Virginia hailed Jim Farley as the "greatest campaign manager of them all."[21]

As president-elect, Roosevelt continued the same winning strategy of inclusivity, gathering a diverse assortment of liberals and conservatives, Democrats, Republicans, and Independents for his administration. He heavily weighted his cabinet with southern conservatives whose support would be crucial to get his legislation through Congress. He appointed the courtly Cordell Hull of Tennessee as secretary of state, Daniel Calhoun Roper of South Carolina as secretary of commerce, and Virginian Claude Swanson as secretary of the navy. There would have been a fourth southerner if Glass—the father of the Federal Reserve Act of 1913 and later Wilson's secretary of the treasury—had not declined to come aboard for another tour as treasury secretary. Other southerners were appointed to positions outside the cabinet: Steve Early of Virginia would serve as the president's press secretary; Robert Fechner of Tennessee would head the Civilian Conservation Corps; Marvin McIntyre of Kentucky would be his secretary for appointments; and the genial and diplomatic Major General Edwin M. ("Pa") Watson, of Alabama and Virginia, a senior aide.

Seeking to broaden his team, FDR also appointed progressive Republicans Henry Wallace and Harold Ickes as his secretaries of agriculture and the interior. In the first appointment of a woman to a cabinet position, he named Democrat—and former Socialist Party member—Frances Perkins as secretary of labor. There were westerners—the Department of War went to Governor George Dern of Utah—and easterners—Connecticut lawyer Homer Cummings accepted the post of attorney general. The president's budget director, Lewis Douglas of Arizona, was a conservative advocate of laissez-faire economics.

"The only principle in the cabinet's make-up," commented James MacGregor Burns, was "its lack of essential principle." For Roosevelt, the diversity and range of his cabinet represented a strength, not a weakness, for not only did it consolidate his broad coalition and fortify his power base but it also permitted brilliant collective leadership from a diverse team of skilled and visionary people. "On the whole Mr. Roosevelt has chosen well," acknowledged the usually disapproving Walter Lippmann. "There is courage, there is ability, there is experience."[22]

After Roosevelt's election victory, conservatives, liberals, Republicans, and Democrats made the pilgrimage to Hyde Park to pay their respects to the president-elect. A warm, ebullient FDR welcomed them all, smiling enthusiastically at their ideas, nodding approvingly at their suggestions, and leaving them with the strong—and often erroneous—impression that he agreed with them. He reassured Senator Pat Harrison of Mississippi, one of his earliest and most devoted supporters, that it would be necessary to cut government spending even below the revised budget figures. After his tête-à-tête with the president-elect, Huey Long, the populist Democratic senator from Louisiana, announced, "I think we've got a great president. Every man, woman and child in the land would be delighted if they knew what I know after this conference." Even Father Charles Coughlin, the radio priest who would later become FDR's raging, infamous foe, gushed: "the New Deal is Christ's deal."[23]

The name of Roosevelt's game during his first term in office was consensus. That had been his strategy in his run for the presidency in 1932, and it remained his strategy for governing the nation in the first years of his administration. And his greatest asset for achieving that consensus was his own calculated charm and skill in friendly persuasion. "He was courtesy itself in receiving suggestions from his advisers," remarked Frances Perkins. White House speechwriter Stanley High remembered many eminent congressional leaders going to the president's office in a state of incipient revolt, only to leave the White House ready to "declare to the world their subscription to things that they did not subscribe to."[24]

Above all, FDR was a master opportunist and pragmatist. Neither ideology nor theory captured his imagination; he was interested only in concrete results. That was his genius. Throughout his many years in office, his favorite saying was "Let's try it!"[25] At the heart of the New Deal, as historian Richard Hofstadter remarked, lay not a philosophy but "a temperament." Roosevelt's top priority was to promote economic recovery and rescue tens of millions of forgotten Americans from the Great Depression. To do that, he intuitively understood that he had to be a master broker, an agile appeaser who could mediate among all the major political and economic interest groups in the nation.

The early New Deal offered transformational legislation—huge and unprecedented—that changed the nature and responsibilities of government. It also offered goodies to many sectors of society. Roosevelt instituted the Securities and Exchange Commission for small investors; mortgage readjustments for homeowners; the Farm Relief Bill for farmers; the Civilian Conservation Corps for the jobless; the Tennessee Valley Authority for the southern states; the National Industrial Recovery Act for businessmen, workers, and consumers. Even isolationists got something: FDR sabotaged the World Economic Conference in London in the spring of 1933, disappointing American internationalists who had hoped for better economic relations among nations. The president's outreach, at least during his first two years in office, was a "skillful, even a miraculous performance," judged Arthur Krock of the *New York Times*.[26]

Curiously, during his first transformational term in office, Roosevelt displayed no interest in building and leading a resolutely liberal Democratic Party. He never repeated the uncompromising partisan message of his Chicago acceptance speech and never took aim at conservatives in his own party. Nor would he even predict the party's survival. Instead he merely voiced the hope that a progressive majority, under any umbrella and any label, would take root under his leadership. After winning the election in 1932, elated by the stunning Democratic victories in both the House and Senate, FDR confessed to Rex Tugwell that "we'll have eight years in Washington. By that time there may not be a Democratic Party but there will be a progressive one." And in the epilogue to his 1934 book *On Our Way*, he even paid tribute to voters with little party loyalty. In a "perfect system of government," Roosevelt mused, the public should vote "solely upon political principles and good administration." But younger voters, he pointed out, were less concerned with party labels, and they admitted that they almost always split their tickets. "That is a happy sign," Roosevelt improbably concluded, "for the future of America."[27]

So anxious was Roosevelt to respond to different political and economic pressures, to annex moderate Republicans and Independents, and cobble together as broad, inclusive, and nonpartisan a coalition as possible that, during the first years of his presidency, he virtually peeled the Democratic label off himself and his administration. Declining to attend Jefferson Day festivities, an old Democratic tradition, he suggested that nonpartisan Jefferson dinners be held instead—with Republicans as well as Democrats in attendance. And when an aide, Charles Michelson, prepared a document underscoring the role of the Democratic Party in the achievements of the New Deal, FDR tossed aside his draft.[28]

Discounting the importance of party, Roosevelt emphasized instead American solidarity around a liberal majority and a progressive agenda. In 1934, he declared to a crowd in Wisconsin that the New Deal "seeks to cement our society, rich and poor, manual worker and brainworker, into a voluntary brotherhood of freemen, standing together, striving together." He told the members of the National Emergency Council in June of that year that it was important to think about government "and not merely about party." Again and again, he reminded Americans that his administration's recovery programs were being accomplished "by men and women of *all parties*." In 1934, he told a group of reporters that he was "trying to get across the idea that if we have the right kind of people the party label does not mean so very much." Members of Congress, Roosevelt rejoiced, had "displayed a greater freedom from mere partisanship than any other peacetime Congress since the Administration of President Washington himself."[29]

That was the line he continued to take in 1935, suggesting that it was more important for people to support the idea of an energetic, competent government than to support a political party. "We must be loyal also to the higher conceptions of *ability* and devotion that modern government requires," he said, dismissing the role of parties in organizing and propelling government action. "Franklin was a Democrat of convenience," remarked Rex Tugwell. According to Tugwell, the president was committed to a liberal and progressive coalition and agenda, not necessarily to Democratic ones.[30]

In election races, too, Roosevelt refused to be constrained by loyalty to the Democratic ticket. He reached out to non-Democrats, offering them his precious coattails. In 1933, he helped the maverick Republican Fiorello LaGuardia, who was running on a "fusion" ticket, defeat his Democratic and Socialist opponents in the New York mayoralty race—although New York Democrats warned Roosevelt that people would resent his intervention in a local race and that his support for a fusion ticket could "boomerang" and hurt the Democratic Party. In the midterm election of 1934, Roosevelt snubbed the Democratic candidate for the Senate in Wisconsin and instead came to the aid of Progressive Robert La Follette in his successful reelection bid.[31]

The same year in California, Roosevelt declined to support longtime socialist Upton Sinclair, who was running on the Democratic ticket for governor. The president instructed his staff to "(1) say nothing and (2) do nothing"—thereby helping the Republican candidate trounce Sinclair. In Minnesota, FDR aided the powerful and popular Farm-Laborite Party's two candidates—Henrik Shipstead for the Senate and Floyd Olson for the governorship. "In Minnesota, *hands off*—don't encourage opposition to Shipstead and Olson," FDR instructed Jim Farley.[32]

And in 1936, Roosevelt happily backed former Republican George Norris of Nebraska, who was running as an Independent for the Senate. Announcing that he was breaking his "rule" of nonparticipation in state elections, FDR declared in a speech in Omaha, "I have made—and so long as he lives I always will make—one magnificently justified exception. George Norris's candidacy transcends State and party lines." And while FDR turned down requests to help Senator Key Pittman of Nevada and Congressman Maury Maverick of Texas in their Democratic primary contests that year, he enthusiastically embraced his ideological foe, Carter Glass of Virginia, who was running for reelection. Few Democratic senators differed more with the president than Glass, who as early as August 1933 had blasted the New Deal as "an utterly dangerous effort of the federal government to transplant Hitlerism to every corner of the nation."[33] Glass had voted not only against the National Industrial Recovery Act but even against Social Security. And yet, when FDR visited Lynchburg in the summer of 1936, he and the diminutive, five-foot four-inch Virginian were photographed warmly hugging each other. With lingering fondness for Glass, whom he addressed as "my dear old friend" and who remained a loyal Democrat despite his policy differences with the president, FDR made it clear that he would welcome the lord of Virginia politics, the father of the Glass-Steagall bill that separated commercial banks from investment banks, back to Washington for another term.[34]

By backing Independents and Farm-Laborites, by throwing support to the La Follette Progressive Party in Wisconsin and to the American Labor Party in New York, by helping a conservative Democrat like Glass and dodging pleas to aid a liberal Democrat like Maverick, FDR demonstrated little interest in building a liberal Democratic Party. Indeed, he was far more preoccupied with his own political needs. Especially in the months leading up to the election of 1936, he was eager to round up politicians regardless of party label—as long as they supported *him*.[35]

Encouraging a variety of progressive, nonpartisan organizations, he put his seal of approval on the Roosevelt Agricultural Committee, which reached out to farmers; the Progressive National Committee, which tried to draw in moderate Republicans; Labor's Non-Partisan League, a new pro–New Deal political party, created by Congress of Industrial Organizations officers John Lewis and Sidney Hillman; and the "Good Neighbor League," designed to mobilize women, blacks, educators, social workers, and clergymen for Roosevelt's reelection.

The president might have considered a plan to channel all of that progressive energy into the Democratic Party and to hoop all those organizations together under the Democratic umbrella. Instead, he hailed the creation of a group like Labor's Non-Partisan League and ignored the warnings of Farley and other Democrats that the creation of more labor parties, resembling the Farm-Laborites of the Northwest or the recently formed Labor Party in New York, might one day turn into the enemy of the Democratic Party. "I am heartened," Roosevelt wrote in a public letter to the Non-Partisan League, "by the conviction that we are all working for the same ideal." His campaign literature rarely contained any reference to the achievements of the Democratic Party. "I do not believe that the President himself mentioned the party by name more than three times in the entire campaign," remarked Stanley High. "He did his campaigning, not as a Democrat but as a New Deal liberal, fighting not for party success but for a cause."[36]

Deeply troubled by the opposition of conservative Democrats to New Deal programs, Roosevelt was tempted by the idea of transcending party politics altogether. At times, he believed that it would be enough to have an enduring liberal majority, under any name or organization, as long as that majority could ensure a lasting liberal bureaucracy in Washington. Such a consolidated bureaucracy, as political scientist Sidney Milkis acutely argued, would be defined by a New Deal consensus and would ultimately marginalize parties, perhaps even making them irrelevant. But while such a bypassing of the vicissitudes of party politics would increase presidential autonomy, it would have the unfortunate consequence of decreasing democratic participation in government and diminishing a dynamic connection between government and society. Still, right on cue, at one press conference in 1938, the president indeed insisted that the common good transcended political parties.[37]

Caught in his own contradictory feelings, he wanted it both ways—he wanted on the one hand a majority liberal coalition that would permit the indefinite continuation of a New Deal "administrative state" and on the other a unified, liberal Democratic Party. For in the spring of 1938, Roosevelt the nonpartisan liberal coalition-builder suddenly proclaimed himself the zealous partisan leader of a soon-to-be-disciplined Democratic Party from which he, as party leader, would boldly banish the faithless conservatives.

In 1938, an angry Roosevelt, smarting from his defeats, wanted to oust his conservative foes from the party. But he also wanted something less personal, less emotional, and more lasting: a change in the political culture of Washington. His long-term goal was to *highlight* the conflict between conservatives and liberals within the Democratic Party and then *eliminate* that conflict—by banishing conservatives and creating a unified, solidly liberal Democratic Party. Then meaningful and vital political sparring could take place—not within a party but between two opposing parties. His goal was to quash conflict in order to reorganize and relocate it.

If the Democrats succeeded in ejecting conservatives from their ranks and if the Republicans absorbed those conservatives, the result, FDR hoped, would be party realignment and healthy, principled conflict between Republicans and Democrats. The Republican Party would embody conservative ideals while united Democrats would rally around liberal and progressive values. Two teams, each with its own clear agenda, each with a broad, national perspective, would combat each other in the political arena of American democracy. And, most important, the president, leading a loyal and united majority team, would be empowered to fulfill his mandate and respond swiftly and effectively to the desperate and urgent needs of the people. Only with a disciplined majority party behind him could the president overcome congressional deadlock, filibusters, and uncooperative committee chairmen.

After years of skillfully offering sweetened deals to conservative Democrats and catering to some Republican and Independent progressives, Roosevelt now began to believe that party polarization would better serve American democracy. First of all, it would spur a crucial national debate on the direction the country should take. And second, polarization would give voters a real choice between two sharply opposing visions. Elections, FDR wrote, "become meaningless when the two major parties have no differences other than their labels." He believed that politicians who ran for Congress by claiming to be Democrats while intending to vote as Republicans not only deceived voters but prevented them from making informed choices about the type of government they wanted for the next few years.[38]

But in calling for two distinct parties, each with its own clear ideology, was FDR attempting to graft onto the American political system an alien model—that of Great Britain?

In the House of Commons, two parties—two ideological teams always prepared to joust and exchange verbal blows—confront each other across an empty space, playing their assigned roles in a supremely choreographed adversarial system. But in Washington, the political architecture has always suggested conviviality rather than ideological confrontation. Unlike the straight, parallel symmetry of the House of Commons, in the Senate and House chambers, senators and representatives are seated in a collegial semicircle. Not only do the two parties bleed into each other, within each party there is also a spectrum of political colors. "The aisles don't mean anything," George Huddleston, the Democratic congressman from Alabama, remarked in 1931, "except a good place to walk in and walk out."[39]

Those architectural differences symbolize the stark contrasts in the British and American systems of government. In Great Britain, the executive and the legislative branches of government are one, united in Parliament; the prime minister heads the government because he is the leader of the majority party in Parliament. There are virtually no checks on the party in power, which is free to enact its legislative agenda. The role of the opposition party is merely to offer its own alternative agenda—it has no power of its own to block the prime minister's government. But American founders like James Madison feared precisely such an energetic, majoritarian government. In order to assure stability rather than energy, they designed a Constitution that separated the executive and legislative branches, giving each of them distinct responsibilities and clashing powers. "Ambition must be made to counteract ambition," wrote Madison, nodding to political collision and deadlock in the new government.[40]

Whereas the disciplined members of Parliament must adhere to the principles and direction of their party's leadership, the American system of separation of powers permits senators and representatives to often act like independent agents—opportunists free to spurn their leaders when it suits them and to move deftly back and forth across party lines. In addition, whereas British voters cast their ballots for a party and its program, Americans pride themselves on voting not for a party but for individual candidates, on the basis of their personalities, their promises, and sometimes their refusal to toe a party line. The sheer independence of the two senators from Nebraska in the mid-1930s—Edward Burke, who was elected as a Roosevelt Democrat yet consistently opposed the New Deal, and Republican George Norris, who criticized Republican leaders at every turn and supported much of the New Deal—would have been inconceivable in Great Britain.

With its inability to impose discipline, the party system in America, remarked the great political scientist V. O. Key, "exists in a continual state of flux." In Washington, within each party—as well as between the parties—alliances are formed and unformed; political partnerships are created and dismantled; allegiances and friendships continually mutate, dissolve, shift. American parties are broad, fluid coalitions. A "national" party in the United States is national once every four years; the rest of the time it serves state and local politicians and officials— from sheriffs and district attorneys to mayors, state senators, and governors. The basis for their party affiliation is as much a question of loyalties, personalities, local interests, and emotions as it is of rational political principles. Such a sprawling holding company for so many diverse groups is inevitably decentralized, disorganized, and undisciplined.[41] Roosevelt hoped that those local and state political organizations would spurn parochial issues for national ones. But his vision of local elections dominated by questions of political ideology and by national issues like workers' rights and the country's security simply did not correspond to the reality of American party politics.

Another problem with Roosevelt's idea of party realignment was that it presumed that the Republican Party would cooperate with him and agree to become the nation's conservative party. While that would have brightened the spirits of the GOP's Old Guard, the party's moderates were unwilling to relinquish their party to die-hard anti–New Dealers. Progressive Republicans—governors Alf Landon of Kansas and George Aiken of Vermont and senators William Borah of Idaho, Styles Bridges of New Hampshire, Charles McNary of Oregon, James Couzens of Michigan, and others—wanted to steer their party back to the middle and to the progressivism of Theodore Roosevelt. And while they had no desire to close ranks with FDR, they knew that it was political suicide to adopt a stance of polar opposition to the New Deal.[42]

The 1936 Republican platform, indeed, had not truly embraced conservatism. While it attacked the "frightful waste and extravagance" of the New Deal and promised a balanced budget, it also approved of Social Security, supported the rights of labor to organize and bargain collectively, and recommended adequate relief aid for the needy. Going beyond the Democratic platform, it even called for "equal opportunity for our colored citizens." Four years later, in 1940, the Republican platform would embrace isolationism, but it would also urge the prompt building up of the nation's defense forces, a "square deal" for African Americans, and a constitutional amendment providing equal rights for women. This was hardly the platform of a party of reaction; and neither of the party's 1936 and 1940 standard-bearers—former Bull Mooser Alf Landon and former Democrat Wendell Willkie—were right-wing conservatives. Real realignment would be a difficult affair. "The president seems to feel that all he has to do," scoffed Landon, "is wave the flag and shout: 'All liberals on this side.' It is not quite as simple as that."[43]

Nor was it that simple for the Democratic Party. "I'm not a member of an organized party," quipped humorist Will Rogers in the 1930s. "I'm a Democrat!"

Discipline—ideological discipline as well as organizational discipline—was foreign to Democrats. It could not have been otherwise, since they represented a mix of incompatible interests and organizations. Still, they had grasped that in order to survive as a somewhat effective party, they would have to swallow and manage at least some of their disagreements.[44]

At the foundation of the Democratic Party lay a bargain. In the early nineteenth century, northern Democrats and southern Democrats had made a pragmatic deal, joining forces in a marriage of convenience and mutual empowerment, not a marriage of love. Northerners had tacitly agreed to give southerners influence and clout in the party in exchange for northern control of the presidency. Southerners accepted their end of the bargain, while northerners, too, honored their promise, respectfully deferring to southern traditions—first to slavery and later to white supremacy in the South. Anchored in the cities of the Northeast, the party was run by the spoilsmen of city machines. In the South it was, according to one observer, "undilutedly Bourbon and unashamedly reactionary." In the North it was industrial and proletarian, in the South agricultural and aristocratic.[45]

Under this unlikely and fragile arrangement, however, the Democrats for decades after the Civil War had found themselves for much of the time relegated to the political wilderness of minority status, controlling the Senate for only ten years and the White House for only sixteen between 1861 and 1933. Democrat Woodrow Wilson was elected in 1912 only because the Republicans split their votes between Taft and third-party Bull Mooser Theodore Roosevelt. In 1916 Wilson barely squeaked by to victory: he won 277 electoral votes against 254 for his Republican opponent, Charles Evans Hughes. In 1920, power shifted back to Republicans. Even in the wake of the egregious corruption of Warren Harding's administration, the Democratic candidate for president in 1924, Wall Street lawyer John W. Davis, was trounced by Calvin Coolidge, winning only 136 electoral votes to Coolidge's 382. In 1928, not only did the Democrats lose, but their party platform sounded as if it had been written by pre–Civil War southerners. It demanded protection for the rights and powers of the states, condemned expansive federal government, and called for a revival of the spirit of local self-government.[46]

But after Roosevelt's victory in 1932, the profile of the Democratic Party began to change. During his first term, the party became broader and more liberal, as new groups—blacks, ethnic minorities, Jews, immigrants, urban workers, organized labor, farmers, intellectuals, some Independents, and even some Republicans—jumped on the New Deal bandwagon. Equally traumatized by the Great Depression, old foes—such as northern industrial interests and southern agrarian interests—joined together in supporting the New Deal, thereby uniting northern and southern elements of the Democratic Party. Roosevelt rejected the fancy three-syllable word "inclusive," commented Frances Perkins. He preferred to say simply that in his government no one would be left out. In 1928 the Democrats had won only 15 million votes, but in the election of 1936, they would garner almost twice as many.[47]

In the 1930s, the party no longer had the South at its core; during FDR's administration, southern politicians did not represent a majority of Democrats as they had in 1920, when 107 of the 131 Democrats in the House of Representatives came from the South.[48] But because of seniority, southerners nevertheless continued to occupy key positions of power in Congress. Joseph Byrns of Tennessee, William Bankhead of Alabama, and Sam Rayburn of Texas served as Speaker from 1935 until Republicans recaptured the House in 1946; and the majority leaders in the Senate, during Roosevelt's terms, were also southerners: Joseph Robinson of Arkansas and Alben Barkley of Kentucky. In the Senate and in the House, southerners chaired most of the important committees. Carter Glass of Virginia headed the Senate Appropriations Committee, Pat Harrison of Mississippi, Commerce, and Ellison "Cotton Ed" Smith of South Carolina, Agriculture and Forestry. While northern Democrats wielded their influence largely through the executive branch, southern Democrats wielded theirs through the legislature.[49]

To keep the southern politicians on board the New Deal ship, FDR made substantial concessions to them. He withheld his support from unions that were trying to organize workers in the South, distanced himself from anti-lynching legislation, excluded agricultural and domestic workers—most of whom were black—from Social Security, permitted New Deal training and relief programs to discriminate against blacks, and tolerated poll taxes, literacy quizzes, and "white-only" Democratic primaries. Those transparent concessions to racism earned him points with southern politicians like Harrison, who candidly admitted that the South would remain loyal to the Democratic Party as long as it "protected the white civilization of the South."[50]

What did Roosevelt get in return? In the House and Senate, his southern loyalists—senators such as Theodore Bilbo and Pat Harrison of Mississippi, John Bankhead and Hugo Black of Alabama, Alben Barkley of Kentucky, and James Byrnes of South Carolina—supported the New Deal during his first term. "No man in Washington . . . has done more for the New Deal than Pat Harrison," wrote *Business Week* in May 1937. Of course, the New Deal had done even more for Mississippi, pouring hundreds of millions of dollars into a state that paid only a few million dollars in federal taxes. "Oh, you can't imagine the hell I have to go through," Senate majority leader Joe Robinson of Arkansas said to Carter Glass one day, asking for sympathy for having to be FDR's point man in the Senate. "In your case, Joe," Glass replied, "the road to hell seems to be lined with post offices." Roosevelt had earned the loyalty—if not the gratitude—of most southerners in Congress. Often they had voted for New Deal bills not because they liked *them* but rather because they liked *him*—as well as the dollars and jobs the programs brought to their states.[51]

Of course, not all southerners in Congress came on board with Roosevelt. He could not count on Glass and Byrd of Virginia, Smith of South Carolina, George of Georgia, Tydings of Maryland, or others who could not swallow the New Deal's fiscal policies or its vast expansion of the national government. But neither the president nor his opponents in his own party had ever declared war on each other—until 1938.[52]

After years spent courting and catering to conservative Democrats, FDR's Dutch was up. In the spring of 1938, after the defeat of his proposals for executive reorganization and court-packing, he decided to break with those obstructionists, repudiate them, and drive them—or at least drive those among them who faced primary contests and reelection in 1938—out of the Democratic Party. But it was a hazardous, high-risk strategy. By intervening in state primaries and opposing popular and powerful incumbents, Roosevelt risked alienating hundreds of thousands of their supporters. He was also bucking the history and traditions of the Democratic Party. And, most worrisome, he was impulsively abandoning his own proven skills for deal-making, compromise, and seduction. It was "wholly out of character," said a baffled Sam Rosenman years later. Roosevelt's usual tactic, Rosenman said, was "to make many compromises so that he would last to fight another day."[53]

On the other hand, in the wake of the brutally disappointing defeat of crucial bills in 1937 and 1938, Franklin Roosevelt had copious evidence that his talent for wheedling, promising, cajoling, pressuring—

and sometimes threatening—had run into a wall. And the broad coalition he had worked tirelessly to cobble together had collapsed under the weight of a bipartisan conservative bloc. If he could rid the Democratic Party of even one reactionary senator or congressman, it would surely be a net gain. And he had little to lose—during his second term, the turncoats in his own party stood in opposition to him; it was unlikely that the situation could become worse. "The struggle was a political one," wrote Rex Tugwell. "It was neither clean nor pretty. . . . Fire had to be fought with fire."[54]

And so the man who had lifted the country out of the Depression with a host of innovative economic experiments was now ready to try a bold political experiment: the purge.

◄ 3 ►

Favorite Son of the South

"FRANKLIN ROOSEVELT COMES BACK HOME THIS MORNING!" trumpeted the headline in the *Atlanta Constitution* in October, 1932. Home, of course, meant Georgia. The Peach State had adopted Roosevelt, and he often referred to "my State of Georgia" and "our South." He contrasted the warmth of southerners with New Englanders who never said "Howdy." That visceral bond with the people of the South made his war with certain southern Democrats all the more surprising and perilous.[1]

Roosevelt first embraced the South in 1924, three years after he was stricken with polio. It was then that he experienced the soothing waters of Warm Springs, seventy miles south of Atlanta, which by 1926 had become his second home. He built a cottage for himself and then bought the resort, pouring two-thirds of his savings—against his mother's advice—into transforming the dilapidated buildings into a modern treatment center for other polio victims, mostly children.

It was not just the warm waters that rejuvenated FDR—it was the satisfaction and pleasure he felt in creating a community of empathy. His work in Warm Springs reminded him that compassionate leadership—as well as leadership that empowered the leader's followers—could transform people's hopes and lives, including his own. "You didn't get anywhere until you came out of the North to Georgia," FDR's

Georgia neighbor Judge H. H. Revill used to remind him. "Then people realized that you must have pretty good sense."[2]

When he was in Warm Springs, Roosevelt swam and exercised in the pool for two hours every morning, and then, after lunch, relaxed on the shady porch of his cottage. "I do wish you were down here," he wrote in 1929 to his New York friend Henry Morgenthau from Warm Springs. "It is heavenly weather and the pool is perfect, especially since all of the new work is completed. Things are booming, and for the third successive month we are full up, with a long waiting list." In his convertible, specially designed for him with hand levers instead of foot pedals, he toured the Georgia countryside, delighting in the southern spring. "You would love the . . . truly languid southern atmosphere of the place!" he wrote to an aunt.[3]

In the South, he fit right in, receiving local politicians, attending community suppers, giving interviews to local reporters. "Mr. Roosevelt has made a great hit with the people of Warm Springs who have met him, and they are extending him a hearty welcome as a prospective regular visitor," reporter Cleborne Gregory wrote in the *Atlanta Journal*'s Sunday magazine in the fall of 1924. Mr. Roosevelt ebulliently pronounced everything in Warm Springs "Great" or "Fine" or "Wonderful." "Say! Let's get one of the hot dogs this man makes just outside the swimming pool," Roosevelt said to Gregory with his usual zest. "They're great!" Sixteen years later, in 1940, he and Gregory crossed paths again in Warm Springs. "Didn't we have a good time in the springs," FDR said, "and weren't those hot dogs good?"[4]

But he drew the line at possum. When he had visited the coastal town of Brunswick, Georgia, in 1913 as assistant secretary of the navy on a reconnaissance trip to see if Brunswick had potential for a deepwater port, his hosts regaled him with a possum banquet. They whipped up possum soup, possum salad, possum stew. "I ate them all," he cheerfully said. But the lukewarm soup, he later confessed, "wouldn't have been good even if it were hot." Still, a good-natured FDR heralded the possum as the "glorious symbol of our freedom."[5]

Roosevelt felt connected to Georgia, but he was not blind to its problems. The exorbitantly high electricity rates—four times the price of electricity in Hyde Park—astonished him.[6] He was also dismayed by the poor quality of public education in the state. "One day, as I sat on the porch of the cottage in which I lived," FDR would later recall of his first year in Georgia, "a boy came over very nervously and shyly and said, 'Mr. Roosevelt, may I speak to you for a moment? We are having a commencement at our school on Wednesday. Do you think you could come over and say a few words and give out the diplomas?' I said, 'Certainly, I will be glad to come. Are you the president of the graduation class?' He said, 'No sir; I am the principal of the school.' I said, 'How old are you?' 'I am nineteen.'

"Have you been to college?" FDR asked. "Yes, sir; I finished my freshman year at the University of Georgia."

"This is a pretty pathetic story when you come right down to it," FDR concluded. Life in Georgia was "a pretty tough game."[7]

While a cultural critic like the acerbic H. L. Mencken took pleasure in performing a facile hatchet job on the South, ranting in 1917 that southern society was replete with "fundamentalism, Ku Kluxry, revivals, lynchings, and hogs" and that southern culture was nothing but "an awe-inspiring blank," a sympathetic FDR recognized the vast potential of the South; he wanted to improve the South, not disparage it.[8]

For two months in 1925, Roosevelt wrote his own column in the *Macon Daily Telegraph*, taking over for a friend, Tom Loyless, who was ill with cancer. "The first week my column was splendid. The second week it wasn't so good and by the third week it was bunk," Roosevelt wrote. But, he added, in those columns he began to develop ideas for dealing with the gnawing economic problems of the South—ideas that would evolve into the New Deal.[9]

With a practical eye, he zeroed in on some of the problems in

Georgia—from the state's shortage of cattle and its reliance on imports of milk and other dairy products to the critical scarcity of timber. Whereas Georgia used to export millions of feet of lumber to other states, FDR wrote in one of his columns, now there was barely enough wood for the state's own needs. Trees were being burned, sometimes by accident but more often by design, raising the cost of home building and even that of paper. And there was no planning for the new growth of trees. "Unless we, in the United States, take immediate steps to compel the growing of new timber by individuals," Roosevelt warned, "I prophesy that it will become a government enterprise in the next generation."[10]

At first, Roosevelt believed that it was possible to propose remedies for these agricultural and economic woes without addressing the political situation in the South. "I must not get mixed up in Georgia politics," he prudently assured his readers in his first column for the *Daily Telegraph*. He had no interest in toppling local elites or criticizing the state's sole political party, the Democratic Party. "You people can mix it up to your hearts' content over all the local matters in the world," he wrote in 1925, "just so long as you come together and work shoulder to shoulder when it comes to *national* issues and the general strengthening and better organization of the Democratic party throughout the United States."[11]

But despite his hands-off declaration, Roosevelt soon came to realize that many of Georgia's entrenched politicians were unwilling to grapple with their state's immense problems. "Last Fall the Governor of this State made a speech on the subject of 'Georgia for the Georgians,'" FDR wrote in a column April 1925. "If every State adopted that attitude, we should have, in a generation, an aggregation of 48 ingrowing, inbred, selfish communities." The governor's provincial and insular slogan "Georgia for the Georgians" might have wide appeal, but Roosevelt was convinced that the combination of suspicion of new ideas, mistrust of the federal government, and a narrow concept of social responsibility would only doom the state to isolation, stagnation, and poverty.[12]

The South ached from low wages, inadequate purchasing power, depleted soil, unemployment, the absence of labor unions, and poor public schools. Child labor was more common in the South than in the North, and women and children had fewer legal safeguards. People suffered from pellagra, a vitamin-deficiency disease resulting in symptoms from skin lesions to dementia. Parasitic hookworm infections could be traced to poor sanitation and a lack of indoor flush toilets. The problems afflicting the South, Roosevelt discovered, were infinitely more complex than cattle and timber.

All these issues needed to be addressed, but change was as lazy in the South, wrote two southern reporters, as an August day in the Delta.[13] Some regions of the South had reform groups and liberal newspapers. And in the 1920s, Mississippi, North Carolina, Alabama, and Louisiana had reform or populist governors in Theodore Bilbo, Cameron Morrison, Bibb Graves, and Huey Long. They improved public education, roads, health, and other public services.

Yet the one-party South, politically as well as economically and socially, was mostly a dying, not a dynamic, culture. In the 1890s, conservative "Bourbon" Democrats had put to death the populist People's Party. Although the Republican Party made some modest gains in the South in the 1920s and showed strength in the 1928 presidential election, the South elected few Republicans to Congress. Without a viable opposition party, Democratic primaries were usually tantamount to elections—but they were closed to black voters. Poll taxes and other obstacles like blank registration forms and registration quizzes prevented millions of poor whites and blacks alike from voting; and state legislatures typically overrepresented conservative rural areas.

In the 1930s, the South did have some liberals—especially at southern universities. But, as historian George Tindall noted, "they were generals without an army" and had little influence among the general population. But for the most part, anticonservative insurgents against the status quo in the South were populists. Often driven by their rage against concentrated wealth and power, the populists sought to free Americans from the tentacles of what they considered a predatory free market economy and restore to them control over their own lives. Like liberals, they demanded economic equity, but unlike them, they hated the idea of expansive, intrusive government.[14]

Populists and liberals also had to contend with the powerful inertia of the conservative establishment and with a tendency, as the southern writer Clarence Cason observed, to avoid the baffling realities of the present by taking refuge in a backward-looking mythology that idealized the Old South. And when that mythology did not idealize life on the land, it rationalized stagnation and poverty and nurtured what Cason called "the dreamy, miasmic lethargy of the southern mind."[15] "The Lord made the land and He put me here to raise crops on it," says a character named Jeeter Lester in Erskine Caldwell's 1932 novel *Tobacco Road,* about Georgia sharecroppers. "I been doing that, and my daddy before me, for the past fifty years, and that's what's intended."

The system in the South appeared paternalistic, commented Thomas Stokes, a liberal reporter for the *Knoxville News-Sentinel,* but that merely masked a "communion of interests of the haves against the have-nots." The governing elite, Stokes wrote, dismissed the have-nots as "poor white trash," leaving them in servitude and ignorance.[16]

Franklin Roosevelt saw that his promise not to get mixed up in local politics was unrealistic. If he wanted to find truly effective solutions to the South's economic problems, he would have no choice but to dirty his hands in the political mud.

As president, Roosevelt grasped that it would take all the energy, resources, and planning of the federal government as well as all the cooperation and goodwill of southern politicians and business leaders to modernize the South and raise the standard of living of millions of people there.

He had long enjoyed warm relations with southern politicians. The reform-minded among them recognized him as a progressive leader and backed him politically. Since 1913, he had been close to Josephus Daniels of North Carolina, his boss when he was assistant secretary of the navy. Daniels, who would become Roosevelt's ambassador to Mexico, was starved for transformational change in the South. "The older I grow the more radically progressive I become," Daniels wrote in 1940 when he was seventy-eight. Other southerners also placed their hopes in Roosevelt. In 1930, just weeks after he was reelected governor of New York, "Roosevelt Southern Clubs" and "Women's Roosevelt Clubs" were established; they were southern-wide volunteer organizations promoting FDR for president in 1932. Poor southerners identified with Roosevelt because he identified with the South and connected with them on a seemingly personal basis.[17]

And wealthier and less progressive southerners, especially the descendants of plantation owners, appreciated him, too. His patrician background appealed to them, and they attributed to him an elitism and sense of noblesse oblige with which they felt comfortable. As early as 1926, Virginia's conservative senior senator Carter Glass had touted Roosevelt for president, hoping that he might be the Democratic candidate in 1928. By 1932, Glass's enthusiasm had not diminished. "Holding fast to sound Jeffersonian principles," he said in a radio endorsement of FDR, "we shall hope to rescue the government and the country from the unendurable confusion and distress into which the Republican maladministration has thrust us." A delighted FDR sent a telegram to Glass: "Wonderful speech last night . . . sincere appreciation."[18]

If Roosevelt was elected, South Carolina's senator James Byrnes predicted in 1932, "I give you my word that South Carolina will be recognized as she has never been recognized by any Democratic President before." When it became clear on the floor of the 1932 Democratic convention in Chicago that the party's nominee would be Franklin Roosevelt, "a rebel yell split the air," the *New York Times* reported. In Georgia, people celebrated the victory of their favorite son that November.

"Georgia's joy of anticipation became joy of realization today," reported the *Atlanta Constitution*.[19]

President Roosevelt would earn the gratitude and affection of millions of southerners. He and his Brains Trust had designed much of the New Deal with the South in mind. Their goals were to improve agriculture, create housing, raise wages, provide access to better education, and upgrade sanitation and health care.

The National Recovery Administration boosted the standard of living; the Tennessee Valley Authority brought flood control, jobs, and low-cost electricity to some of the poorest regions of the country, from Virginia to Mississippi; the Civilian Conservation Corps constructed roads and airports; the Agricultural Adjustment Act stabilized crop prices and increased farmers' incomes; the Farm Credit Association and the Farm Security Administration prevented foreclosures and permitted tenant farmers to purchase their own land; the Soil Conservation Service instructed farmers in scientific farming methods; the Rural Electrification Agency spread electricity and modern conveniences from refrigerators to radios to millions of rural homes; and the Public Works Administration put people to work transforming the nation's landscape—constructing schools, hospitals, highways, and parks. The PWA built dams—like the eight-mile-long Santee Dam in South Carolina that provided hydroelectric power to the state—and bridges—like the Overseas Highway connecting Key West to the Florida mainland.

The New Deal and its magical alphabet soup of agencies—NRA, TVA, WPA, CCC, REA, FERA—meant jobs, food, and money in almost every corner in the South. Mississippi sold its state's rights back to the federal government, said William Faulkner, only half in jest. "Our economy is the federal government." Though the South, in fact, may have profited less from federal largesse than other sections of the country, the effects of New Deal programs were more transformational there.[20]

In just one county in the mountains of North Carolina, there were four active Civilian Conservation Corps camps and one large Federal Emergency Relief program. When he opened the program's office in Clayton, North Carolina, in the bleak winter of 1933, Frank Smith recalled looking out onto the main street in town and seeing the faces of hundreds of waiting men, some too weak to stand up. With the help of FERA, they found jobs and began to live again. Until the late 1950s, Smith wrote, a framed portrait of Roosevelt hung in the local farmers' market in downtown Clayton. Letters praising the president poured into the White House. "You were the first to come to our rescue," Mrs. Lamar Rutherford Lipscomb of Atlanta wrote to the president.[21]

Many southerners knew that FDR was on their side—and they were on his. "The people of Georgia," editorialized the *Atlanta Constitution* during the summer of 1935, "will not turn away from the man whose leadership is primarily responsible for the kaleidoscopic change from despair to optimism. Not only will Georgia support President Roosevelt to succeed himself but his renomination and reelection are assured." That same year, Joe Starnes, an Alabama representative, affirmed that 80 percent of the people in his district wanted to reelect Roosevelt.[22]

Not once did Roosevelt carry his mid-Hudson home district in New York—the conservative Dutchess County—in a presidential election. But he always carried the South. In all four of his presidential races, he won in his Warm Springs, Meriwether County, district—once by the crushing margin of fifty to one. In the 1936 election, FDR received 255,364 votes in Georgia, compared to a meager 36,942 for the Republican candidate, Alf Landon. In the upper South and the border states, the vote was closer—about two to one. But the deeper the South, the greater Roosevelt's victory: in Alabama he won 238,196 votes compared to Landon's 35,358. In South Carolina he won 98.6 percent of the vote, and in Mississippi 96 percent. For the southern masses, remarked Georgia newspaper editor John Temple Graves, "Roosevelt was the Democratic Party, the rebel yell, Woodrow Wilson, and Robert E. Lee rolled into one present help in trouble."[23]

An anecdote about a southern schoolteacher and her class told by Ferrol Sams, Jr., a physician and writer from Fayetteville, Georgia, encapsulated Roosevelt's quasi-divine status below the Mason-Dixon line.

"Children, who paved the road in front of your house?"

In response, the chorus, "Roosevelt!"

"Who put electricity into your house for you?"

"Roosevelt!"

"Who gave your uncle a job in the WPA?"

"Roosevelt!"

"Who got your granddaddy an old age pension?"

"Roosevelt!"

"All right, children. Now. Who made you?"

After a moment of silence one little boy asserted stoutly, "God."

Whereupon a barefoot towhead leaped up in the back row and yelled, "Throw that sorry Republican out of here!"[24]

But while millions of southerners cheered and voted for Franklin Roosevelt, some southern politicians who had initially supported him felt betrayed. The New Deal triggered their instinctual aversion to public debt, high taxes, and the intrusion of the federal government in the affairs of their states. And, as historian George Tindall remarked, many New Deal policies, such as ones on crop limitations and government credit, also challenged the South's power elite, the industrialists, landlords, bankers on whom many southern politicians were dependent. One of the issues that ignited southern senators' most fervent objections was the minimum wage.[25]

Low wages plagued much of the nation but presented an especially critical problem in the South. The national minimum wage was $12 per week, but many southern factory workers earned less than half that. One woman whom reporter Thomas Stokes interviewed was proud to be earning $7 per week working in a factory from 7 A.M. to 4:30 P.M. with half an hour for lunch. The woman stood all day in front of a machine, putting biscuits in boxes, working a treadle with her foot while both hands were busy. She and people like her had no complaints, for they were the lucky ones. They had jobs. Stokes, who wrote movingly about the dark and brooding South that he hated, pitied, and loved, had faith in the New Deal.[26]

Roosevelt's key proposal in 1937 to end starvation wages in the South was the Fair Labor Standards Act, also known as the Wages and Hours Bill. Hope for prosperity hinged on good wages. Since one of the principal causes of the Depression was "underconsumption," FDR knew that higher wages would give workers real purchasing power; increased purchasing power would create demand for consumer goods; demand for goods would stimulate industry, helping businesses large and small. Most economists believed that higher wages would also improve productivity.[27]

In addition, higher wages would create more taxable income, providing revenue for schools, hospitals, a modern system of highways, and countless other necessities. So obvious was the importance of increasing wages and purchasing power that even the Republican Party platform of 1936 acknowledged the need to regulate maximum hours, minimum wages, and working conditions.[28]

The National Labor Relations Act of 1935 looked after the rights of workers who were able to organize—and strike—if they wanted to do so, but the Wages and Hours Bill aimed at protecting the forgotten workers in the country, those who did not have enough power to organize and bargain, those who worked the longest hours for the lowest wages, those who had little if any legislative protection. The bill also sought to bar child labor and prevent communities from trying to attract new industries by offering cheap labor. The Fair Labor Standards

Act, FDR wrote, was a critical part "of a democratic picture which grows more logical and simple the more we analyze it."[29]

But in 1937 the bill ran into a wall of opposition—especially in the South. The southern elite—the "banker-merchant-farmer-lawyer-doctor-governing class"—was above all interested in tempering what it considered the radical aspects of the New Deal and in maintaining the status quo. Politicians and businessmen bitterly objected to the bill's provisions for a 40-cents-per-hour minimum wage, a forty-hour maximum work week, and a minimum working age of sixteen. They argued that low wages actually helped the South by placing the region in a strong competitive position. When northerners complained that southerners wanted to keep wages low in order to lure northern industries to the South, those southerners nodded enthusiastically in agreement.[30]

Higher wages, some southern politicians contended, would be a fatal blow to the New South. For decades, the South had cast itself as the victim of northern colonialism; now many of its senators and representatives insisted that the North was once more threatening the South with economic and political strangulation. "This whole bill," exclaimed Senator Ellison "Cotton Ed" Smith of South Carolina, "is determined to check the inevitable rise of the South from the lowly condition in which the war between the States left it." As if he still felt the sting of southern defeat, Smith wanted nothing of northern panaceas.[31]

Even reliable southerners who had steadily supported the New Deal balked at the Wages and Hours Bill. Senator Pat Harrison of Mississippi, Roosevelt's formerly faithful ally, led the assault, arguing against too much rapid economic change. "Perhaps I do not want to travel as fast as some people," said Harrison, in a strange, rambling disquisition, "because I might get out of breath. I have often felt in sympathy with the old ox down in my country in July days that had been worked all day in the sun, who sees over in the distance a little shade under a tree, and you could not hold that ox back; he wanted to get under that shade." Harrison declared that he, too, needed to rest in the shade—and that he was against letting economic policy be made by people who believed stereotypes about the South, such as the one that "our women wear no shoes."[32]

On hearing of Harrison's bizarre speech, Roosevelt sighed that his old friend "has gone off the deep end." But what also came through in Harrison's words was the expression of a certain southern torpor, passivity, pessimism, and skepticism about northern promises of prosperity. Of course, it was not just higher wages to which some people in the South objected: they also feared that the bill might introduce a greater measure of racial equality. "You cannot prescribe the same wage for the black man as for the white man," pronounced Texas congressman Martin Dies.[33]

Southern conservatives found unlikely allies in the labor movement. Some labor leaders feared that a minimum wage would become a maximum wage, while others worried the bill would undermine their raison d'être—collective bargaining—and take away the unions' prime role. When the beleaguered—and watered-down—Wages and Hours legislation reached the Senate on July 31, 1937, it was passed by a vote of 56 to 28. But in the House, the chairman of the powerful Rules Committee, Democrat John O'Connor of New York, was determined to bury the bill in his committee. This congressman had become one of the New Deal's most zealous enemies, cheered on by three southerners on his committee: Martin Dies, Edward Cox of Georgia, and Howard Smith of Virginia.[34]

Unable to take action on the bill, Congress simply adjourned on August 21, 1937. No matter that it had passed only one vital piece of legislation—the Wagner Housing bill—from the president's ambitious agenda. Just nine months after Roosevelt's landslide election, opposition in his own party had grown assertive, militant, and confident—and the New Deal had come to a standstill.

It was pointless and absurd for these conservatives to remain in the Democratic Party, cried Pennsylvania senator Joseph Guffey in a radio address in late August, pointing especially to three western Democrats in the Senate—Wheeler of Montana, Burke of Nebraska, and a recent turncoat, O'Mahoney of Wyoming—who deserved to be repudiated at the polls. "I believe that the twenty-seven million who voted for Mr. Roosevelt dislike ingrates and ingratitude," Guffey said, predicting that voters would soon bury "in the oblivion of defeat" the Democrats who voted against the Wages and Hours legislation and the president's court bill. "It was a good speech," FDR wrote to Guffey. "You said vigorously many things that needed to be said." In fact, Guffey had preceded the president by a year in publicly raising the idea of a Democratic purge.[35]

"An Unchanging Roosevelt Drives On," read the headline of a profile of FDR by Anne O'Hare McCormick in the Sunday *New York Times Magazine* on August 15, 1937. "Despite the physical and the political heat of Washington," McCormick wrote, "he looked cool, comfortable and fit, the smile as wide and instant as ever." The president hadn't really changed since she first interviewed him in 1932. "Physically he ages remarkably little. His hair is thinner, his face and figure thicker, the shadows more deeply etched round his eyes. The characteristic expression, the backward jerk of his head when he laughs, the laugh itself, are the same." But whether or not his usual good humor and magnanimity extended toward the deserters in the Democratic ranks, she wrote, that was "another question."[36]

A few days later the president answered that question. On August 18, on Roanoke Island, North Carolina, he gave a speech in which he spewed out his frustration. He lashed out at all manner of conservatives—the U.S. Chamber of Commerce, the Liberty League, the National Association of Manufacturers, editorial writers. These men were interested only in protecting their own property and restraining the less privileged in the nation, those they labeled the "malcontents." Vacuously they maintained that all that was required to return the nation to prosperity was "tranquility and cheerfulness," never offering a word about improving the living conditions of the poor, increasing their wages, or helping them find steady work. In response to those selfish reactionaries, FDR proclaimed, "My anchor is democracy—and more democracy!"[37]

The president had said nothing about going after conservative Democrats in the primary elections the following year, but ever since White House insider Stanley High revealed that a crackdown was imminent in his *Saturday Evening Post* article in early 1937, the story was reported almost as fact. No one paid attention to White House denials. *Newsweek,* in its coverage of the Roanoke Island speech, predicted that the president would soon seek to oust Democrats who were "obstructing popular rule," while in late August the *Chicago Daily Tribune* reported that the president would shortly make a trip to the West Coast during which he would carry out "reprisals against the opposition elements of the party."[38]

Jim Farley, the national Democratic chairman, denied those reports. "There will be no reprisals," he categorically stated, dismissing the notion that the administration would punish Democrats. "It's entirely up to the voters whether they want their present representatives or new ones." For their part, voters agreed. According to a Gallup poll, they wanted to make their own decisions at the polls.[39] In fact, there would be reprisals—but, contrary to Farley's denials and the reports in *Newsweek* and the *Tribune,* reprisals would not take place for another year.

In late September 1937, the president, his wife, and the rest of his entourage boarded his ten-car private train and set out on a two-week journey for the Northwest.[40] Whereas the king of England traveled only with his immediate party, the American president was accompanied not only by family and friends but by Secret Service agents, secretaries, staff, reporters, radio broadcasters, cameramen, photographers, telegraph operators, cooks, barbers, and valets. In addition to the sixty people on the train, several thousand others were directly involved in the operation. The rear car of the train, reserved for the president, contained a sitting room, dining room, and several bedrooms. In front of the presidential car were office, dining, club, and sleeping cars for staff, guests, reporters, and railroad officials. Preceding the president's train was a "pilot train" that scrutinized and cleared the track, making sure that no moving trains would pass the president's in either direction.[41]

Whizzing across Iowa, Nebraska, Wyoming, Idaho, North Dakota, and Oregon, the Presidential Special passed cornfields, cattle, golden haystacks, farmhouses, and irrigation ditches. In Wyoming, Franklin and Eleanor Roosevelt, bundled in blankets in the sunny forty-degree weather, motored in an open car through Yellowstone, past snow-topped peaks, geysers, hot springs, Civilian Conservation Corps camps, and curious brown and black bears who lumbered out of the woods to stare at them.[42]

At each of the president's train stops, hordes of local politicians swarmed into the cars, while excited crowds gathered expectantly around the rear platform. After a calculated period of suspense, the president made his appearance and, smiling warmly, delivered his remarks. He spoke mostly about conservation and the protection of natural resources. In Marshalltown, Iowa, he talked about stable crop prices; in Cheyenne, Wyoming, he spoke about cattle and beets, confessing that he was more interested in the ten men who have a hundred head of cattle apiece than in the one man who has a thousand head of cattle. At the site of the stupendous new $50 million Bonneville Dam in Oregon, he talked about the importance of providing affordable electrical power to hundreds of small communities and mentioned his plans for more regional power authorities like the Tennessee Valley Authority. In the Mount Hood National Forest, he dedicated the Timberline Lodge, a project of the Works Progress Administration. And at the gigantic Grand Coulee Dam in Washington, he reminded listeners of the enduring significance of this spectacular feat of engineering that when completed would not only generate electricity but also supply water for irrigation to a parched region twice the size of Rhode Island and create a lake 155 miles long stretching all the way to Canada.[43]

Although he mostly avoided the controversial subjects of his court reform bill and the Wages and Hours Bill, he did not shrink from attempting to reward his congressional allies and rebuff his critics. In Idaho, Roosevelt and Republican Senator William Borah greeted each other effusively, a pointed reminder to Democrats that the president valued support for his programs more than party membership. Roosevelt told a Boise crowd that he and Borah thought alike; they both focused not just on the issues of the moment but on the "bigger objectives of American life"—on *national* problems from peace to prosperous agriculture and regional planning.[44]

But in Montana, Wyoming, and Nebraska, he hoped to wound the three senators—Wheeler, O'Mahoney, and Burke—whom Guffey had singled out a month earlier, although none of those senators was up for renomination in 1938. While Roosevelt gave the nod to Montana's Senator James Murray, one of the court bill's supporters, he wanted to demonstrate his dissatisfaction with the state's other Democratic senator, Burton Wheeler. In 1930, Wheeler had been one of the first Democrats to call for a Roosevelt presidency and up until 1937 had supported the New Deal. But more recently he had not only led the fight against the court bill but slammed the president as a would-be American dictator. Roosevelt wanted the pleasure of snubbing Wheeler in Montana, but two can play the snubbing game; Wheeler beat him to the punch by sneaking off to California. His flight marked the final bitter break between two former friends and allies.[45]

In Wyoming, a chilly Roosevelt tried to keep his distance from Senator Joseph O'Mahoney, another of the court bill's fierce opponents. O'Mahoney had not received an invitation to join the president on the train, but the senator, refusing to stand on formalities, drove furiously from Chicago to Wyoming in time to squeeze onto the rear platform. He was the "unwanted guest who cannot be turned out," wrote one reporter. Still, O'Mahoney's presence at FDR's side did nothing to stop the president from telling a crowd in Casper how much he scorned those who give "lip service" to New Deal objectives while doing nothing to attain them. In Nebraska, he gave the cold shoulder to Senator Edward Burke—one of the few Democrats to oppose the National Labor Relations Act and a stern foe of the court bill—by pointedly not inviting him to board the presidential train and by arranging his schedule so that the train crossed Nebraska in the middle of the night. No reprisals, no scalding blasts of criticism—but an artful president managed to express his displeasure with his Democratic adversaries without directly rebuking them. In any case, voters would be making no decision about the fates of Wheeler, O'Mahoney, and Burke until 1940.[46]

The trip may have helped slightly to strengthen the president's hand and the liberal wing of the party, inasmuch as a prodigal son like O'Mahoney showed himself anxious to climb back on board the president's train. But the journey served another important purpose too—that of buoying the president's spirits and reminding his critics of just how popular he was. Although a Gallup poll published that month revealed that a majority of Democrats in Wyoming, Montana, and Nebraska approved of their senators' stands against the court reform bill, those same Democrats also loved Roosevelt.[47]

Wherever he went, excited crowds jammed the streets; people covered him with confetti and torn strips of newspaper while others ecstatically ran alongside his motorcade. They cheered when he spoke of the importance of raising wages and "tackling the problems of the day." "I feel that I regain my strength," he confided to a crowd in Boise, "by just meeting the American people . . . and saying 'Howdy' today, just like the plain folks like all of us are." One of those plain folks was a thirty-four-year old itinerant who climbed on board the Presidential

Special. "They told me I was lucky I didn't get shot," he said after Secret Service agents arrested him in Pocatello, Idaho.[48]

Back in Washington in October, Roosevelt returned to the Wages and Hours Bill. Adamant that Congress address the plight of the poorest paid workers in the country, he called legislators back into session to reconsider it, as well as several other key farm, housing, and regional planning bills. Members groaned at the summons—especially those who were in Honolulu, working hard, no doubt, as they investigated Hawaii's application for statehood.[49]

The autumn of 1937 was a cruel season. In October, the stock market sank for the second time that year as stocks lost 12 percent of their value. A nervous Henry Morgenthau, the secretary of the treasury, feared that the country was headed for another depression. As industrial production dropped by a third, two million people lost their jobs. The president, who only a few months earlier had hailed the prospect of a balanced budget and cuts in federal spending, was perplexed by the jolting economic downturn, soon to be dubbed the "Roosevelt Recession." As if that wasn't enough, his defeats in Congress and news of fascist gains throughout the world made the president's gloom palpable. An abscessed tooth darkened his mood even more. His head throbbing from the pain, he postponed plans for a cruise in the Florida waters and cancelled a Thanksgiving holiday in Warm Springs.[50]

In late November, the president—with his jaw still visibly swollen—finally left windswept Washington for Miami and a vacation cruise with Jimmy Roosevelt, "Pa" Watson, Ickes, Hopkins, and assistant attorney general Bob Jackson. But the tour, on rough seas, turned out to be as miserable as everything else that fall. To the holiday mood, Ickes and Hopkins contributed only their own despair. Secretary of the Interior Ickes, prone to seasickness, was more comfortable in the interior than on coastal waters; Hopkins was still distraught over the recent death of his wife—and was already suffering from the stomach cancer that would be discovered a few weeks later. Even Jackson was suffering from an ailment he diagnosed as "neuritis." The president caught mackerel, barracuda, and yellowtail and occasionally joined the evening poker games, but he bitterly confessed to Eleanor that he felt like a "boiled owl." The tortured cruise was cut short.[51]

Politics in Washington did nothing to improve FDR's mood. In a shocking repeat performance, John O'Connor's Rules Committee once again refused to discharge the Wages and Hours Bill. This time, however, the House Labor Committee embarked on an intensive campaign of deal-making and horse-trading to wrest the measure from O'Connor. "They have swapped everything today but the Capitol," remarked Rules Committee member Martin Dies. The committee did finally release the Wages and Hours Bill, but on December 17, a majority of House members—some fearful that higher wages would worsen the recession—decided once again to recommit it to committee. Voting to recommit were 133 Democrats, including 81 of the House's 99 southerners. The southern bloc broke out into a triumphant roar of applause when the final tally was announced. The vote, FDR bristled, was "pure selfishness."[52]

The special congressional session the president had convened in October adjourned a few days before Christmas in December 1937. Only a few trivial pieces of legislation had been enacted during that three-month period, including one to lend four portraits to an art gallery. Representatives and senators had not passed a single one of the important measures they had been summoned back to consider. The whole session, Republicans gloated, was a "goose egg affair"—meaning that Roosevelt had scored a zero. The president was "fighting like a cornered lion," Henry Morgenthau wrote in his diary. He "did not want to be tamed, yet . . . did not know where to put his strength."[53]

In December, after Japanese bombers sank the United States gunboat *Panay* near Nanking, China, killing three Americans, Roosevelt moved to expand American naval power. The nation would begin to rearm and ready its guns. At least in foreign affairs, the president knew where to put his strength.

Southern Insurgents

ON DECEMBER 3, 1937, just before the House sent the Fair Labor Standards Act down to its second defeat, the junior senator from Virginia, Harry Byrd, hosted a luncheon in one of the private dining rooms in the Capitol for a small group of conservative senators. Among his guests were Democrats Josiah Bailey of North Carolina, Carter Glass of Virginia, Walter George of Georgia, Cotton Ed Smith of South Carolina, Royal Copeland of New York, William King of Utah, and Frederick Van Nuys of Indiana and Republicans Arthur Vandenberg of Michigan and John Townsend of Delaware. The guest of honor was Lewis Douglas, a zealous economizer who had resigned in 1934 as Roosevelt's budget director after falling out with New Dealers.[1]

Byrd and his friends, convinced that the nation was fed up with the New Deal, were buoyed by the idea that conservatism was on the rise. And as one of them remarked to a reporter, now it was their turn to "take the initiative away from the President." No longer did they feel as demoralized as they had been the year before. At the Democratic Convention in 1936, their behind-the-scenes fight against the party's liberal platform had come to naught, and their power ebbed even more when the convention abolished the "two-thirds" rule that had given the South a virtual veto on the presidential nominee. But now their fortunes seemed to be turning. In 1937, they had defeated the president's court plan, opposed his Fair Labor Standards bill, secured a Senate resolution branding sit-down strikes "illegal and contrary to public policy," watered down Senator Wagner's bill for slum clearance and low-cost housing, and blocked an anti-lynching measure. The president's glitter had been tarnished, and they were pleased.[2]

During Roosevelt's first term, many conservative Democrats had happily supported their president. "I feel that we should stand by the administration and not attack it," Bailey asserted in 1935. True, he had disagreed with Roosevelt on some key matters, but, he said, "never have I thought of going back on him as the head of our Government and the head of our Party." Bailey and his friends realized that it was Roosevelt's popularity that had given Democrats commanding majorities in Congress, ending decades in the minority outback. And it was also Roosevelt's political success that had empowered them as committee chairmen. And, of course, they knew how welcome New Deal programs were with their constituents back home. Bailey boasted that he had helped thousands of North Carolinians find jobs with federal agencies. He was just as prepared to act the part of fox and opportunist as the master fox himself.[3]

These conservative Democrats had believed that they were merely leasing out their party on a short-term basis to Roosevelt and his progressive agenda. They assumed that the New Deal meant little more than the government's response to the economic emergency of the Great Depression and that the Democratic Party and the nation would before long revert to the old status quo. "We will return to reliance upon private enterprise and individual initiative," Bailey wrote in 1934, "but not to greed, not to unconscionable profits, not to speculation. This, as I understand, is the essence of the New Deal." But slowly it dawned on them that FDR was making more transformational changes than they had counted on and that much of the New Deal would be irreversible.[4]

Dismayed, they saw their party changing before their eyes—and stolen out from under them. Whereas it had once stood for small, frugal government and for states' rights, it was metamorphosing into a party of big spending and an expansive, intrusive federal government. These conservative Democrats objected to federal relief, they hated the crop controls of the Agricultural Adjustment Act, and a few of them—Byrd, Glass, Smith, and Tydings—despised Social Security and declined to vote on the measure. "Children are supposed to look after their parents," Harry Byrd had sternly sermonized. Old age pensions, he believed, wrongly relieved children of that responsibility. The conservative mantra was fiscal restraint and rugged individualism. Any desire to address the needs of desperate Americans was trumped by a devotion to the status quo, a probusiness ideology and, as historian V. O. Key remarked, an "adding-machine mentality."[5]

Even more disconcerting to them, the Democratic Party was becoming hospitable to African Americans. Indeed, in the election of 1936, virtually all northern black voters had shifted their allegiance from the GOP to the Democratic Party. Bailey, Carter Glass, and others voiced fears that the party traditionally committed to preserving white supremacy might become, at least in the North, a "negro party" advocating racial equality. South Carolina's senator Cotton Ed Smith even staged his own high-profile protest at the 1936 Democratic Convention in Philadelphia. Not only did thirty black delegates attend the convention, but a black minister was chosen to give the invocation. When the clergyman rose to deliver the prayer, Smith stormed out of the hall. "He started praying and I started walking," said Smith, as he recounted—again and again for admiring southerners—his theatrical exit from the convention. White supremacists might have been placated by the president's refusal to back anti-lynching legislation, but the words and deeds of the president's wife in favor of racial equality fueled their alarm. In the segregated South, photos circulated of Eleanor

Roosevelt, accompanied by black students from Howard University, attending civil rights meetings with other African Americans.[6]

The most obvious solution was for southern Democrats to bolt from a party that had betrayed and abandoned them—and Republicans like Senator Vandenberg extended an invitation to them to move to the other side of the aisle. Vandenberg even offered to support a conservative Democrat like Nebraska's Burke for the presidency in 1940. In 1936, a front-page editorial in the stoutly Republican *New York Herald Tribune* urged the GOP's national convention to nominate a conservative Democrat for vice president. Such a choice, the *Tribune* wrote, would appeal to "the millions of Democrats who distrust the Roosevelt administration" and would help to begin the "liquidation" of the New Deal.[7] And with blacks having left en masse the party of Lincoln for the party of Roosevelt, Republicans felt that they could offer southern Democrats a friendlier political home. Roosevelt and the New Deal, a Mississippi newspaper editorialized, had "absolved southerners from any further obligation of loyalty" to a party that had once courageously stood for the preservation of white supremacy. From the other end of the political spectrum, the left-leaning *Nation* bluntly told conservative Democrats to "take a walk."[8]

The problem was that, seventy years after the Civil War, "Republican" was still a fighting word in the South, and conservative southern Democrats had a far greater aversion to the party of Abraham Lincoln than to New Deal Democrats. Under "no conditions," stated Harry Byrd, would he join a coalition with Republicans. Despite what they considered the administration's sinister and perilous course, conservative Democrats had no intention of leaving their party. "I am unable to see much difference between Roosevelt and Landon," Glass said in 1936, "except that the former is a first-class New Dealer and the latter a second-rate New Dealer."[9]

These Democrats might have been backward-looking, but they were also pragmatic and ambitious—and realized that it would be political suicide to leave the Democratic Party. After all, even in their own states, Roosevelt was more popular than they were. Josiah Bailey won 563,969 votes in the 1936 election in North Carolina, but FDR polled 616,141. They had nothing to gain by disrupting their own local organizations and giving up their party seniority and committee chairmanships to join a powerless minority Republican Party. Though some southern Democrats "cordially disliked" the views of many members of their own party, as historian James T. Patterson observed, they distrusted Republicans even more.[10]

In addition, party realignment in the South would also inevitably entail black enfranchisement, and conservatives could only shudder at that prospect. If the one-party white-majority South split into a two-party South, elections would become competitive, and, if African Americans voted in large numbers, they might hold the balance of power—and in some states, like South Carolina, almost the preponderance of power. The southern journalist Henry W. Grady had already made that point in the late nineteenth century: "The worst thing that could happen," he wrote, "is that the white people of the South should stand in opposition factions, with the vast mass of ignorant or purchasable Negro votes between." Decades later southern whites continued to fear that a competitive political arena—in which decisions were made in real elections and not in white-only primaries—would empower blacks to demand reforms and use their votes to transform their third-class status.[11]

The disquieting aspects of a two-party South had convinced white southerners of the need to maintain party solidarity. A division in the Democratic ranks would merely spell the election of a Republican— "and neither you nor I," Josiah Bailey wrote to his campaign manager in 1935, "desire to be a party to any such consequences." A Democrat in the South, Carter Glass underscored, "would as soon think of deserting his church as deserting his party." On second thought, party was probably more important than religion, Glass added, for "it involved the very preservation of Anglo-Saxon liberty"—by which he meant the survival of a segregated society.[12]

The Democratic Party might have been divided and at odds with itself, but it still mattered deeply to southerners. It represented far more than a political label and far more than a political machine. It embodied their traditional home, one with deep historical, regional, emotional, and racial resonances. The party stood for their way of life—white supremacy, states' rights, and a conservative, agrarian society. "The Democratic Party was nurtured in the South," the *Atlanta Constitution* reminded its readers early in 1938, crediting southern leaders with having shaped the party's basic principles and policies.[13]

The historian of southern politics V. O. Key speculated that a certain lassitude—"the inertia of traditional partisan attachments formed generations ago"—also explained the reluctance of southern Democrats to leave a party that was becoming more and more foreign to them. But southern patricians like Carter Glass would have responded that it wasn't lassitude: it was loyalty. In 1935, Glass firmly pronounced himself "a *Democrat*, not a half-way Democrat." Party regularity was simply an article of faith. Josiah Bailey, too, announced in 1935 that he backed the Roosevelt administration because it was "the Administration of my Party, and if I did not support it, I certainly would have no other to support."[14]

But by 1937, the situation had changed dramatically. Bailey no longer equated Roosevelt's administration with the Democratic Party. Radical New Dealers, he grumbled, "have come into the house which was built by others and intend to take possession and drive the builders out." Now Bailey was prepared to fight back against liberals and "socialists" for the soul of his party. "We'll not let anybody take the Democratic party away from us," he declared.[15]

Nor was Cotton Ed Smith of South Carolina prepared to switch parties. After he famously stormed out of the 1936 convention when the black pastor began to give the invocation, that pastor remarked that if Smith was "looking for a party without Negroes, it looks like he will have to form his own little party right there in South Carolina." But Smith shot back, "I don't have to form my own party. The party already exists. It was born in the red-shirt days of the Reconstruction period when the gentlemen of South Carolina donned red shirts to rid our State of carpetbaggers, scalawags and Negroes."[16]

During FDR's second term, Democrats like Glass, Bailey, and Smith sought a way to capitalize on the growing resistance to the New Deal, blunt Roosevelt's ascendancy, and reclaim the party that since the early nineteenth century had been theirs. "Their aim is not to smash the Democratic Party," the *Nation* astutely wrote in the summer of 1937, "but to capture it." In fact, the left-leaning journal foresaw a two-pronged strategy: first, the conservatives would freeze any more liberal economic and social legislation, and second, they would wrest control of the party from Roosevelt and his New Dealers and command the choice of the presidential nominee in 1940. "The Old Guard is after the scalp of the New Deal and *not* of the Democratic Party," wrote the *Nation*.[17]

The problem with this conservative strategy—and it was a fundamental one—was that by seeking to shift the Democratic Party to the right, these men envisioned the coexistence of two conservative parties in the United States. It was a doomed, shortsighted plan. Not only would two conservative parties have offered no meaningful choice to voters, running counter to the very reason that makes a competitive two-party system essential in an open, vital democracy, but these southerners appeared to forget that the vast majority of American voters in the 1930s were liberals—Roosevelt's Democratic Party reflected most Americans' needs, values, and goals.

But conservatives—especially southern ones—didn't see it that way. The Democratic Party had belonged to *them* for a century. They were convinced that it was *their* party, the party of *their* South. They were prepared to mount all their political skills and clout to obstruct and defeat the New Deal.

For his part, Jim Farley, the chair of the Democratic National Committee, papered over the fissures developing within the party. Denying the rumor of an internal split, he assured the press in the fall of 1937 that any differences among Democrats would be "ironed out within our party." Senator Vandenberg's invitation to conservative Democrats to join the Republican Party, Farley said, was a "meaningless gesture." It was nothing less than absurd to think that Democrats, who disagreed with the president on a few issues, would follow Vandenberg "into a bankrupt political organization that doesn't even know the United States is living in the twentieth century." Byrd, Bailey, and company would have agreed with Farley about the GOP, but they had a plan of their own in mind.[18]

As the men lunched on quail—supplied by Republican senator John Townsend of Delaware—at their private luncheon in the Capitol, former budget director Douglas gave an informal talk that, though predictable, stiffened the senators' resolve. Echoing Herbert Hoover's repeated attacks on Roosevelt's devotion to "the magic of spending," Douglas held his former boss and the New Deal's "extravagant" economic policies responsible for the recession of 1937. Unless the government cooperated with the Republican Party and the business community to meet the new emergency, he warned, there would be a "day of reckoning."[19]

In the days following Douglas's talk, the group expanded to include Democrat Millard Tydings of Maryland and Republican Warren Austin of Vermont. Rhode Island's Democratic senator Peter Gerry hosted two dinners during which the men discussed the situation, vented their frustrations with Roosevelt and the New Deal—and agreed on a strategy. They decided to assert themselves by formulating a set of conservative principles around which they could rally. Ideas were floated, drafts were circulated.

The result was a ten-point "manifesto" outlining their political creed and presenting practical suggestions for economic recovery. The manifesto called for a reduction in taxes, especially the capital gains tax, curtailment of government spending for relief "with the view toward encouragement of individual self-reliance," respect for the rights of the states, and "just relations" between management and labor, with minimal intervention by the federal government. This statement of principles offered neither a new vision for the future nor any recognition that the recent recession and increase in unemployment were caused precisely by Roosevelt's decision in 1937 to cut spending.[20]

The manifesto contained no calls for action, no concrete legislative proposals—that is, other than the standard Republican calls for tax cuts and praise for a balanced budget. In the middle of a deep recession, it obtusely called for "reduced public expenditures at every point practicable." It was a bland, complacent appeal to the past, a probusiness document that enthused about the American system of competition and individual initiative and stressed the key role of the private sector in stimulating economic recovery. As such, the manifesto fell flat, already tired and platitudinous at its birth. Its advocates began staking out the Senate cloakrooms, hoping for a large number of signatures—thirty to forty. But outside of their small group, they could find no other senators, not even some of the most conservative ones, who were willing to sign a document that smacked of a "manifesto."[21]

Prematurely leaked to the syndicated columnist Joseph Alsop on December 14—by the moderate Republican leader Senator Charles McNary of Oregon—the manifesto was scorned in much of the press and ridiculed by liberal senators like Claude Pepper of Florida and Sherman

Minton of Indiana. Panicked at the idea of being seen as rebels conspiring with the GOP, the conservative gang of Democrats ran for cover. Gerry denied to reporters that he and Vandenberg had anything to do with the phrasemaking. As for Republicans, Vandenberg privately denounced McNary's treachery for foiling their "patriotically dramatic contribution to the welfare of the country," while McNary derided the notion of any Republican signing on to the document. "Anyone who signs that thing is going to have a Liberty League tag put on him," McNary warned, referring to the ultraconservative, New Deal–bashing organization of wealthy businessmen.[22]

Was there no one willing to be the "father of this waif at this gladsome Christmas time?" challenged Senator Minton on the Senate floor. In that jittery atmosphere, Josiah Bailey decided to step forward, accept paternity, and read the manifesto out loud on the floor of the Senate.[23]

On December 20, 1937, spectators packed the visitors' gallery. Representatives, eager to be present for the start of the counterrevolution, hurried across the Capitol lobby to the Senate chamber. Jack Garner, Roosevelt's anti–New Deal vice president, left the rostrum to take a seat closer to Bailey, keen to hear every word.[24]

The manifesto, Bailey reassured his colleagues, was not "anything like a secret matter, or anything like the formation of a bloc." Nor did the Liberty League play any part in it, he said. Putting a conciliatory spin on the document, Bailey insisted that it criticized neither the president nor the New Deal. The emergency spending of the early New Deal had been "wise and necessary," he judged, but he contended that such spending would not work again. More unbalanced budgets would lead only to national financial disaster. "Stand up for the American system of enterprise," Bailey cried. "Give enterprise a chance, and I will give you the guarantees of a happy and a prosperous America!"[25]

Seeking to broaden his insurgency, Bailey suggested that his group's platform was still open to reasonable changes. "If there is a thing wrong in that statement, strike it out. If there is anything in it that offends you, condemn it. If you have a better paragraph, write it in. But, in God's name," he exclaimed, raising the specter of socialism, "do not do nothing while America drifts down to the inevitable gulf of collectivism!"[26]

But Bailey was clearly torn, for he had been not only a party man but something of a Roosevelt loyalist. A year after voting against the National Labor Relations Act but for Social Security and relief appropriations for the Works Progress Administration, Bailey declared, as he seconded FDR's nomination at the 1936 Democratic National Convention, that he admired the president for "the enemies he has made!" If the president decided to try for a third term and win the 1940 nomination again, Bailey and others hardly wanted to commit political suicide by balking at his leadership. Could Bailey possibly manage to be both a rebel and a loyalist, a mutineer and a Roosevelt man? Bailey worked through this problem by improbably convincing himself that he and Roosevelt could remain on good terms and that FDR was even seeing the light. "There are good evidences here," Bailey confided to a colleague later that day, "that the President wishes to turn decidedly to the right."[27]

After Bailey finished speaking, other New Deal critics who had not attended the conservative group's luncheon and dinners—O'Mahoney of Wyoming, McCarran of Nevada, Holt of West Virginia, and Wheeler of Montana—rushed to his side, showering him with praise and congratulations. Vermont's Warren Austin suggested that the manifesto might be used as the platform of some party in the future. Bailey mailed out a million and a half copies of the manifesto, while dozens of businesses also printed it up, in lots of a hundred thousand. Across the country, Chambers of Commerce hailed Bailey's speech and endorsed the manifesto.[28]

But the escapade imploded: few Democrats, even among the most hard-core conservatives, were willing to tie themselves to the manifesto, declare war on the administration, or publicly collaborate with Republicans. Moderates like Mississippi's Pat Harrison and South Carolina's

Jimmy Byrnes fled from the document. Republicans, for their part, may have been happy to play a role in heightening a split in the Democratic ranks, though they themselves were split between moderates like McNary and dyed-in-the-wool conservatives like Vandenberg.[29]

Still, despite the fiasco of the manifesto, conservative Democrats had not given up: they remained determined to oppose the New Deal and overrule FDR's huge popular mandate.

Roosevelt knew that the New Deal had been only half dealt. He believed passionately that the government needed to continue to help improve citizens' lives. It could not stand still. "Once you build a house you always have it," he said in a radio talk to the nation. "On the other hand, a social or an economic gain is a different matter." Those kinds of gains, made under one administration, he explained, could evaporate under the next. Much of Theodore Roosevelt's progressive legacy, for example, was squandered by his successor, William Howard Taft, and many of Woodrow Wilson's accomplishments were similarly liquidated by Warren Harding. If American democracy ceased to move forward as a living force, FDR said a year later, "then Fascism and Communism, aided, unconsciously perhaps, by old-line Tory Republicanism, will grow in strength in our land."[30]

Roosevelt had begun that radio chat by talking about a real house, one he was having built in Hyde Park. "Top Cottage," a small, simple two-bedroom stone house on a hill overlooking the Hudson River, had special meaning for him. It would offer an oasis of tranquility and stability in a world growing every day more violent and dangerous.

During the bleak winter months of 1937 and 1938, Roosevelt found relief in drawing up plans for his hilltop escape from the estate's "big house," still presided over by his formidable mother, Sara Delano Roosevelt. At his new private retreat, he looked forward to relaxing with his friends. Playing the amateur architect, he designed the floor plan himself. The house would be, for the most part, handicapped-accessible—with no entry stairs or saddles in the doorways. It would be a simple cottage—with no air-conditioning, no telephone, no screens on the porch, and no landscaping—just the trees.

Construction would begin in the spring of 1938 and coincide with his efforts to eject conservatives from his party. He hoped that Top Cottage and the transformed, liberalized, and unified Democratic Party would both be permanent.[31]

◄ 5 ►

The Partisan Leader Takes His First Steps

"JACK, I AM GOING to reassert leadership," Roosevelt said to his vice president, Texan Jack Garner, at a cabinet meeting on January 2, 1938. The main item on the agenda was FDR's draft of his state of the union message. He wanted to test it out on the members of his cabinet.

The president looked tired, and Garner said as much to him. Roosevelt even agreed that he felt weary. The engine of his second term was sputtering: Congress had buried his Fair Labor Standards Act, slashed funds for Senator Wagner's urban housing program, and forced the president to accept an emasculated court reform bill. Trying to even the score, in August 1937, Roosevelt nominated one of the most left-wing senators, Alabama's Hugo Black, for the first Supreme Court vacancy since 1932. But senators struck back; dispensing with the courtesy they usually extended to one of their own, they refused to waive hearings for their colleague. The president, Harold Ickes thought, seemed "punch drunk" from the relentless series of punishing blows.[1]

But at the start of the new year, Roosevelt's "Dutch was up," and in his annual message to Congress, he was resolved to take the offensive and even set off some sparks.

The following day, January 3, Roosevelt delivered that address to a joint session of Congress. From the podium he looked down at his cabinet members, elegantly attired, seated in the front row and, around them, the dour, stony-faced Democratic senators from the South. When the president was introduced, they barely moved, clapping only perfunctorily, their mouths set in icy indifference.

In his cultivated, warm patrician voice, the president spoke quietly, but with deliberate emphasis. It had become apparent, he said, that vast numbers of American farmers were living in abject poverty, *"more abject* than that of many of the farmers of Europe whom we are wont to call peasants."* He refrained from singling out the South as the most blighted region of the nation, though he had originally intended to do just that. Instead he had accepted the advice of his cabinet members to tone down his criticism.

Once again, the president hammered home the message that Congress needed to pass the Wages and Hours Bill and at last put an end to starvation wages and intolerable hours for the nation's poorest citizens. Once again, he pointed out that the communities in which family income was pitifully low also had the poorest schools and worst health care. The ability to pay taxes, support effective local government, and maintain adequate public services all depended on workers earning a livable salary.

Hoping to mobilize support for the bill, Roosevelt appealed to southerners, making it clear that he was not seeking uniform wages throughout the country. He appealed to big business by announcing that the changes he sought were not "drastic." And he assured labor leaders that, in the future, higher wages would continue to be the result of collective bargaining.

Then came the meat of his speech: progress would be possible only if politicians rose above the insular, parochial traditions of their local regions and took a broad, national perspective. "No government," he declared, "can help the destinies of people who insist in putting sectional and class-consciousness ahead of general weal." It was critically important for all members of Congress, Republicans and Democrats alike, to be "national in outlook."[2]

But behind that message was in fact a threat—if a subtle one. The president expected Democrats in particular, and especially those from the South, to relinquish their sectional biases, rise above local interests, and support their national party, its platform, and its leader. They got the point. When Roosevelt exited the chamber to enthusiastic applause, the grim Southern clique remained frozen, their hands folded. "As they say on the East Side in New York," FDR whispered to one of his congressional escorts, "I guess that's telling 'em; that's not askin' 'em."[3]

Back at the White House, Roosevelt felt that he had earned some relaxation—and playtime. Although it was the middle of the day, he took out a deck of cards. Around the poker table with him sat the men he most trusted—Harold Ickes, Henry Morgenthau, "Pa" Watson, Steve Early, Marvin McIntyre. On a side table, servants had set up cheese and crackers, sandwiches, coffee, whiskey, and beer. FDR and his friends played for a few hours, until 7. "We had a very good time," Ickes wrote in his diary, relieved that he had lost only $8 in the game.[4]

Two days after his state of the union speech, the president received news from Alabama that seemed to confirm his hope that the South was becoming more liberal. On January 4, a special Democratic primary was held to fill the Senate seat vacated by Hugo Black. Running for the nomination—tantamount to election—were J. Thomas Heflin, a sixty-nine-year-old former senator, and forty-three-year old Lister Hill, a liberal-leaning congressman who chaired the House Military Affairs Committee.

Heflin, eccentrically attired in his trademark sombrero, tailed frock coat, high-standing collar and black sash of a bow tie, was a white supremacist and race-baiter who had further distinguished himself in the Senate by spewing out hatred against Negroes, the pope, and the Catholic Church. In 1928, he had attacked the Democratic presidential nominee and Catholic Al Smith as the "Roman candidate" and staged an anti-Smith "walkout" at the national convention. In 1930 Alabamans kicked him out of the Senate and elected John Bankhead, paying Heflin back for his desertion in 1928.[5]

During FDR's first term, Heflin had tried to make amends, praising the president and the New Deal. Roosevelt returned the favor, appointing Heflin to jobs in the Federal Housing Administration and the Justice Department. But the ex-senator, who had once forcibly ejected an African American from a Washington streetcar and then tried to shoot him, wounding a white bystander instead, ultimately proved too radioactive for the White House to support.[6]

For his part, Lister Hill was lukewarm about Roosevelt's court reorganization bill, but he championed the Wages and Hours legislation—and that bill, which a broad swath of Alabamans opposed, became the key issue in the campaign. After meeting with Hill in December, Roosevelt bestowed his blessing on the challenger. By a stunning two-to-one margin, Hill trounced Heflin. It was a major victory for Roosevelt and the New Deal that boosted the president's confidence and would set the stage for a more aggressive stance.[7]

Four days after Hill's victory, on January 8, the president spoke at a traditional Democratic event—the Jackson Day dinner—held at the Mayflower Hotel in Washington. All the major broadcasting companies carried the speech live on the radio. This time Roosevelt wore his party leader hat, not his presidential one. Fortified by Hill's win, he used the occasion to hammer out another strong and plain warning to conservatives in the Democratic Party. Guessing what was coming, many of those Democrats had run for cover. James Byrnes of South Carolina, Roosevelt's liaison man in the Senate, and Pat Harrison of Mississippi, who had helped steer key measures like the National Industrial Recovery Act and Social Security through to passage, conspicuously absented themselves from the dinner. And it was not surprising that Senator

Bailey, whose apartment was in the Mayflower Hotel, similarly declined to attend the gathering. Catching Bailey in an elevator in the Mayflower, a reporter asked him why he was skipping out on the dinner. "I like Jackson, but the Jackson I know is not named 'Bob,'" Bailey replied, referring to Bob Jackson, Roosevelt's assistant attorney general who had recently gone on the offensive against the business community.[8]

When the president took his place at the microphone in the Mayflower ballroom, a full minute of applause greeted him. He started off on a comfortable, friendly nonpartisan note, expressing pleasure that his Jackson Day audience was not limited to active Democrats. Although he came from a Democratic family, he reminded his audience, there were Republicans in his past. "In 1904 when I cast my first vote for a president, I voted for the Republican candidate, Theodore Roosevelt, because I thought he was a better Democrat than the Democratic candidate."[9]

Roosevelt was not, however, suggesting that the Democrats make nice with Republicans. On the contrary, he was pointing out that what matters are political principles, not labels. He then stressed three key points about the Democratic Party: first, that the party represented "the essential unity of our country." By this he meant that it stood for the common good around which all citizens could rally and unite. Second, it was a national party, concerned with the welfare of the majority. And third, as a national party, it could not continue to be a home to those who placed sectional interests ahead of the interest of the majority. It was therefore imperative, he concluded, that the Democratic Party "*slough off* any remains of sectionalism and class consciousness."

With the verb "slough off," a term simultaneously aggressive and dismissive, Roosevelt sent a stern, confrontational warning to his opponents inside the party. It was an unsubtle threat, giving notice that there was no home in the liberal Democratic Party for reactionaries who placed conservative principles or southern traditions ahead of the national interest. Anti–New Deal Democrats could either join the mainstream of their party or set up new quarters.[10]

And so, less than three weeks after Josiah Bailey bravely introduced the conservative "manifesto" on the Senate floor, FDR had come back swinging.

In March, Roosevelt traveled to Georgia for ten days of vacation, accompanied by his secretary and traveling companion Missy LeHand and his old law partner Basil O'Connor—the brother of his spiteful congressional foe, John O'Connor of New York. On his way to Warm Springs, the president stopped in Gainesville, Georgia, to give a short address dedicating Roosevelt Square, the town center that was reconstructed with federal aid after two tornadoes, striking together, ripped through the heart of the "queen city" of North Georgia in the spring of 1936, destroying practically every downtown building and leaving thousands homeless and two hundred dead.[11]

On March 23, two weeks before the House of Representatives buried his executive reorganization bill, as many as fifty thousand people traveled to Gainesville by car, bus, train and mule cart to hear the president. In a gay holiday mood, buzzing with excitement, they all jammed into the new square. Warm, enthusiastic introductions by Governor Ed Rivers and Senator Walter George paid tribute to the president's commitment to rebuilding Gainesville; George, who had voted against the president on several recent bills, nevertheless showered him with praise, calling him "the greatest leader among English speaking people at this hour anywhere on earth!"[12]

When the president rose to speak, the crowd erupted in deafening cheers and whistles that went on for five minutes. They happily smiled and nodded with pleasure when the president began by paying tribute to their courage in the wake of the tornado. With the help of federal and state funds, the citizens of Gainesville did more than restore the old—they created the new. "You were not content with rebuilding along the lines of the old community," Roosevelt said admiringly. "You were determined in the process of rebuilding to eliminate old conditions of which you were not proud; to rebuild a better city; to replace congested areas with parks; to move human beings from slums to suburbs."[13]

Expecting more such genial, congratulatory remarks, people were not prepared for what came next. "I speak to you of conditions in this, my other State," Roosevelt said as he launched into a sober, scolding lecture on the economic ills in the lower South in general and the consequences of low wages in particular. Those consequences were clear and dire—weak purchasing power, empty stores, industry at a standstill, poor schools, poor health care, and poor roads. And there was no mystery about the identity of the culprits: they were the selfish, privileged few who opposed raising wages in the South, men who believed in rugged individualism and whose creed, Roosevelt said, was "I am *not* my brother's keeper."

Ratcheting his attack up another notch, the president then lashed out at those reactionaries who believed "in a wholly different theory of government than the one our Constitution provides." Indeed, the conservatives who would hold back progress and prosperity for millions of Americans considered that "the feudal system is still the best system." And what was the twentieth-century incarnation of feudalism? "When you come down to it," Roosevelt told the Gainesville crowd, "there is little difference between the feudal system and the Fascist system. If you believe in the one, you lean to the other." Having been called a Hitler by some politicos and editorial writers, FDR relished turning the table on his critics. Now it was his turn to slap the fascist label on the men who clung to their selfish ideology of the "survival of the fittest." These were the same people, he pointed out, who "owned the government of the United States from 1921 to 1933."

Having laid out the fundamental economic problems and identified the guilty party, Roosevelt then tried out his purge scenario. He explained that it fell to American voters to move the nation forward, to rid Congress of conservative obstructionists and elect in their stead progressive candidates responsive to the needs of the people and supportive of the president's programs. "To those in and out of public office, who still believe in the feudal system and have leanings to the Fascist system," Roosevelt dramatically concluded, "the people of the United States and in every section of the United States are going to say 'We are sorry, but we want people to represent us whose minds are cast in the 1938 mold and not the 1898 mold.'"[14]

By branding conditions in the South "feudal" and by lambasting the southern ruling elite, Roosevelt was seeking to persuade southerners that there were alternatives to the backwardness of their region and to the conservatism of their politicians. The next step, he suggested, would be a grassroots movement to liberalize the South. In a departure from his written remarks, he had singled out for praise Governor Rivers and Georgia congressman Frank Whelchel—but he pointedly made no mention of Walter George, who had introduced him to the crowd.[15]

The president had delivered a memorable, compelling, even profound address, but reactions varied wildly—from anger to puzzlement, from defensiveness to jubilation. Had Roosevelt come to Gainesville to pelt mud at southerners in their own backyard? some asked. Others expressed irritation that the president had presumed to intrude in local political races. A few, however, were elated. "I exulted as he spoke bitterly of the South's feudalism," wrote Knoxville reporter Thomas Stokes, gratified that the truth was finally being spoken.[16]

"President Declares Increasing Buying Power Necessary for Permanent Prosperity in U.S." announced the headline the next day in the *Atlanta Constitution*. Next to the text of Roosevelt's address appeared an advertisement for 15-cent Bayer Aspirin that read, "The Poorest

Family in America Can Afford This Relief." It was a sad reminder of the wrenching conditions in the South.[17]

Those three speeches that FDR gave in the early months of 1938 signaled the start of a major shift in the White House. On three different occasions—a formal state of the union address, a partisan Jackson Day dinner speech, and a nonpartisan talk to folks in Gainesville, Georgia—Roosevelt had adopted a confrontational tone, portraying himself as the leader of a progressive nation and an indisputably liberal party in which there was no place for reactionaries and "feudalists." In all three contexts, he complained, castigated, and threatened, capitalizing on his mandate, exploiting his authority and power, and giving notice that he could be a tough, hard-hitting partisan.

But a fourth speech that spring—a fireside chat in April—suggested that it was not quite that simple—and that perhaps the president was at least somewhat mistaken about the feudalists he considered his foes.

Roosevelt drafted the talk at the last minute. "Oh, I'm tired, let me go to bed," he said at 1 A.M., when his secretary Missy LeHand and his speechwriters and advisors implored him to work on his speech. "You just have to get something down on paper tonight," Missy said. He leaned back on the sofa with an air of resignation, shut his eyes, and then started to dictate. "Mah F-r-a-a-nds," he said in such an exaggerated drawl that everyone laughed. But he continued to work until 2:15 A.M.[18]

The purpose of the fireside chat was to announce his plans for huge new government spending. After another stock market slide a few weeks earlier that deepened fears about the "Roosevelt Recession" and after months of fumbling about and ignoring advice from the British economist John Maynard Keynes to spend, spend, spend, he finally grasped the wisdom of Keynes's recommendation. Massive government spending was indeed the most effective weapon against the economic depression. Roosevelt was requesting from Congress billions of dollars—so much money that Treasury Secretary Morgenthau threatened to resign—for the Works Progress Administration, the Civilian Conservation Corps, Public Works Administration projects, highway construction, housing, and farm security.

On the evening of April 14, 1938, after a nap and a light dinner, the president spoke with tens of millions of Americans. The purchasing power of the consuming public, he explained, had not kept pace with production. Thus the economic slump could be attributed to the combination of overproduction and underconsumption. The aim of the funding he would request was to increase the national income, put more people to work, and give security to all Americans.

And yet, the ultimate goal, he implied, was not economic growth, jobs, food, education, or health. It was something even more important: the survival of the American republic. Several great nations in Europe, he soberly reminded his listeners, had recently turned to fascist dictators. It was not that the people of those nations disliked democracy, he said, "but they had grown tired of unemployment and insecurity, of seeing their children hungry while they sat helpless in the face of government confusion." In desperation those people sacrificed liberty in the hope of getting something to eat. In other words, economic depression was the incubator of totalitarianism and war. At stake, therefore, was "not only our future economic soundness but the very soundness of our democratic institutions." Above all, his goal was to strengthen and protect democracy. "History proves that dictatorships do not grow out of strong and successful governments," he said, "but out of weak and helpless governments."[19]

To grasp the import of the president's words, Americans had only to read the front pages of their newspapers. Just a few weeks earlier in March, Hitler had annexed Austria. As if presaging Roosevelt's point, the *New York Times* reported that although the Austrians were bitter over the Nazi conquest, "the possibility of better times *economically* was helping to temper their resentment and assuage their fears."[20]

*   *   *

The security of the American democracy depended on economic prosperity. And yet the president knew that the nation's ultimate security hinged even more on a muscular foreign policy—and especially on military preparedness—at a time when the German octopus hungered and plotted for more power in Europe, when Japan was expanding its reach in Asia, and when more Americans were inclining to "peace at any price" appeasement. The isolationist business leaders who simultaneously called for the resumption of prosperity and appeasement of Nazi Germany were, Roosevelt believed, tragically misguided. That isolationist formula, he wrote two days after his fireside chat, "would only be breeding far more serious trouble four or eight years from now."[21]

Some of the representatives and senators who best understood the gravity of the fascist threat were precisely those men whom Roosevelt wanted to purge from the Democratic Party. Ironically, some of his New Deal cheerleaders were isolationists, whereas many of the Democratic senators and congressmen who opposed the president on key bills, from court-packing to fair labor standards, were strong internationalists.

The fight over the "Ludlow amendment" in January 1938, six months before the purge began, was a case in point. Louis Ludlow, an isolationist Democratic congressman from Indiana, proposed a constitutional amendment that would prevent the United States from waging war unless it was *actually invaded* by a foreign force. The amendment would stipulate that in all cases where there was *not* such an invasion, there must be a nationwide referendum prior to a congressional declaration of war. As more and more members of Congress declared themselves in favor of the amendment, an astonished and dismayed FDR wrote to Speaker Bankhead that it would "cripple any President in his conduct of foreign relations."[22]

In the end, the amendment's proponents in the House could not come close to mustering the necessary two-thirds vote—or even a simple majority. The final vote to bring the proposal to the House from committee was 209 nays to 188 yeas. But many of the representatives who helped sink the misguided plan were Roosevelt's conservative adversaries, the very Democrats he would soon seek to "slough off." Not only John O'Connor of New York but every member of the solidly Democratic Alabama and Virginia delegations voted against the amendment. Even Senator Millard Tydings of Maryland, who would become a prime target on Roosevelt's hit-list, denounced the Ludlow amendment as a "standing invitation to aggression" and declared that the way to keep the United States out of war was to have "a navy second to none."[23]

In addition to Tydings, conservatives like Walter George, Carter Glass, Harry Byrd, Josiah Bailey, and other potential "purgees" would wholeheartedly back the president's authority to defend the nation militarily and help America's allies. Indeed, their aggressive, internationalist stance on defense should have cast doubt on the whole concept of the purge and given the president second thoughts about it.

After the Japanese bombing of the U.S. gunboat *Panay* in December 1937, the outbreak of civil war in Spain, and his own warnings about the fascist threat in Europe, there could have been little doubt in the president's mind that war was at least a possibility. And he might reasonably have understood that many of the members of the conservative Democratic bloc—like Tydings, who had spoken out against Hitler's anti-Semitic policies as early as 1933—would be among the staunchest supporters of his military policies. But despite the gravity of Japanese aggression in the Pacific and the fascist threat in Europe, Roosevelt's top priority—at least in 1938—was still economic recovery and the fulfillment of the New Deal. And the sting of his losses in Congress on key bills like court reform, executive reorganization, and fair labor standards was so frustrating, so infuriating, and so personal, that he could not overcome his resentment and live—and compromise—with the economic conservatives in his party who put national security ahead of domestic reform. On the contrary, he could only think of striking back at his congressional foes.[24]

Two weeks after Roosevelt warned Americans that democracy was fragile in a world besieged by fascist dictatorships, a midwestern governor tried his own hand at building a fascist-style party. On April 28, 1938, five thousand people gathered in the Livestock Pavilion in Madison, Wisconsin, to hear Governor Phil La Follette announce the creation of the National Progressive Party. On the stage, behind the small and studious-looking governor, was an immense banner bearing the party's emblem—a blue cross in a red circle. It was a shocking and unmistakable takeoff on the Nazi Party's symbol—some called it a "circumcised swastika." Around the pavilion stood national guardsmen in shiny steel helmets, emblazoned with the party's jarring insignia.

The old parties were "fumbling the ball," La Follette told the excited, roaring crowd. The good intentions of President Roosevelt were being "sabotaged, undermined and hamstrung" by dissension in the Democratic Party and especially by its reactionaries. For liberal Americans who longed for change, the National Progressives, he proclaimed, was not a third party but rather "*the* party of our time."[25]

The party platform, however, puzzled some observers. "We are near the end of the road," La Follette exclaimed. "The time has come when a *new trail* must be blazed." Exactly what kind of trail did he have in mind? The governor refused to offer "blueprints." What kind of progressivism was he offering then? He ruled out "failed capitalism," insisting that capitalism had become obsolete. His brand of progressivism, he said, meant no more "coddling or spoon-feeding of Americans." The executive branch needed the power "to get things done."

But he opposed military preparedness and hammered FDR's naval buildup.[26]

His statements were alarmingly, ominously vague. "We must have a method and be able to act collectively, but preserve at the same time individual initiative." In a frightening emotional appeal that made short shrift of reason, he declared that only true believers—"those who come with complete conviction and without reservation"—were welcome in his party.[27]

A darkly shadowed photo in *Life* of La Follette on the podium with his arm outstretched, as if giving the Nazi salute, captured for many the menacing drift of his party. When asked about the party insignia, La Follette gave the improbable explanation that the gigantic X stood for the cross that citizens marked on their ballots, a symbol of their inalienable rights. Interviewed by writer Max Lerner in his office, where he displayed a photograph of Mussolini, La Follette, who had visited Germany in 1933, spoke admiringly of the Führer's "positive achievements" and energy.[28]

La Follette's National Progressive Party managed to inspire some Americans—and it also aroused one former president, Herbert Hoover. The new party, Hoover slyly remarked, might be just the wedge needed to divide Democrats and return Republicans to power. "If the Republicans continue to stand together," he said, "and the liberal and conservative Democrats continue to widen the breach between them, as they have recently, we should be able to regain leadership."[29]

The National Progressive Party was not the kind of party realignment Harold Ickes and FDR had in mind. Ickes understood how disruptive and unpredictable a third party ticket could be—he remembered that Phil La Follette's father, "Fighting Bob" La Follette, had run for president in 1924 on a third party ticket and won 5 million votes, making a Coolidge victory all the more likely. "You cannot divide the liberal movement into two or three parts and hope it would succeed," Ickes warned.[30]

For his part, Roosevelt was seriously worried about a third party threat, though he joked about the grotesque Nazi resonances of the National Progressive Party, whose very name recalled Hitler's National Socialist Party. Writing to his friend William Phillips, the ambassador to Italy, the president described La Follette's dedication of his new party emblem on a twenty-foot-wide banner. "All that remains," he wrote, "is for some major party to adopt a new form of arm salute. I have suggested the raising of both arms above the head, following by a bow from the waist. At least this will be good for people's figures."[31]

In public FDR took a more diplomatic approach. First, the White House let it be known that the president believed that both La Follette brothers—Governor Phil as well as his brother, Senator Bob—were acting on "none but genuine" motives. The more numerous liberal organizations were in the country the better, the unflappable president pronounced at a press conference.[32]

On May 13, a mere two weeks after the rally in the Livestock Pavilion, Roosevelt invited Bob La Follette and his wife to join him on a weekend cruise on the Potomac River and Chesapeake Bay. Sporting the disconcerting emblem of his brother's party, Bob La Follette along with his wife set out with FDR on board the cruiser under heavy rain. Joining them was Missy LeHand, Senator Theodore Green of Rhode Island and his wife, and James Roosevelt and his wife, Betsey Cushing.[33]

Roosevelt the scrootch owl was clearly going after another hen. By remaining on friendly terms with the La Follettes—Senator Bob was one of only twenty senators to vote with the president on court-packing—and by displaying not the slightest irritation, FDR gave neither publicity nor traction to the National Progressive Party. His maneuver exemplified his typical breezy and beguiling self-confidence. He even fancied making a deal with Bob La Follette: if Roosevelt successfully ran for a third term in 1940, he briefly imagined offering La Follette the job of secretary of state.[34]

With his usual acute political instincts, Roosevelt helped defuse the potential threat of the National Progressives. Within months the infant party imploded. With no discernible platform, principles, or programs, Governor Phil had staged a one-man show, built on a scaffolding of hollow slogans. The National Progressive Party was a dud. "Any sound political realignment must be built state by state," he had written. "We learned in my father's campaign in 1924 that it can't be done overnight in the nation, but must be developed in the states after a great deal of organization work." He stressed the importance of organizing at the grass roots. Ironically, Phil La Follette failed to grasp the implications of his own message—but so did FDR.[35]

The president had spoken passionately about the need for all Democrats to work together on the same team—but words were not enough. The real challenge was to fortify the liberal wing of the Democratic Party at the grass roots, and nurture a new cadre of young progressive Democratic leaders in the South. In April 1938, FDR expressed confidence that the South "is going to be a liberal democracy."[36]

But was he willing to channel enough of his energy and resources into creating real change? Was he motivated enough to aim for lasting results that would not disappear within a few years? Liberal groups in the South desperately needed assistance. The Southern Policy Committee, a group that sprang from the turn-of-the-century social gospel movement and stressed the obligation of Christians to fight for social justice, had no effective organization. Other progressive groups, like the Southern Conference for Human Welfare and the populist Alabama Policy Committee, also had difficulty getting off the ground. Even state Democratic committees pleaded for more help from the White House. In the spring of 1938, North Carolina representative Lindsay Warren, the chairman of his state's Democratic convention, wrote frantically to Steve Early, FDR's press secretary, pleading for the White House to send him a militant letter he could read out loud at the convention in Raleigh, which more than five thousand Democrats were expected to attend. Building up the liberal base would require more work and planning than a few biting speeches.[37]

As FDR and his advisors contemplated a possible crackdown on dissidents, they seemed to be thinking only in terms of hurried shortcuts. The president had the grit and the heart for a fight—but did he have the staying power?

Two exemplary primary contests in the spring of 1938, in Florida and Iowa, offered the president crucial cautionary lessons about his purge strategy. In Florida, it was conservative Democrats who took the initiative and wanted to engineer a purge of their own. Boldly stepping up to the plate, Mark Wilcox, a congressman and New Deal foe, decided to challenge the thirty-eight-year-old liberal incumbent senator, Claude Pepper, and put the conservative stamp back on the Democratic Party in Florida.[38]

Pepper and Wilcox exemplified the deep ideological rift within the Democratic Party. Pepper, who was chosen for the Senate in a special election in 1936 to fill the vacancy created by the death of Duncan Fletcher, was a passionate New Deal ally and one of the few southern supporters of the court-packing plan and the Wages and Hours Bill. He longed to see social, economic, and political conditions in the South improve. "I want to make the state liberal, which it has never been," he wrote. Pepper indeed could take credit for many of the popular New Deal projects that came to Florida.[39]

In his campaign speeches in 1938, Pepper told his listeners that it was about time for someone in authority to "do some fighting for the poor white man in the South." Though one of the leading southern liberals in the Senate, he was no champion of racial equality. Not only had he opposed the anti-lynching bill, which would have established federal jurisdiction over local officials who countenanced lynchings, he filibustered it for more than four hours on the Senate floor. Still, Pepper left no doubt that he would do everything in his power to help Roosevelt, "the man who was trying to help you and whom you chose to serve as your leader by a three-to-one majority. Friends, I am proud of my record in Washington!"[40]

Opponent Wilcox was a fierce critic of the New Deal. Elected to the House of Representatives in 1932, Wilcox hated the Fair Labor Standards Act and opposed FDR on executive reorganization. His strategy was to portray himself as a "cracker boy," a man with deep roots in the South. "Cracker Boy Wilcox," wrote *Time*, "has helped crack many a pet project of Franklin Roosevelt," needling him for claiming personal responsibility for the defeat of New Deal bills. "President Roosevelt is not God," declared Wilcox at his campaign stops. "He is a man just like all of us. He is bound to make mistakes. When he does, I will vote against him." As for Pepper, Wilcox branded him a "Roosevelt rubber stamp."

The Democratic Party in Florida—unlike other state parties such as that of Virginia, where politicians like Harry Byrd had their own effective statewide organizations—was so atomized and disorganized that the struggle in Florida was a free-for-all—a five-way race with three other candidates vying for the nomination in addition to Pepper and Wilcox.

Although FDR had made several combative speeches that spring, signaling his willingness to act the part of strong party leader, he declined, as was his custom, to intervene directly in a primary race. It was his son and secretary Jimmy who fired off an urgent memo to his father. "Don't you think we should do something really active to try to help him?" he wrote, referring to Pepper. Slowly awakened to the plight of his Florida ally, Roosevelt saw to it that he received a check for $10,000 and asked Jimmy to endorse him. Traveling in Florida in late January and early February, Jimmy stopped in Palm Beach at the home of Joseph P. Kennedy, the ambassador to Great Britain, and announced at a press conference that it was "*our* sincere hope" that Pepper would be returned to the Senate. Ecstatic at the endorsement, Pepper sent a telegram to Jimmy. "From the bottom of my heart," he wrote, "I am grateful to you for this invaluable help you have given and I shall try to prove to be a faithful coworker for the common cause."[41]

For his part, Wilcox tartly responded that the state of Florida was "waiting with bated breath" to see what positions FDR's two young grandchildren, Sistie and Buzzie, would also take in the primary. *Time* credited Cracker Boy Wilcox with making the best wisecrack of the campaign. The *New York Times* prematurely concluded that Jimmy Roosevelt would have "fared much better had he kept silent and enjoyed his swimming."[42]

When the primary results came in late on Election Day, May 3, Pepper as well as the White House had reason to celebrate. The senator won an impressive 58.4 percent of the vote, trouncing Wilcox, who received less than 30 percent. Pepper's bracing victory, FDR cheerfully wrote, proved that "the voters' hearts (and heads!) seem still to be in the right place."[43]

Once again, the New Deal was riding high—or so it seemed. Jimmy Roosevelt guessed that the sizzle of the Florida primary results would help jar the Wages and Hours Bill loose from the Rules Committee and drive its passage in the House—and he was right on target. On May 6, House Democrats, including twenty-two southerners and even some Republicans, rushed to the well of the House to be among the first to sign the discharge petition, permitting representatives to vote on the bill. Secretary of Labor Frances Perkins called it a "stampede." The scene was so chaotic that the Speaker called the sergeant at arms to help keep the members in line and in order. Representatives cheered when a southerner or a Republican signed his name. The uproar of cheers and applause even made it necessary to temporarily halt proceedings. Given the surge of enthusiasm, the next day the leaders of the southern bloc announced that they would no longer oppose the wage bill.[44]

Three weeks later, on May 24, the House finally passed the Fair Labor Standards Act by an overwhelming vote of 314 to 97, and a few weeks later the bill passed on a voice vote in the Senate. The law banned—finally and forever—child labor, set the minimum wage at 25 cents per hour, limited the work week to forty-four hours, and provided that the hourly wage would rise to 40 cents and the hours in the work week fall to forty hours within several years. Although the final bill allowed for no geographical wage differentials—differentials that took into account the cost of living had been one of the key demands of the South—it did exempt most agricultural workers as well as domestic service workers and small businesses; and it established industrial boards that would be permitted to consider local conditions in order to raise the minimum wage for certain interstate occupations. Despite these compromises, the law, Senator Bailey pronounced, was "manifestly unconstitutional," while Senator Glass let it be known that he was used to working eighteen hours a day. Other opponents warned that the wage legislation "opened the door to an industrial dictator," but proponents celebrated a "great humanitarian victory."[45]

"That's that," Roosevelt said as he signed the bill. Some of the exemptions and other compromises were disappointing, yet the legislation still represented a historic victory. He had finally prevailed, he remarked, over the "calamity-howling executive with an income of $1,000 a day" who had claimed that a wage of $11 per week would have a "disastrous effect" on American industry. Because the minimum wage affected millions of unorganized workers, one Labor Department statistician termed it "the most vital social legislation" in the nation's history. Almost a million factory workers would see an increase in their pay, and almost 3 million Americans would work a shorter week. Roosevelt's recovery of his power was a "historic feat," pronounced the *New York Times*. Thanks to Pepper's win in Florida, the president seemed to have regained control of Congress. [46]

The Pepper experience—his primary win and the stampede in the House to pass the Wages and Hours Bill—made it all look deceptively easy, as if liberal Democrats, with a few words of support from Jimmy, could win primary contests against conservative opponents. But Pepper was the incumbent, and he had the backing of the White House and of Harry Hopkins, who bestowed thousands of popular Works Progress Administration jobs on Florida. Roosevelt might better have concluded that it would be tough to beat incumbents, especially those who, unlike Pepper, had effective statewide organizations.

That would have been the safe course—but a few weeks later, Roosevelt injected the White House into a primary in Iowa.

"I don't think Senator Gillette is a strong candidate," FDR said. "If we could get a real liberal, we would have a strong ticket." A tall, handsome, white-haired, fifty-nine-year-old Iowan, Guy Gillette had served two terms in the House before being elected to the Senate in 1936 to fill a two-year vacancy. Gillette fashioned himself as an independent Democrat—a smart survival tactic in a traditionally Republican state. His record of loyalty to the president was mixed. A moderately faithful supporter of the New Deal, he reserved the right to "use his own judgment," as he said, on individual bills.[47] He had voted for rural electrification, flood control, and the CCC and opposed the NIRA, the AAA, more federal spending for relief, and the Fair Labor Standards Act. But his vote against court-packing earned him Roosevelt's smoldering enmity. Perhaps to make amends for casting that vote as well as others, Gillette supported the executive reorganization act—but then proceeded to vote against the Wages and Hours Bill.

Otha Wearin, a thirty-five-year-old third-term congressman, stepped forward to challenge Gillette in the Democratic primary. Physically, at least, he was no match for Gillette. Diminutive in stature and undistinguished in appearance, he was once denied admission to the House floor. In Congress he was known for his trademark bright red ties and for the hog-calling prizes he had won. He was famous, too, for his annual proposals to move the nation's capital from Washington to the Midwest. His support for the New Deal, however, was lukewarm. He had voted against the AAA, the NIRA, and some tax bills, but more recently he had supported executive reorganization and the Wages and Hours legislation.[48]

Was the president supporting Wearin? It was not at all clear. Wearin claimed to have White House backing, but Steve Early said that those assertions were a "surprise to me." Still, three weeks before the June 6 primary, Jimmy Roosevelt traveled with Wearin to a rally for Young Democrats in West Virginia, and their smiling faces appeared together on posters throughout Iowa. More controversially, WPA administrator Harry Hopkins weighed in. "If I voted in the Iowa primary," he told a reporter from the *Des Moines Register* on May 24, "I would vote for Otha Wearin on the basis of his record." Those seemingly inoffensive words touched off a firestorm of protest in Iowa and in Washington.[49]

The backlash in Iowa was fierce. The governor, Democrat Nelson Kraschel, fired off a telegram to FDR and Jim Farley, attacking Hopkins for his assault on "the freedom and independence of the primary voters." The *Cedar Rapids Gazette* accused Hopkins of using WPA funds as "a political whip," and the *Council Bluffs Nonpareil* branded Wearin a "presidential puppet." Even Roosevelt's secretary of agriculture, Iowan Henry Wallace, gave aid—clandestinely—to Gillette. For his part, Gillette at first offered only the low-key response that "If Mr. Hopkins lived in Iowa, Mr. Wearin would have one more vote."[50]

But there was a more enduring backlash in Washington against Harry Hopkins's endorsement of Wearin. Conservative Democratic senators Burton Wheeler, Patrick McCarran, Bennett Champ Clark, and a half a dozen others, who feared that their own political scalps might eventually be on the line, raked Hopkins and the White House over the coals. With Hopkins responsible for billions of dollars for relief, Wheeler charged that the White House was "playing politics with human misery." Accusing Hopkins of trading Works Progress Administration jobs for votes for Wearin and for Claude Pepper, Democratic Senator Carl Hatch of New Mexico sought a legislative remedy. He sponsored an amendment to a relief spending bill that would bar officials as well as employees of all federal relief programs from engaging in partisan political activities. On the floor of the Senate, Hatch's ally, the fervently reactionary Democrat Rush Holt, shouted that "politics oozed" from Hopkins's WPA. Arguing against Hatch's amendment, Roosevelt's point man in the Senate, majority leader Alben Barkley, noted that other federal officials and employees, paid out of the same treasury, would be left free to "roam around and play politics to their hearts' content." Hopkins might have committed an "indiscretion" in endorsing Wearin, Barkley conceded, but he insisted that Hopkins was no more guilty than members of Congress who expressed their political views.[51]

After a bitter all-night session, the Senate rejected Hatch's proposal by a close vote of thirty-nine to thirty-seven.[52] But the following year, after more questions about WPA activities in other campaigns, Congress would pass the Hatch Act. Born from Hopkins's endorsement of Otha Wearin, the Hatch Act, still today, prohibits all federal employees from engaging in partisan political activity.

On his home turf in Iowa, Gillette proved himself a determined and effective campaigner. While declaring himself "a Democrat from the soles of my feet to the tips of my hair," he denounced certain unnamed White House officials for interfering in Iowa's primary. They were a "gang of nonresident political termites," he ranted, comparing them, in the fashion of the day, to European dictators. Throwing the blame on Hopkins for his "devious and dubious" tactics, Gillette claimed to believe that the president was sincere "in his statements of neutrality."

Gillette had the support of almost all elected state officials in Iowa, including Governor Nelson Kraschel. "Otha and his gang," exclaimed Kraschel in a radio endorsement of Gillette, "would prostitute the basic principles of American government." In Washington, Iowa's other senator, Clyde Herring, announced that he would cast an absentee ballot for Gillette. And thanks to the intervention of South Carolina senator James Byrnes, Gillette received monetary assistance in his campaign from financier Bernard Baruch.[53]

From the White House, in defense of the beleaguered Wearin: silence. At a press conference, a visibly angry president insisted that he would say nothing publicly about primary candidates. Jimmy Roosevelt, laid up at the Mayo Clinic in Minnesota, sent a public telegram apologizing for not being able to help "his friend" Wearin in person. Henry Wallace remained silent and neutral. And Harry Hopkins, days before the election, was admitted to a Long Island hospital with a "sore throat." Steve Early sent him a telegram, suggesting that "one way to avoid throat infections is to keep your mouth shut; you will be surprised to learn how well this works." And so, when Otha Wearin was challenged to prove that he had the backing of the White House, he came up pitifully short.[54]

On June 6, when Iowans went to the polls, the turnout was the largest in state history. Gillette pummeled Wearin, 81,605 votes to 43,044. The election was "a vindication for democracy and repudiation of the backseat drivers here in Washington," gloated Senator Wheeler. "Their attempt to pack the court failed and their attempt to pack the Senate will fail," he predicted." Meanwhile, Wearin announced that he would not seek another term in the House. Hog-calling was less stressful than politics.[55]

From the botched Iowa experience, the president concluded that the White House should have intervened in the race less indirectly and more forthrightly. But had the White House been willing to listen and learn, the Iowa election could have served as a first-rate political manual replete with useful lessons and dos and don'ts.[56]

The first mistake was that the White House had operated outside the Democratic Party. Aside from one brief visit by Tommy Corcoran to Iowa, the White House clique ignored the state Democratic machines and officials, aiming instead at appealing to public opinion.[57] Making the situation even more contentious, Jim Farley, the head of the Democratic National Party, let it be known that he disagreed with the prime object of ousting conservative Democrats.

The politicos in the White House also failed to recognize how deeply an incumbent senator like Gillette was entrenched in the political life of his state. The party's turf, it turned out, could not be easily invaded by Washington. Gillette had deep statewide support, including that of the governor, senator, and chair of the state Democratic committee. And he had at his disposal the local political machines as well as the power to perform countless favors for constituents.[58]

Another persistent problem was the dearth of experienced, attractive progressive candidates to challenge incumbents. In contrast to the well-established Gillette, Wearin was young, weak, and eccentric—and had dubious New Deal credentials. The White House support for Wearin was also dubious—the administration's mixed messages might have confused New Deal loyalists in Iowa while angering others.

And the last chapter in the lesson book was that Iowa was not as liberal in 1938 as it had been in 1936. In November 1938, Gillette would go on to win reelection to the Senate—but by a very slim margin. And Governor Kraschel would lose to a Republican in the fall election. Had a more liberal candidate than Gillette won the Democratic primary in 1938, that candidate might well have lost the general election. In 1940, Wendell Willkie, not Roosevelt, would carry Iowa; and, in 1945, Iowa's entire delegation of representatives and senators would be Republican. If President Roosevelt had been able to read the tea leaves, he might have concluded that in all cases, even when purge tactics seemed justified and necessary, it would always be helpful to work with, energize, and solidify a state's Democratic organizations.

Some lessons, however, Roosevelt didn't need to be taught. A week after the primary, he reverted to his familiar role as charming scrootch owl, inviting Gillette to a reconciliation tête-à-tête in the White House. Shedding their suit jackets in the ninety-five-degree heat, they lunched alone in Mrs. Roosevelt's second-floor study. "We talked about the farm situation and the President's coming western trip and other matters," Gillette told reporters, adding, "I have always been a liberal." Roosevelt had gambled, lost, and sensibly tried to cut his losses.[59]

Still, he had done relatively little to inspire confidence in himself as a party leader. His clandestine meetings with challengers, his public denials of support, his haphazard improvisations, his many tactical errors, the ambiguous role of Jimmy Roosevelt—none of that instilled support for his languid party leadership. On the other hand, although Wearin had lost in Iowa, Roosevelt had helped secure wins for Hill and Pepper in Alabama and Florida.

In the spring of 1938, the president's score in the primary jamboree was two to one—in his favor.[60]

Rolling Westward

ON JULY 7, 1938, two weeks after his fireside chat in which he announced his plans for a "purge," Roosevelt's ten-car, air-cooled train pulled out of Washington's Union Station and rolled westward. For ten days, he was going to zigzag across the continent; then, from San Diego, sail down the Pacific for several weeks of vacation, pass through the Panama Canal, disembark in Florida, spend a night in Warm Springs; and then tour the Southeast before finally returning to Washington in late August.

A lively entourage of about eighty other passengers joined the president on board the train—secretaries, assistants, military aides, a few friends as well as radio engineers and announcers, newsreel cameramen, photographers, and thirty reporters. More journalists traveled with him than were assigned to cover his reelection campaign tour in 1936.[1]

The first stop, on July 8, was Marietta, Ohio, a pretty—and thoroughly Republican—town of broad streets, overarching trees, and orderly, comfortable Victorian houses. Festooned for the occasion in red, white, and blue bunting, Marietta was celebrating the 150th anniversary of the opening of the Northwest Territory and the unveiling of a monument to the pioneers. In the Muskingum Park, where the Muskingum River flows into the Ohio, a band dressed in orange and black played as thousands of people gathered—coatless men, women waving palm-leaf fans, chattering, laughing children.[2]

On the rostrum with the president stood Ohio senator Robert Bulkley and former governor George White, who was challenging Bulkley
in the Democratic primary. After an introduction by White—whose
hometown was Marietta—the president spoke.

Deftly, Roosevelt tied the early pioneers in the Northwest Territory
to present-day Americans—including himself. Just like the pioneer
settlers of Ohio, he, too, was "pushing on" to find solutions to social
and economic problems. "I am sure," he told the crowd, "that you will
push on with me." And just as the early pioneers had reached out to
government for help, the president continued, Americans in 1938 also
saw an ally in their government. By "government," he explained, he did
not mean a power *over* the people but the power *of* the people. The very
concept of "government" really meant "another form of the cooperation of good neighbors." The reaction of the crowd was polite and
curious—not demonstrably enthusiastic.[3]

Would the president dip into politics and say anything on behalf of
Senator Bulkley—a man he had known since his Harvard days when
they had worked together on the Harvard *Crimson?* "The cavalry captain of the old days who protected the log cabins of the Northwest,"
Roosevelt said, "is now supplanted by legislators, men like Senator
Bulkley, toiling . . . so that the protection and help of government can
be extended to the full." Referring specifically to Bulkley's bill to build
a network of superhighways across the United States, the president remarked that Americans were "not afraid . . . to choose forward-looking
representatives to run their government."[4]

The president's remarks were not effusive, but they left no doubt
that he favored the incumbent senator. He was even giving Bulkley
slightly more support than Bulkley had given to the New Deal, for the
Ohio senator had voted against the National Industrial Recovery Act,
against the Tennessee Valley Authority, against the Agricultural Adjustment Agency, against a major relief bill to fund the Works Progress
Administration, against soil conservation, and against the Wages and

Hours legislation. But he had been one of the few Democrats to back Roosevelt on court-packing and executive reorganization, and the president—perhaps fearing that an even more conservative candidate might win the primary—was returning the favor.[5]

As for White, whom the president had not deigned to recognize or mention, he took the endorsement in stride. "It was about as mild as he could make it," White said to reporters, adding that "it didn't do any harm."

A few hours later, under a blazing sun, Franklin Roosevelt's train arrived in Covington, Kentucky, a railroad labor center. It was the hottest day in years, and a few people fainted from the heat. Still that did little to quash the enthusiasm at the Latonia Racetrack in Covington. While the president frequently mopped his brow, thousands of people strained to see him. Everyone—especially politicians—pushed to get near him, as if they wanted some of his magical powers to rub off on them. But the president had come to Kentucky to rescue the state's Senator Alben Barkley, who was being challenged in the Democratic primary by the young governor, Albert "Happy" Chandler.[6]

In the summer of 1938, the president could indeed bask in his popularity. The spending of billions of dollars more in federal aid had eased the pinch of the recession for millions of average citizens. A poll taken that summer revealed that 73 percent of lower-income citizens had confidence in Roosevelt and the New Deal—while only 33 percent of upper-income Americans favored his administration. Roosevelt's popularity could also be measured geographically. In the southern states, 67 percent approved of the job he was doing, 54 percent in the midwestern states, and 64 percent in the far western states. But in New England, only 43 percent of voters supported him. In the summer of 1938, he was wisely staying away from the Northeast.[7]

Roosevelt had come to Covington on a mission. "Jim, I'm going to go to Kentucky to help Barkley," Roosevelt had told Farley. "I'm going to make a speech for him. Barkley must win." When Governor Chandler had gone to the White House in early February to discuss a possible run for Senate, the president tried to dissuade him, suggesting that Chandler wait his turn. But Happy decided to oppose Barkley in the Democratic primary—even though, just three years earlier, Barkley had helped Happy win his race for governor. "I wish they could both win," Farley told FDR, averse—as usual—to conflict within the party.[8]

The president needed Alben Barkley, a stalwart New Deal leader and loyalist, and was willing to go to bat for him. The Kentuckian had recently won the race—by only one vote—for Senate majority leader against Pat Harrison of Mississippi, and the president wanted him, at all costs, to remain in that role. Roosevelt considered Barkley an "integral part of the administration."[9]

In the heat of the sweltering day, Roosevelt addressed the crowd of thousands in the grandstands at the racetrack, joking with them that he was just passing through their state. "I am glad to be back in Kentucky," he said. "Some Republicans have suggested that I have come to Kentucky on a political mission. But I assure you the only reason is that I cannot get to Oklahoma without crossing Kentucky."[10]

The president then recalled a trip he had made to Kentucky in 1932 when he was campaigning for the presidency and described what he saw as his train moved slowly from Covington to Louisville. "Hunger, stark hunger, stared out at me from the faces of men and women and little children. There was scarcely a new dress or a new suit of clothes in the crowd. It was a chilly day . . . and for the actual want of clothes people stood there shivering." Roosevelt was not alone in witnessing southern poverty; Alben Barkley had traveled and campaigned with him. "Yes, tears were in our eyes that day," Roosevelt said. But he and Barkley had more in common than empathy: they both wanted action and results. Barkley, Roosevelt passionately told the crowd, was "a man who had fought valiantly, voting against doing nothing, voting in favor of action to meet the growing needs of the Nation."

Surprisingly, the president put in a good word for Happy Chandler, too. "Your Governor deserves due credit for getting this state on a sound financial basis," he said, adding that he considered Chandler a friend who "has done a good job as the Chief Executive of his State." Chandler indeed had proved himself a competent, progressive governor—he had balanced the state budget, reduced debt, built roads, revamped welfare in the state, and repealed an unpopular sales tax and replaced it with a graduated income tax.

Then came the president's strong advice to voters, and it began with warm words for Happy. "I have no doubt that Governor Chandler would make a good Senator from Kentucky," the president said to the crowd. Lowering the axe, he added, "But I think he would be the first to acknowledge that, as a very junior member of the Senate, it would take him many, many years to match the national knowledge, the experience and the acknowledged leadership in the affairs of the nation of that son of Kentucky of whom the whole nation is proud, Alben Barkley."

Roosevelt had just nimbly cast the governor as a young, somewhat green politician—certainly not as a villain. A show of courtesy and warmth was the order of the day. He was being careful not to burn his bridges with Chandler or alienate voters—in case Chandler won the race. He was willing to help friends like Barkley—by speaking out and raising money for them, sending members of his family to their fundraising events, talking up their chances for the 1940 presidential nomination, and letting the Works Progress Administration drum up support among the tens of thousands of its workers in the state.[11] But he was not yet interested in publicly disparaging anyone. In a final flourish of goodwill and respect for the independence of voters, he diplomatically said, "You have the absolute right to vote for any candidate in accordance with the dictates of your conscience. No outside source is out to dragoon you."

The perpetually ebullient Happy disguised whatever disappointment he felt. "Any time the President can't knock you out, you're all right!" he chirped. So adept was he at hogging the spotlight that he managed to get into every newspaper photo that was taken that day, brazenly stealing the limelight from the man on whom Roosevelt had come to bestow his blessing. He had of course been on hand at the Covington station to welcome the president. After Roosevelt had taken his usual place on the right-hand side of the back seat of his car, Chandler, wearing his usual gleeful grin, leaped over FDR and plopped himself down between the president and Barkley. All the newspapers had photos the next day showing Roosevelt on the left, the irrepressible Chandler smiling in the middle, and Barkley glumly relegated to the far right of the picture. A few weeks later, when Barkley went to the White House, Roosevelt enjoyed imitating how Chandler had outmaneuvered the senator in the car seat.[12]

On the campaign trail, the tall, athletic Happy was a natural, "a sweating, laughing, singing, hand-shaking, baby-patting dervish," reported *Time*. Indeed, he was such an effective campaigner that for once Jim Farley believed that Roosevelt's appearance in Kentucky to exert his influence in a Democratic primary might be necessary to guarantee a win for his favorite candidate. At rallies, Happy could often remember the first names and nicknames of people in the crowd, and, when he couldn't, he would call oldsters "Dad" and "Mom" and African American men "Uncle." He bestowed his infectious, buoyant smile on all and occasionally effervescently burst into his campaign theme song, "There Is a Gold Mine in the Sky."[13]

As far as the governor was concerned, the president had given him a good enough endorsement. "The President said, 'I have no doubt but that Chandler would make a good Senator.' What more do you want?" he asked the crowds. When he met people wearing Barkley buttons, he walked up to them and ripped them off. "You can't do that to me! I'm the best Governor you ever had!" One of his tactics was to make a joke of the president's support for Barkley. He told the crowds on the campaign trail that when Barkley prayed, he said, "Please God, don't send Jimmy. Send the President." But a more astute tactic was Chandler's successful introduction of legislation to open the Democratic primary to Republicans, for he guessed that some Republicans would be delighted to knife the president's man, Barkley.[14]

The strategy of the slightly pompous Barkley was to campaign as the servant of Roosevelt's leadership. When Happy accused him of being a "yes man" to FDR, Barkley proudly pleaded guilty. Around the state, the senator's supporters hung up small red-and-white signs indicating that a road or a bridge was built by the WPA. He could also boast of the support of powerful labor unions and important state newspapers, while the right-wing Liberty League backed Chandler.[15]

The age difference, too, came up in the campaign, with the dynamic, forty-one-year-old Happy charging that Barkley, at sixty-one, had become too old, too soft, and too out of touch with Kentucky. But before the race was over, it was Happy who found himself in the hospital, claiming that he had intentionally been served poisoned ice water. Barkley milked the episode for laughs. Every time someone poured him a glass of water at a speaking engagement, he held it up, looked at it quizzically, and waited for people to yell out, on cue, "Careful! It may be poisoned!"[16]

At 10 A.M. the following morning, July 9, Roosevelt's train stopped at the railroad station in Booneville, Arkansas, where three hundred people had gathered. Stepping out of his air-conditioned railcar, perspiring in the heat, the president listened as Senator Hattie Caraway, the only woman in the Senate, introduced him. In his brief talk, the president mentioned that he had known Mrs. Caraway for a quarter of a century, underscoring that she was "my very old, old friend and a friend of yours." But he offered no other words of praise—even though Caraway was a liberal on everything except anti-lynching bills. The White House believed that she had only a fifty-fifty chance of reelection—and the president was being very cautious. Nor was it evident that his restrained and tepid pat on the back for Caraway would even resonate in the largely rural state of Arkansas, where most farmers had no radios and only a weekly newspaper. More helpful to Caraway was the support of labor unions, the American Legion, and important Democratic women's groups.[17]

The president had no words at all for Caraway's Democratic opponent, Representative John McClellan, who had voted against both the Wages and Hours Bill and executive reorganization and who now was running on the antifeminist slogan "Arkansas needs another man in the Senate."[18]

In Arkansas, Roosevelt seemed more interested in keeping the New Deal flame alive than involving himself in local politics. "We're going to town and we're going to keep going to town, for the people!" he told the small crowd in Booneville. His meager efforts were a far cry from the week that the Kingfish, Huey Long of Louisiana, had gallantly spent in neighboring Arkansas back in 1932, stumping for Caraway while jubilantly making mincemeat of her opponent.[19]

Soon the presidential train was rumbling off to Oklahoma. It was the first time a sitting president had ever visited the state, and Roosevelt received an ebullient welcome. It seemed as if all of Oklahoma City's three hundred thousand citizens had come out to cheer and wave at the president as he rode by in an open car along flag-lined streets on his way to the state fairgrounds. There, in the sweltering, sun-baked grandstands, an overflowing crowd of fifty thousand Oklahomans excitedly waited for him.[20]

The political situation was complicated in Oklahoma, where two candidates were challenging the incumbent senator, sixty-two-year old

Elmer Thomas, in the Democratic primary. The state's junior senator, Josh Lee, was worried that Thomas might lose and appealed to the White House for help. Not only did Harold Ickes come out with a strong endorsement of Thomas, but the state WPA administrator urged his workers to support Thomas, while Harry Hopkins secured an executive order to raise the salaries of these workers in Oklahoma by almost a third.[21]

Thomas was a liberal who had a mostly positive record of support for the New Deal—he had backed the president on most bills, including executive reorganization, but opposed him on court-packing and some farm bills. Still, FDR approved administration aid to Thomas and had discouraged a liberal congressman, Wesley Disney, from running against him.[22]

Challenging the incumbent was Representative Gomer Smith, whom the White House had placed on its blacklist. But Smith, a talented orator whom some called the "rising Huey Long of the Southwest" and whom the *New Republic* considered "the most serious of our home-grown Führers," was the favorite in the race. A populist, he was the former national vice president of the Townsend old age pension movement—a plan concocted by Dr. Francis Townsend in 1933 to give all Americans over the age of sixty a monthly check of $150, funded by a 2 percent national sales tax. It had been a popular proposal in Oklahoma, where there were four times as many senior citizens per capita as in New York.[23] Smith campaigned on a platform demanding less government interference in the lives of citizens. If the present situation continued, he told Oklahomans, every time a calf was born, government representatives would be sure to show up.

The third candidate was Governor Ernest Marland. While he often supported the Roosevelt administration, he could also be unpredictable, on the one hand taking some conservative positions distasteful to the White House, on the other promoting populist panaceas that, as one historian wrote, "made old Dr. Townsend look like a spokesman for the Better Business Bureau."[24]

When the president suddenly appeared on the platform at the fairgrounds, accompanied by Senator Thomas and Governor Marland, people erupted into ecstatic cheers and whistles. Under the sweltering sun, constantly mopping his brow, Roosevelt spoke to the crowd and on a live radio hookup. First he made a few remarks about the many visible Works Progress projects in Oklahoma and about the importance of water control in the Arkansas River valley. Then he plunged into politics.

For social and economic progress to continue, he said, the government had to remain liberal and national in its outlook. And voters, too, needed to have a national outlook—and keep New Deal liberals in power. In choosing candidates, voters should "look into men's hearts." Do the candidates really mean what they say? Are they truly devoted to bettering conditions—or are they "Yes, but" men? Some people at the fairgrounds surmised that Roosevelt included Governor Marland among those "Yes, but" men. Still, the president recognized Marland with a reference to "your Governor," and in the realm of Democratic politics, four syllables uttered by Roosevelt were precious. Marland couldn't complain.[25]

The president's demolition job on Representative Smith, on the other hand, was ferocious. Roosevelt relegated the congressman, without explicitly mentioning his name, to the category of people who campaign "on impossible pledges and platforms—people with panaceas for reforming the world overnight." Trotting out his cousin Theodore Roosevelt for help, the president mentioned that TR used to refer to such people as the "lunatic fringe."[26]

Against the spooky backdrop of the lunatic fringe, the president's backing of Senator Thomas was unmistakably enthusiastic as he departed from his lukewarm remarks about Thomas in his prepared speech. "It was due to the persistent effort of my old friend, Senator Thomas," the president said, that the Grand River Dam project was under way. "Senator Thomas has been of *enormous help* to me and to the Administration in keeping me advised as to the needs of your state, and as to how we, in Washington, could help meet them." Roosevelt's bouquet for Thomas drew a loud cheer from the crowd.

The president's train traveled on south through Oklahoma, making stops in Shawnee, Holdenville, McAlester, and Wister. Wildly enthusiastic crowds greeted the president when he stepped out on the back platform for a few extemporaneous remarks.

In McAlester, where twelve thousand people thronged around the sun-baked station, the president explained the reason for his journey: "This is a tour primarily of inspection," he said. "I am occasionally mentioning a few words of politics but, of course, not in a partisan way. What I am seeking is . . . to maintain a liberal government in the capital."

Liberal—but not partisan; an inspection tour, not a political tour. It was a cautious, obfuscating message—for although the president had come out strongly for Thomas, some of his advisors were concerned about his thrusting himself into heated primary contests, especially those where candidates like Caraway and Thomas had only an even chance of victory. In addition, a Gallup poll in early July found that only 31 percent of Democratic voters answered yes to the question "Do you think that the Roosevelt administration should try to defeat in the primary elections Democratic senators who had opposed the President's plan to enlarge the Supreme Court?" Most of those who favored the purge felt that "the New Deal needs a unified front." But a majority of Democrats, 69 percent, felt that "senators have right to their own opinions and should voice them."[27]

The crowd, however, was unfazed by the subtleties of the president's mixed signals and roared its approval when he ended his talk on a peppy note: "As my boys would say, we are going places and I want to keep on going places!"

Three days later, on July 12, voters in Oklahoma went to the polls and—to Roosevelt's relief—renominated Thomas. "Your visit was most timely and beneficial," a grateful Thomas telegramed the president.[28] A young liberal, Mike Monroney, was nominated to take the House seat vacated by Gomer Smith.

"He was just like a daddy to me always," Lyndon Baines Johnson said about Franklin Roosevelt. "He was the one person I ever knew—anywhere—who was never afraid. I don't know that I'd have ever come to Congress if it hadn't been for him. But I do know I got my first great desire for public office because of him—and so did thousands of young men all over the country."[29] At least the young congressman was not ambivalent about Roosevelt, as many other Texans were—including Roosevelt's vice president and his own son Elliott.

When the president's train pulled into the Fort Worth station on a hot Saturday July night, six thousand people were waiting for him. Thousands more lined the motorcade route from the station to Elliott's hilltop ranch, ten miles outside Fort Worth, in rolling, grass-covered country. At the ranch, Roosevelt gave a short radio talk from a hookup on the lawn. Elliott, who managed a radio station in Texas and also had his own twice-weekly program, introduced his father. "In times of emergency," Elliott stated, "the Liberal says, 'try anything once.' The Conservative says, 'stop, look and listen before you leap.' Which is the best school of thought for the people of Texas to follow? I, for one, am not prepared to answer that question."[30]

While Franklin Roosevelt championed vast liberal, experimental programs, his son had veered to the right of the Democratic Party, questioning the very philosophy of the New Deal and locating wisdom in the do-nothing philosophy of a Herbert Hoover. It was an odd, somewhat troubled beginning for the president's swing through Texas.[31]

Politics in Texas—as in the president's own family—was turbulent. Roosevelt's own vice president, Jack Garner, snubbed him. Vacationing at his home in Uvalde, west of San Antonio, Garner declined to venture to northern Texas to meet FDR. It was "too far to walk," Garner telegraphed, with no expression of regret for his conspicuous absence. "Hope the fishing is good and not too strenuous," the president politely replied.[32] Roosevelt got the message that even though all of Texas's twenty-one representatives and its two senators were Democrats, he would have to tread lightly in the state. And so the trip through northern Texas would be filled with mild talk, not purge talk.

In his radio address from Elliott's ranch, the president avoided speaking about Democratic Party primaries, mentioning instead the problems of raising cattle and cotton and the importance of good wages in new industries in Texas. But most of all, he flattered his listeners by portraying himself as a fan of the Lone Star State. "I am proud of the spirit of Texas," he said at the end of his talk. "And now, as I sit here in a garden on top of a hill, with a breeze blowing and the sunset coming, surrounded by a very delightful gathering of Texans, all I can think of is that I want to come back again, many, many times in the days to come."[33]

There were some primary confrontations for renomination to the House in 1938, though there was no Senate race that year. The state's senior senator, old-timer Morris Sheppard, who had served in the upper house since 1913, was a loyal New Dealer. Tom Connally, the other senator, whose flowing hair, bow tie, and Texas wit were his Senate trademark, had a more mixed record; through 1936 he had backed most New Deal measures, with the exception of the National Industrial Recovery Act and the Guffey Coal Act of 1935. But lately he had opposed court-packing and executive reorganization as well as the Wages and Hours Bill. Still, Connally accompanied the president on his swing through the state and spoke from the rear platform about his "proud part" in the conventions of 1932 and 1936.[34]

But Roosevelt, reporters noticed, was "cool" toward the senator, never mentioning or referring to him in any of his rear platform talks, and Connally himself was convinced that the president wanted to humiliate him. At one of the stops in Texas, the president announced the appointment of the progressive governor, James Allred, to the federal bench, passing over the man Connally had recommended for the judgeship. In an icy rage, Connally believed that it was a calculated gesture to belittle him in public.[35]

The president had stepped into a Texas minefield—and in the twenty-one congressional races, there was little he could do. A few of Texas's conservative representatives were unopposed; others—like Martin Dies, Hatton Sumners, and Fritz Lanham—did have challengers, but they were either not viable candidates or even more conservative than the incumbents. For example, the Democrat who challenged Dies, H. G. Hendricks, had branded the New Deal "economic quackery" and predicted that it would lead "to destruction—a complete washout with unbelievable tragedy and sorrow."[36] Sumners rode with the president out of Fort Worth through the panhandle. But though Roosevelt, amiable as always, chatted with him on the train, he snubbed him in his platform talks.

In Amarillo, under a drenching rain, a crowd of more than one hundred thousand people and a band advertised as having between four and six thousand pieces greeted the president in Ellwood Park. Bareheaded, squinting to make out the words on his soggy text as water poured down his face, the president competed with explosive thunderclaps and driving rain to make himself heard. As he spoke about water and land conservation and his administration's farm policy, he laughed when he came to a passage about dust storms in the great American desert. Winding up his talk, he remarked that "this little shower that we've had is a mighty good omen."[37]

Though his speech in Amarillo was not political, the president squeezed in "honorable mentions" for five congressmen who accompanied him on the train: he referred to Johnson, Lanham, Marvin Jones, William McFarlane, and Maury Maverick as his "friends."[38]

While they were undoubtedly grateful to be recognized, one of them, the stocky, five-foot-tall Maverick, doubted that a few bland words would resound sufficiently 550 miles away in his home district of San Antonio. Maverick was more than a politician. During the last years of the Hoover administration, he had assumed the life of a hobo, sharing the miserable existence of the down-and-out transients living at the edge of San Antonio and eventually helping create a self-help organization for them. Elected to Congress in 1935, he became a member of a group of young radicals who tried, as some said, to outdeal the New Deal—for example, he was the only southerner in the House to vote for the anti-lynching bill. The exuberant Maverick had energetically backed the president's court-packing plan, his executive reorganization proposal, and the Fair Labor Standards Act. But not only did Maverick represent one of the most conservative districts in Texas, he had also managed to alienate the American Federation of Labor, which was powerful in San Antonio, as well as the city's political boss, Mayor C. K. Quinn, who arranged for the brother of his police chief to oppose Maverick in the 1938 primary. The ultraliberal congressman was desperate for help from the White House.[39]

Roosevelt had told Maverick that he could "write the prescription and I'll fill it"—and he approved funds for an airfield as well as a slum clearance project in Maverick's home district. Harold Ickes also responded to Maverick's plea for help with a strong letter of support.[40] Accompanying the president from Fort Worth to Amarillo aboard the Presidential Special, Maverick heard the president mention his name to the crowds along the way and link him to the projects under way in San Antonio. But would all of that help be enough to return him to Washington?

Lyndon Johnson's Tenth Congressional District was also 530 miles from Amarillo, but Johnson, unlike Maverick, was a born politician.

First elected to the House of Representatives in a special election in April 1937, he had made his support for FDR's court-packing scheme the central issue in that campaign. While Maverick focused on ideology, bypassing if not alienating his constituents, Johnson lavished all his attention on serving the men and women in his district. He quickly mastered the art of funneling New Deal jobs and money to his district and tirelessly dispensed personal favors. That formula guaranteed him deep and enduring support at home. When Texans went to the polls on July 23, they renominated Johnson—but not Maverick—for Congress.[41]

As for the president, he had capitalized on his own popularity in the Lone Star State. In 1940, he would win 840,000 votes in Texas to 199,000 for Wendell Willkie; and in 1944 he would crush Thomas Dewey by an almost identical margin. And the Lone Star State's entire delegation in Congress would remain 100 percent Democratic until 1954.

On to Colorado rolled the president's train. Roosevelt continued to play it safe there, repeating the same nonconfrontational scenario. "I did not come out here for political reasons," he told folks in Grand Junction. It was simply his "annual look-see," he said. He invited on board his train Colorado's Senator Alva Adams, who was up for renomination. Adams might have been in the doghouse for opposing the president on several key bills, but he was a shoo-in to be renominated. His father, "Big Alva," had served two terms as governor and his uncle Billy had served in that office for three terms—and the Adams family political machine now belonged to "Little Alva." Adams was so far out in front, Harold Ickes observed, that there was no chance to beat him.[42]

At the train stop in Pueblo, his hometown, Adams stood next to the president on the rear platform as Roosevelt addressed a crowd of fifteen thousand. Shifting nervously from one foot to the other, Adams waited to see if the president would help—or hinder—his renomination. But Roosevelt did neither. He made no reference, positive or negative, to Adams—or to his opponent. Instead, the president focused solely on local problems—irrigation, land reclamation, reforestation, power development, and flooding on the Arkansas River that starts west of Pueblo. "That river isn't just the problem of one state or one community," FDR said. "It calls for national planning. . . . We are thinking of all of our problems in national terms. We have been trying . . . to make this nation conscious of the fact that it is a nation."[43]

At another stop in Colorado, Roosevelt did venture into politics—but Utah's, not Colorado's. When Utah's governor, Henry Blood, asked the president—in private—how prospects looked for Senator Elbert Thomas's reelection, the president replied that it appeared almost certain that Thomas—who had supported him on executive reorganization—would win. That offhand remark earned the senator—who had no opposition in the Democratic primary—a banner headline in the *Salt Lake Tribune:* "Roosevelt Bestows Blessing on Senator Thomas." That was the only direct help Thomas received from the president. He didn't need it.[44]

In 1938 Nevada's junior senator, Pat McCarran, was up for reelection. The handsome, white-haired sixty-two-year old senator, a former chief justice of the Nevada Supreme Court, had refrained from openly attacking the New Deal in the early years of the Roosevelt administration, but he had caused the White House many a headache. And more recently, from his perch on the Judiciary Committee, he had helped sink the president's court reform plan.

In the Democratic primary, McCarran faced two opponents, who were both 100 percent New Dealers but who posed no serious challenge to him. Dr. John Worden, the state's health commissioner, considered himself a socialist and campaigned on the slogan "Little man, improve your condition. Send to the Senate a New Deal physician!" The second challenger was a young Reno lawyer known more for his wisecracks than for his abilities: Albert Hilliard. Hilliard's platform was simple: President Roosevelt "has never been wrong and never will be wrong." The president bestowed his grace on Hilliard by referring to him as "Brother Hilliard" and his "friend Al."[45]

McCarran was virtually certain to be renominated, and FDR, unable to come up with a better opponent than Worden or Hillard, had decided not to try to dislodge him. McCarran told his friends that he would consider it a personal victory if he received no worse than the silent treatment from the president. But McCarran did better than that—like Happy Chandler, he would prove himself adept at stealing the spotlight.[46]

As the president's train passed through Nevada on July 13, with both McCarran and Hilliard on board, the senator succeeded in overshadowing his challenger. At a stop in Carlin, after Roosevelt had started speaking from the rear platform, McCarran suddenly appeared at his side. "Hello, Pat!" someone called out. The crowd interrupted the president with applause for their senator. Upstaged, the president smiled, stopped speaking for a moment, and shook hands with McCarran.[47]

McCarran's clever maneuvers succeeded. In Imlay, Nevada, when the president said that things looked better in Nevada than they had a few years ago, McCarran led the little group assembled there in clapping and cheering for the president. Returning the gesture, the president remarked: "Your senator has given me some Nevada trout for lunch and I'll have it again for dinner." Roosevelt had not mentioned McCarran's name, but he said "your senator" with a smile, and for McCarran that was a bonus from heaven. At another stop, the president had to leave the back platform to make a call to Washington, and McCarran, beaming, quickly took center stage. What more could a senator in the doghouse have hoped for? Jim Farley remarked that McCarran had turned Roosevelt's excursion through Nevada "into a rally for himself."[48]

★   ★   ★

While McCarran basked in the limelight, some newspaper reporters interpreted Roosevelt's failure to crack down on formerly dependable senators who had turned against the New Deal—politicians like Mc-Carran and Colorado's Adams—as the premature demise of the purge, barely a week after it had begun. Other reporters concluded that the president had adopted a cautious tack, surrendering, as a *Washington Post* columnist remarked, to an "impulse to prudence."[49]

They were right: Roosevelt was indeed being prudent. Unwilling to stump for a losing cause, he was playing it safe; the purge was, at least temporarily, on hold. Making the best of the political situation, he had decided not to oppose conservative, entrenched Democrats like Adams and McCarran.

Nor was Roosevelt interested in challenging Senator Bennett Champ Clark of Missouri, who was also up for reelection in 1938. Since Clark had opposed the AAA, the NRA, tax reform, the court plan, and executive reorganization, he was popular with Republicans as well as with conservative Democrats. By 1937 he had become one of the organizers of the conservative coalition in Congress. There was even talk that Clark, the son of James Beauchamp "Champ" Clark, Speaker of the House during Woodrow Wilson's presidency, might step forward as a "compromise" candidate for the presidency in 1940.[50] That would have been quite a compromise: in 1941, Clark would join forces with the isolationist America First Committee and oppose Roosevelt on the Lend-Lease Act, as well as on all his preparedness policies. But in Missouri in 1938, Bennett Clark's position seemed impregnable.

Roosevelt also shied away from trying to oust another one of the stars on his blacklist, Frederick Van Nuys of Indiana. A member of the Senate Judiciary Committee, Van Nuys had written a scathing report on the court-packing bill. In July 1937, the Democratic governor of Indiana, after meeting with the president, announced on the White House steps that the state's Democratic Party would refuse to renominate Van Nuys. But Van Nuys threatened to run as an Independent, and Roosevelt feared that such a move would split the Democratic vote and give the seat to a Republican. In addition, a group of senators including Wheeler, Bailey, Byrd, Copeland, and Tydings vowed to stump for Van Nuys. So in Indiana, too, the president agreed to a marriage of convenience, as one reporter wrote, between the Van Nuys Thistle and the New Deal Rose.[51]

Roosevelt also saw that there was no point in opposing Connecticut's Senator Augustine Lonergan, who, like other lukewarm and unreliable Democrats, had voted against court-packing and executive reorganization. And so the president declined to help Lonergan's opponent, Congressman Herman Kopplemann.[52]

It made some sense for the president not to wage losing battles in Colorado, Nevada, Missouri, Indiana, and Connecticut. But it was much harder to fathom his decision not to travel to Idaho, where Senator James Pope, a 100 percent New Dealer, was facing a strong challenge in the Democratic primary from a young congressman, Worth Clark. The thirty-five-year old Clark had been one of the first members of the House to publicly declare his opposition to the president's court plan. Not only had Clark voted against court-packing, executive reorganization, and the Wages and Hours Bill, he was also an isolationist adamantly opposed to FDR's internationalist foreign policy.[53]

Few had been warmer or a more loyal supporter of the administration than the fifty-four-year-old Pope. When he first ran for the Senate in 1932, Pope had seemed to anticipate the New Deal; like FDR, he spoke about the "little man" and demanded relief for poor Americans. The only thing wrong with the American system of government, Pope said, was "the men who have worked our system for their own selfish advantage." In 1937, he had enthusiastically backed Roosevelt's court reform bill, arguing that it was "incongruous, inappropriate and out of accord with the sprit of our Constitution" for justices to set aside laws that reflected the wishes of the people, Congress, and the president. He even proposed a resolution of his own requiring a two-thirds majority on the Supreme Court to overturn any law enacted by Congress.[54]

Ten months earlier, in the fall of 1937, Roosevelt had traveled to Idaho, where he had embraced progressive Republican Senator William Borah. Borah introduced Roosevelt to a cheering crowd, hailing him as "our great president"—and Roosevelt showered the senator with effusive praise. But in 1938, as he zigzagged across the continent and through the West, Roosevelt declined to make a detour to Idaho and bestow on Pope the same kind of personal endorsement he had given to Borah, Barkley, Bulkley, and Thomas. Nor did he even take the opportunity to capitalize on federal largesse in Idaho—a $10 million hydroelectric power and irrigation project on the Snake and Boise rivers in Idaho.[55]

Perhaps Roosevelt and Pope were both overly cautious, fearful that in conservative Idaho the president's intervention might do more harm than good. Instead of making personal appearances in Idaho and bestowing his blessing on Pope, Roosevelt dispatched Jim Farley to speak for him. Passing through Boise on his way to Alaska, Farley put aside his negative feelings about intervening in primaries and told the crowd that it was "highly important" that Idaho elect a senator who would support the president and his programs. But Farley stopped short of explicitly stating that Pope was Roosevelt's choice in the contest. Secretary of State Cordell Hull, on the other hand, did endorse Pope, lauding in particular the senator's stand on agricultural trade treaties. But Hull's support may have been more of a minus than a plus in Idaho, where Borah, one of the most fervent isolationists in the Senate, had accustomed people to look with skepticism on the internationalism Pope outspokenly espoused. Clark promised Idahoans that, if elected, he would work "to thwart those sincere but misguided folk who would take us into the league of nations or would have some other scheme for us to pull Europe's chestnuts out of the fire."[56]

Pope faced a severe uphill struggle, not least because the Democratic state legislature—in a move that seemed designed by anti–New Deal Democrats to sabotage Pope—had approved an open primary, permitting voters, whatever their party affiliation, to cast ballots in either party's primary.[57] That new law gave the green light to Republicans—especially Borah-style isolationists—to vote against Pope in the Democratic primary.

On August 9, in a jolting blow, Pope lost to Clark by a few thousand votes. At a press conference in late August, Roosevelt denounced the Idaho primary for defeating the whole idea of giving party voters the right to choose their own candidates for public office. The primary system in Idaho, he fumed, had been "morally and completely violated." A few days later, Pope traveled to Hyde Park to discuss with Roosevelt the possibility of running for the Senate on a third party ticket. But FDR worried about splitting the Democratic vote and weakening the tenuous hold the Democratic Party had in Idaho. Judging that Clark was a lesser evil than an even more right-wing Republican, he vetoed Pope's idea.[58]

The president and his party left the train in Crockett, California, north of Berkeley, and motored a few miles north to Mare Island Navy Yard. Then they crossed the glistening new Golden Gate Bridge—just completed by the Public Works Administration in 1937—to San Francisco, where a rousing reception greeted them. On the city's streets, people, standing six deep, cheered and waved flags, hats, and anything else they could grab as the motorcade went by.[59] Though FDR's popularity had declined a bit in the state—from 69 percent in 1936 to 63 percent in 1938—Californians still loved him and the New Deal. This was nothing new—they had deserted the Republican Party as well as the state's native son, Herbert Hoover, in 1932.

After viewing the new Golden Gate International Exposition grounds, the president and his entourage crossed another PWA bridge—the Bay Bridge—to Oakland and proceeded to their final destination: the Treasure Island Naval Base in the middle of San Francisco Bay. There the president, who had served as assistant secretary of the navy during World War I, boarded the USS *Houston* and reviewed sixty-five naval craft—so many battleships, destroyers, submarines, and aircraft carriers that they could barely fit into the huge bay. Aboard the ship, the president and his entourage heard a twenty-one-gun salute ring out.

Before boarding the *Houston,* the president spoke to an enthusiastic crowd on Treasure Island. "Rarely in my life have I been thrilled as I am today," he said, impressed by the stunning new bridges he had just crossed. The Works Progress Administration and the Public Works Administration, he reminded the crowd, were pouring tens of millions of dollars into the state. Then, turning to world affairs, he expressed both optimism and pessimism. On the one hand he hoped that the Golden Gate International Exposition would be a harbinger of peace and goodwill among nations. But he added that despite his hopes for peace and despite the fact that money spent on armaments did not create permanent income-producing wealth, he believed in the necessity of arming the nation. The fleet he was about to review was more than a symbol; it was a "potent, ever-ready fact in the national defense of the United States."[60]

The president had spoken about prosperity, progress, peace, and war—not about politics or candidates. Or about Senator William Gibbs McAdoo. Elected to the Senate in 1932, the seventy-five-year old McAdoo was being challenged in the primary by progressive Sheridan Downey.

Roosevelt and McAdoo were old friends. The two had worked together during World War I when McAdoo, Woodrow Wilson's son-in-law, served as Wilson's treasury secretary. And it was McAdoo who, after initially backing Jack Garner at the 1932 Democratic convention, turned to Roosevelt on the decisive fourth ballot and helped deliver, as he declared on the Chicago convention floor to wild cheers and resounding boos, "the forty-four votes of California for Roosevelt!" In the Senate, McAdoo supported Roosevelt on executive reorganization but opposed him on court-packing. Generally speaking, pronounced Harold Ickes, McAdoo "does line up for the administration."[61]

Sheridan Downey, on the other hand, had backed Roosevelt on the first ballot at the 1932 convention, while McAdoo flirted with Garner. Two years later, in 1934, Downey was the running mate of socialist Upton Sinclair when Sinclair ran for governor of California. And Downey was the personal lawyer of Dr. Francis Townsend, the founder of the old age pension movement. Though the *New Republic* had dubbed Downey a member of the "lunatic fringe of . . . the extreme left," Downey posed a serious threat to McAdoo, especially because his main issue—"$30-every-Thursday" old age pensions for every Californian over fifty, to be financed by a 2 percent state sales tax—was highly popular with voters.[62]

In March 1938, McAdoo had pleaded with the president for his endorsement and even drafted a sample letter himself that he showed to Jim Farley, who passed it on to FDR. After reading with a wry face the tribute McAdoo had composed for himself, the president agreed to write an endorsement, but one that was "not so sugary." Though Roosevelt, in private, berated Downey's "$30-every-Thursday" plan as a half-baked "short-cut to Utopia" and agreed with McAdoo that it was a "cruel delusion," no other help for McAdoo was forthcoming from the White House—that is, not until Roosevelt decided that he would finally speak out in Los Angeles.[63]

On the morning of July 16, a thousand invited guests waited at the railroad station while the Los Angeles Police Band raucously played "California Here I Come." When the president's train pulled in at 9 A.M., Roosevelt made some brief extemporaneous remarks.[64]

Then he turned to Senator McAdoo, standing next to him. "Last March, I wrote a letter to an old friend of mine expressing the very definite hope that he would run again for the Senate," Roosevelt told the crowd. Then, smiling broadly at McAdoo, he said, "And I might add that I meant I hoped he would be re-elected, too." It was a clear—though restrained—statement of support.[65]

"Reelection of M'Adoo Urged in Train Talk" read the headline in the *Los Angeles Times*. But Downey, who had also been in the president's fifty-person entourage at the Los Angeles railroad station, countered with a statement of his own. "McAdoo autocracy has run its course," he declared, adding that throughout his life he had been devoted to the liberal cause. "In the future, as in the past," Downey promised, "I shall continue to support all liberal, labor and New Deal objectives." Downey's campaign was picking up steam, and the president, wary of alienating him in case he won, had carefully refrained from being effusive in his praise of McAdoo.[66]

Leaving the train for an open-topped automobile, Roosevelt, along with Senator and Mrs. McAdoo, motored slowly through the streets of Los Angeles. It was a beautiful, breezy, sunny day. Thousands of people flanked the route as the thirty-car motorcade wove its way through the sprawling city; people ran into the streets after the president; some showered the motorcade with paper streamers and confetti. When the president passed in front of the Orthopedic Hospital, where children in wheelchairs sat outside along the curb and sidewalk, he recognized a nurse from Warm Springs. "Hello! How are you?" he jovially called out.[67]

As they headed south to San Diego, the crowds thinned out. Along the road, families quietly held up American flags; a small group of Japanese-American boys and girls held a sign reading "We Wish You Luck." Near Long Beach, the president saw other groups holding signs—"Ford Strikers Welcome President Roosevelt"; "Longshoremen are for President Roosevelt—Send New Dealers to Washington!" On the route through Long Beach, thousands more lined the streets.

Along the ocean highway the president gazed out at the blue Pacific. One man held up his rod and two fish, showing his good luck to the president, who was about to leave on a fishing cruise himself. In the beach towns, residents, some in their bathing suits and a few holding surf boards, greeted the motorcade. A few held signs: "Please stop and chat with us" and "We Like You But We're Thru with McAdoo."[68]

After a picnic stop at the San Clemente State Park, the motorcade continued into San Diego, where twenty-five thousand people waited for the president to dedicate the new Civic Center Plaza, a PWA project. Afterward, the president and his party once again boarded the USS *Houston*. Roosevelt was off to the Galapagos Islands and the Cocos Islands for three weeks of fishing.

Desperate for dramatic news, newspaper reporters were disappointed. They had hoped for much more. During the ten days since the president's departure from Washington, there had been no fireworks—no bitter, hostile, or even dismissive remarks about conservative senators like Adams and McCarran. No political throats were slit. There had been no crackdowns, no denunciations—and not even any condescending scoldings. Just a few mild snubs. "The Roosevelt 'Purge' Fails to Materialize" blared the headline in the *New York Times* on July 17.

In the wake of his daring fireside chat in June, Franklin Roosevelt's ten-day crosscontinental journey had started off as a bold, partisan political sortie into critical primary elections. He had stumped for Barkley in Kentucky, Thomas in Oklahoma, and McAdoo in California. But in primaries in Texas, Colorado, and Nevada, he refrained from taking stands, and he had completely ignored races in Indiana and Missouri where the conservative incumbents were popular. He even shunned a race in Idaho out of fear that in a conservative-leaning state, his liberal stands might do more to damage than help the liberal incumbent. His fiery denunciations in the spring of 1938 of the "Yes, but" men had softened and metamorphosed into the prudent motto "First do no harm." And so the journey had become a tour to assist some incumbents but also a tour to help himself. From Union Station in Washington to

San Diego, the president had staged his own triumphal march across the continent, including some places he had not yet visited.

Even at the railroad stations where it was known that the presidential train would not pause, people gathered anyway, hoping that as the train briefly slackened its pace they might catch a passing glimpse of Roosevelt, a smile or maybe a wave. Where the train stopped, joyous crowds were eager to see him and hear his words. "Pour it on, Mr. President," shouted one man. "Pour it on!" His effect on crowds was "instantaneous," the *Times* commented. What was the secret to his magic?[69]

In part, it was his happy, infectious smile, his zest for life. But it was also his ability to discuss local problems with people across the country simply and intelligently. Summoning a vast store of topical information, the president could talk with knowledge and empathy about the problems of different communities. He could address flood control in Arkansas, Ohio, and Kentucky and the challenges of drought in the dust bowls of Texas, Oklahoma, and Nevada; mining in Colorado and naval defense in California.[70]

Even though there was no bloodletting, it was nevertheless a tense experience for the senators, congressmen, and governors who stood beside him on the rear platform of his train or on the podium at stadiums and fairgrounds. Longing for a friendly nod, a mere mention of their names, they knew that any acknowledgment of their existence— however slight—could change their political fortunes. But so far the president had rarely been effusive with his support. Was it his intention to keep most of his political capital for himself? Was he trying to enhance his own political standing with voters? Was he thinking about his own political future—in 1940? To all the above: Yes.

On July 16th, the *Houston*, newly scrubbed, renovated, and equipped with escalators and other modern comforts rarely found on warships, set sail for the Galapagos Islands. "All goes well on board," the president wrote to his appointments secretary Marvin McIntyre. "I take it you have a screamingly funny time over primaries!! Here we don't care who wins! As ever."[71]

On the ship, tackle, reels, and rods dominated the day—along with reading, discussion, sleep—and work. News about domestic politics and crises in Europe easily made its way to the group on the *Houston*. In late July, while the president sailed serenely on the ocean, the British prime minister, Neville Chamberlain, vigorously assured Parliament that the European situation had taken a turn for the better. Four months after Nazi Germany annexed Austria and six weeks after Hitler proclaimed his decision to smash Czechoslovakia, Chamberlain chirped, "We all feel the atmosphere is lighter." He was responding to Sir Archibald Sinclair, the Liberal Party leader, who had begged the government to change its foreign policy and confront Hitler's aggression more forcefully while there was still time. But members of Parliament, even those who interrupted Chamberlain with derisive taunts and calls for his resignation, were anxious to end debate and begin their own three-month summer holidays. In Washington, U.S. Navy Commander Charles Rosendahl, just back from festivities in Germany marking the one hundredth anniversary of the birth of Count Ferdinand von Zeppelin, urged that the United States sell helium to Germany. Secretary of the Interior Ickes, who controlled the nation's helium supply, sneered at Rosendahl's hollow contention that airships had no place in Germany's war plans—and gave a flat and angry no. Germany, however, needed neither zeppelins nor helium. Its military buildup of tanks, bombers, and U-boats was advancing with bewildering speed.[72]

On the blue Pacific, for three precious weeks, Franklin Roosevelt and his friends—military aide "Pa" Watson, an expert deepwater fisherman who liked talking to his catch as he reeled it in; former law partner Basil O'Connor; cousin Frederick Adams, and a few others—focused on yellowtails, groupers, and sharks. Sailing and fishing were the two sports the paralyzed president could enjoy. He happily landed a thirty-eight-pound yellowtail—and was even prouder to catch a 230-pound shark after an unusual battle of patience and will that lasted an hour and a half. "I got tired just watching," said O'Connor. Also caught were some unknown species, which were turned over to another companion on board, Professor Waldo Schmitt, who added them to the Smithsonian Institution's collection of marine life specimens. Schmitt discovered a new genus of palm that he named the "Rooseveltia Frankliniana." The biologist was such a success, Roosevelt later quipped, that "we decided to change the Smithsonian to 'Schmittsonian.'"[73]

Occasionally they picnicked on a deserted palm-shaded beach. Anchored near one island in the Galapagos, they sent ashore food, supplies, and magazines for the island's twelve inhabitants. But mostly they fished all day under sunny skies. In the evenings, chilled by the cold Humboldt Current that runs up from the Antarctic regions through the Galapagos, the friends, wrapped in coats and blankets, watched movies on deck. "Roosevelt Loafs in Cool Breezes" was the headline in the *Atlanta Constitution*. On the way home, they passed through the Panama Canal. Roosevelt, relaxed and tan, pronounced his vacation "a grand cruise, a real holiday."[74]

Before disembarking on August 9 in Pensacola, Florida, where a cheering, whistling, waving throng of one hundred thousand awaited him, the president met with reporters. He mentioned that he had begun working on the speeches he would give in two days in Barnesville and Athens, Georgia.[75]

Would the talks be political? reporters wanted to know. Well, they were still in the rough draft stage, he hedged, and he wasn't yet sure. Might they become even rougher when he went over the rough drafts? one reporter asked. The president laughed.[76]

It was a good question.

★   ★   ★

Ahead were still more crucial primary elections, in which some of the most conservative and obstructionist Democrats in the Senate—Walter George of Georgia, Cotton Ed Smith of South Carolina, and Millard Tydings of Maryland—were up for renomination. And as ever in the one-party South, renomination in a Democratic primary was tantamount to reelection.

So far, Roosevelt had backed—or at least not opposed—incumbents. He had warmly praised Barkley; Bulkley, Caraway, and McAdoo received mild endorsements. McCarran and Alva Adams got the silent treatment—but no worse. The president had been mostly cautious and prudent.

Would he be brasher and more aggressive in the South against George, Smith, and Tydings? Had the sea air—and the 230-pound shark—reinvigorated him and fortified his resolve?

In Senate races since January 1938, he had racked up an impressive list of victories, with wins for New Deal allies Lister Hill in Alabama and Claude Pepper in Florida. In Oklahoma and Ohio, Thomas and Bulkley won their primaries; in Kentucky, Barkley received 56 percent of the vote compared to 43 percent for Chandler; and in Arkansas Caraway was also renominated. The only race in which the president had approached an active role and lost was in Iowa, where he had wavered on support for Otha Wearin, who was predictably defeated by the incumbent, Guy Gillette.[77]

In Warm Springs, on the morning of August 10, two months after his fireside chat announcing and outlining the "purge," Roosevelt discussed with Harry Hopkins and a few others—political aide Joseph Keenan and Georgia governor Ed Rivers—how to handle the Georgia Senate primary. Also present was Lawrence Camp, a U.S. Attorney from Atlanta, who was challenging the incumbent, Walter George.

One person who was absent from the powwow in Warm Springs was the Democratic national chairman, Jim Farley. "Walter George is my friend, and I am Walter George's friend," Farley had recently remarked. And that past June, a brand-new, warmly inscribed photograph of Farley had suddenly appeared on George's desk. The photo seemed to symbolize the deepening division between the Democratic chairman and the White House on the subject of the purge. Farley knew that George's supporters had backed Roosevelt even before the 1932 Chicago convention—and he had told Democratic conservatives Wheeler, George, and Smith that the president had nothing to gain by giving vent to a spirit of vindictiveness.[78]

And so it was without any input from Farley that Roosevelt, Hopkins, Keenan, Rivers, and Camp analyzed the situation one final time. The men knew that already that past June, twelve out of thirteen Democratic county chairmen in Georgia had predicted that Walter George would be renominated in the Democratic primary on September 14. But they also knew that George had been one of the key New Deal obstructionists. The question was whether the president was willing to alienate untold numbers of southern Democrats by trying to oust George from the party.[79]

At a luncheon that day, the president, seated at the head table next to Rivers and Camp, greeted the patients at the Warm Springs Foundation. "We are very much honored today in having as guests of Warm Springs Governor Rivers, who is an old friend of ours," Roosevelt said, "and also a gentleman who I hope will be the *next Senator from this State,* Lawrence Camp." The president's aides were startled; they had just assured reporters in Warm Springs that the president would have nothing newsworthy to say.[80]

But Roosevelt had indeed made news. For the first time since the purge began, he was going to try to oust a sitting Democrat.

Just four days earlier, on August 7, the *New York Times* had reported that Roosevelt's purge had been "called off." It simply had not "materialized," the *Times* wrote, applauding the president's restraint and "sagacity." But after the president's pointed remarks in Warm Springs, the *Times* back-tracked. "Move Is a Surprise" announced the headline on August 11.

Eight weeks after his fireside chat about the "purge," the president would finally unleash his anger.

"All this made interesting reading in Alaska," Jim Farley later remarked.[81]

◄ 7 ►

Marching through Georgia

ON AUGUST 11, a dry, scorching day with temperatures in the mid-nineties, the president emerged from his private train car at the tiny Barnesville station in Georgia. With a population of only three thousand, Barnesville had become, at least for a day, the focal point of the state—and the nation. Officially the president had come to dedicate a Rural Electrification project that would supply power to the central parts of Georgia. But some of the more than forty thousand people who drove in their automobiles to Barnesville in the searing heat suspected that the events of the day might be more confrontational than celebratory.[1]

Along the short, dusty parade route, lined with soldiers from Fort Benning, the president's motorcade made its way to the Gordon Institute's stadium, built out of a swamp with Works Progress Administration funds. There, with the sun burning down from the bright blue sky, with the scent of pine and peaches in the air, Georgians waited for the president to arrive, fanning themselves with folded newspapers and anything else that was available. "Mama is that him? Mama is that him?" asked squirming children. It was early afternoon, and people swarmed around the lunch stands, concession booths, and carnival rides.[2]

Finally, the president, wearing a light-colored summer suit, appeared, looking tanned and vigorous after his vacation cruise. The crowd cheered when he flashed his famous smile. They loved their president. That summer, George Gallup had polled Americans to gauge the popularity of Franklin Roosevelt. Indeed, many of Roosevelt's most enthusiastic, loyal, and appreciative followers lived in Georgia, where almost three-quarters of the people supported their president.[3]

On the speakers' platform—gaily festooned with stars and stripes and red, white, and blue bunting—were the president, Senator Walter George, Governor Ed Rivers, the state's junior senator, Richard Russell, and Lawrence Camp, George's primary opponent. Occasionally, George, his face as emotionless as a mask, gave a half-yawn.[4]

Senator Russell was the first to speak, hailing President Roosevelt as "the greatest exponent of liberal democracy and equality of opportunity of his generation." Then Governor Rivers rose to introduce the president to the stadium crowd. The governor was running for reelection and wanted to make the most of his moment in the sun. He, too, was a reformer who promised a "little New Deal" for Georgia. He had made important changes in the state, especially improvements in public education, guaranteeing a seven-month school term. At length, he lavished praise on Mr. Roosevelt, happily describing him as a "taxpayer, resident and part-time citizen" of Georgia and extolling his "great character, his matchless intellect, and his irresistible personality." Someone in the impatient crowd finally shouted "Turn him off!" and Rivers wound up his encomium. His voice rising, he presented "the greatest human lover of human rights of all times, our fellow Georgian, the Honorable Franklin Delano Roosevelt, President of the United States of America!"[5]

At last it was the president's turn to speak, and he began by looking back on one of the transforming events in his earlier life. "Fourteen years ago, a democratic Yankee, a comparatively young man came to a neighboring county in the State of Georgia, in search of a pool of warm water wherein he might swim his way back to health." And indeed, he found all that he was looking for. But there was one discordant note in his first stay at Warm Springs. "When the first of the month bill came in for electric light for my little cottage, I found that the charge was . . . about four times as much as I was paying in another community, Hyde Park, New York," Roosevelt said. "We hear you!" shouted a voice in the crowd. Someone else yelled, "They were just trying to rob us poor people!" After smiling at these interruptions, Roosevelt continued.[6]

He reminded the crowd that electricity was a modern necessity, not a luxury. "That necessity ought to be found in every village," he declared, "in every home and on every farm in every part of the United States. The dedication of this Rural Electrification Administration project in Georgia today is a symbol of the progress we are making—and we are not going to stop."

Roosevelt did not exaggerate the achievements of the Rural Electrification Administration: It was one of the great New Deal successes. Before it, the free market economy had left much of rural America literally in the dark. The few state power authorities that did exist, such as the one created by Roosevelt in 1931 when he was governor of New York, collapsed a few years later. But the REA, established in 1936, offered subsidies to private companies, public agencies, and consumer-owned "cooperatives." Barely two years later, it had spread electricity to sparsely populated regions in forty-five states where private utility companies had found it unprofitable to invest.[7]

But the economic and social problems facing the South were far more complex than its electric power infrastructure. Dampening the crowd's festive mood, the president plunged into a diagnosis of the many ills affecting the South. "It is my conviction," Roosevelt told his surprised listeners in Barnesville, "that the South presents right now the Nation's Number 1 economic problem—the Nation's problem, not merely the South's. For we have an economic unbalance in the Nation as a whole, due to this very condition in the South itself. It is an unbalance that can and must be righted for the sake of the South and of the Nation."

The president explained that the very day he disembarked from the USS *Houston* in Pensacola, he received the final report he had requested a few months earlier from a special committee of experts on the persistent problems plaguing the South.

The idea for a study of the South had come from Clark Foreman, a Georgia-born, Harvard-educated economist. Foreman had first suggested that the White House publish a pamphlet outlining the benefits the New Deal had brought to the South. Roosevelt decided instead that the study should focus not on the New Deal but rather on the economic and social conditions in the South. The report would not even have to suggest remedies. Once people understood the scope of the problems in the South, he said, the remedies would be apparent to all.[8]

Roosevelt assembled a blue ribbon panel of experts—all southerners—to draft the study, and now, in Barnesville, he announced that the panel had completed its job and released its findings. To some extent, the report synthesized data that had already been collected by Howard Odum, a sociologist at the University of North Carolina, who in 1936 had published *Southern Regions of the United States;* Odum's conclusions were then popularized in Baltimore journalist Gerald Johnson's book *The Wasted Land.*

The panel's stinging sixty-page report spared no one's feelings as it documented the facts of southern poverty and analyzed the dilemmas facing the region. Although the South was blessed with great natural resources, its people were still the poorest in the country. "The richest state in the South ranks lower in per capita income than the poorest state outside the region," the report stated. The average income of an individual in the South in 1937 was $314, while in the rest of the country it was $604. Whereas the average farmer outside the South had an annual gross income of $528, farmers in the South grossed $186. Tenant farmers, who made up the majority of farmers—53 percent—in the South, earned less than half that, and sharecroppers even less. The wages of industrial workers in the South were less than half the wages in the North. New York spent five times more on education for each child than Mississippi. Banks held deposits of $150 per capita in the South and $471 per capita in the rest of the nation.[9]

Problems in the South ranged from a lack of industrial development, depleted soil, and child labor to deficient education, poor housing, inadequate sanitation, and substandard health care. The South was a region of farms and yet it imported food; it prided itself on its tradition of gracious living and yet did not even provide a subsistence level of living to many citizens.

Perhaps to encourage acceptance of the report's findings, there was no mention of race—even though in Mississippi and South Carolina close to half the population was black.[10] Segregation and its baneful effects—especially on education—were omitted. Half a million copies of the report were printed and were distributed across the country to civic groups and schools.

Without going into the details of the report, Roosevelt told the crowd that it was divided into fifteen short sections, covering subjects of vital importance such as economic resources, soil, water, population, private and public income, education, health, housing, labor, ownership and use of land, credit, use of natural resources, industry, and purchasing power.

The reason for mentioning all fifteen sections, the president explained, was to demonstrate that there was no one single simple answer to so many diverse problems. "Talking in fighting terms," Roosevelt said, "we cannot capture one hill and claim to have won the battle, because the battlefront extends over thousands of miles and we must push forward along the whole front at the same time."

But how, then, to conquer all those hills? Everyone in the stadium knew it was coming: the president would talk about leadership and the purge. There were two kinds of politicians he had no use for, he explained: those who had simplistic, all-purpose remedies for complicated problems and those who had absolutely no worthwhile remedies to offer but merely tried to kill all measures for progress.

Roosevelt's conclusion was that only a certain kind of politician was prepared and equipped to deal with the difficulties and dilemmas confronting the South: "The task of meeting the economic and social needs of the South," he declared, "calls for public servants whose hearts are sound, whose heads are sane, whose hands are strong." Indeed, the people of Georgia, Roosevelt insisted, needed senators and representatives who were "willing to stand up and fight night and day."

Now the crowd smelled blood. They were more interested in hearing the president swoop down for the political kill than in listening to a talk about electricity rates and southern problems. It was time for political theater.

Lest there be accusations that he was interfering in the internal politics of Georgia, Roosevelt took care to stress that Georgia voters had a "perfect right" to choose any candidates they wished. "Hurrah for George!" some people shouted, interrupting the president. "Good-bye George!" others yelled out.[11]

Suspense was building. Interestingly, as early as August 1937, after his vote opposing Roosevelt on court-packing, Senator George had predicted, on the floor of the Senate, that the president might "attempt to control the state primaries," but at a cost of "party harmony."[12] Now, after Roosevelt's endorsement of Camp in Warm Springs, the senator, dressed in a blue suit, his grey hair blowing in the slight breeze, fully expected the president to brazenly try to sabotage his bid for renomination. But how would Roosevelt go about it, with the courtly senator sitting only a few feet away from him? "Let me preface my statement," Roosevelt began, "by saying that I have personally known three of the candidates for the United States Senate for many years."

The audience in the sun-baked stadium was also acquainted with the men running in the Democratic primary. The sixty-year-old Senator George, the son of a tenant farmer in South Georgia, had attended Mercer University in Macon, where, at twenty, he had won an oratorical contest with a speech on the Constitution. After working as a lawyer, he went on to become a judge on the state Supreme Court and then senator, in a special election to fill a vacancy in 1922. Attired in his dark, double-breasted suit, white pocket handkerchief peeking out, the formal, chivalrous southern senator—he always referred to his wife as "Miss Lucy," and she called him "Mister George"—seemed to come from central casting. Not a flamboyant speaker, he was nevertheless serious and effective—if humorless. Whereas Roosevelt prided himself on being a "part-time" resident of Georgia, George wanted to make it clear in his stump speeches that he was a "full-time Georgian." "I have always lived in and worked for Georgia," he said. "And I expect to die in Georgia." If he was a Georgian first, he was a Democrat second. "I am a Democrat," he declared in his stump speeches. "I fought the party's battles in Congress and have fought the party's battles upon the hustings." George had a strong base of supporters in Georgia—this was his first contested primary since 1926.[13]

But how good a Democrat was he really? In 1933, George had supported Roosevelt's proposals, including the National Industrial Recovery Act, the Tennessee Valley Authority, and the Agricultural Adjustment Act; later he voted for Social Security, the National Labor Relations Act, and other New Deal measures. And during the 1936 presidential campaign, George had backed Roosevelt effusively and stressed the importance of a record turnout for him. "Every vote we poll for our great President and part-time Georgian will be just that much more for his popular majority over the nation." But during FDR's second term, George had cast votes against some key administration bills, including housing bills, court reform, the executive reorganization bill, and the Wages and Hours Bill. Were those votes enough to disqualify George for membership in FDR's Democratic Party? Or was George basically a New Deal ally?[14]

A senator's voting record in some cases could be deceptive. Often senators and congressmen strenuously opposed a measure in committee and on the floor. But if it appeared that a bill would ultimately be passed, conservatives could stay on Roosevelt's good side by voting for it on the final roll call. Columnist Raymond Clapper also noted that George had a string of New Deal votes behind him—indeed, a better New Deal voting record than Bulkley of Ohio, who won FDR's support. "I don't consider George a New Dealer," Clapper wrote. "Yet when I try to diagram the proof out of the record I can't do it. You have to give George a Scotch verdict—guilty but not proven."[15]

That is why, in his Barnesville speech, the president was less concerned with George's voting record than with the question of whether a candidate "really, in his heart, deep down in his heart," believed in the objectives of the New Deal. And it could not be said that George had fought for the New Deal. Tied to powerful business interests like the Georgia Power Company and the Coca-Cola Company, George was not even an enthusiastic backer of rural electrification.[16]

Still, George was neither a die-hard reactionary nor a rash, outspoken adversary of the president, and he was anxious to maintain good relations with him. Frances Perkins, for one, was on George's side. "I remember being shocked," she recalled years later, "when I heard that George was marked for destruction. . . . It seemed to me that he was nothing to be alarmed at." Perkins considered George one of the "better-brained men in the South" and felt that he had never done anything that would annoy anybody—except for his stand on the Supreme Court. Though she remembered George as being "puzzled" by some of the New Deal proposals, Perkins viewed him as a mostly loyal and intelligent ally.[17]

After Roosevelt's fireside chat in June announcing the purge, George suspected that he might be on the hit list and humbly tried to make amends. "I hasten to assure you," he wrote to the president, "that I have never meant to be offensive to you. . . . I may have, and regret it, too little self-control at times but I am unwilling to have you think I have . . . at any time felt anything but deep affection for you." And Senator George was also one of the few southern politicians to approve the president's decision to look into the economic conditions in the South. Though George was less enthusiastic than Alabama's senator Lister Hill and governor Bibb Graves, he diplomatically announced that he would "welcome and support any program lifting the purchasing power of the south." Most other southern politicians simply declined to comment on the president's decision to commission the report—or professed to be too busy to read his statement announcing the study.[18]

But FDR had stood his ground, responding that while he appreciated George's "mighty nice note," he feared that George's brand of conservatism would "destroy the Party in a few years, and second, jeopardize the Nation and its government."[19]

Despite the civil exchange of notes, Roosevelt was determined to flush George out of the party and the Senate. "Boss, I think you're foolish," Jim Farley said. "I don't think George can be beaten." But Roosevelt insisted. "I am going to endorse someone, if I have to pick my tenant farmer, Moore!" he snapped. The White House clique united not around tenant farmer Moore but around Lawrence Camp as the challenger to George. Camp seemed to have a strong background. In 1938, he was the U.S. Attorney for Atlanta and had also served as the state attorney general of Georgia, a nonelective post. And yet, though he had been Senator Russell's campaign manager in 1936, he seemed a newcomer to the political arena. He entered the race on June 1, at the last filing deadline, apparently encouraged—or pushed—to do so by the president's aide Marvin McIntyre, who just happened to be in Atlanta on the same day, picking up an honorary degree from the Atlanta Law School and playing a round of golf with Bobby Jones. Indeed, in a sign of the hapless, disorganized campaign to come, Camp paid the $350 fee just fifteen minutes before the deadline.[20]

Running against both George and Camp was the third candidate in the race, Eugene Talmadge, the former governor of Georgia, known as the "wild man from Sugar Creek." Always decked out in his trademark red suspenders, Talmadge was certainly a more colorful candidate than George and Camp, but the colors were black and menacing. "This man is darkness," wrote the novelist John Gunther. "All you have to do is look at him. Lank hair flapping sideways on the forehead; cold malicious eyes full of hate."[21]

Neither Talmadge's law degree nor even his Phi Beta Kappa key stopped him from chewing and spitting tobacco. On the contrary, he reveled in his image as an uncouth, rednecked racist. Sneering at Roosevelt's paralyzed legs, Talmadge branded the Warm Springs Foundation a "racket" that was "disguised under the name of charity." The president's problem, he diagnosed, was that he "can't walk around and hunt up people to talk to." According to Talmadge, the whole New Deal, hatched out of a Russian primer, was designed for "loafers and bums." But the problem went beyond the New Deal. Intoxicated with hatred, Talmadge explained that Georgians had three enemies: "Nigger, nigger, nigger!" As governor, he had starved social services and locked up striking workers behind barbed wire. He did not exaggerate when he pronounced himself "as mean as cat shit."[22]

Roosevelt began the final part of his talk with a brief lesson on presidential leadership. The president's job, he explained, was to work with congressmen and senators to translate progressive objectives into action. But some of them gave only "lip service" to those objectives, without even raising their little fingers actively to attain them. Then, Roosevelt— the object since 1933 of accusations of dictatorship—decided to play the dictator card himself, accusing powerful, reactionary businessmen and their supporters of trying to establish their own dictatorship, contrary to the wants and needs of the American people. Too often the few conservatives in Congress, he said, "have listened to the dictatorship of a small minority of individuals and corporations who oppose the objectives themselves. That is a real dictatorship and one which we have been getting away from slowly but surely during the past five years. As long as I live, you will find me fighting against any kind of dictatorship!" "That is right!" shouted people in the crowd.

Then, for a moment, Roosevelt sought to defuse the tension—and play the diplomat. "Now, my friends, what I am about to say . . ." A voice shouted, "We know what you are going to say!" The president continued, "will be no news. Let me make it clear," he said, that Senator George "is, and I hope always will be, my personal friend. He is beyond question, beyond any possible question, a gentleman and a scholar."

But then, with George quietly perched a few feet behind him on the podium, powerless to do anything but look studiously and stoically ahead, Roosevelt took aim—and coldly and mercilessly lowered the axe, as his voice pierced through the buzz of the crowd. "Here in Georgia, my old friend, the senior Senator from this State, cannot possibly in my judgment be classified as belonging to the liberal school of thought," he said, adding that "on most public questions he and I do not speak the same language." At this tough talk, Senator Russell stole a glance at Senator George, who stiffened but continued to stare into space.[23]

For a man who valued the friendships he had cultivated over the years with politicians across the political spectrum, it was an impetuous act to rebuke the courtly southerner—but it was also a courageous act. And so the president forged ahead. Did George display "a constant active fighting attitude" on behalf of the New Deal? Did he truly believe in the New Deal's objectives? "I regret," Roosevelt pronounced, "that in the case of my friend, Senator George, I cannot honestly answer either of these questions in the affirmative."

As for the candidate of darkness, Eugene Talmadge, who had denounced the New Deal when he ran unsuccessfully—and with the support of the ultra-right-wing Liberty League—for the Senate in 1936, the president was contemptuous and dismissive, to the delight of the crowd.[24] "I have known him for many years. His attitude toward me and toward other members of the Government in 1935 and in 1936 concerns me not at all. But, in those years and in this year I have read so many of his proposals, so many of his promises, so many of his panaceas, that I am very certain in my own mind that his election would contribute very little to practical progress in government." Before Roosevelt could finish his sentence, many in the crowd broke out into the loudest cheers of the afternoon. "That is all I can say about him," the president scornfully remarked, as people in the stadium laughed in approval.

Roosevelt's final praise for Lawrence Camp, his favorite in the contest, was concise. "I regard him not only as a public servant with successful experience but as a man who honestly believes that many things must be done and done now to improve the economic and social conditions of the country, a man who is willing to fight for these objectives. Fighting ability is of the utmost importance. . . . I have no hesitation in saying that if I were able to vote in the September primaries in this State, I most assuredly should cast my ballot for Lawrence Camp." More mischievous shouts of "Good-bye George!" filled the air, along with a few cheers for the beleaguered senator.

This was the first time that Roosevelt had spoken so openly, bluntly, and negatively against a Democratic incumbent. But for his part, Senator George handled the situation as a gentleman. Roosevelt's speech over, a seemingly unfazed George left his seat and approached the president. Reaching over to take FDR's hand, George said for all to hear, "Mr. President, I regret that you have taken this occasion to question my democracy and to attack my public record. I want you to know that I accept the challenge," and then added, "in the friendly spirit in which it was given." Shaking George's hand, Roosevelt said, "God bless you, Walter. Let's always be friends." Disconcerted by George's unexpected gesture, the president left the platform, forgetting to throw the switch to begin the flow of electricity to several hundred families living along 144 miles of rural power lines. But he had delivered a different kind of jolt to the surprised Georgians in his audience. He had awakened them to the threat faced by the New Deal—and he had also startled them with an unchivalrous attack on their gentlemanly senator.

Roosevelt returned to his car, where, after wiping perspiration from his face, he greeted local residents and then posed for photographers with Lawrence Camp.

Later the same sultry day, FDR gave the commencement address at the University of Georgia in Athens. Before an audience of fifteen thousand people in the Sanford Stadium, Roosevelt spoke about the economic and social problems of the South. When he first came to Georgia, the president told his audience, the South had offered a picture of despair. Anguished southerners questioned why their pay was so low, their roads so bad, sanitation and medical care so neglected, teachers inadequately paid, schools so antiquated.

It all came down to improving the quality of life by creating more wealth—and a greater tax base—to support a variety of essential social services, from education to health care. But even in this nonpolitical, nonconfrontational speech, Roosevelt could not avoid dipping—at least sideways—into politics. At heart, he said, Georgia was devoted to the "principles of democracy." There had been lapses, he pointed out, when Georgians had been fooled by demagoguery and feudalism "dressed up in democratic clothes."

The audience applauded when the president said that it was better for people to have "constant progressive action" than to follow the lead of politicians who wanted to slow down progress—presumably Senator George—or those who "promise they will hand you the moon on a silver platter," a reference to Talmadge. Roosevelt urged the audience to join him in working responsibly for the future. For twenty years, he noted, he had given thought to helping the South tackle its economic problems. "So you will see," Roosevelt said, "that my thoughts for the South are no new thing. Long before I had any idea of reentering public life I was planning for better life for the people of Georgia."

A few Georgian and southern newspapers supported the president. "What man in the White House has ever done so much for the rank and file in the South? What man there has done so much for Georgia?" the *Walker County Messenger* editorialized. "We believe in the great social and economic objectives of the president . . . and to obtain these objectives he must have cooperation. And he best knows who is cooperating with him. . . . We therefore are for Lawrence Camp."[25]

Roosevelt could also feel buoyed by the dozens of letters that poured into the White House from Georgians, urging him to persist in his effort to oust George. "There are thousands like me who are depending on you to carry this thing through," wrote Dr. J. M. McAllister from Rochelle. An Atlanta lawyer wrote to say: "We have a traitor within our ranks, a Doctor Jekyll and Mr. Hyde, a wolf in sheep's clothing, a Republican by the name of Walter F. George, parading under the misnomer of a Democrat." W. G. Hollomon, of Brooklyn, Georgia, wrote to the president to say that his Barnesville talk "was the best speech I have ever heard . . . you are the only president the nation has ever known to give one thought to the underprivileged. . . . I do not believe the people want to see the nation slip back into Hooverism." And a few "man in the street" interviews conducted by the *Atlanta Constitution* also turned up some favorable reviews. "I have a high regard for Senator George, but I have a higher regard for President Roosevelt," said a teletype repairman from Adamsville. "The president wants congressmen who will support him. I think he ought to have cooperation. I'll do my bit to help him. The people shouldn't bite the hands that feed them."[26]

But most of the commentary on the president's visit slammed him. A Gallup poll taken a few days after the Barnesville speech demonstrated that while Roosevelt remained overwhelmingly popular throughout the state, 75 percent of Georgia voters disapproved of his march into Georgia politics.[27]

Washington was Washington, and Georgia was Georgia, and many Georgians, as reporter Thomas Stokes pointed out, simply did not view the two as being connected. National elections were one thing—and state elections another. People in Georgia elected their senators and congressmen and then did not pay a great deal of attention to what they did in far-off Washington. Nor did they realize that southern senators and congressmen had formed a bloc to defeat the New Deal. When a politician returned home, Stokes explained, he simply told voters that he had voted for their interests—and they took what he said on faith.[28]

As for the president's comments on the report on the economic conditions in the South, one columnist for the *Atlanta Constitution,* Ralph McGill, commended the president for focusing attention on the South's problems. Even if Roosevelt had calculated the release of the report to coincide with his visit to Georgia, as some people charged, the report, McGill wrote, was "the finest thing that has happened to the South."[29]

But McGill was in the minority, for most people in the South, upset that the North seemed to be judging them and finding them wanting, reacted angrily and defensively to the report. Headlines like "Giving the South a Bad Name" appeared in southern newspapers. Instead of responding to the president's substantive speech about the South and his message that he needed a united, liberal Democratic Party in order to improve conditions there, it was so much easier to skirt those issues entirely. Instead of broaching questions of jobs, higher wages, improved housing, schools, and health care, editorial writers and journalists righteously proclaimed their outrage at Roosevelt's invasion of Georgia, their refusal to permit their politicians to be his "rubber stamps," and their rejection of a presidential dictatorship.[30]

Their strategy proved effective. Since the New Deal was extremely popular with voters, conservatives knew that they had nothing to gain by criticizing Roosevelt's policies or raising the issue of social and economic conditions in the South. It was far easier to distract voters from those crucial issues and win support for Senator George by whining about the president's tactics and his infringement on state "sovereignty."

The *Atlanta Constitution* fumed that it was a "historic first" for a sitting president to enter Georgia and call for the defeat of one of the state's leading politicians. Roosevelt, the *Constitution* charged, had "ruthlessly and savagely" attacked Senator George. "Georgians hate a dictatorship," editorialized the *Savannah Evening Press.* "They resent being told how they must vote." The question should be, the *Roanoke World News* proposed, "whether a sovereign state is to choose its own senator, untrammeled by the dictates of presidential prestige." "What right has Mr. Roosevelt," demanded the *New Orleans States,* "to dictate to the people of a sovereign state how they shall vote?" No mention of the presidential report on conditions in the South, no recognition of the need for change and progress.[31]

Letters to the editor of the *Atlanta Constitution* echoed the complaints of dictatorship. One insisted that "the people don't like the President telling them who to vote for." Someone else believed that the speech revealed "the dictatorial streak" in Roosevelt. "I couldn't help but think of Hitler and Mussolini."[32]

The day after Roosevelt's talks in Barnesville and Athens, Walter George began his campaign in earnest. He was in a strong position with endorsements from the American Federation of Labor and the Georgia Federation of Labor and campaign money from financier Bernard Baruch, an old friend of the president.[33] "We have just begun to fight!" George exclaimed from the balcony of his hotel in Atlanta, pointedly borrowing Roosevelt's famous phrase from his 1936 campaign. Born and raised to respect the southern code of chivalry and courtesy, George was determined to be assertive—but not rudely personal. He would have to walk a verbal tightrope—on the one hand avoiding criticism of the popular president and on the other insisting on Georgia's independence from Washington and from the Roosevelt administration.

On one steamy afternoon in Waycross, his suit wet with perspiration, George politely told a crowd of his supporters that the president had been "misinformed" in questioning his record. He refused to let the White House define him as an opponent of the New Deal. In order to avoid discussing his voting record and personalizing his rift with the popular president, George always declared himself an admirer of "that great and good man" Franklin Roosevelt and insisted that he supported 80 percent of the New Deal. But he also indignantly denounced outside interference in Georgia politics. "I serve notice now that you cannot buy Georgia!" he declared in Waycross, as audience members broke out in the long quavering trills of rebel yells.[34]

One campaign event, on August 20 in a downtown Atlanta hotel, summed up George's campaign. After a brass band played "Glory, Glory to Old Georgia" and then "Dixie," George declared to the over-flow crowd, "We have given our President a great deal of power, but we haven't given the President power to prescribe Democracy and read me out of the party which I have served all my life."

Then, in a surprise move designed to awaken Georgia pride, he summoned the ghost of Tom Watson. To loud applause, George declared, "Imagine Tom Watson taking dictation from anyone outside of Georgia!"[35]

Four months earlier a young historian at the University of Florida, C. Vann Woodward, had published a biography entitled *Tom Watson: Agrarian Rebel*. Reviewed on the front page of the *New York Times Book Review* on April 3, 1938 by the eminent Columbia University historian Allan Nevins, Woodward's book made a significant intellectual splash.

It told the story of the strange career of one of the South's most ideal-istic—and hate-filled—politicians.[36]

Watson served as a representative in the Georgia state legislature in the 1880s and then as a U.S. congressional representative for one term in the 1890s, and then ran for vice president of the United States in 1896 on the Populist Party ticket headed by William Jennings Bryan, who was also the Democratic presidential nominee that year, running on that ticket with Arthur Sewall. In 1904, Watson ran for president as the Populist Party candidate. Sixteen years later, he won election to the Senate; he died after serving just one year.

In the 1880s and 1890s Watson was a radical reformer—"a red-headed populist with fire in his eye and mutiny in his voice" who, Woodward wrote, spoke on the stump to crowds of ragged, impoverished farmers "with the raw corn liquor of revolt racing in their veins." A bold cru-sader, Watson had a program for economic reform that included re-straining corporate capitalism, placing railroads and the telephone and telegraph industries under government control, assuring free rural de-livery of the mail, helping industrial workers as well as white farmers and black sharecroppers, and securing equal political rights for both races. "The accident of color can make no difference in the interests of farmers, croppers, and laborers," Watson proclaimed. The races were kept apart, he maintained, "that you may be separately fleeced of your earnings." In many respects, his proposals went much further than the New Deal.[37]

But between 1896 and 1908, something crucial changed in Watson; he experienced some essential frustration, disappointment, or disillu-sionment, for he emerged from those years of transition a bleary-eyed demagogue, apostle of prejudice, Jew-hater, Catholic-basher, and Ku Klux Klanner whose name became associated with mob violence and lynching. Instead of proposing better schools, jobs, and decent wages to the poor and discontented, he offered racial and religious hatred.

"How could such a man," asked Woodward, "be taken seriously as the symbol of anything but the worst?"[38] Why did Walter George summon the memory of Watson?

When Senator Tom Watson died in office in 1922, Atlanta businessmen chose Walter George to run for the late senator's seat. George won the election—and often referred approvingly to "my predecessor in the Senate." But the courtly, reserved George was no Tom Watson. He embraced neither Watson's early radical populism and spirit of revolt nor his later toxic hate-mongering. Yet Watson's anger and despair as well as his strange radical and reactionary politics spoke to the 1930s. Woodward later said that his biography of Watson was "a book *for* the 1930s and *of* the 1930s, a book for hard times and hard scrabble, when rebellion was rife and the going was rough." As if to prove Woodward's point, the Georgia legislature, in 1932, during the very depths of the Great Depression, commissioned a bronze statue of Watson and placed it at the foot of the front steps of the Capitol in Atlanta, a monument to frustration, suffering, and rage.[39]

And now in his campaign speeches, Senator George, under assault from the president of the United States, rekindled the intoxicating fever of provincialism, defiance, and resentment associated with Watson and Georgia's populist tradition of revolt against an intrusive national government. He sought to flatten the mild liberalism of a Lawrence Camp and co-opt the populist anger of a Eugene Talmadge by summoning the rebellion if not the fury of Tom Watson. While not directly criticizing the president, George did lace into the president's advisors, expressing his contempt for that "little group of Communists" led by Corcoran and Cohen. By lingering on the Jewish and Irish names "Benny Cohen" and "Tommy Corcoran," George deftly exploited the anti-Semitism and anti-Catholicism Tom Watson had whipped up twenty-five years earlier.[40]

But when it came to channeling Tom Watson, George had nothing on Eugene Talmadge. *Atlanta Constitution* columnist Ralph McGill recognized the type. "You may be sure," McGill wrote in mid-August 1938, "the man from Sugar Creek has studied his Tom Watson." Rabble-rousers like Talmadge, he pointed out, told a few jokes, compared their opponents to jackasses, called up the ghost of Tom Watson—and won the election. And like Watson, Talmadge depended on the rural poor; he knew how to turn middle-class town-dwellers into his whipping boys.[41]

Talmadge claimed to be pro-Roosevelt yet vehemently denounced every act of Roosevelt's administration and every New Deal program. He was rumored to have been negotiating with Huey Long of Louisiana to form an anti–New Deal alliance—a plan cut short by Long's assassination in 1935. Talmadge did not disagree that the South was the nation's number one economic problem, but he placed the blame on the Roosevelt administration's "communistic, free-spending" policies. "I want to go to Washington," he shouted, "to protect the President from such men as Wallace, Tugwell, Frankfurter and Ickes."[42]

An "orgy of exploitation" was taking place in the nation's capital, he declared, and it would not end until men like him were elected who would stand up to the president. One of his solutions to the problems of the Depression was to "take the five billion dollars they have set aside for relief" and buy each of the ten million unemployed Americans $500 worth of land from absentee landlords. "Ah'll make America another Garden of Eden," was his refrain. One story that circulated was about a man from southwestern Georgia who explained, "I'm for Gene Talmadge and President Roosevelt. Talmadge will give me forty acres of land, and the President will pay me not to work it. Yes sir, that's my ticket."[43]

Talmadge might have reasonably argued that the ragged children of the South had not received their fair share of help from the New Deal— and he might have agreed with Roosevelt that low wages were starving southern workers. But rational arguments drowned as he wildly lashed out in every direction against government programs. Still, people regarded him, like Tom Watson, as a champion of the underprivileged rural poor. The South, Roosevelt had explained at a press conference in the spring of 1938, "because it is still educationally behind the rest of the nation, is peculiarly susceptible to the demagogue. Fair? Fair statement?"[44]

Though farmers were pro-Roosevelt, during the summer of 1938 the Agricultural Adjustment Act's system of production quotas helped Talmadge. The Georgia tobacco quota had been fixed at 76 million pounds, while the tobacco output in Georgia in 1938 approached 100 million pounds. To unload their surplus, farmers had to pay a penalty tax of 50 percent of the selling price, and the anger of tobacco farmers and of sympathetic cotton farmers helped Talmadge in rural counties.[45]

How could the diffident Lawrence Camp compete with the likes of George and Talmadge? Camp's organization proved amateurish at best; neither it nor the White House even thought to arrange for the president's Barnesville endorsement of Camp to be broadcast on the radio throughout Georgia. Camp had some labor backing, but he had few if any newspapers behind him and little money. "Camp has no organization, no management, no money, no vision and—apparently no following. Never has a campaign been so bitched up," wrote one astute observer at the time.[46]

Nor did Camp even have his good friend, Georgia's junior senator Richard Russell, or the pro–New Deal governor Ed Rivers on his side. Why would they have wanted to alienate George—or get involved in the mess Roosevelt was making in Georgia?[47] And they may have been worried that Camp's candidacy could result in the nomination of Talmadge, a prospect far more frightening to them than the renomination of Senator George. "I'm neutral on the senatorship," Rivers said. "I'm for the New Deal and the President, but I'm staying out of everything except my own race for re-election." Spurned by Rivers's political organization, the White House instead sent Joseph Keenan and Clark Foreman to help organize and galvanize the campaign. Foreman tried to energize Georgia voters with his own daily radio program, "Georgia

Marches On with Roosevelt," in which he discussed how federal funds were spent in various Georgia communities. The White House also persuaded a reluctant Jim Farley to chime in from Michigan with an all-purpose statement for Michigan voters—that could also be read by Georgians—that they needed to send senators and representatives to Washington who were "in accord with the President's objectives." And in the days before the primary, federal money rained down on Georgia, including $53 million in WPA funds for building projects in Georgia that promised to create thirty-five thousand jobs.[48]

On the stump, Camp's speeches were well-meaning but bland. On the magnetism scale, he scored a zero. Focused more on Washington than Georgia, Camp wrapped himself tightly in the popular president's mantle. He called on Georgians to "uphold the hands of the President in his determination to help us" and to fight for President Roosevelt's "humanitarian program." On campaign posters, the slogan underneath Camp's photo read, "If he's good enough for Franklin D. he's good enough for me." He left the job of summoning the ghost of Tom Watson to George and Talmadge—and to Jim Farley. A week after Roosevelt's speech in Barnesville, Farley, who was postmaster general as well as party chairman, hailed Watson as the father of free rural mail delivery at a meeting of the National Association of Rural Postal Carriers in Washington.[49]

Still, Camp managed a few zingers. Disputing the notion that southern industry could be competitive only if wages were kept low in the South, he insisted that southern workers "are worth as much as the northern workers." Camp was most forceful when he rebutted the charge that the president was dictating to Georgians how to vote. "The President," Camp said, "has attempted no dictatorship but is fighting the dictatorship of Wall Street and the power trust who want Georgia to send Senator George back to the Senate." But even when Camp's words were well chosen, he recited his speeches awkwardly, not deviating from his prepared script, unable to connect with voters. Next to

Talmadge's radicalism and George's traditionalism, Camp's mild liberalism failed to draw on the energy and the anger of the southern populist tradition and to ignite deep support.[50]

At least it was clear where Camp stood politically: he was a New Deal liberal. George avoided discussing politics; instead he lambasted the Washington "Communists" and underscored the importance of his own "independence." As for Talmadge, he relished diving into politics—the politics of rage.

But on one subject all the candidates—including Governor Ed Rivers, a member of the Ku Klux Klan—heartily agreed. They all denounced the anti-lynching legislation that was debated in Congress. Talmadge relished lambasting Eleanor Roosevelt for her disapproval of lynching. George prided himself on having filibustered the anti-lynching bill. But the president's man, Camp, scoffed at George's paltry filibuster effort. "George spoke for *only one hour* in the filibuster against this bill, yet he has spent 25 hours over Georgia telling the folks about that one-hour speech," Camp declared, adding that George was not even present for the final vote. "When I get to the Senate," Camp promised, "I'm going to speak just that many hours against the anti-lynching bill and then vote against it!" Apparently Roosevelt and his team were so out of touch with racist sentiment in Georgia and with Camp's own commitment to white supremacy and segregation that the person they sent to help organize Camp's campaign was none other than Clark Foreman, who had belonged to the Commission on Inter-Racial Cooperation, a fact George capitalized on with relish.[51]

The landmark report on the economic conditions of the South, which Foreman himself had inspired, was lost in the dust. Appeals to local pride, fantastic promises, denunciations of Roosevelt's "dictatorship," and free-floating anger at Washington overpowered the president's deep concern for the economic future of the South.

*   *   *

A southern writer named Clarence Cason had remarked a few years earlier that southerners, their nerves irritated by the heat, liked pepper in their food, strong coffee, and the excitement of fights—and that explained why they were far more interested in elections than in government. The primary election in Georgia indeed had all the elements of a rousing brawl.[52]

On Election Day, September 14, voters who had paid the poll tax flocked to cast their ballots. Turnout was extraordinarily high. As the first returns trickled in that evening from poor, rural counties, Eugene Talmadge was in the lead. Blood ran cold. It would be a nasty joke indeed if Roosevelt's attempt to sabotage Walter George merely resulted in the nomination of someone infinitely more unpredictable and hate-filled. When urban areas began to report their tallies, many people breathed sighs of relief; now George was in the lead.[53]

The election would be decided not by the popular vote but rather by county unit votes, an egregiously malapportioned system that privileged sparsely populated rural counties at the expense of growing urban centers. Each of Georgia's 159 counties had a certain number of winner-take-all unit votes; Atlanta's Fulton County, for example, with forty thousand registered voters, had six unit votes, whereas rural counties, in which perhaps only four hundred people went to the polls, had two, the minimum number allotted to a county. Interestingly, this anti-majoritarian system was defended in 1908 by none other than Tom Watson, who grasped that his own political future depended on the disproportionate power of poor, uneducated, white rural voters. Defenders of these country districts, which also served as U.S. House districts, insisted that the best government came out of rural areas, untainted by the socialistic ideas that ran rampant in cities. A quarter century later, the U.S. Supreme Court would hold such gross malapportionment unconstitutional. Legislative and election districts, the Court ruled, had to be roughly equal in population to comply with the principle of "one man, one vote." It was "one of the most momentous political decisions of the century in Georgia," wrote Jimmy Carter, who ran for the first time for state senator when the county unit system was abolished in 1962. But in 1938, Roosevelt had to contend with this all-white antimajoritarian system that left him little chance of success.[54]

The outcome was devastating. A candidate needed 206 out of 410 county unit votes to win. George won 142,074 popular votes and 246 unit votes. Talmadge won 102,602 popular votes and 152 county unit votes. Lawrence Camp limped in, a distant, ignominious third with 78,223 popular votes and only 16 unit votes. He carried Warm Springs but not even his own home county of Fulton. Talmadge, ever the malevolent clown, insisted that he was robbed. Citing evidence of fraud in thirty counties, he refused to concede defeat. It was not clear what role the eighteen thousand registered Republicans might have played in the race. A Georgia Republican committeeman had urged Republicans to cross over and vote for George in the Democratic primary, though the Democratic candidates had displayed no interest in courting the Republican vote.[55]

When news of George's victory reached the hundreds of his supporters milling around in the Henry Grady Hotel in Atlanta, they cheered as the band struck up "Dixie." But for his part, an elated, pink-faced Walter George struck a conciliatory note. "There must be differences of opinion in a democracy," he told the crowd. "We cannot afford any bitterness after this primary. . . . I pledge you now, as before, to support every piece of legislation which is to benefit the people of the state and the nation."[56]

"What about the primaries?" Jim Farley was asked a few days after the Georgia vote.

"Well, they are about over now," he sighed.

"Did you say 'Thank God'?" asked a reporter.

"All right," Farley replied, "make it, 'Thank God.'"[57]

⋆   ⋆   ⋆

In the November election, George beat his only opponent, an Independent, attorney Charles Jiles, by twenty to one, and voters also returned Governor Ed Rivers to the statehouse. But whereas almost four hundred thousand people had voted in the Democratic primary, only about fifty-five thousand bothered to cast ballots in the November senatorial election.[58]

In late December, the Georgia Democrats who had recently pummeled one another in their primary campaigns made nice at a formal dinner in Atlanta. Rivers, Talmadge, and Camp were all on hand, along with aides representing George and Russell. "I am sorry the two senators from Georgia could not be here tonight," said Talmadge. "They are the two best senators in the United States!" And Camp added the useful information that Georgia Democrats are not "liberal Democrats" or "conservative Democrats" but just "Democrats." "All Democrats can come together on one common ground—the interest of the party," Camp pontificated.[59]

"Down here in Georgia," Roosevelt wrote to Jim Farley from Warm Springs in late November 1938, "there is a rather definite tendency to quit fighting the Administration and to try to 'make up,'" but, he added, this "does not yet apply to Walter George." It would take Roosevelt and George considerably longer—almost another year—before they were ready, or almost ready, to repair their relationship.[60]

Their moment of reconciliation would come almost a year later.

"Boss, I want to say something you may not like," Jim Farley said to the president in September 1939. "The time has come," Farley counseled, "for everyone along the line to forget the past and try to help in every way they can." The president, Farley suggested, should send a get-well note to Walter George, who had just undergone eye surgery. "I'll send him a telegram," the president vaguely promised.[61]

That October, after refusing to repeal or even modify the nation's neutrality law in July 1939, George transcended his personal pique with the president, made an about-face, and voted with a majority in the Senate to repeal the arms embargo. In late 1940 and early 1941, as chairman of the Senate Foreign Relations Committee, George helped steer through Congress the Lend-Lease bill. One of the most critical pieces of legislation of the war years, it permitted FDR to sell, transfer, lend, or lease ships, planes, tanks, and guns to the Allies—especially Great Britain.

While some senators, such as Democrat Burton Wheeler of Montana, attacked and even tried to filibuster the bill, Walter George declared that he would "do what the American people want done."[62] In the moment of grave national crisis, George came to the support of the president—and the world. He ridiculed the filibustering critics of the Lend-Lease bill, exhorting them to stop making a "foolish spectacle" of themselves on the Senate floor. Of the thirteen Democratic senators who voted against the Lend-Lease bill, not a single one was from the South.[63]

Even if some Georgia voters and politicos were cool to FDR's economic policies and irked by his unmannerly intrusion into the politics of the Peach State, the president's immense popularity did not suffer. On the contrary, in the election of 1940, he garnered 265,194 votes compared to Wendell Willkie's pathetic 23,934.

Still, Roosevelt appeared to have learned a lesson. In 1941, when George served as the chair of the Finance Committee, the president sought the senator's support for a certain tax program, which he felt would be popular with voters. "Walter, if I know anything about Georgia politics . . ." the president began with some urgency. At that point, George caught the president's eye. ". . . and certainly I don't," Roosevelt finished with a good-natured, knowing laugh.[64]

"Not to be trusted on the President's coat tail," August 1938. Grover Page, *Louisville Courier-Journal,* © *The Courier-Journal.*

"Qualifying Test for Supreme Court Jobs," February 12, 1937. *New York Herald-Tribune.*

"Step by Step,"
February 11, 1937.
Bill Warren, courtesy of
the *Buffalo News*.

Senate Judiciary Committee considers FDR's court-packing plan, 1937.
Senators seated left to right: Borah (ID), Ashurst (AZ), McCarran (NV);
standing left to right: Van Nuys (IN), Burke (NE), Austin (VT), Pittman (NV),
McGill (KS), Hatch (NM). Harris & Ewing Collection, Library of Congress.

"A Master of Both Instruments," November 18, 1934. Edwin
Marcus, *New York Times*. Permission of the Marcus Family.

Little White House, Warm Springs, Georgia. Franklin D. Roosevelt Presidential
Library and Museum, Hyde Park, New York.

FDR swimming at Warm Springs, c. 1930. Franklin D. Roosevelt Presidential Library and Museum, Hyde Park, New York.

Senators James Byrnes (SC), Carter Glass (VA), and Josiah Bailey (NC) celebrating Glass's 79th birthday, January 4, 1937. Harris & Ewing Collection, Library of Congress.

Jim Farley, Eleanor Roosevelt, FDR, and Tommy Qualters at Jackson Day Dinner, Mayflower Hotel, Washington, D.C., January 1938. Franklin D. Roosevelt Presidential Library and Museum, Hyde Park, New York.

From left, FDR, Governor Albert "Happy" Chandler, and Senator Alben Barkley in Covington, Kentucky, July 1938. AP/Wide World Photos.

FDR shakes hands with young Congressman Lyndon B. Johnson of Texas; between them is Texas Governor James Allred, May 1937. Franklin D. Roosevelt Presidential Library and Museum, Hyde Park, New York.

FDR in the well deck of the USS *Houston* with a shark he caught in the Galapagos Islands, July 1938. U.S. Naval Historical Center, courtesy Naval Historical Foundation.

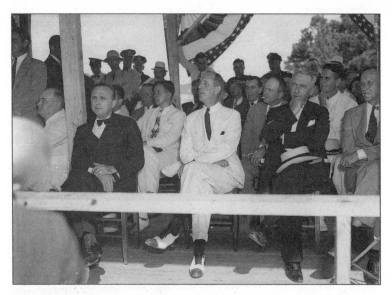

Georgia Senators Richard Russell (in white suit) and Walter George (his hat on his knee) listening to FDR's speech in Barnesville, Georgia, August 11, 1938.
Kenneth G. Rogers Collection, Kenan Research Center at the Atlanta History Center.

In this detail of a photo taken after FDR's Barnseville, Georgia, speech on August 11, 1938, the president bids farewell to U.S. Attorney Lawrence Camp.
Kenneth G. Rogers Collection, Kenan Research Center at the Atlanta History Center.

"Seeing Eye to Eye,"
August 28, 1938.
Fred O. Seibel, *Richmond
Times-Dispatch*, image
courtesy of Virginia
Commonwealth
University.

"The Music Master,"
September 4, 1938.
Fred O. Seibel, *Richmond
Times-Dispatch*, image
courtesy of Virginia
Commonwealth
University.

FDR casts his vote in Hyde Park, Eleanor Roosevelt on the left, November 8, 1938. AP/Wide World Photos.

Purge targets Senators Millard Tydings and Walter George pleased after their election victories, December 1938. Senator Josiah Bailey is between them.
Harris & Ewing Collection, Library of Congress.

FDR and Jim Farley at the Jackson Day Dinner, January 1939, Mayflower Hotel, Washington, D.C. Thomas D. McAvoy/Getty Images.

President Lyndon Johnson signing the Civil Rights Act, July 2, 1964. Cecil Stoughton, White House Press Office. Courtesy Lyndon Baines Johnson Library & Museum.

◄ 8 ►

"Cotton Ed"

"AW, HELL, ED, tell us 'bout Philideffy!" As the rumpled, quick-talking, tobacco chewing and spitting "Cotton Ed" Smith made the rounds on the campaign trail in South Carolina, people wanted to hear more about how their senator stormed out of the 1936 Democratic Convention in Philadelphia when a black minister rose to give the invocation. Cotton Ed always obliged, happy to launch into different versions of the famous episode. He had hardly taken his seat on the convention floor when out onto the platform walked a "slew-footed, blue-gummed, kinky-headed Senegambian. By God, he's as black as melted midnight! And he started praying and I started walking. . . . It seemed to me that old John Calhoun leaned down from his mansion in the sky and whispered . . . you did right, Ed." "Hot damn," people in the audience chortled in delight. "Old Ed's pourin' it on tonight!"[1]

That tale of white supremacy cemented the support of Smith's followers in South Carolina, though at one campaign event he had a heckler. "If you were in heaven and a colored angel walked in," the heckler inquired, "would you walk out?" Thinking quickly while people laughed, Smith said, "Keep your shirt on, brother. Whatever I do in heaven, you won't be there to see it." The crowd was his again, pleased that he made no concessions to integration.[2]

Born in 1864, Ellison Du Rant Smith grew up during the Reconstruction days, absorbing the hate and provincialism that infused life in

South Carolina. During the presidency of Theodore Roosevelt, Smith, along with Tom Watson and others, helped organize the short-lived Southern Cotton Association, a movement that sought to help growers raise the price of their cotton by adjusting production to demand. The association died in 1908 but, the same year, nevertheless catapulted Smith into the U.S. Senate, where he had served ever since. Campaigning in 1908, his message had been all about cotton, the biggest and most important crop in South Carolina. "My sweetheart, my sweetheart," he crooned, lovingly addressing the cotton boll he wore in his lapel, "others may forget you, but you will always be my sweetheart." Every cotton farmer in South Carolina, it was said, considered "Cotton Ed" a personal friend.[3]

Cotton Ed understood South Carolina. Every time he ran for the Senate, the price of cotton rose, boosting his popularity with voters. Cotton growers could even plan for a prosperous year when he was up for reelection. Over the years, he voted for Prohibition and against women's suffrage. "The women run things anyway—what more do they want?" he barked. But when he strayed from the traditional southern path, for example by supporting in 1926 the World Court, which the Ku Klux Klan opposed, he barely squeaked by to victory.[4]

In 1938, this seventy-four-year-old "conscientious objector to the twentieth century," as one reporter put it, was seeking election to a sixth term in the Senate. Though Smith had been an early and enthusiastic supporter of Roosevelt—voting for the National Industrial Recovery Act, the Emergency Relief Appropriation Act that funded the Works Progress Administration, Rural Electrification, and Social Security—he soon began grumbling loudly about bureaucracy, centralization, and regulations. From 1933 to 1944, Smith chaired the Senate Agriculture Committee, but he barely understood the New Deal's agricultural policies, drowning in the complexities of rates and quotas. He "was getting quite old," commented one AAA official. "He reached the stage that he didn't fully comprehend what we were trying to do." In public, he supported the president's agricultural legislation, but in private he did his best to sabotage it.[5]

During Roosevelt's second term, Smith rebelled publicly against the New Deal. He opposed the president's court-packing plan and, loyal to cotton farmers more than to mill workers, he voted against the Wages and Hours Bill, labeling it a "Yankee plot." But, always happy to raid the Treasury to help cotton farmers, he impatiently dismissed the notion of a balanced budget. The budget might be balanced, he suggested, "about the year 1999, or perhaps in 2040."[6]

Challenging Smith in the 1938 Democratic primary were two liberal candidates: state senator Edgar Brown and Governor Olin Johnston. Brown campaigned as a New Dealer who would "bring home the federal bacon" from Washington to South Carolina. He had come within five thousand votes of defeating Smith in 1926 and was ready to try again.[7]

Roosevelt favored Johnston, an ardent disciple of the New Deal who, as governor, had made many important reforms in South Carolina. On May 16, on the steps of the White House, Johnston announced his candidacy, telling reporters that Roosevelt had invited him to Washington and suggesting that the president had endorsed him. But at a White House news conference the same day, Roosevelt surprisingly refused to confirm Johnston's claim. The fact that Johnston declared his candidacy at 1600 Pennsylvania Avenue did not mean that he had his endorsement, Roosevelt said. Lots of people were coming to the White House these days, he added. Just a month before his fireside chat announcing the purge, Roosevelt was still wavering as to what strategy to adopt in the upcoming primaries. Hardly a militant party leader, he was clearly ambivalent and cautious about his role.[8]

A few hours after Johnston announced his candidacy, Smith came upon him by chance at a luncheon in the Senate dining room. All the steadfast liberals were there with Johnston: Claude Pepper, Hugo Black, Harry Truman, Lister Hill, Theodore Green of Rhode Island, together with White House elimination committee member Joseph Keenan. "What is this, a conspiracy?" Smith demanded. He then strode over to Johnston. "Congratulations, Governor," he said, patting Johnston on the back. "I'm going to beat you so badly you'll never know you've been in a race." After giving Lister Hill a friendly head massage, captured by a *Chicago Tribune* photographer, Smith told some reporters standing nearby, "When I get ready to announce my candidacy I'll make the announcement on a pine board platform in my home town in South Carolina and not on the steps of the White House after trying to grab myself a piece of the President's coattail."[9]

Although Smith was on Roosevelt's hit list, the president was advised to tread lightly, for the popular Smith knew how to play South Carolina. Cotton Ed, one reporter remarked, drew his strength "from the ancient soil of his home state, right up from crossroads, creek, and river-bottom." When the left-leaning secretary of agriculture, Henry Wallace, visited Smith's two-thousand-acre plantation, which was farmed by black tenants, he humbly deferred to the southern mythology Smith had created for himself. "As the Senator and I sat on the broad veranda after breakfast," Wallace told reporters, "I felt I was close to the secret of why our country is great and respected."

Many of the state's politicians urged the president not to intervene in the race. Johnston was a poor candidate, argued the state's junior senator, James Byrnes, warning Roosevelt that his election four years earlier to the governorship had been "a political fluke." Pro–New Deal South Carolina Democrats also explained to Roosevelt that Cotton Ed and his supporters were ready to make a White House endorsement of Johnston the paramount issue in the contest. Presidential advisors Marvin McIntyre and Harry Hopkins also tried to dissuade Roosevelt from intervening in South Carolina.[10]

But by mid-July the president was seriously considering taking his case to South Carolina voters and began to make plans to speak there after his stops in Georgia. An alarmed McIntyre, knowing that Smith was leading in the polls and that any attempt to sabotage him would boomerang against the White House, took matters into his own hands. He urged Steve Early to delay the departure of the president's train out of Georgia—or find a way to slow the train down—so that it would arrive close to midnight, when the crowd at the railroad station in Greenville would be small and the president's words would vanish into the warm night.[11]

But on August 11, when the presidential special arrived at the Greenville station near midnight, a noisy crowd of ten thousand was still waiting. Roosevelt flashed his radiant smile and shook hands with state politicos.

Suddenly, out of the dark, came Cotton Ed. Puffing and panting, he raced to squeeze onto the rear platform. In the glare of klieg lights, he grabbed the president's hand and smiled exuberantly for photographers. Olin Johnston, who had ridden up with the president from Barnesville, also stood on the rear platform, along with Edgar Brown, and Jimmy Byrnes. Dozens of other local leaders scrambled onto the car to bask in a few rays of the Roosevelt aura. When Byrnes nervously asked FDR what he was going to speak about, the president answered that he wanted to talk about his recent fishing trip. "Wonderful," replied Byrnes. "We can all agree on fishing."[12]

Not only was Roosevelt's train several hours late but he undiplomatically told the crowd in Greenville that he had already given two speeches that day and had not had the "time or opportunity" to prepare a third—and so he advised them to check their local newspapers and read what he had said in Georgia.

Speaking for less than two minutes, the president made the general recommendation that if South Carolinians agreed with his goals—wider distribution of national income, better conservation of natural resources, a decent minimum wage, and greater purchasing power for farmers—they should send representatives and senators to Washington who "will work toward those ends."

His train about to pull out, the president hurriedly closed by saying that he had two more points to make. First, "I promised Governor Johnston that I would come down some time this year to visit the capital of the State of South Carolina. I have never been there—but I am coming!" Observers wondered if he planned to return to South Carolina in the event of a runoff election between the two highest vote-getters, presumably Smith and Johnston. Then—his second and last point—he tossed the grenade: "The other thing is that I don't believe any family or man can live on fifty cents a day."

That throwaway line was a clear attack on Smith, for the president was referring to a remark the senator had made on the Senate floor in the summer of 1937 when he rose to speak against the Wages and Hours Bill. Both Johnston and Brown had been slamming Smith's words around for months, ridiculing him for suggesting that 50 cents a day was enough to live on. The trouble was that they misrepresented what Smith had actually said.

"If South Carolina living conditions are so kindly that it takes only 50 cents a day to live reasonably and comfortably, and in New England it takes a dollar and a half," Smith had argued on the Senate floor, "then must we raise the wages in the south to a dollar and a half?" His point was simply that the cost of living was different in the different regions of the country and that wages in the South did not necessarily need to correspond to the cost of living in the North. Johnston and Brown, as well as FDR, were taking a cheap shot at Smith—yet at bottom they were right, for Smith not only opposed a decent minimum wage for the South but sneered at the "philanthropic and eleemosynary spirit" of the wages and hours bill.[13]

"I stepped on the gas in Georgia and South Carolina on my way North," Roosevelt boasted a few days later to Harold Ickes.[14] But despite his self-congratulations, it seemed more like he was stuck in second gear. While he had succeeded in infuriating Smith, he had not even ventured to endorse Johnston. He had referred to the governor only in passing, barely giving him a pat on the back, not even deigning to call him an old friend. Despite McIntyre's worries, Roosevelt was taking few chances; he was deferring to Byrnes—and playing it very safe.

Over the next few weeks, as the temperature soared to a wilting 110 degrees, the three candidates toured all of the state's forty-six counties together, as was the custom in South Carolina—a group political road show that sometimes resembled a three-ring circus. In the towns and remote counties, amid the handshaking and backslapping, Smith impatiently tried to set the record straight. Declining to criticize the president publicly, he graciously—and shrewdly—held instead that Roosevelt had unfortunately been "misinformed" about his 50-cent comment and suggested that the culprit was probably Olin Johnston. Smith explained that he had made that observation only "for illustration" of the different costs of living in the different parts of the country.[15]

Moving into overdrive, Smith's campaign manager mailed twenty thousand copies of Smith's Senate speech to white voters in South Carolina. Newspapers around the South gladly bought his rationale—and the 50-cent story boomeranged, adding to Smith's appeal.[16]

Smith found himself in a strong position; he had the backing of some of the state's major newspapers—the *Greenville News* proclaimed him the "poor man's friend"; he had the support of Senator Byrnes and his political machine; and his chairmanship of the prestigious Agriculture Committee also boosted his popularity in this largely rural state.

For his part, Governor Johnston presented himself as a staunch backer of the New Deal, completely loyal to the "humanitarian policies of Franklin Roosevelt." He even went so far as to stress the importance of increasing liberal southern power in Washington. With liberals like Claude Pepper and Lister Hill in mind, Johnston remarked in a radio address in late August that "the sons of the South are in the saddle in Washington" and that it was the "mighty responsibility" of South Carolinians to send to the Senate a man who would "cooperate wholeheartedly with these Great Southerners."[17]

Though Johnston and Brown both pummeled Smith—as "Old Sleepy"—for his failure to bring South Carolina its fair share of New Deal goodies, there was one subject on which all three candidates could come together as one: race. In South Carolina, where almost 43 percent of the population was African American but barred from voting in the all-white Democratic primaries, white supremacy was a given, a campaign theme shared by all the candidates. It was only a question of how bitter and incendiary the racist rhetoric would be. Johnston wanted to leave no doubt that he was every bit as much of a white supremacist as Cotton Ed Smith, even berating Smith for once opposing segregation on railroad trains. "Why, Ed Smith voted for a bill that would permit a big buck Nigger to sit next to your wife or daughter on a train!" charged Governor Johnston.[18]

Not to be outdone, Smith predicted that if he was defeated, "a peal of joy will ring through the nigger-loving East." Cotton Ed relished playing the race card; there was no more effective strategy for distracting voters from his opposition to the New Deal and the benefits it brought to white as well as black South Carolinians. He told crowds in South Carolina that "every red-blooded white man" in the state should vote for him "because outside organizations are seeking to defeat me because of my stand for white supremacy." If outside agitators and labor organizations succeeded in their goals, he warned, white workers in South Carolina would find themselves "placed alongside Negroes at the looms in the cotton mills." White supremacy was a "time-honored tradition," he sermonized, that could not be "blotted out of the hearts of South Carolinians."[19]

For his part, candidate Brown made the conciliatory observation that "we are all anti-nigger in the black belt." But he went on to attack Smith's lack of accomplishments in the Senate. "You can't eat states rights and you can't live off white supremacy," he said, suggesting— almost courageously—that a discussion of genuine issues was being stifled by the obsession with race.[20]

But just seventy-two hours before the election, Brown abruptly pulled out of the contest. Upon hearing that news, Johnston made the premature announcement that Brown's withdrawal assured him of an overwhelming victory. Brown, however, refused to endorse Johnston, reminding voters instead that Johnston had invited Huey Long to South Carolina "to vilify and abuse the [Roosevelt] administration."

Polls still placed Smith ahead, but Roosevelt judged that Johnston now had a reasonable chance to win. While on a working vacation in Hyde Park in late August, he decided that he could finally risk throwing his support behind the governor.[21]

In a public statement two days before the August 30 primary, Roosevelt said that Brown's withdrawal "clarified" the issue. Now, since no runoff election would be necessary, voters had a clear choice between two candidates "representing entirely different political schools of thought." One of the candidates "thinks in terms of the past and governs his actions accordingly, the other thinks in terms of 1938 and 1948 and 1958 as well." The election, he reminded voters, would have important, far-reaching consequences, deciding whether average Americans— farmers, laborers, storekeepers—would get "fair play." The choice, he concluded, was "in the hands of the people of South Carolina."[22]

The president had finally climbed into the ring and taken a stand— and yet he still did not even mention Johnston by name. Perhaps that omission was a small, symbolic peace offering to Jim Farley, with whom he had met earlier the same day—their first meeting since early July.[23] Farley, of course, still disapproved of Roosevelt's campaign to dislodge incumbent Democrats, and he surely dreaded having to straighten out ruffled feathers in the months ahead. And perhaps, by naming no names, Roosevelt was also deferring to the South Carolina Democrats who had urged him not to intervene in the primary. In either or in both cases, he was displaying his characteristic caution.

If Roosevelt was trying to be subtle or cagey in his endorsement of Johnston, the ploy did not work, for within hours Smith fired back, expressing regret that the president had seen fit "to inject himself" into South Carolina politics and make an "eleventh-hour" attempt to influence the primary. And Smith reminded voters that not only had he supported "over 80 percent of the president's program," he had also voted for the executive reorganization bill, which would have expanded the president's powers. Moreover, if South Carolina sent him back to the Senate, Smith promised, he would follow the Roosevelt administration "except when to do so will be in direct conflict with what I consider the best interests of South Carolina."[24]

Voter turnout was tremendous. When the results came in on August 30, Smith had won 55.4 percent to Johnston's 44.6 percent. The election could not be interpreted as a "repudiation of the New Deal," editorialized the *Atlanta Constitution*, putting a positive spin on Johnston's defeat. Smith's renomination, the *Constitution* wrote, only proved "the right of free Democrats to cast their ballots uninfluenced by federal interference." "Well, you beat me in that election down there," Roosevelt said good-naturedly to Jimmy Byrnes when they met in the White House after the primary.[25]

In his acceptance speech in Columbia, Smith portrayed his win as a hard-fought victory against powerful foes, a triumph for independence and freedom, in the spirit of the American Revolution. "We conquered in '76," he cried, "and we conquered in '38. We fought with bullets then, but today, thank God, we fought with ballots." For Roosevelt's part, when he was informed about Smith's victory, he wearily sighed, "It takes a long time to bring the past up to the present." One university professor in South Carolina agreed with the president but was more caustic. "I am sure you are rejoicing," he wrote sardonically to a friend after Smith's victory, "that states' rights, white supremacy, Bourbonism, low wages, long hours, and the right to ignorance, prejudice and superstition are no longer in jeopardy in South Carolina."[26]

It seemed that "Philideffy" had triumphed over the progressivism of the New Deal. Still, Roosevelt's popularity remained intact. In South

Carolina in the presidential election of 1940, FDR would win 95,470 votes compared to 1,727 for Wendell Willkie.

On August 30, the same day as the South Carolina primary, the primary in California brought more bad news to Roosevelt. Sheridan Downey swamped FDR's candidate, McAdoo. Out of about seven hundred thousand votes cast, Downey won by one hundred thousand. In the West as well as in the South, Roosevelt's cross-country journey was looking like a bust. But FDR the scrootch owl lost no time in making nice with the victors. Downey was a true liberal in the general sense of the word, the president stated at a news conference in early September. And in a letter to the senator-elect, the president allowed that California had "every right" to try out its $30 per week pension plan, though Californians ultimately chose not to do so. As for the national chairman of the Democratic Party, Jim Farley wired a message to Downey proclaiming his "hearty support." So much for McAdoo.[27]

But the president offered no such conciliatory gesture to Cotton Ed Smith. On the contrary, a few weeks after the South Carolina primary, Roosevelt declined to meet with a group of senators from cotton- and wheat-producing states—Bilbo and Harrison of Mississippi, George and Russell of Georgia, and Cotton Ed. After waiting impatiently for the president for three hours only to be told finally that he was unavailable and that they could meet instead with two AAA officials, Cotton Ed Smith erupted. "This isn't a democracy," he indignantly shouted. When asked by a reporter if he wished to be quoted, he replied, "Hell yes! Why not?"[28]

And yet, a year later, in 1939, when the so-called true liberal Sheridan Downey proposed a ban on all sales of munitions to all foreign nations and when Roosevelt's independent-minded buddies, William Borah and Robert La Follette, also came out as staunch isolationists, voting against a repeal of the arms embargo and denouncing the "shrewd and persistent propaganda of the British," Cotton Ed, along with Walter George and Josh Bailey, waged battle against the isolationists in Congress and voted to repeal the arms embargo. Indeed, with the exceptions of John Overton of Louisiana and Robert Reynolds of North Carolina, southern senators voted solidly for embargo repeal. Smith even put some icing on the cake, taking a slap at Charles Lindbergh, the pilot who famously crossed the Atlantic solo and now urged Americans to "keep out of European wars entirely." The aviator, Smith sneered, "should stick to the air."[29]

Still, grudges remained. In 1940, Cotton Ed charged that by seeking a third term, President Roosevelt was giving "a green light for totalitarianism and a dictator." While South Carolina's other senator, James Byrnes, called the anti-third-term tradition "a myth," Smith asked, "If a third term, why not a fourth? If a fourth, why not a fifth, and if a fifth, why not for life?" and threatened to organize a walkout at the Democratic National Convention. Instead he remained neutral in the race between FDR and Willkie. The day before voters went to the polls in 1940, Cotton Ed declared that he had made plans to go fishing. "I don't think it will be necessary for me to vote," he told reporters.[30]

Ellison "Cotton Ed" Smith, who was born in 1864, would die in office, just weeks after losing the 1944 primary to none other than his 1938 challenger, Olin Johnston, who would finally win a Senate seat for himself. In that contest, however, the president remained silent.

◄ 9 ►

The Maryland Shore

"TAKE TYDINGS' HIDE OFF and rub salt in it," Roosevelt muttered to Harold Ickes. Roosevelt wanted the hide—or the scalp—of Millard Tydings, and this time, even Jim Farley—back in Washington after his six-week trip to Alaska—jumped on the purge bandwagon. Roosevelt and Farley might have felt some affection for a conservative like Walter George, but they had nothing but loathing for Tydings.[1]

The Maryland Democrat, who was seeking reelection to a third term in the Senate, had opposed nearly every New Deal measure. He had voted against the NIRA, the TVA, the AAA, the National Labor Relations Act, relief appropriations for the Works Progress Administration, housing bills, revenue acts, court reform, and executive reorganization. Even on Social Security, which was approved by all but six senators, he demurred, voting only "present." After Congress approved FDR's request for $5 billion in 1935 for the Federal Emergency Relief Appropriation, Tydings took to the Senate floor to lash out at the government for "running on hot air." He also spoke darkly about "subversive trends" in Washington and the threat of a home-grown dictatorship. Yet, very well aware of the president's extraordinary popularity among the constituents whose judgment he would face in 1938, Tydings improbably insisted that he embraced the "bone and sinew" of the New Deal and labeled claims to the contrary "silly propaganda."[2]

The forty-eight-year old Tydings was young, tough, and very conservative. From a modest family in Havre de Grace on the Chesapeake Bay, Tydings delivered newspapers as a child, worked his way through the Maryland Agricultural College, enlisted as a private in World War I, fought in the trenches of France, and left the service with several medals. But after his election to the Senate, he enjoyed hobnobbing in elite Washington circles and, in 1936, married an heiress and socialite, Mrs. Eleanor Davies Cheeseborough, whose father was FDR's ambassador to the Soviet Union. The dapper senator was a "bloated aristocrat," charged columnist Drew Pearson, who also wrote a parody entitled "The Life and Times of Milord Tydings."[3]

Tydings even managed to alienate the temperate, purge-averse Jim Farley, who hated him for refusing to play the game by the rules. Tydings accepted favors, Farley grumbled, but was slow to return them; and Farley had never forgotten that he had had to bludgeon Tydings into making a seconding speech for the nomination of FDR in 1932. Tydings also brought out Roosevelt's vindictive streak. After the Maryland senator pushed through a bill for a bridge crossing the Chesapeake Bay, the president vetoed it; and when Tydings pushed through another bill for a bridge south of Baltimore, Roosevelt killed it, too.[4]

For months, the members of the White House elimination committee had been hunting around for a strong candidate to challenge Tydings. But once again, their effort was a masterpiece of disorganization and miscues.

First, because they neglected to inform Maryland's junior senator, George Radcliffe, that Tydings was on their hit list, Radcliffe agreed to serve as campaign manager for Tydings, who had helped him a few years earlier in his own campaign. A close friend and former business associate of Roosevelt, Radcliffe was distressed to find himself in the enemy camp. But it was too late for him to backtrack, and so this champion of the New Deal found himself in the Tydings corner.[5]

Second, the White House politicos delayed choosing a candidate to oppose Tydings. After considering the president of the University of Maryland, then the Maryland attorney general, and even Harold Ickes, who owned a farm in Maryland, they eventually settled on David J. Lewis—but only after Lewis had announced that he would seek reelection to his seat in the House of Representatives. By then, county organizations had already endorsed Lewis for the House and Tydings for the Senate.[6]

Third, the diminutive, sixty-nine-year-old Lewis was not well known outside of his district. He had first been elected to the House in 1910, the same year that FDR ran for the first time for a seat in the New York State Senate. In 1916 and again in 1922, Lewis tried unsuccessfully for a U.S. Senate seat. Twenty-two years later, Lewis was taking a big chance in running again for the Senate, for he was giving up certain reelection to the House in order to challenge a powerful, popular incumbent. Lewis also lacked a skilled organization and financial support. Making matters worse, the Democratic candidates for governor and mayor of Baltimore decided to remain neutral in the Senate race while other Maryland politicos were pledged to Tydings.

What Lewis did have was a strong pro–New Deal record and a compelling personal story. From a dirt-poor family of coal miners in western Maryland, Davey Lewis never attended school. He worked in the mines from the age of nine until he was twenty-three and learned to read only because a Sunday school priest gave him lessons.[7]

Lewis's experience in the mines had made him sympathetic to the needs of workers, and he had the strong backing of labor unions. One of the first to sponsor a workmen's compensation act in Maryland, Lewis received endorsements from the American Federation of Labor and from John Lewis, the militant president of the Congress of Industrial Organizations. Unfortunately, the Maryland Communist Party also praised him—though it was running its own candidate in the race—for his clear record of support for the New Deal. But its admiration was equivalent to a bouquet of poison ivy.[8]

"I'm no enemy of organized labor," Tydings retorted on the campaign trail. "If you want a CIO senator, don't vote for me. Democrats, stand to arms! Do you want to turn this State over to a Senator run by John L. Lewis?" The crowds shouted back "NO!" Trying to break labor's support for Davey Lewis, Tydings appealed to unorganized farmers who were reeling from falling commodity prices.[9]

Back and forth flew the accusations. Tydings attacked Lewis for missing 42 percent of House votes during his terms in office and mocked him for not showing up for several joint speaking engagements. "I'm going to lick the whole damn crowd," Tydings cried at one rally. Lewis shot back that Tydings was a Democrat in name only, pointing out that the senator had members of the anti–New Deal Liberty League campaigning for him and large numbers of Republicans attending his rallies around the state. "Let him call a spade a spade," Lewis exclaimed. "Let him come out in his true colors as a Tory Republican."[10]

But behind Tydings was an adept organization—his staff checked registration rolls and even automobile licenses for potential voters— and campaign funds from financier Bernard Baruch. Also behind him were the editors of the state's major newspapers. The *Baltimore Sun* cast Lewis as "the puppet of Mr. Roosevelt, of Mr. Farley, of Mr. Hopkins, of Mr. Ickes" while it portrayed Tydings as a hero, championing a balanced budget, willing to sacrifice his last drop of blood for liberty. Tydings also had youth and energy on his side as he raced around the state from one speaking engagement to another, while the elderly Lewis spoke at only a few events.[11]

Enter Franklin Roosevelt. His efforts were belated—but he understood that Lewis's campaign needed a rapid infusion of money and inspiration. He tapped his ambassador to Italy, who was a Maryland native. "Will you call Breck Long," Roosevelt wrote in a memo to Marvin McIntyre, "and ask him how he can help in Maryland both personally and financially?" And why was undersecretary of state Sumner

Welles, another Marylander, vacationing in Europe when he should have been back home helping Lewis? Or did Welles simply not have the "guts to fight?" Josephus Daniels asked FDR. The president dispatched Harry Hopkins to Maryland and mobilized the postmistress of Salisbury, Maryland, Maude Toulson—a move that sparked a flurry of Senate and Justice Department investigations of Toulson for possible violations of federal postal regulations.[12]

And Roosevelt also spoke out himself for Lewis. In a radio speech in mid-August, he praised Lewis as one of the "legislative fathers" of Social Security. At a press conference in his office the following day, the president, in shirtsleeves and smoking a cigarette, read approvingly from a *New York Post* editorial arguing that Tydings "had betrayed the New Deal in the past and will again" and that the Maryland senator was trying "to run with the Roosevelt prestige and the money of his conservative Republican friends both on his side." And he concurred with the *Post*'s conclusion that it was "the President's right and duty to tell the people what he thinks of Millard Tydings."[13]

On August 29, Roosevelt announced that he would visit Maryland in person over Labor Day weekend. Accompanied by Davey Lewis, Jim Farley, Congressman Alan Goldsborough, and a few others, he would drive to tiny Morgantown, on the western side of the Chesapeake Bay, twenty miles south of Washington, to inspect the site of a proposed bridge across the Potomac River. Then he would board his yacht for an overnight cruise down Chesapeake Bay. He would disembark the next day in Crisfield, near the southernmost point on the eastern side of the Bay, and slowly drive north, along a circuitous two-hundred-mile route on the Eastern Shore, to Denton, where he would deliver a Labor Day address.[14]

In Morgantown, where Roosevelt began his swing through the state, he spoke to a small crowd of five hundred, praising the planned new bridge as important for coastal defense and noting that he hoped to return for its inauguration. No mention was made of the senatorial contest or of Davey Lewis. When the president disembarked from his yacht in Crisfield, the town's mayor declined to welcome him. His reception on the Eastern Shore was indeed mixed. That part of the state was Tydings's base. An isolated, flat, lush region, it was home, since the Revolutionary period, to Tories and conservatives.

Along the president's route, Tydings banners and signs outnumbered Lewis signs by three to one. In Berlin, people held signs reading "Keep Democracy Democratic. Vote for Tydings." In most villages, Roosevelt received a polite reception and spoke from his automobile. In Salisbury, the largest town on the Eastern Shore, a crowd of ten thousand jammed into the town square while the high school band entertained them. In Sharpton and Federalsburg, the president was also greeted by enthusiastic crowds.[15]

When Roosevelt arrived in Denton, a village of sixteen hundred people, on September 5, seven thousand people had shown up, having traveled from miles around. In a holiday mood, they picnicked under the sycamore trees surrounding Caroline County's red brick courthouse; they ate hot dogs at refreshment stands; they bought Roosevelt buttons from hawkers. A local hotel on the village square sold "reserved seats" on its second-floor porch for 75 cents each. But when Roosevelt rose to speak, behind him were huge signs reading "We Want Tydings" and "Vote for Senator Tydings—Not for a Rubber Stamp."[16]

In his speech, broadcast nationally on the radio, the president went through the well-known purge talking points—his determination to keep the Democratic Party liberal, the selfishness of the "cold-blooded" plutocrats who tried to blind average people to the common interest, the need for a "humane and modern standard of living" for the vast majority of working Americans, the importance of brotherhood and the Golden Rule, the American tradition of equality. He also spoke about "Economic Lesson Number One"—that "men and women on farms, men and women in cities, are partners."

Turning to his candidate of choice, Roosevelt remarked that a young Maryland legislator named David Lewis pioneered the first Workmen's Compensation Act ever to be passed in the United States. Ten years later, when he was governor of New York, Roosevelt added, he had followed Lewis's lead, working to steer through the New York State legislature a similar law. "Maryland," Roosevelt said, "you are fortunate in having a man who not only has seen visions but has lived to make his dreams come true."

Declining to put on his boxing gloves and slam Tydings by name, the president, tossing his head and sticking out his jaw, said only that a politician had the right to be liberal, conservative, and even reactionary, but that "the nation cannot stand for the confusion of having him pretend to be one and act like the other."[17]

The speech was decent, but long, meandering, and without punch. "It's a bust," Jim Farley muttered to some reporters.[18] When FDR was asked if he enjoyed campaigning in Maryland, he snapped, "Did you ever campaign in Maine?" referring to one of the two states in the nation that voted against him in 1936.

Tydings's response to Roosevelt's assault was evasive and brilliant. Rather than answer the fundamental accusation that he was an anti–New Deal Democrat trying to win reelection by capitalizing on Roosevelt's popularity, he tried to blur the issue by insisting: "I am not running particularly as an Old Dealer nor particularly as a New Dealer but I hope as a square dealer." Aware that FDR had the economic and social issues on his side, Tydings realized that it was in his interest to turn the primary into a states' rights contest. He railed against Roosevelt's invasion of Maryland, claiming that he was trying to deny Maryland voters the right to choose their own representatives. "I am confident," Tydings declared in a radio address, "that on September 12th the people of Maryland will act, and act decisively to let the Federal Administration and all the people of the country know that the Maryland Free State shall remain free!" Sneering that David Lewis was excusing the president's "invasion," Tydings shouted that "Maryland will not permit her star in the flag to be 'purged' from the constellation of the States." At one rally, Tydings histrionically announced that he had been chosen by fate to "lift to the masthead the banner of democracy."[19]

Rallying to Tydings's side, the American Legion commander in Maryland charged that Roosevelt's intervention in the primary was a move toward "dictatorship." The *Washington Evening Star* echoed that accusation. Roosevelt was Stalin, Mussolini, and Hitler "rolled into one" with "a Harvard accent and a billion dollar smile." In a bizarre editorial, the *Chicago Daily Tribune* voiced confidence that Maryland voters would "realize that the issue is not one of liberals against conservatives, or even of Democrats against Republicans, but of Americanism against communism."[20]

As it had elsewhere, the administration threw federal money into the battle. Three days before the election, Harold Ickes approved funds for the construction of two bridges in Maryland—one at Havre de Grace across the Susquehanna River and the other over the Potomac at Morgantown, where Roosevelt had just spoken. Coincidence? The decision to approve the two projects, the *New York Times* noted, "was made purely at the personal request of the President." Apparently missing the point of Roosevelt's blatant tactic, the *Times* suggested that in the future, the president should use "greater caution in timing these announcements."[21]

By coincidence the September 12 primary fell on Defenders' Day, a holiday commemorating a battle during the war of 1812 when soldiers at Fort McHenry defended Baltimore from the British, the battle that inspired Francis Scott Key to compose "The Star Spangled Banner." Tydings was determined that Defenders' Day would mark the state's repulse of FDR's invasion.

In the primary election, Tydings won 59 percent of the popular vote to Lewis's 39 percent. It was a convincing three-to-two margin and a humiliating defeat for Lewis—and for FDR, too, who had trounced Alf

Landon in the 1936 election in Maryland. Voters bought Tydings's argument that his responsibility was to his constituency and not to the national party or its leader. But Tydings also benefited from the fact that sixty thousand black voters who had backed FDR in 1936 were registered Republicans barred from voting in the Democratic primary.[22]

The following day, Farley mentioned to the president that he wanted to send Tydings a congratulatory telegram. "I think I should at least express hearty congratulations," Farley said. "Leave out the 'hearty' and all the other adjectives," Roosevelt snapped. "Boss, I think I ought to send him the same kind of wire I've sent to all the other successful primary candidates," Farley said. "Suit yourself but leave me out of it," the president retorted. Conversation over.[23]

Well, not quite over, for Tydings would ultimately prove to be a courageous internationalist. A few days before the November election, Tydings joined other members of Congress in asking Great Britain to keep Palestine open for Jewish refugees fleeing persecution in Nazi Germany.[24]

A cautious interventionist at first, Tydings moved more and more over to the side of preparedness and internationalism in the years leading up to the war. After meeting with Senator Robert Wagner in the fall of 1939, Jim Farley happily reported to FDR that Tydings might support repeal of the Neutrality Act's arms embargo. "Bob says Tydings is strong for national defense." When a Maryland delegation visited Tydings in the Capitol to demand that he vote against repeal, the Senator held his ground. "I don't care for hell and a brown mule," he snapped. "I'm going to do what I think is right." In the summer of 1940, Tydings was one of the most energetic supporters of the Selective Service Act, which created the compulsory draft. "I would rather have it and not need it," Tydings said, "than need it and not have it." While seventeen Democratic senators opposed military conscription in peacetime and denied that there was an imminent danger of war, Tydings emotionally reminded his fellow legislators that it was necessary to make "sacrifices for preparedness." And Tydings joined most other Democrats in voting for the Lend-Lease Act in 1941.[25]

A decade later, Tydings, by then chair of the Armed Services Committee, steered through the Senate landmark legislation to consolidate the Navy and War departments in a new Department of Defense. And eleven years after opposing FDR's executive reorganization plan, Tydings would agree with the recommendations of the Hoover Commission on the Reorganization of the Executive Branch, thereby finally approving Roosevelt's original aim of streamlining the government.[26]

In 1950 Tydings chaired a subcommittee of the Senate Foreign Relations Committee; his mission was to look into allegations of Communist infiltration in the U.S. State Department. The charges had been brought by Senator Joseph McCarthy of Wisconsin, a Republican elected to the Senate in 1946, defeating the incumbent, Progressive Robert La Follette. While most senators cowered before McCarthy's reckless charges, Tydings stood up to him. After four months of investigation and testimony, Tydings delivered a two-hour-long speech on the Senate floor, declaring that McCarthy's accusations were "a fraud and a hoax."[27]

Now, a dozen years after FDR's campaign against Tydings, Harold Ickes, one of the purge's most fervent champions, made an about-face and praised Millard Tydings for throwing his weight "on the side of truth and fairness" and for exposing McCarthyism for what it was, "a thing obscene and loathsome."[28]

Tydings's principled, icy aloofness, however, was no match for McCarthy's raucous showmanship. Calling Tydings President Truman's "whimpering lap dog," the Wisconsin senator defiantly replied that "today Tydings tried to notify the Communists in Government that they are safe in their positions. However, I want to assure them that they are not safe." Later that year, McCarthy attempted a purge of his own, pouring his energy and the resources of his propaganda machine into a campaign against Tydings's reelection, going so far as to publish a faked composite photograph showing Tydings standing with the former head of the American Communist Party. So alarmed was Ickes at the prospect of Tydings's defeat that he rushed to make peace with his old enemy. "I am sure that I am not the only citizen of Maryland," Ickes wrote to Tydings, "who has been persuaded to vote for you on November 7, by Senator McCarthy."[29]

But Ickes's vote of confidence was not enough. While U.S. representative John F. Kennedy dined with McCarthy at Kennedy's parents' home in Hyannisport, while his brother Robert served as an assistant counsel to McCarthy's own subcommittee, and while Minnesota Democrat Hubert Humphrey introduced a Senate bill making membership in the Communist Party a felony, Tydings paid the price for his courage. Seeking a fifth term in the Senate, he lost the election to McCarthy's man, John Butler.[30]

By taking down the prime target on Roosevelt's hit list of 1938, McCarthy accomplished what Roosevelt could not. And yet, what would FDR have thought of the defeat of his implacable New Deal foe at the hands of Joe McCarthy? Might he have decided that, given the vicissitudes of politics, his best bet in 1938 would simply have been to play, as best he could, the hand he was dealt? Or did he simply relish a principled, challenging fight?

Tydings would die in 1961. Senator Bob La Follette, McCarthy's first victim, would end his life in 1953 with a pistol shot to the head.[31]

◄ 10 ►

New York Streets

"THE HAVE-NOTS ARE GOING to take everything away from the haves—and don't you fool yourself!" shouted John O'Connor as he campaigned in the late summer of 1938 to keep his seat in the House of Representatives. His agitated warning to a group of wealthy New Yorkers about the potentially violent and vindictive fury of downtrodden Americans was strange, not because he was whipping up fears of class warfare but because he was running for office as a Democrat.[1]

Well, a nominal Democrat. An anti–New Deal Democrat. A Democrat who felt no loyalty to his party. A Democrat who was running not only as an incumbent in the Democratic primary but also running simultaneously as a Republican in the Republican primary—giving new meaning to "opportunism." "In this emergency," O'Connor told voters, "whether you are a Republican or a Democrat does not count. What does count is whether you put your country first!"[2]

As chairman of the House Rules Committee and one of the highest ranking Democrats in the House, O'Connor, who had served in Congress since 1923, had been a determined and skillful saboteur who relished knifing New Deal programs. He worked to defeat the executive reorganization bill and schemed to bottle up in committee the Fair Labor Standards Act. Hammering the New Deal, he mocked the Americans who "go to the public trough to be fed."[3] And yet, despite his scorn for the have-nots, his district—a narrow strip of Manhattan stretching from Fourteenth Street to Sixty-third Street and from Park Avenue to the East River—was populated by men, women, and children crushed by the Great Depression.

In 1935 the play *Dead End* opened on Broadway. It was set in O'Connor's Sixteenth District, on a riverfront block in the East Fifties, where fashionable, palatial new apartment buildings—on Sutton Place and Beekman Place—were rising up amid the squalor of old tenements, gas tanks, electrical works, and coal chutes. "The tenement houses," wrote the playwright, Sidney Kingsley, in his stage directions, "are close, dark, and crumbling. They crowd each other. Where there are curtains in the windows, they are streaked and faded; where there are none, we see through to hideous, water stained, peeling wall-paper, and old broken-down furniture. The fire escapes are cluttered with gutted mattresses and quilts, old clothes, bread-boxes, milk bottles, a canary cage, an occasional potted plant struggling for life." The play's characters—a young woman on strike for better pay, an unemployed architect, idle teenagers looking for trouble, and a notorious murderer—all fight to survive on mean streets.[4]

John O'Connor was virtually a stranger in that riven district. Storekeepers and tradesmen in his neighborhood claimed not to know him. The *New York Times* revealed that although he had a "voting residence"—a two-room apartment—in the Sixteenth District, this Brown University and Harvard Law School graduate made his permanent home in wealthy Bayport, Long Island, fifty-three miles outside of Manhattan.[5]

"Mr. President, have you anything to say about the forthcoming primaries in New York where Congressman O'Connor is running against Jim Fay?" a reporter asked Roosevelt at a press conference in mid-August.

"I knew that somebody would ask the question so I have a perfectly good statement here," the president said, and then proceeded to read aloud from a *New York Post* editorial that echoed his own thoughts, the same editorial that denounced Millard Tydings. "Week in and week out," he said, "O'Connor labors to tear down New Deal strength, pickle New Deal legislation. Why shouldn't the responsible head of the New Deal tell the people just that?" "Let's have it out!" O'Connor barked in reply a few days later.[6]

What mattered most to Roosevelt was defeating O'Connor in the Democratic primary. If O'Connor lost that, he would automatically lose the powerful chairmanship of the Rules Committee. Then, even if he won the Republican primary and went on to win reelection as a Republican, he would return to the House as a freshman member of the minority party. In fact, columnist Heywood Broun mused that it would be "sweet" to see O'Connor seated in Congress in the benches of the GOP, for he would be living testimony to the president's assertion that conservatives of O'Connor's stripe had profited from the Democratic label while, in their hearts, they were allied with Republicans. But majority leader Sam Rayburn added a note of caution, warning that O'Connor might create even greater trouble for the White House "if the Administration takes an interest in opposing him and then he should be renominated and elected." The president, though, was undaunted and was determined to unseat his toxic foe.[7]

Roosevelt's candidate for O'Connor's House seat was the thirty-nine-year old James Fay. A World War I veteran who had lost a leg in combat and won the Purple Heart, Fay had served as a deputy commissioner of hospitals of New York City and also worked as a field deputy for the Bureau of Internal Revenue. And he was a longtime resident of Manhattan's East Side. But more important, he had the potential to be a strong challenger. In 1934, Fay had faced off with O'Connor in the Democratic primary and lost by fewer than two hundred votes.[8]

Fay had the backing of various labor organizations, some New York politicians, the *New York Daily News,* the Works Progress Administration, and federal workers—as well as the support of the president himself. Well, at least his behind-the-scenes support. For unlike in Georgia, this time Roosevelt listened to the local politicos who urged him to take a back seat. When FDR asked Bronx Democratic boss Ed Flynn to go to bat for Fay, Flynn accepted—but only on the condition that the White House stay out of the campaign. Thus Roosevelt made no direct statements on behalf of Fay—and even cancelled a meeting with him in Hyde Park.[9]

Aid for Fay also came from City Hall. Mayor Fiorello LaGuardia's executive assistant, William Walsh, served as Fay's campaign manager. A major in the army during World War I, Walsh excelled in putting together a tight, disciplined team. And LaGuardia himself gave a boost to Fay by hammering O'Connor. "I served in Congress with him for ten years—hence my opposition," explained the mayor.[10]

Fay relished the challenge of running against O'Connor and understood the art of political campaigning. Presenting himself as a 100 percent New Dealer, he skewered O'Connor for his "shameless knifing of the great leader Franklin D. Roosevelt." "Are the people of the Sixteenth Congressional district going to have a man in Congress who represents them," he would ask, "or one who represents Park Avenue and Wall Street?" And what more could Fay have wished for than the chance to run against a man with two political faces? In a radio speech entitled "You Can't Pitch for Both Teams," he derided O'Connor's political masquerade. O'Connor's prime goal, Fay declared, was to "do the most damage to the great program of social progress represented in the New Deal."[11]

It did not help Fay's campaign, however, that Israel Amter, the Communist Party candidate for governor of New York, called for O'Connor's defeat. And it helped even less that fake "Communist petitions" endorsing Fay were being circulated in the district.[12]

For his part, O'Connor had the encouragement of New York's famed Tammany Hall Democratic machine—but the power of that once invincible organization was, in the words of Jeremiah Mahoney, who had run for mayor in 1937, "at the bottom of the sewer." The cause of the decline? First, a weakening of Tammany's base as the number of immigrants in the city dropped. Second, as even O'Connor admitted, the fact that Tammany had had "some stupid leadership in recent years." And third, LaGuardia's election as mayor in 1933. The Republican "Little Flower" had ousted Tammany from City Hall, depriving its "sachems" of the power of patronage.[13]

Nor did it improve O'Connor's chances—at least not in the crucial Democratic primary—to receive the blessings of some of FDR's most bitter enemies. Raymond Moley, a former member of Roosevelt's inner circle who had turned against the president, bestowed his seal of approval on O'Connor. The people who backed Fay, Moley charged, were "pinks, reds and internationalists," while he himself supported O'Connor "because I am an American."[14]

Father Charles Coughlin, the anti-Semitic radio priest from Michigan who had first hailed FDR as the savior before deciding he was satanic, devoted the September 12 issue of his weekly newsletter, *Social Justice,* to the virtues of O'Connor. Unfortunately for the congressman, the same issue—which the O'Connor campaign unguardedly mailed to all voters in the district—also contained excerpts from the notorious anti-Semitic tract *The Protocols of the Elders of Zion.*[15]

Dubious aid for O'Connor also came from Congressman Hamilton Fish, the archconservative who represented an upstate district that included Roosevelt's own Hyde Park. Republican Fish urged Democrats to vote for O'Connor in their primary. As chairman of the Rules Committee, Fish explained, O'Connor would have "far more power over legislation than Senators Tydings and George combined," and the stakes could not have been higher. The battle was really between American freedom and Soviet-style communism, inasmuch as the president, according to Fish, "has the full and open support of the Communist party."[16]

In the Republican primary, O'Connor was running against a moderate Republican, Allen Dulles. The intelligent and temperate Dulles had endorsements from the *New York Times* and the *Herald Tribune,* and he had the blessing of Republican moderates like Bruce Barton, who represented Manhattan's "Silk Stocking" district, which bordered O'Connor's Sixteenth District and where the president owned a town house. While hard-line conservative Republicans like Colonel Theodore Roosevelt, the son of the former president, smiled on O'Connor, Dulles won the approval of the Republican Party in New York. New York Republicans had recently been trying to liberalize their party's image, broaden its base, and cleanse it of any association with President Hoover and the reactionary Liberty League. Young Republicans even agreed with most New Deal policies but promised to administer them more efficiently.[17]

Dulles spoke out in favor of many of Roosevelt's social and economic reforms, though he took issue with what he called the president's "executive dictatorship." With war clouds darkening in Europe, Dulles had sensibly proposed canceling Great Britain's World War I debt. But the isolationist O'Connor slammed him for "selling out" the United States to England, and the beleaguered Dulles retreated from his position, denying that he had ever proposed any such policy.[18]

O'Connor's challenge, of course, was how to position himself to run simultaneously in the primaries of two opposing parties. His pitch was simple: the "grave danger to our way of American life" obliged him to make a sacrifice of party loyalty. "I am not one to wrap myself in the American flag," he declared.[19] But, in fact, he was doing exactly that. His strategy was to elude the real issues of the day and blur all meaningful party distinctions—in short, he was determined to win any way he could. There was even the possibility that he could win in both primaries and then run against himself in November, turning a democratic election into a comic farce. At Democratic rallies, O'Connor praised many New Deal programs; at Republican events, he outlined his opposition to them.

He was, O'Connor maintained, a consistent advocate for political sanity and prudence. It was perfectly logical for him to run in both primaries, he explained, for the real distinction was not between Democrats and Republicans or between conservatives and liberals. Most of them, including himself, were simply "liberals." The crucial distinction, he argued, was between liberals and "radicals." And by radicals, he meant Roosevelt and his New Deal fanatics. Their brand of extremism, he warned, led to fascism and communism. Whereas the goal of Roosevelt's purge was to give voters a meaningful choice between candidates and parties at election time, O'Connor not only wanted to obliterate those party distinctions but, oddly, even wanted to exclude Roosevelt's New Deal popular majority from the political mainstream. And while O'Connor was branding New Deal Democrats as fascists and communists, Roosevelt was issuing the opposite warning—"old-line Tory Republicanism," he suggested, would unwittingly strengthen communism and fascism in America.[20]

The last days before the primaries sparked a flurry of rallies and speeches. The final exchange between O'Connor and Fay brought up the subject of war. In a blistering attack, O'Connor charged that Roosevelt was willing to plunge the nation into war merely to assure his own reelection in 1940. Fay counterattacked. "This is equivalent to accusing the President of treason," he responded, adding: "This kind of wildness is not new for O'Connor."[21]

Fortunately the weather on primary day was calm—because on the following day, September 21, the famous hurricane of 1938 struck New York and New England, flooding streets, uprooting trees, destroying more than a hundred thousand homes and buildings and leaving in its wake six hundred dead. But on Tuesday, order reigned. In accordance with state law, no alcoholic beverages could be sold from the time the polls opened until they closed. Fifty-eight additional inspectors from the State Liquor Authority prowled the city to make sure that voters flocked to the polls and not to the bars. For Fay, however, it was a difficult day: he was hospitalized with an infection in the stump of his amputated leg.[22]

Late that night Roosevelt received a telephone call from Tommy Corcoran. Victory for Fay! The margin might have been small—but O'Connor was out. "Tommy," said Roosevelt, "I have never had such a lift in my spirits in my life."[23]

Ever since the Presidential Special had pulled out of Union Station in early July, Roosevelt had been bent on war against incumbent conservative Democrats, hoping that they would be defeated in the Democratic primaries. Ironically, the one contest in which he was successful was the last one—and also the one in which he was the least involved.

After the many failures of the president's purge, the *New Republic* rejoiced: "This single victory is enough to justify the whole effort." O'Connor's run as a Republican was a harbinger of party realignment, the journal predicted. "Let the anti–New Deal Democrats in Congress align themselves openly with the conservative Republicans." But that realignment was decades away.[24]

O'Connor was not a total loser: he beat Allen Dulles in the Republican primary. "I congratulate the Republican party on its new member," Harold Ickes dryly responded when reporters asked him for a comment.[25]

With Dulles out of the picture and O'Connor now running as a Republican against the Democrat Fay in the November election, O'Connor's true political colors finally came out. Admitting that his hero was Herbert Hoover, he praised the former president as a "great American." Unlike Roosevelt, Hoover did not "play politics with human misery," according to O'Connor. But knowing that he needed the votes of Democrats to win the election, O'Connor tried to persuade Democrats that Republicans were the "real Democrats." Only if Real Republicans and Real Democrats all stood "shoulder to shoulder for American principles of government" would they be able to vanquish New Deal extremism. His strange script outlining a new political realignment was as delusional as Orson Welles's radio broadcast "War of the Worlds" that October. Welles's news bulletin—"Ladies and gentlemen, incredible as it may seem, strange beings who landed in New Jersey tonight are the vanguard of an invading army from Mars"—sent thousands of panicked listeners to the highways to save themselves from the interplanetary conflict.[26]

New York Times columnist Arthur Krock, however, bought into O'Connor's bizarre scenario and obtusely predicted that should O'Connor win the Republican seat in Congress, Democrats in the House might very well reward him and permit him to retain his committee chairmanship! Fortunately Adolph Sabath of Illinois, next in line for the chairmanship of the Rules Committee, set Krock and O'Connor straight, making it clear that he "did not and cannot" endorse O'Connor."[27]

Nothing was simple in the November contest, for once again O'Connor was on the ballot twice—as the candidate of the Republican Party and of the Andrew Jackson Party. Campaigning on an "Old Hickory" ticket, O'Connor claimed to be a Jacksonian Democrat. Outraged that O'Connor was confusing voters in the general election by calling himself a Democrat, Fay sued to restrain him from using the word. "Old Hickory must have turned over in his grave," Fay said.[28]

"I'm still a regular Democrat, and I'm still a member of the Democratic Party," O'Connor insisted to a New York judge on November 1, a few days before New Yorkers went to the polls. Fay's lawyers argued that the use of the word "Democratic" in conjunction with the Andrew Jackson Party was "misleading and deceiving to the voters." Fay won the first round and later the appeal. Political candidates and independent parties, the court ruled, could not use words from other party labels to confuse voters.[29]

During the closing days of the campaign O'Connor predictably accused Fay of being a Communist while Fay charged that O'Connor "faked" his residence, "faked" his allegiance to the New Deal, and "faked" sympathies for the people. On election day, O'Connor lost—

and blamed his defeat on Harry Hopkins and the Communists, "which is the same thing," he noted.[30]

In December 1938, O'Connor moved into a new law office in Washington. "I'm not through with politics," he said. In 1939 he tried to recruit five hundred former congressmen to prevent any "radical" New Deal Democrat from being nominated for president. In 1940, he predictably supported Republican Wendell Willkie in the presidential race against FDR. That year, trying for a comeback as a fervent advocate of American isolationism, O'Connor would run again in the Democratic and Republican primaries—and lose in both. In the general election in November, the Republican candidate, William Pheiffer, went on to defeat incumbent James Fay. But two years later, in 1942, Fay would run again against Pheiffer—this time successfully—and serve one final term.[31]

As for the Rules Committee, which under O'Connor had so often blocked action on New Deal measures, there was no salutary transformation after his defeat. A conservative majority confronted the new chairman, Adolph Sabath, an old friend and Roosevelt loyalist. In addition to the committee's five Republicans, five southern Democrats—including archconservatives Howard Smith of Virginia and Martin Dies of Texas—made life difficult for Sabath. The new chair could count on only three votes, in addition to his own.

Sabath was often forced to resort to odd ruses. Once, when he failed to convince members to adjourn their meeting, he pretended to faint, almost falling out of his chair. After the committee adjourned and the members had left the room, he lifted his head from his desk and whispered, "Have they gone yet?" Assured that they had, he strolled out of the room.[32]

John O'Connor was gone—but Roosevelt had still not mastered the Rules Committee.

In late November 1938, with the purge over, Roosevelt met with Jim Farley. "Well, I've been giving a lot of time to the study of the election returns," the president said, "and I find they demonstrate the result around the country was due in every case to local conditions." With this singular admission, the president conceded that the White House had been unable to penetrate the web of local power brokers and local issues. The national Democratic Party and the congressional Democratic Party were indeed separate entities.

From the very beginning, however, Farley had warned the president against the purge, and now Roosevelt was annoyed that Farley had been right all along. He took his disappointment and frustration out on his friend. "From that time on the President began to see less and less of me," Farley later wrote in his memoirs, "as if I were to blame for the defeat I had counseled against. . . . My appointments came further and further apart. . . . Outwardly we were as friendly as ever. It was just that I found myself outside the White House door. True, it had not been slammed in my face, but it was locked and barred nonetheless."[33]

Frances Perkins, Roosevelt's secretary of labor, who had more than once seen the president "freeze out" people he was angry with, corroborated Farley's version of events. "He just froze him," she recalled, "froze him solid in looks, in manner, in lack of speech, not saying anything. When Jim would say anything, FDR would say, 'Really, really, indeed.' That was all."[34]

Two years after the purge, Farley would seek to even the score. A strong opponent of presidential third terms, he would challenge his old friend FDR for the Democratic nomination in 1940.

◄ ‖ ►

The Dynamics of the Purge

THE LITTLE FRAME TOWN HALL in Hyde Park was surrounded by reporters scribbling in their notebooks and photographers snapping shots of the crowd outside the green and white building. It was Election Day, November 8, 1938, and the president, his wife Eleanor, his eighty-five-year old mother Sara, and his secretary Missy LeHand stood in line with everyone else to cast their votes. "Your name please," said the election official. "Franklin D. Roosevelt," came the confident reply.[1]

Cane in hand and supported by an aide, Roosevelt entered the polling booth, closing the curtain behind him. When he emerged only three minutes later, the reporters shouted their questions. Had he voted the straight Democratic ticket? "It's a secret ballot," Roosevelt answered with a smile, adding that he had left his "good luck" watch chain at home.[2]

That evening, while the president and Harry Hopkins listened to the election returns on the radio in Hyde Park and made phone calls to Democratic leaders around the country, more than one hundred thousand people jammed into Times Square. As they watched the results displayed on the electric crawler on the *New York Times* building, the skies opened and a drenching rain poured down, dispersing the crowd. Holding umbrellas or newspapers to shield their heads, ten thousand hardy souls remained, staring up at the crawler as it spelled out the mixed returns for the Democrats. By 11:30, only a handful of people were still standing in the cold rain. The four newsreel companies that had waited all evening to film the midnight crowds left disappointed.[3]

Those glum feelings saturated Democrats across the country, too. With the exception of 1934, when enthusiasm for FDR and the New Deal had been high, the sitting president's party invariably suffered losses in midterm elections. But this time the Democrats took a real drubbing, a stunning reversal after the 1936 landslide. Probably it was the combination of labor strikes, the recession of 1937, the president's court proposal, and the "purge." Or perhaps voters just wanted to taste a little change.

Certainly they got it. Republicans picked up 8 Senate seats, increasing their numbers from 19 to 27, and they nearly doubled their forces in the House from 88 seats to 169. They also gained a dozen new governorships. Although Democrats still held large majorities in Congress—with 69 senators and 262 representatives—the Republican Party seemed to be recovering from its Depression-induced eclipse and making a comeback. The columnist Walter Lippmann, who had grown ever more conservative since he had dismissed FDR in 1932 as an amiable lightweight, now wrote that it was "not too rash" to forecast a Republican landslide in 1940. A few weeks after the election, the chairman of the Republican National Committee would mail out his Christmas cards emblazoned with a happy elephant emerging from a doghouse.[4]

Did the president expect to encounter any "coalition opposition" to the New Deal? a reporter asked at an Oval Office news conference on November 11. "No, I don't think so," Roosevelt brightly answered—and then joined in the laughter when the sassy reporter retorted, "I do!"[5]

The truth was that the president's purge had backfired. Roosevelt's "iridescent dream of a perfectly pure liberal party untainted by conservatism and reaction," commented the old Republican journalist from Kansas, William Allen White, "has been knocked into a cocked hat."[6]

Some of the candidates FDR had helped in various degrees on his trip out west did succeed in winning reelection: Alben Barkley of Kentucky, Elmer Thomas of Oklahoma, Hattie Caraway of Arkansas, and Lyndon Johnson of Texas. But several Democrats for whom the president had stumped went down to defeat. Maury Maverick of Texas lost his seat in the House; William McAdoo of California failed to win renomination; and the president's lukewarm ally and old Harvard friend Senator Robert Bulkley of Ohio was beaten in the general election, replaced by conservative Republican Robert Taft.

Even worse, four of the purge's main targets sailed to renomination and reelection, easily brushing Roosevelt's onslaught aside: Walter George of Georgia, Cotton Ed Smith of South Carolina, Millard Tydings of Maryland, and Guy Gillette of Iowa. As for the entrenched conservative Democrats, whom the president had declined to oppose— Bennett Clark of Missouri, Alva Adams of Colorado, Pat McCarran of Nevada, and Frederick Van Nuys of Indiana—they, too, swept to reelection. Another conservative Democrat in whose race the president had decided not to intervene, Augustine Lonergan of Connecticut, won his primary but lost in November to an even more conservative Republican, John Danaher, a passionate isolationist and biting New Deal critic. Roosevelt had only one big consolation: the lone casualty of the purge was the defiant representative from New York's Sixteenth District and chairman of the House Rules Committee: John O'Connor.

Constitutionally averse to admitting any personal weakness, Roosevelt put on a good face and gave the debacle a positive spin. "Frankly, our officeholders and our candidates had not measured up," he confided to a friend, placing the blame on others. To his old boss, Josephus Daniels, he sounded a cheery note. "I am not only wholly reconciled to last Tuesday's results," he wrote after election day, "but believe that they are on the whole helpful." A few bad apples—Mayor Frank Hague of Jersey City, Governor Martin Davey of Ohio, James Michael Curley in Massachusetts, as well as O'Connor—had been eliminated, and he breezily predicted: "We will have less trouble with the next Congress than with the last." The press was less convinced.[7]

"Purgin' Time Down South" was the theme of one of the skits at the December 17 Gridiron Club dinner, attended by the president and hundreds of other guests. Reporters, costumed as Senators Tydings, George, and Smith, visited the cotton patch to sing "We'll put you Yankees right where you belong!" Another reporter took the role of Cotton Ed for a tune about "the cause of white supremacee," and a chorus of "southerners" crooned "God bless you, Franklin, stay out of the South!" Other reporters, dressed as black cotton pickers, proclaimed that "they got no more chance o' purgin' Cotton Ed than they have o' puttin' Jimmy Roosevelt on the dole." The president, observers said, appeared to laugh.[8]

A month later, in January 1939, Roosevelt spoke at the Jackson Day dinner in the ballroom of the Mayflower Hotel, a few blocks from the White House. A thousand Democratic Party stalwarts, including Carter Glass, Jim Farley, Vice President Garner, and Speaker William Bankhead, feasted on turtle soup and filet mignon and listened to the president acknowledge the Republican comeback—and try to make peace with his fellow Democrats.[9]

Roosevelt faced reality. Claiming to welcome the surge in Republican strength and the reestablishment of a two-party system, the president challenged Republicans to play the role of an effective, united, conservative opposition party instead of continuing to compensate for their "impotence" by voting in Democratic primaries and seeking other ways to sabotage the Democrats and "destroy our party's unity and effectiveness."

That new Republican muscle, Roosevelt said, would also serve to strengthen Democratic unity by bringing together "real Democrats" and others who believe in the "liberal gospel." He admitted that there were some "nominal Democrats" who wanted a conservative party— "a Democratic Tweedledum to a Republican Tweedledee." But—as though asking his audience to forget the purge—he argued that differences among Democrats constituted no more than "honest debate" and "an honest effort to work things out for the good of the country." There was no bad blood among Democrats, he maintained, dismissing the notion of internal dissension as nothing more than a Republican myth. Debate within the party was healthy, and he insisted that in the six years since 1932 it had "borne six crops of good fruit."

With politicians like Glass and Farley in his audience, Roosevelt sought to trumpet a message of party unity that would obliterate lingering bad feelings about the summer's purge. "If we Democrats lay for each other now," he warned, "we can be sure that 1940 is the corner where the American people will be laying for us."[10]

And FDR meant it—he would not again intervene in primary fights between Democrats. Two years later, when Senator Harry Truman of Missouri asked for help in his primary, Roosevelt had his aide Steve Early unceremoniously pour cold water on the idea. "While Senator Truman is an old and trusted friend of the President's," Early replied, "his *invariable* practice has been not to take part in primary contests. . . . The President must stand aloof regardless of any personal preference he might have."[11]

Harmony, teamwork, unity, no bitter feelings. As far as the White House was concerned, the purge was forgotten—it had never even taken place. The politicians FDR had targeted, however, were not so sure.

Some of the economic and social conservatives whom Roosevelt had sought to banish from his party would ironically become his staunchest allies as he battled congressional isolationists over America's role in the mounting world crisis. As country after country—Poland, Austria, Czechoslovakia, Norway, Denmark, Belgium, Holland, France—fell to Hitler's armies from 1938 to 1940, and as Japanese tentacles grasped

China and French Indochina, Roosevelt desperately needed the support of internationalists and "interventionists" in Congress. Their cooperation was critical if the president was to help Great Britain and France while also preparing the United States militarily for possible war. But Roosevelt first had to win back the trust of those Democrats.

In the months following the purge, many of them were in no forgiving mood, and even those who agreed with the president on crucial foreign policy issues still distrusted his motives. Although Virginia's Carter Glass wished to see "England and France shoot Hitler off the map," he suspected, as he wrote in January 1939, that Roosevelt's "war scare" was a red herring "to divert attention from the reckless expenditures that have already bankrupted the nation." Nor was Josiah Bailey of North Carolina an isolationist, but he, too, was wary, insisting in March 1939 that he opposed "any step calculated to get this country into a war." The president talked up war, he said, "to capture the vote of the Jews in New York City."[12]

Roosevelt had no choice but to butter up the senators he had riled—and by the fall of 1939, Bailey was crowing with pleasure at the White House's ceasefire. "The President is in a very conciliatory attitude," Bailey remarked. "Certainly he is cultivating us in a very nice way." The two men even chatted fraternally about their common dermatological problem of athlete's foot infecting their hands. Frances Perkins later wrote that what she admired most about FDR was that he always adapted "to new circumstances, always quick to understand the changing needs and hopes of the people and to vary his action to meet changing situations." She never forgot the president's personal rule—"Be flexible in all dealings with human beings"—a rule he himself had forgotten in the summer of 1938.[13]

With the nation's security at risk as the European situation continued to deteriorate, Roosevelt poured on the charm. He courted Tom Connally of Texas; he cajoled Mississippi's Senator Pat Harrison. "I need you here on lots of things," Roosevelt deferentially wrote to

Harrison. He mollified Harry Byrd—one of the two most conservative Democrats in the Senate—by agreeing to name a Virginian to a position in the Treasury Department.[14] And he paid special attention to the eighty-one-year-old Glass. Meeting with the Virginian in September 1939, after the British and French formally declared war against Germany, the president gushed, "Well, it took a war to get us together again. I hope it will take an earthquake to separate us!" To cement their reconciliation, he and Eleanor sent him a bouquet of flowers when they heard that he was ill. Even though Glass had vociferously opposed a third term for FDR in 1940 and even though Roosevelt had crowed that he had trounced the old-line Democratic conservatives at the 1940 Democratic Convention and won a "great victory," the president supported Glass's appointment in 1941 to the Senate Foreign Relations Committee, where he helped steer through passage of the Lend-Lease bill. And after FDR had intensely ruffled Glass by appointing Virginia judges to the federal bench without consulting him, deliberately ignoring the tradition of senatorial courtesy, the harmony-seeking president now invited the Virginia senator to the White House to discuss judicial appointments.[15]

Roosevelt's attitude toward conservative Democrats, he confided to his advisor on party politics, Attorney General Homer Cummings, had become "all milk and honey." The goodwill that the president now fostered within his fractured party amused Jim Farley. "You know, I'm getting suspicious of what is going on around here," Farley said laughingly to FDR. "There seems to be no dull moment around here. Bailey and Glass are trooping in here regularly, and now I suppose you'll throw out the welcome mat for your old friend Happy Chandler." The president would indeed welcome Happy to the White House. Contrary to Farley's preconceptions, Chandler—the man who had unsuccessfully challenged Kentucky's Alben Barkley and who had been awarded a Senate seat in 1939, when the state's junior senator Marvel Logan died— would unhesitatingly join the ranks of Roosevelt allies on defense and war bills.[16]

Still, Roosevelt could not win over Democratic isolationist holdouts in the Senate like Burton Wheeler of Montana—who would successfully insist on a noninterventionist foreign policy plank in the 1940 Democratic Party platform—and Bennett Clark of Missouri, Worth Clark of Idaho, Guy Gillette of Iowa, David Walsh of Massachusetts, Pat McCarran of Nevada, and Robert Reynolds of North Carolina, who would all vote against the Lend-Lease Act as well as other internationalist legislation. But in the reshuffling of domestic politics, almost all of the conservative southern Democrats who had opposed the president on economic issues rallied to his side on aid to Britain and the military buildup.[17]

In the fall of 1939, Senator Connally—who had opposed court-packing, executive reorganization, and the Fair Labor Standards Act—led the fight, with encouragement from the White House, for repeal of the American arms embargo so that the United States could aid Great Britain and France. For two and a half hours he spoke on the Senate floor, pleading for help for the Allies as well as for a two-ocean navy, a strong army and air corps, and more coastal defenses. Bailey, too, stood up against the isolationists. In August 1940, he assured the White House that southern Democrats would be "voting right and with the president on every question before the Senate, particularly conscription." A year later, still before the Japanese attack on Pearl Harbor, he continued to support FDR's military policies. "I am advocating intervention with all its implications," Bailey announced to a hushed Senate in the fall of 1941. "Security comes before prosperity. Security comes before peace."[18] Carter Glass complained not that Roosevelt's war policies were too bellicose but rather that they were too cautious. Convinced that the dire European situation placed America's democratic institutions "in mortal peril," in the summer of 1941 Glass worried that the United States was "not moving fast enough" against Hitler. While Roosevelt battled isolationists from both the left and the right and while they battled him, he continued to receive some of his strongest support on military policy from the South. In September 1940, 70 percent of southerners—18 percent higher than the national average—believed that it was important for the United States to aid Great Britain against Hitler and Nazism "even at the risk of war." Popular opinion in the South left the isolationist Senator Vandenberg of Michigan to grumble that southern Democrats had become the president's "rubber stamps," meekly following their leader.[19]

Why was the South the most internationalist region in the nation? Why, more than other Americans, did southerners favor action against Nazi and Japanese expansion, as opinion polls showed? The South had ancient cultural and blood ties to Great Britain as well as lingering gratitude to the British for their sympathy toward the Confederacy. More than any other region of the country, the South had a strong military tradition, a plethora of military academies, a cult of chivalry, honor, and dueling, pride in the valor and fighting ability of its sons, and, as one historian suggested, an "indifference to violence."[20] Carter Glass would have agreed with that description. "Virginia has always been a leader in the vanguard of the fight for freedom," he wrote in the spring of 1941. "She is ready today as in the past to give virile leadership to the nation." And, in the one-party South, there was also loyalty to a Democratic president. The isolationist stance of "peace at any price" was doomed to arouse no enthusiasm in the South. The only southern state in which the isolationist America First Committee had some success was Florida, and even there its supporters—Republicans and former or part-time northerners—were intimidated into silence.[21]

There was also the factor of self-interest. Southerners feared that German conquests in Europe would disrupt their cotton and tobacco trade. When war finally did come, the South would reap a bounty of material rewards and would benefit from an economic defense boom, with the construction of shipyards, training camps, powder mills, aircraft plants, petroleum refineries and pipelines, and new orders for its textile mills.[22]

With the vigorous support of the internationalist, interventionist South, the president was able to push through Congress key measures like the Selective Service Act of September 1940, which made universal military service compulsory. That law, sponsored in the Senate by Edward Burke of Nebraska, a court-packing foe whom FDR had artfully snubbed when he toured western states in the autumn of 1937, found enthusiastic support in the South. "I am in favor of universal conscription," declared Carter Glass on the Senate floor, blasting "Adolf Hitler, the Central European Assassin." His fellow southerners Harry Byrd and Walter George agreed, and Tom Connally, who would soon succeed George as the chairman of the Senate Foreign Relations Committee, added that George Washington, too, had favored mandatory peacetime military service. Senators John Overton of Louisiana and Richard Russell of Georgia, supported by representatives John Rankin of Mississippi and Overton Brooks of Louisiana, believed that industry, too, should be conscripted. They amended the Selective Service bill to allow the government to seize industrial plants if their owners refused to accept government contracts. And a nonsoutherner, Senator Alva Adams of Colorado, who had opposed FDR on court-packing and executive reorganization, successfully proposed another amendment limiting profits for war materiel produced for the government to 7 or 8 percent. When the Selective Service bill passed in the Senate by a vote of 58 to 31, only one southern Democrat, Cotton Ed Smith, voted against it.[23]

In a remarkable reversal, virtually all of the conservatives who had opposed—and continued to oppose—much of FDR's New Deal legislation had come to serve as his unfaltering foreign policy allies. In the spring of 1941, George, Smith, and Tydings as well as Glass and Byrd all backed the president and his point man in the Senate, South Carolina's Byrnes, in the climactic and successful battle on the Lend-Lease Act. Ironically, the only southern senator to vote against Lend-Lease, which supplied Great Britain and other allies under siege with war matériel in exchange for military bases, was Robert Reynolds of North Carolina, one of the few senators who had sided with the president on court-packing.[24]

As national security trumped economic policy, the purge and its criteria appeared all the more irrelevant and ill conceived. Now Roosevelt could not dispense with the support of men like Tydings and Glass, Connally and Bailey. "Foreign policy," wrote historian James T. Patterson, "destroyed what little hope there had been for party realignment after the 1938 primaries and elections." Equally ill conceived, Patterson insightfully suggested, were the attempts of Republicans like Senator Vandenberg in 1937 to attract southerners to their party. With war approaching, internationalist southerners had less incentive than ever to join the ranks of isolationists like Vandenberg and a party largely blind to the fascist threat.[25]

In targeting certain conservative Democrats for exile in 1938, Roosevelt had divided politicians into good and bad, depending on where they stood on his New Deal policies, especially his court reform bill and executive reorganization. But he seemed to have forgotten that the art of politics is the art of the deal. "Men in politics cannot be divided into white knights and black knights," remarked journalist Thomas Stokes in 1940. "It is best to take them over the long pull, placate them and win their support when you can, let them stray occasionally if they must—always remembering that there is another day and another battle when they will be needed."[26]

Ultimately, the president was forced to shower his Democratic adversaries with charm instead of bile. He relearned the lesson that as president and party leader he had to conciliate his party, not coerce it. After the purge's failure, as Patterson remarked, Franklin Roosevelt ate a generous helping of humble pie.[27]

Why had Roosevelt, a canny, instinctive politician, failed so dramatically in the purge? His political vision of party realignment was compelling—the famed political scientist E. E. Schattschneider, who favored stronger and more centralized national parties, hailed it as "one of the greatest experimental tests of the nature of the American party system ever made"—and yet the execution of Roosevelt's plan was hurried, amateurish, and replete with not only miscalculations but also deep ambivalence about party government.[28]

First of all, the members of his informal "elimination committee"—Harold Ickes, Harry Hopkins, Tommy Corcoran, Ben Cohen, and Joseph Keenan—were all administration insiders who, unlike the president himself, had no experience in grassroots politics. They underestimated the power of incumbents and their machines and failed to appreciate how little control the national Democratic Party had over local party organizations. The president similarly miscalculated; he believed that he could capitalize on his great popularity, make a direct, personal appeal to voters, and bypass local organizations. But he, too, underestimated the clout of political machines, the long-standing relationships between politicians and their constituents, as well as the influence of local newspapers. The president may have been skillful and experienced in politics, but his real strength—according to FDR's attorney general Robert Jackson, whom he would appoint to the Supreme Court in 1941—lay neither with Congress nor with party leaders but "with the great masses of warm-hearted people who saw in him a champion and enlisted in his cause."[29]

In addition, the White House had not foreseen the indignant backlash the president would fuel by intruding in local elections. Roosevelt's personal popularity did not suffer—67 percent of southerners and 55 percent of Americans nationwide still backed him, according to a September 1938 Gallup poll. But he antagonized not only the targets of his purge, who would remain on the scene in Congress to spar with him, but voters and newspaper editors. "I knew from the beginning," wrote Jim Farley, "that the purge could lead to nothing but misfortune, because in pursuing his course of vengeance Roosevelt violated a cardinal political creed which demanded that he keep out of local matters. In any political entity voters naturally and rightfully resent the unwarranted invasion of outsiders."[30]

Even Harold Ickes had second thoughts about the purge. Although in the spring of 1938 he had urged the president to fight back—no holds barred—against conservatives in the party, by September he was backpedaling and even putting the blame for the purge's failure on the president. There would have been fewer "serious repercussions," Ickes cravenly wrote in his diary, if the president "had not actually gone into the states of the candidates himself but had announced his position from Washington."[31]

Nor did Roosevelt and his team in Washington grasp the depth of the ideological breach between the national party and local organizations. Two decades later, Roosevelt's speechwriter Sam Rosenman remarked that although the president was angry that conservative Democrats ran on his coattails while simultaneously betraying the party platform, he failed to recognize, first of all, that most politicians didn't need his coattails to win their elections, and second, that many voters would have been astonished if they had read some of the planks of the party's liberal platform.[32]

And perhaps the White House's most obvious blunder was to undertake the purge in the absence of impressive challengers to conservative incumbents. "Where could you find a man in Georgia with great strength who was ready to run against Walter George in the Democratic primaries?" Rosenman told an interviewer in 1959. "You could find good and qualified people, but not people of any outstanding political reputation. I think every one of the people who ran in the primaries, if he had been elected, would have made a good Senator or a good Congressman. But they were weak politically."[33] And making matters worse, the White House was parsimonious with its economic assistance as well as with its gestures of support—whether to challengers like Lawrence Camp in Georgia or to incumbents it wanted to keep, like Pope in Idaho and Maverick in Texas.

And finally, from the outset, Roosevelt's purge strategy resembled, in part, a personal vendetta. The president and the members of his inner circle had begun thinking about a "purge" during the painful months of the court-packing episode in 1937. And although FDR had denied that he harbored a grudge against the senators who had opposed the plan, Sam Rosenman later said that "the basis of the purge arose out of the determination to get rid of the people who opposed him during the Court fight. You must remember that in 1937, the disaster of the Court fight . . . left a deep impression on the President's mind."[34]

When the president announced to the public his intention to pick favorites in state party primaries, he said that he was doing so to rescue the New Deal and reform the party. But he was also was personalizing his political conflicts with conservative Democrats, casting himself dramatically as wrongful victim and heroic avenger in a play all about loyalty—to himself.

There was a precedent—and perhaps an unheeded warning—of this defeat: Roosevelt's court reform plan. Both episodes reflected his determination to rescue the New Deal from a powerful clique of obstructionists. And both episodes sparked flurries of accusations that he had overreached and harbored dictatorial ambitions. But there was a deeper similarity between court reform and the purge, for in both schemes the president employed slapdash methods.

In the case of court-packing, FDR had resorted to the quick and easy remedy of changing the Supreme Court's membership, when he might instead have courageously confronted the dubious—and constitutionally nonexistent—claim of the Court to striking down legislation. He might have proposed a constitutional amendment or searched for other ways to roll back the Court's unilateral appropriation of the power of judicial review.

In the matter of the purge, too, the president chose to go on a head-hunting expedition. He missed the opportunity to devise a far-reaching, well-planned strategy for party building and realignment. He neglected to deal with the core problems of nurturing new political talent and creating and consolidating a permanent New Deal majority coalition. He did not dedicate his time, energy, and resources to providing direction and support to grassroots liberal Democrats or to stimulating the growth of liberal groups within the party. Instead, he simply concentrated on nudging a few bad apples out of the party.

Both plans were hurried—but did the president have a choice? In the case of court-packing, he wanted to prevent the justices on the Supreme Court from striking down more New Deal legislation—and it might have taken years to secure a constitutional amendment, too much time to halt the damage the Court was inflicting on his programs. Similarly, he opted for the purge because it might have taken a decade— if not half a century—to dealign and then realign the two parties. With much of the nation still reeling from the Great Depression, Roosevelt felt the urgency of continuing and extending the New Deal. The political situation, too, was pressing: he wanted to control the selection of the party's nominee in 1940 and prevent the nomination of a conservative like his vice president, John Garner—if not run for a third term himself.

Neither in the court-packing episode nor in the purge did Roosevelt demonstrate the kind of intellectual commitment that is indispensable for truly transformational leadership. Rather, he allowed pique to control him. The type of party realignment he envisioned was not about to magically transpire after the ouster of a few conservatives from the Democratic Party.

But perhaps, dooming the purge, there was a deeper, less visible factor. The purge ultimately failed because, at bottom, Roosevelt was deeply

ambivalent about partisan party politics. When he first publicly announced the purge in his June 1938 fireside chat, he had cast himself as
the combative Democratic Party leader who would strengthen and
unite his party around liberal principles. And yet both before and after
1938, he often shunned that kind of militant partisanship.

Ever since his quest for the presidency in 1932, when he cultivated
southern conservatives in order to secure the Democratic nomination,
he had tried to transcend party strife. As president, he courted, charmed,
and placated Democratic conservatives in order to get crucial New
Deal legislation through Congress. So committed was he to political
harmony that he even tried to shed party labels. "The recovery and reconstruction program," he told Democrats in 1934, "is being accomplished by men and women of *all parties.*" That year he delivered a
similar message to the National Emergency Council. "We are thinking
about Government," he said, "and not merely about party." A few
months later, he told a group of bankers that good government was
"essentially the outward expression of the unity and leadership of all
groups."[35]

Not even during the "purge" did he completely abandon that anti-
party stance. Principles mattered more than party labels, he said in
early September 1938. "If there is a good liberal running on the Republican ticket," he told reporters at a press conference, "I would not have
the slightest objection to his election," adding: "The good of the country rises above party." His message was greeted with incredulity in the
South, where the Democratic label still mattered tremendously. And
five days before the November 1938 election, he urged voters to send
liberals—but not necessarily Democrats—to Congress. His advice to
voters: "Pick those who are known for their experience and their liberalism." A dozen times in that talk he used the word "liberal"—but not
once did he utter the words "Democrat" or "Democratic Party."[36]

So where did Roosevelt ultimately stand on party leadership and
party realignment? In the end, hard to tell, so often did he waver and

tack. In August 1939, he again briefly cast himself as militant party leader, warning the convention of Young Democratic Clubs of America that if Democrats nominated conservative candidates on "strattle-bug platforms" they would bring about the "unfortunate suicide of the old Democratic Party." Roosevelt insisted that he would sooner bolt the party than have any active part in that.[37]

But then, as the world crisis demanded a new political strategy, one of Republican support for a bipartisan foreign policy, Roosevelt donned his nonpartisan cap again. At the 1940 Jackson Day dinner, he underscored the importance of devotion to country above party. He recounted a humorous story about the schoolteacher who, after describing heaven in golden terms, asked her class of small boys how many of them wanted to go to heaven. One boy didn't hold up his hand. "Why Charlie, you don't want to go to Heaven? Why not?" "Teacher," Charlie said, "sure I want to go to Heaven, but—pointing to the rest of the boys in the room—not with that bunch!" The president then glanced at the three empty chairs at one of the banquet tables and wondered aloud why the three Republican leaders who had been invited had declined to attend. "I guess the real reason is that, like the small boy, they did not want to go to Heaven with this bunch!"[38]

Roosevelt's point was that democratic government, like heaven, should be inclusive; there is no place for political tribalism only. Politics should merely serve the purpose of good, progressive, effective administration. "The future," he said, "lies with those wise political leaders who realize the great public is interested more in government than in politics." He bestowed praise not on party leaders or party rank and file but on the men and women who toiled in the federal bureaucracy. "Back of the jockeying for party position, back of the party generals, hundreds of thousands of men and women," Roosevelt said, "have to get a good job done, have to put in day-after-day of honest, sincere work in carrying out the multitudinous functions that the policymakers in modern democracy assign to administrators in modern democracy." Parties did have a useful role, he hastened to add, as effective vehicles for presenting and explaining issues to the public, getting out the vote at election time, and recruiting talented candidates for office. But parties' claims on their members' loyalty merely diverted energy away from unified teamwork for common goals.

That was why Roosevelt now refused the crown of party leader. "People tell me that I hold to party ties less tenaciously than most of my predecessors in the Presidency," he earnestly declared at the 1940 Jackson Day dinner, "and that I have too many people in my Administration who are not active party Democrats. I must admit the soft impeachment."[39]

But FDR did not, in the end, give up on the importance of political parties, for he also believed in healthy—and even polarizing—partisanship. Seven months after that Jackson Day dinner, the president had drafted an irate talk to the delegates assembled at the July 1940 Democratic National Convention in Chicago, declining the party's nomination. He intended to deliver the message if the delegates did not nominate his choice of liberal Henry Wallace as their vice-presidential candidate. In the message, which was never delivered, Roosevelt warned Democrats that their party would fail if it strayed from the path of progressivism and liberalism and did not shake off the "shackles" of conservatism and reaction. "The party, he wrote, "must go wholly one way or wholly the other. It cannot face in both directions at the same time."[40]

Later that fall Roosevelt sent his son Franklin Jr., around the country to campaign for him. In Miami, at a meeting of the Young Democratic Clubs, the young man read aloud a letter from the president, still bent on clear party realignment. "There always will be two parties in this country," he said. "Their names may change but the issues between them are definite. Inevitably the struggle must be between the forces of liberalism and the forces of reaction. That struggle will go on as long as selfishness finds a place in the heart of man."[41] So much for inclusiveness and common purpose. For FDR, the Democratic Party alone was the organ of democracy and progress.

But Roosevelt ultimately was never able to use his personal popularity to transform the party into a united, liberal political machine or to commit himself to the role of vigorous party leader—in other words, to New Dealize the Democratic Party. Temperamentally, he was comfortable exploiting his charm, magnetism, and political dexterity for short-term ploys—which included enhancing his own popularity and standing with voters—rather than for long-term, coherent political planning. Although his marvelous flexibility as well as his opportunism had often served him well, they could also weaken his ability to stick to a long-range strategy. More an intuitive, wily tactician than a patient strategist, Roosevelt always kept open, as historian James MacGregor Burns noted, alternative lines of action, including a line of retreat. He was "less a great creative leader," Burns wrote, "than a skillful manipulator." In the purge, Roosevelt's spectacular talent for improvisation finally failed.[42]

And yet the hope for a strong, unified liberal party lingered, and in 1944 Roosevelt once again revisited the idea of party realignment. That spring, he learned that Gifford Pinchot, a progressive, forward-looking Republican, environmentalist, and old friend of Theodore Roosevelt, had recently spoken to FDR's 1940 Republican presidential rival, Wendell Willkie of Indiana, about creating a coalition of liberal Republicans and Democrats. Roosevelt was jubilant at the idea of joining forces with Willkie on such a plan. "We ought to have two real parties—one liberal and the other conservative," Roosevelt excitedly said to Sam Rosenman. "As it is now, each party is split by dissenters. Of course, I'm talking about long-range politics—something that we can't accomplish this year. But we can do it in 1948. . . . From the liberals of both parties Willkie and I together can form a new, really liberal party in America."[43]

Roosevelt had trounced Willkie in the election of 1940, winning 449 electoral votes to his rival's 82 after a bitter campaign. Prodded by Republican isolationists, Willkie had accused the "third-term candidate" of having a "dictatorial complex" and being a "warmonger." But Roosevelt knew that Willkie, a former Democrat, was really a moderate and an internationalist who had supported most New Deal goals.[44]

After the election, the president invited Willkie to the White House. "You know," he said to Frances Perkins after their January meeting, "he is a very good fellow. He has lots of talent. I want to use him somehow. I want to offer him an important post in the government. Can you think of one?" When Roosevelt learned that Willkie was going to England in January 1941, he asked him to be his personal representative, giving him a letter for Prime Minister Winston Churchill. In February, after visiting bombed-out sites in London, Coventry, and Birmingham, inspecting war-production factories, and meeting with Churchill, Willkie reported back to FDR on his trip and then testified in Congress as a strong proponent of the Lend-Lease Act and more aid to Britain. That fall, when a few senators, along with the isolationist and anti-Semitic "America First Committee" and their spokesman, aviator Charles Lindbergh, denounced Hollywood studios as the province of Jews seeking to push the country into war through their movies, the leaders of the film industry retained Willkie to represent them. "The motion picture industry," Willkie declared, "has shown only a pale portrayal of the terror and cruelties of Nazi Germany."[45]

Now, in 1944, Roosevelt hoped to join forces with Willkie to reshape the American party system. But for Willkie it was a delicate moment. After he lost the presidential nomination in 1944 to New York governor Thomas Dewey, Republicans on the right were pressuring him to back Dewey, while those on the left hoped he would come out for Roosevelt.

Willkie decided to remain neutral—and avoid any contact with the president until after the election.[46]

But, assured that the discussion would concern only party realignment and not the coming election, Willkie consented to a secret meeting with Roosevelt's emissary, Sam Rosenman, early in July 1944 at the St. Regis Hotel in New York. So fearful was Willkie that he might be recognized and the story leaked to the press that he stepped into the bedroom of the suite when the waiter arrived to serve lunch.

Roosevelt "wants to team up with you," Rosenman told Willkie, "and he thinks the right time to start is immediately after this election . . . whether he wins or loses in November." Willkie agreed, lamenting that "both parties are hybrids." He was enthusiastic about the prospect of fighting with, rather than against, Roosevelt. "You tell the president that I'm ready to devote almost full time to this," Willkie said. "A sound, liberal government in the United States is absolutely essential to continued cooperation with the other nations of the world."[47]

Later in July, Roosevelt wrote to Willkie, offering to meet with him "here in Washington or, if you prefer, at Hyde Park—wholly off the record or otherwise, just as you think best." But then Roosevelt committed a faux pas. Though he was aware that his contact with Willkie had to remain secret, he nevertheless mentioned to someone—probably to a visitor or a dinner guest—that he had written to Willkie, and that person leaked the news to the press. The incident was intensely embarrassing for Willkie. "The interesting thing is how word of my note to you got out to the Press," Roosevelt disingenuously apologized to Willkie in August. "I am awfully sorry that there was any leak on a silly thing like this."[48]

Apology accepted. Willkie was still bravely open to meeting with the president. He drafted a letter to Roosevelt, saying that he remained "intensely interested" in the project of party realignment. "I am fearful, however, that any talk between us before the campaign is over might well be the subject of misinterpretation. And I do not believe, however much you and I might wish or plan otherwise, that we could possibly have such a talk without the fact becoming known. Therefore, if it is agreeable with you, I would prefer postponement of any such talk until after the November election."[49]

In early October 1944, while the presidential campaign was in full swing, Willkie published an article in *Collier's* entitled "Citizens of Negro Blood" in which he revealed a key aspect of his thinking about party realignment. Deeply disappointed by both parties' weak platform positions on the subject of the rights of black Americans, Willkie charged that Republicans as well as Democrats were "overanxious" to win the approval of their conservative voters. Neither party was willing to mobilize its liberal supporters and give leadership to the millions of Americans who believed in equality for all. The only logical solution to the problem of such "cowardice," he implied, was political realignment. He did not, of course, mention to his *Collier's* readers that he and the president expected to have a serious discussion about just such realignment immediately after the election.[50]

But no talk between Roosevelt and Willkie ever took place. Willkie suffered a heart attack in a New York hospital on October 8, 1944, a day after his article in *Collier's* appeared. The fifty-two-year old lawyer, who had never held elective office, died as he had lived, a lone wolf, never having endorsed Thomas Dewey. Five months after his November re-election, on April 12, 1945, the sixty-three-year-old Roosevelt, too, would be dead. They never had the opportunity to discuss party realignment or make the transformational sea change to the American landscape that they both envisioned.

In politics, "timing is everything"—and in 1944 the timing was off, although neither Roosevelt nor Willkie could hardly have controlled the finality of death. But in 1938, FDR's usually superb sense of timing did fail him, for the moment was not ripe for an event as revolutionary as party realignment. Conservative Democrats, especially southerners, were still ardently loyal to their party. For them to abandon the Democratic Party, they would have needed a far more compelling and incendiary catalyst than the economic measures of the New Deal. That triggering issue, as Willkie had presciently discerned in the weeks before his death, would be race.

◄ 12 ►

From the Purge to Realignment

IN 1938, FRANKLIN ROOSEVELT'S Democratic coalition had become unworkable, and he realized that southern conservatives, New York liberals, and African-American autoworkers in Detroit could not continue indefinitely to cohabit the same political party. For his part, he knew in what direction he wanted the party to go: to the left—and to the completion of the New Deal. His hope was that Democrats would jettison their right wing while Republicans jettisoned their left so that the nation—and especially the South—could have two vital, responsible political parties.

If Roosevelt had really wanted to purge conservatives from the Democratic Party, though, all he would have had to do was take an unambiguous position on the question of race and support equal rights for blacks. That would have done the job, effectively sparking a mass exodus of southern conservatives. It would, however, also have pushed out many of the region's progressives and populists, a price FDR was not willing to pay. Democrats in the North and South had agreed on social welfare and agricultural assistance, but they were not about to find a consensus on civil rights. Men like Florida's Claude Pepper and Mississippi's Theodore Bilbo loyally supported the New Deal, but they were white supremacists, too. Filibustering an anti-lynching bill early in 1938, Bilbo warned that the measure would "open the floodgates of hell in the South."[1]

So instead, Roosevelt pirouetted around the issue of race, declining to threaten the status quo. In the absence of a strong stance on civil rights, southern conservatives had little reason to abandon the Democratic Party, their political home.

Even so, some prescient southerners recognized the signs of a future realignment. Josiah Bailey, Carter Glass, and others pointedly warned party chieftains not to challenge white supremacy. Bailey put Jim Farley on notice in 1938 that southerners would stay in the Party as long as it remained "the white man's party of the South." "We intend, and I think I speak for every Southern state, to keep the negroes out of our party," Bailey said in a speech that year to Young Democrats. "Should the Democratic Party fail to take this course, you may be assured that a white man's party would arise in the South."[2]

Roosevelt's tactics came straight from the fox's playbook. In 1934 and again in 1937, he refrained from pushing for—or even endorsing—anti-lynching bills. And he limited the reach of some New Deal programs in order to placate southern politicos. For example, neither the higher wages called for in 1933 by the National Recovery Administration nor the benefits guaranteed by the Social Security Act of 1935 applied to agricultural and domestic workers, many of whom were black.

Once, in the fall of 1938, the president strayed from his usual safe course by criticizing poll taxes, one of several methods used in the South to prevent blacks and poor whites from voting. Senator Pat Harrison of Mississippi quickly scolded him, and FDR just as quickly backtracked, explaining that he had expressed merely his own opinion. "At no time and in no manner," the chastened president wrote, "did I ever suggest federal legislation of any kind to deprive states of their rights directly or indirectly to impose the poll tax." In order to keep southern Democrats on board, Roosevelt had little choice but to appease them, praise them, and understand them. He was not unmindful, he told a meeting of southerners in 1940, "of the efforts which the southern people have made and are making toward the solution of their problems." The South, he said, should be proud of what it has been able to accomplish from its available means, but, he added, "we must find a way to increase its means." But Lyndon Johnson, who admired Roosevelt, nevertheless would express deep disappointment that he never submitted one civil rights bill in twelve years. "Roosevelt didn't have any Southern molasses compassion," Johnson said in 1969, adding that he "never faced up to the problem."[3]

But FDR believed that he was only being realistic. His goal was to help Americans, and he understood that not only would legislation like an anti-lynching bill fail to pass in Congress but that, under the circumstances, underprivileged blacks as well as poor whites would be better served by broader New Deal reforms, like raises in the minimum wage, limits on working hours, job creation, public works, and public housing. Indeed, the success of those measures made Roosevelt immensely popular in the black community. And so did his relatively rare but courageous acts, such as his 1936 declaration that there should be "no forgotten men and no forgotten races," his creation of a Civil Rights Section in the Department of Justice, his appointment of over a hundred blacks to administrative posts, his selection of a black judge, William Hastie, for the federal bench, and his signing in June 1941 of an executive order forbidding employment discrimination in defense industries and in government. The African-American weekly newspaper the *Chicago Defender* enthusiastically endorsed him for president in 1940, calling him "a great champion of the common people" who had helped "the Negro attain the full measure of citizenship."[4]

And yet, despite the failure of Roosevelt's purge and his cautious position on race, the tectonic plates of white supremacy and liberalism were ineluctably inching toward a grinding collision throughout the 1940s. He had expected party realignment in the South to be based on attitudes toward the New Deal, not on attitudes toward race. But that was not what happened. Race—later accompanied by other political, economic, and social issues, such as communism, Vietnam, law and order, taxes, and abortion—would take center stage and propel a migration of southern Democrats to the GOP. That realignment would start and stop and start again, continuing haltingly and erratically. But continue it did, as the two parties slowly redefined and reshaped themselves over the next seven decades.[5]

The first stage of the political transformation was the *dealignment* of parties—a period of transition in the 1940s, 1950s, 1960s, and 1970s during which voters' ties of loyalty to their parties loosened. Some switched parties, others joined the ranks of Independents, and still others fled to third parties. The second stage, in the 1980s and 1990s, was *realignment,* as the bases of the Democratic and Republican parties changed and as voters' loyalties to their new parties solidified.

As for Roosevelt's principal concern, the South, many Democrats, defending their citadel of white supremacy, would first flirt with a third party, the Dixiecrats, and then, in the 1960s, 1970s, and 1980s, proceed to swallow their distaste for the Republican label, join the GOP, and make it the majority party in the South. Franklin Roosevelt had wanted to oust southern conservatives from the Democratic Party. Could he have imagined anything as supremely ironic as the South turning the tables and ousting the Democratic Party?

One of the first steps in the long, fitful process of dealignment and realignment occurred in 1944. With a president and a Congress unwilling to take a strong stand on civil rights, the Supreme Court—now packed with FDR's appointees—did. In Texas as in some other southern states, blacks were barred from voting in Democratic primaries, with the party claiming that it was a "voluntary association" that could select its own members. And of course, in the one-party South, the only meaningful election was the primary; the decision in November merely ratified that of the primary. In the landmark case *Smith v. Allwright,* the Court outlawed "white only" primaries, ruling that a party was not a private organization and that a state could not nullify the right of citizens to participate in the choice of elected officials. The *Allwright* decision marked an epochal constitutional step forward for equality, but its effects were not immediate. In the 1946 Texas primaries, only seventy-five thousand African Americans cast ballots, out of more than five hundred thousand of voting age. Still, *Allwright* shook the fortress of white supremacy and opened the Democratic Party in the South to change.[6]

At the National Democratic Convention in July 1944, Democrats responded—by evading the issue of racial discrimination. While the party platform called for a constitutional amendment guaranteeing equal rights for women, black Americans were offered only platitudes. "We believe that racial and religious minorities," the platform blandly stated, "have the right to live, develop and vote equally with all citizens and share the rights that are guaranteed by our Constitution." The platform called for no measures to realize those ideals. Its plank on race was nothing more than a "splinter," scoffed an impatient Walter White, secretary of the National Association for the Advancement of Colored People (NAACP).[7]

The Republican platform that year had ventured much further—denouncing poll taxes, opposing lynching, supporting a permanent fair employment practices commission, and promising to investigate segregation in the armed services. Unlike the Democrats, Republicans had little to lose in the South by making strong appeals for African American votes. White southerners, after all, still resented the GOP as the party of Lincoln and the emancipationist northern armies of the Civil War. And the support of black voters in urban centers in the North would surely help Republican tickets. Earl Warren, California's Republican governor and the nation's future chief justice, emphasized that "the platform of this convention will be one on which all of us can stand together—not divided by race or creed."[8]

If the Democratic platform committee chose to play it safe in the election year of 1944, so did the president—but not the vice president.

"There must be no inferior races," Henry Wallace declared at the convention. "The poll tax must go. Equal educational opportunities must come."[9] Exit Wallace. In truth, Roosevelt had decided even before the convention to dump Wallace, who had become anathema to a wide swath of Democratic leaders. Far more acceptable was the moderate senator from Missouri, Harry Truman, who got the vice presidential nod instead. In that election, FDR won 432 electoral votes to New York governor Thomas Dewey's 99. He held onto the entire South, but it would be the last time a Democrat would perform such a feat.

Less than three months after his fourth inauguration as president, FDR was dead of a cerebral hemorrhage. "I have a terrific headache," he said as he posed for a portrait at his Warm Springs retreat, the place that had always freed him from the burdens of state. Expressions of disbelief echoed in the halls of Congress. "I am too shocked to talk," said the Senate majority leader, Alben Barkley. "It is a world tragedy," grieved the president's friend James Byrnes of South Carolina.[10]

Harry Truman now was president. "He is friendly to the South [and] respects its traditions," said the speaker of the Mississippi House of Representatives three days after Truman took the oath of office in April 1945. "He sounds practically like a Virginian," the *Richmond Times-Dispatch* reassured its readers. But a surprise awaited them, for on race and civil rights, Truman would go further than any Democratic president before him—and further, too, in unsettling the political landscape. His progressive stance on civil rights stemmed from his own convictions about equal rights, equal opportunity, and fair play. But he was also responding to outside pressures. The Cold War rivalry with the Soviet Union made a segregated society untenable in a nation presenting itself as the "leader of the free world"; New Deal liberals challenged Truman, a border-state Democrat, to prove his liberal credentials; groups like the "Committee Against Jim Crow in Military Service and Training" threatened the administration with a campaign of civil disobedience; and the NAACP petitioned the United Nations to persuade the United States "to be just to its people."[11]

In 1946, Truman created a Committee on Civil Rights that would return with a daring program to advance racial equality. "We cannot wait another decade or another generation," he declared in a June 1947 address to the NAACP. "We can no longer afford the luxury of a leisurely attack upon prejudice and discrimination." In February 1948, the president delivered to Congress a bold plan, drawn from his Committee's recommendations, that would provide federal protection against lynching, protect the right to vote, bar discrimination in interstate transportation, and establish a fair employment practices commission.[12]

As Truman began to chart a liberal path on race for the nation, his proposals were too tame and halfhearted for some and too radical for others. On the left, Henry Wallace challenged him by creating a third party. "There is no real difference between the Democratic and Republican parties," Wallace explained, adding: "Jim Crow is a full-fledged member of *both* old parties."[13]

The more serious threat came, though, from southern Democrats. In the House of Representatives, seventy-four southerners signed a manifesto early in 1948 warning Democrats not to put any of Truman's civil rights proposals into the party platform. A Louisiana congressman asserted that Truman, "the chieftain of the National Democratic Party," had declared war against "the traditions and Caucasianism of the South." For months, southern senators filibustered the president's civil rights legislation, ultimately killing it. Letters of protest from the South poured into the White House. "Your recent stand and utterances on the Negro question," wrote one North Carolinian to Truman, "will cost you hundreds of thousands of white votes." "You won't be elected dogcatcher in 1948," predicted a Florida minister. Mississippi's governor, Fielding Wright, put the party on notice, warning it not to accept legislation "aimed to wreck the South and our institutions." It would be painful to abandon his party, Wright conceded, "but vital principles and eternal truths transcend party lines."[14]

While Wright contemplated leaving the Democratic Party, he invited blacks to contemplate leaving Mississippi. "There will continue to be segregation in Mississippi," the governor decreed. "If any of you have become so deluded as to want to enter our hotels and cafes, enjoy so-cial equality with the whites, then kindness and true sympathy require me to advise you to make your home in some state other than Missis-sippi." South Carolina's governor, Strom Thurmond, followed suit. The forty-six-year-old Thurmond, a World War II veteran who had led para-troopers in the invasion of Normandy, had been a relatively liberal gov-ernor, even on matters of race, but in 1948 he tailored his appeal to the South's white supremacists. "All the laws of Washington, and all the bayonets of the Army," he declared, "cannot force the negroes into [white southerners'] homes, their schools, their churches and their places of recreation and amusement." In a state that outlawed miscege-nation and brutally enforced segregation, the fact that twenty-three years earlier Thurmond had fathered a daughter with his family's black maid, had supported her financially, and had met with her secretly while governor did nothing to soften his message of intolerance.[15]

For his part, Truman sought to avoid a confrontation with the South. At the 1948 Democratic National Convention, he desired no more than a brief and vague paragraph on civil rights in the party platform. While even that was too much for some southerners to swallow, northern lib-erals pressed for more. Decrying the nation's failure to fulfill the prom-ise of equality of the Declaration of Independence, Minneapolis's fiery mayor, the thirty-seven-year-old Hubert Humphrey, urged Democrats to "get out of the shadow of states' rights and walk forthrightly into the bright sunlight of human rights." Ultimately the convention's plat-form, stronger than what the president had originally sought, commit-ted the party to basic human and political rights for racial and religious minorities. It did not, however, attack or even mention segregation.

Even so, the plank deeply embittered delegates from the South. "If we are defeated," said one delegate from Tennessee as the platform came to a vote, "you are witnessing the dissolution of the Democratic Party in the South."[16]

For decades, the party had tried to paper over internal disagreements and breaches, but now the convention was openly polarized between North and South. "Things have gone so far at this heart-breaking convention," wrote columnist Joseph Alsop, "that one began to expect the Mississippi delegation to propose repeal of the anti-slavery amendments of the Constitution."[17]

After the South lost the platform fight, some of its delegates rebelled. First, all the Mississippi delegates and half the Alabama delegation stormed out of the convention hall, exiting—to jeers and boos—down the center aisle. Nine and a half southern delegations remained in the hall, but of those 265 delegates, only 13 supported Truman for the presidential nomination; the rest cast symbolic votes for Senator Richard Russell of Georgia, a New Deal Democrat who was liberal on many issues—from court reform to relief spending—but not on race.[18]

A few days after the convention, the political leaders of Mississippi and Alabama—along with a motley assortment of convention delegates, college students, and onlookers from eleven other states—gathered in Birmingham, Alabama. At an uproarious meeting, amid shouts, cheers, and rebel yells, they paraded on the floor beneath a portrait of General Robert E. Lee and then proceeded to form their own States' Rights Democratic Party.[19]

The leaders of the new party, which came to be known as the Dixiecrats, chose for their candidates the chief executives of the two states with the highest proportions of black citizens. They nominated Governor Strom Thurmond of South Carolina for president and Mississippi's Fielding Wright as his running mate. The Dixiecrat platform called for the defeat of both President Truman and his Republican opponent, Governor Thomas Dewey of New York. But above all, the States' Rights

Party—"states' rights" being the traditional code word for segregation and white supremacy—stood for the separation of the races and the "racial integrity of each race." Roosevelt might have viewed the Dixiecrat Party as his wish come true: conservative southern Democrats had performed a "self-purge" in abandoning their party. "I thought it was a very good thing for the Democratic Party," Roosevelt's close advisor Sam Rosenman later wrote, "for the Dixiecrats to leave the party."[20]

Still, most political leaders from southern states declined to jump on the Dixiecrat bandwagon. "My fellow Southerners, for a century and a half the Democratic Party has sheltered you," declared Florida's Claude Pepper, pleading for party unity. North Carolina's former governor, Cameron Morrison, also made it clear that he did not "want any of this revolting business." He and his southern cohort could handle Truman. If the president was elected in November, "we'll let our Congressmen and Senators beat him down when he needs beating." Democratic organizations in Florida, Texas, Arkansas, and a few other states also remained loyal to the party.[21]

Even though the Democratic National Convention had chosen Kentucky senator Alben Barkley as Truman's running mate in the hope of possibly salving some southern wounds, Truman was not optimistic about his chances of carrying the South—not surprising, since a week after the Dixiecrats' convention he signed executive orders desegregating the federal workforce and the armed services. During the fall campaign, he made only two southern stops—in Miami and Raleigh, where he urged audiences to use "reason and debate" and cautioned them against "walking out in a huff." Reluctant to deepen the split within the party, he mostly avoided talk about civil rights. Late in October, the *New York Times* noted that ever since the national convention that past summer the issue of racial equality had "lain in limbo" in the Truman campaign. Only a week before the election did the president finally venture into civil rights territory with a rally in Harlem.[22]

In an election fought more on foreign policy than on other issues, Truman won a stunning and substantial victory—303 electoral votes to 189 for Dewey. The Democrats had managed to hold together the strained New Deal coalition, with Progressive Party candidate Wallace winning only 1,157,328 votes nationwide. Truman's support for civil rights helped him with African-American voters in California, Ohio, and Illinois, three states essential to his victory, given his low standing in the South. Indeed, the Dixiecrats captured, by impressive margins, Mississippi, Alabama, Louisiana, and South Carolina—the states that were among the first to secede at the outset of the Civil War. On the ballots in those states, Thurmond had maneuvered to have his ticket declared the "official" Democratic Party ticket, while he lost in the states in which he ran as a third-party candidate. Even so, by voting for Thurmond, a majority of voters in those four states were signaling that, at least for the right candidate, they were willing to turn away from the regular Democratic Party.

The Dixiecrat revolt marked the beginning of the breakup of Roosevelt's coalition, the weakening of southern voters' bonds to the Democratic Party, and the slow unraveling of the solid South. For the time being, though, the South still remained solid: virtually all of its representatives and senators were Democrats. And if some voters began to identify as Independents, they were not ready to call themselves Republicans. The GOP in the South, remarked political scientist V. O. Key in his 1949 book *Southern Politics,* still resembled an "esoteric cult on the order of a lodge" more than a political party.[23] Yet Key underscored that the essential ingredients in any dynamic, open democracy were a vigorous two-party system and a citizenry engaged in meaningful debate about two different, competing visions of the public good. Both Truman's rejection of racial discrimination and the Dixiecrat rebellion can be credited with having sparked the movement toward that dynamic two-party South.

But Democratic Party leaders in the 1950s were not convinced that a two-party South was in their interest. Whereas Roosevelt had challenged conservatives to leave the Democratic Party and join the GOP—and whereas Harry Truman had boasted after the 1948 election, "I don't want the Dixiecrat vote. We won without New York and without the Solid South, and I am proud of that"—Democrats in the 1950s fought to hold onto southern conservatives, even if that meant dodging once again the issue of race and civil rights. At the very end of the fourteen-page Democratic Party platform of 1952 lay a brief, evasive mention of civil rights—as if an afterthought. According to the platform, racial discrimination was mostly a problem for states and local governments to resolve, though the platform also recognized a role for federal legislation. The Democratic Party found itself in the anomalous position, historian Richard Hofstadter had remarked a few years earlier, of being a party of liberalism "whose achievements are subject to veto by a reactionary faction."[24]

For its presidential nominee, the 1952 Convention turned to a compromise candidate, Adlai Stevenson, the witty, eloquent, and intellectually sophisticated governor of Illinois, a graduate of Choate and Princeton, who captivated liberals and intellectuals with quotations from Shakespeare and rarefied pontifications about "mass mediocrity."[25]

In a move to conciliate the South and bring the Dixiecrats back to the party, convention delegates chose as his running mate Alabama's fifty-two-year-old senator, John Sparkman, who had helped draft the compromise plank on minority rights. Despite his liberal record on most domestic issues, Sparkman had militantly refused to support Truman in 1948. "I greatly deplore his so-called civil rights program," he had said at the time, calling it "a colossal political blunder." And Sparkman had helped drum up support for the Dixiecrats. The director of the

National Negro Council labeled the Stevenson-Sparkman ticket "a Democratic-Dixiecrat coalition."[26] Indeed, in 1964 and 1965 Sparkman would vote against civil rights and voting rights bills.

Describing his campaign strategy, Stevenson confided to the governor of Virginia, John Battle, that he would not adopt a "sledge hammer approach" to "the civil rights business." Indeed, he desperately wanted to distance himself from Truman and his civil rights record, for "Trumanism" had become almost a curse word in the South. "I'm a Virginia Democrat, a true Democrat. I am not a Truman Democrat," declared Senator Byrd, evoking the venomous southern disapproval of the former president.[27]

Judging that it was in his and the Democrats' interest to recapture the South, Stevenson labored to woo back southern voters, often reminding them of his family's southern roots. "I have so many kinfolk," he told one gathering in Florida, "they are my secret weapon." One of those secret weapons, a distant cousin, was Georgia's white supremacist senator Richard Russell. Speaking in Richmond, the capital of the Confederacy, Stevenson shunned talk about civil rights, reducing racial discrimination and segregation to a mere footnote. He included "anti-Negroism" in a list of the various prejudices he deplored—anti-Semitism, antisouthernism, and self-righteousness—and he defended his Virginia hosts against "contemptible" northern charges that the South was a prison for blacks. Democrats in Richmond cheered him, rebel yells rang out, and the band played Dixie.[28]

Republicans, too, were now splitting on the issue of race. In the divisions among Democrats, they saw a chance to make inroads among southern whites for the first time in their history. Yet they also wanted the votes of blacks in the North. It was a delicate, if not impossible, high-wire act. Republican moderates insisted on federal laws to end discrimination and segregation, but the party's presidential candidate, General Dwight Eisenhower, opposed federal action.[29] Drawing cheers from southern crowds, Ike hammered northern Democrats for "taking the South for granted."[30]

Campaigning south of the Mason-Dixon Line, the general spoke in broad terms about equality for "all Americans." Though he exhorted southern audiences to protect the rights of their neighbors, "whatever the color of their skin," he declined to say just how, in the absence of federal laws, equality could be brought about. "I do not believe that we can cure all the evils in men's hearts by law," he said, suggesting that, with the right kind of leadership, the states would naturally do the right thing. But then up North, campaigning in Chicago, he announced that he would appoint a black man to his cabinet, if he could find one of "merit." "Looks like he's got both eyes shifted to Harlem, now, doesn't it?" growled Georgia's governor, Herman Talmadge, a Democrat who, just days earlier in Atlanta, had amiably introduced Eisenhower as a "friend of the South."[31]

Some northern blacks and southern whites were unsure which direction to take in the election of 1952. Black Democratic leaders like New York congressman Adam Clayton Powell and NAACP leader Walter White swallowed hard and supported Stevenson, despite the unappealing presence of Sparkman on the ticket. In the South, however, it was a different story. While a few former Dixiecrats like Fielding Wright stuck with Stevenson, other influential Democrats exited toward the right and the GOP: FDR's old ally, James Byrnes, now governor of South Carolina, who had been the mastermind behind Roosevelt's nomination for a third term in 1940; Louisiana's governor Robert Kennon; Virginia senator Harry Byrd; and Governor Allan Shivers of Texas, along with the entire Texas Democratic Party.[32]

In the November election, Eisenhower swept the nation—442 electoral votes to 89 for Stevenson. The Democrats carried only nine states; in addition to recapturing the four Dixiecrat states of 1948, they held onto Arkansas, Georgia, North Carolina, Kentucky, and West Virginia. But that was all. Stevenson failed to carry even his home state of Illinois. Even worse news for Democrats was that Eisenhower won three stunning southern prizes: the critical states of Virginia, Florida, and even Texas, the sixth largest state in the country with twenty-four

electoral votes. It was only the second time since Reconstruction—
and the first since 1928—that a Republican carried any of those three
states.

Although the South's representatives and senators still remained almost entirely Democratic, Ike's victory, as the *New York Times* editorialized, had given the South "a lever to start building a Southern Republican
party, if they really want to establish one." Interestingly, almost 40 percent of the districts carried by Truman in 1948 went for Eisenhower in
1952, whereas most of the southern districts that had voted for Thurmond in 1948 returned to the regular Democratic Party in 1952, swayed
by Stevenson's subtle appeal for southern votes or simply returning to
their ancestral political home. Thus, although Thurmond's third-party
bid in 1948 cannot receive full credit for sparking the shift in the South
to the GOP, a migration to the GOP had nevertheless begun.[33]

Two weeks after the election, at their semiannual dinner, Gridiron
Club members paraded around on the stage waving Confederate flags.
To the tune of "Dixie," they sang: "Away down South in the land of cotton / Harry Truman's done forgotten." In one skit, set on a remote
Pacific isle, Captain Adlai Bly Stevenson and other survivors of the
"Mutiny on the Bounty" revived a 1926 tune to lament their fate, that
the "Southland gave birth to the blues!" In another spoof, Rip Van GOP
awakened from his long slumber, bewildered by the victory celebration
taking place around him. The Republicans were back in business.[34]

What lessons might bruised Democrats have drawn from their defeat in 1952? By studying the electoral map and poll results, they might
have seen that their appeal for southern votes had backfired in the rest
of the country, that many southerners remained *in* but not really *of* the
Democratic Party, and that the party's future resided in its liberal
wing.[35] And especially as the civil rights movement began to gain traction nationwide in the 1950s, Democratic leaders might also have realized that the defection of many white southerners was inevitable, that
it would entail party realignment, and that they might as well try to

steer and adjust to that realignment for their own benefit. And if they gave up on their self-defeating strategy of appealing to southern conservatives—especially since Truman had won in 1948 without Louisiana, Alabama, Mississippi, and South Carolina—they could devote themselves instead to building up party strength in other regions of the country. In the South itself, they could work at nurturing a cadre of talented liberal and moderate politicians in the mold of Tennessee's senators Albert Gore, Sr., and Estes Kefauver and Texas's Ralph Yarborough and Lyndon Johnson.

But there was still no Democratic will to relinquish the South. Its senators and representatives were almost entirely Democratic; the Speaker of the House until 1961 would be Sam Rayburn of Texas, while another Texan, Lyndon Johnson, would serve as the Senate majority leader. In the spring of 1953, the head of the national party, a Chicago lawyer named Stephen Mitchell, set off on a tour of the southern states, pleading for party unity and extending an olive branch to the conservative dissidents who had fled to the GOP in 1952. He wanted peace, not southern flight and realignment.[36]

As president, Eisenhower improved the Republican standing in the South. "There is no longer a Solid South," he declared to a GOP rally in Kentucky. "The Republican Party is in the South to stay!" An astute party leader who understood the value of a forty-eight-state strategy, he insisted that if Republicans worked long and hard, "there can be no such thing as a hopeless state."[37]

And then the bombshell of *Brown v. Board of Education* exploded in 1954.

Presided over by Chief Justice Earl Warren, an Eisenhower appointee, a unanimous Supreme Court extended to hundreds of thousands of black school children the right to equal education in integrated schools. Morally, the *Brown* decision struck a blow for the American ideal of equality; ideologically, it marked the beginning of an era of civil rights legislation; psychologically and sociologically, it would reshape the South's attitudes and behavior; and politically it would spur the exodus of southerners from the Democratic Party.

In the aftermath of *Brown,* neither party took a firm stand on civil rights. Eisenhower evaded the issue when he could. In desegregation cases in South Carolina and Texas in 1956, he sided with those states' segregationist governors who resisted *Brown*'s mandates. And in 1957 he would reluctantly send federal troops to enforce a court order to integrate schools in Little Rock, Arkansas. "I do not believe," he wrote, "that prejudice . . . will succumb to compulsion."[38]

The Democrats hardly showed more courage or spoke with greater clarity. Campaigning again for the nomination for the presidency in early 1956, Stevenson announced his preference for an unhurried, "gradualist" approach to racial equality. Speaking in Oregon in February 1956, he claimed that the burning question of civil rights was too hot to handle and that it was "essential" to keep the subject out of the presidential campaign. It was a disservice to the country, he said, to "exploit for political ends the tensions that have followed in the wake of the Supreme Court decision." When he did venture into civil rights territory, he disappointed many of his liberal listeners by opposing cuts in federal funding for segregated schools.[39]

Nor was Stevenson alone in tilting southward. Hoping to be chosen the vice presidential nominee, Hubert Humphrey, who had led the successful floor fight for a strong civil rights plank at the 1948 convention, now moved to the center and urged a plank acceptable to the South. The "erstwhile liberal" Humphrey, complained the *Chicago Defender,* was playing the same old "shell game." True, but like Stevenson, he was maneuvering for the party's nomination as well as for a winning strategy for November. Both men were betting on the center and the South. The convention, however, went with another southerner for the second place on the ticket, Tennessee's Senator Estes Kefauver.[40]

As the party's presidential candidate, Stevenson told an interviewer that to achieve his paramount goals for the nation—an improved school system, an expansion of medical and welfare services, and a rise in living standards for all Americans—"no new ground, political or philosophical, has to be broken to accomplish these things." By underlining that "we don't need reforms or groping experiments," he distanced himself from the nascent civil rights revolution. Indeed, he made himself so unobjectionable to the white South that the two Dixiecrat leaders, Fielding Wright and Strom Thurmond, both voiced support for him. Senator Walter George, too, stayed on board. Any party bolt by southerners, George warned, would be "unwise and suicidal." The South's political strength, these southerners realized, resided in its unity. "If the South does not present a solid front," said Georgia Senator Richard Russell, it would be "engulfed in the evil consequences" of school desegregation.[41]

But not all Democrats approved of a southern strategy for their party. Disgusted, Roosevelt's close advisor Sam Rosenman commented that the Illinois candidate possessed "no trace" of the New Deal spirit. And Harry Truman grumbled: "Stevenson won't carry any more states than he did four years ago." He was right. Stevenson suffered an even more damaging defeat in 1956. Tagged as the candidate of the South, he carried six southern states and Missouri—and nothing else. Republican efforts to forge a new majority had paid off—in the South as well as in the urban North. Not only did Eisenhower capture five southern states, he won a greater percentage of the votes of African Americans in all sections of the country than he had in 1952. "Now both the Democrats and the Republicans know they can't ignore us if they want our votes," said one black man in 1956 to a pollster. Paradoxically, southern whites and African Americans were registering protest votes against the Democratic Party as well as against each other by voting for the same man, Dwight Eisenhower.[42]

Even so, southern voters, satisfied that the views of their congressional Democrats were more conservative than those of the national party's chieftains, continued to elect Democratic senators and representatives to Congress. In 1957, only two Republicans would be sent to the new Senate from the South and just six to the House. But in presidential elections, those voters felt less loyalty to the national party.

But how much longer would the national party remain loyal to them? Just as Eisenhower had trouble governing with congressional Republicans who were to the right of him, a Democratic president would have faced the same thorny problem with his own right-leaning congressional party. Given that the 1956 election gave control of both chambers of Congress to the Democrats, if Stevenson *had* won that election, he would have confronted the almost impossible challenge of getting even mildly progressive legislation past a bloc of conservative Democrats, led by powerful southerners inflamed over segregation and civil rights.[43]

Thus, while some Democrats continued to favor a compromise with the South on civil rights, others would push, as had FDR, for party realignment, convinced that the Democratic Party had to unite behind liberal principles. "No one likes to have a split," said the Oregon party chair, "but if we have to lose somebody, I'd rather lose the South." The chair of the Connecticut party also favored a strong stand on civil rights. "What the South does," he said dismissively, "is their business."[44]

The outcome of the argument was ambiguous. In 1960, the liberals in the Democratic Party managed to secure an earnest, wide-ranging section on civil rights in the party platform. It promised to end discrimination in voting, schools, courtrooms, jobs, and housing and at lunch counters. But for its presidential candidate, the convention chose Senator John F. Kennedy of Massachusetts, who had hardly shown a profile in courage on the issue of civil rights. To the outrage of liberals and activists, Kennedy had favored burying in the Judiciary Committee the 1957 civil rights legislation, which had contained provisions to enforce school desegregation. So delighted was Mississippi senator James

Eastland that he promptly announced his support for Kennedy for president. Three years later, Kennedy joined other Democrats in voting for the desegregation part of a civil rights bill, possibly because it had little chance of passing. His early stand on civil rights, his discerning aide Theodore Sorensen later commented, was "shaped primarily by political expediency instead of basic human principles."[45]

For his vice presidential running mate, Kennedy selected Lyndon B. Johnson of Texas. It was a shrewd move designed to keep Texas in the party fold and perhaps hold onto the broader South, though a Mississippi newspaper called Johnson a "traitor" and a Florida one branded him a "Southern Benedict Arnold" after he tried to push civil rights legislation through the Senate in 1960.[46]

In 1960, to more southerners, it was becoming thinkable to leave the political party of their ancestors. Southern Democrats would find it much more "congenial" to become Republicans, wrote the editor of the *Richmond Times-Dispatch,* Virginius Dabney, in the fall of 1960, "if they put out of their minds the fact that to their grandfathers the Democratic Party was only slightly less sacrosanct than the Army of Northern Virginia." But Dabney's invitation to Democrats to leave their party was premature, for the Republican presidential candidate in 1960, Richard Nixon, had repeatedly spoken up for the rights of racial minorities and praised the Warren Court. Nixon, moreover, had first offered the vice presidency to New York governor Nelson Rockefeller, a left-winger by southern standards, and then settled on another eastern moderate, Henry Cabot Lodge. Was there really a meaningful choice for southerners between the two parties?[47]

In the 1960 election, the South once again split three ways. A third-party candidate, Harry Byrd of Virginia, carried Mississippi and Alabama; Nixon won in Florida, Tennessee, and Virginia. And Kennedy and Johnson held on to Arkansas, Georgia, Louisiana, North and South Carolina, and Texas—though their margins of victory in Texas and South Carolina were disturbingly small. Senator James Eastland and Texas's former governor Allan Shivers believed that without Johnson on the ticket, Kennedy would not have won a single southern state.[48]

As president, Kennedy was ambivalent about pushing hard for civil rights legislation, suspecting that it would not pass and fearing that it would alienate the South. But after years of bus boycotts, church bombings, showdowns over integration at southern universities, and lunch-counter sit-ins, the nation's moral conscience was brutally awakened by a confrontation in April 1963 in Birmingham, Alabama. A peaceful demonstration against segregation, led by Martin Luther King, Jr., and members of his Southern Christian Leadership Conference, was violently stopped by the city's commissioner of public safety, Eugene "Bull" Connor, and his police dogs and fire hoses.

After weeks of hesitation, the president finally came to grips with the crisis and decided to speak to the nation. "Are we to say to the world," he asked on June 11, 1963, "that this is a land of the free except for the Negroes; that we have no second-class citizens except Negroes?"[49] A week later he called on Congress to pass measures to integrate schools and ban segregation in public facilities—proposals that predictably ran headlong into a wall of congressional delay and deadlock, mobilized by the updated version of the same old coalition of Republicans and conservative southern Democrats.

Within six months, JFK was dead. Now President Lyndon B. Johnson declared that he would act. "We have talked long enough in this country about equal rights," he told Congress five days after the assassination in Dallas. "It is time now to write the next chapter, and to write it in the books of law."[50]

"I think we just delivered the South to the Republican party for a long time," LBJ conceded in July 1964, after putting his signature on the Civil Rights Act. The bill had finally reached the president's desk, after months of filibusters by southern senators that took up more than six thousand pages of the *Congressional Record*. It was ironic that the Texan Johnson—the first southern president since 1865, when another Johnson from Tennessee, also brought to the highest office by the assassination of his predecessor, occupied the White House only to work against equal rights—would finally spur the mass exodus of conservative southerners from the Democratic Party. But it was also as a southerner that he had acted on civil rights, seeking to heal the wounds left by the Civil War, end the isolation of the South, and help make the nation, as he declared to Congress in November 1963, "a united people with a united purpose."[51]

The 1964 bill outlawed segregation in public accommodations and gave the attorney general authority to initiate suits to desegregate schools and other public facilities. It barred discrimination in employment on the basis of race, color, religion, sex, or national origin. While only six Republicans voted against the Civil Rights Act in the Senate, twenty-one Democrats opposed it, all of them from the South.

Now the contest between the two parties heated up, as the ideological battles lines between them hardened. For while the Democratic Party shifted to the left in 1964, the GOP moved sharply to the right—with a coup by the party's conservative wing. After a brutal primary campaign for the presidential nomination, moderate northeastern liberals were all defeated by Senator Barry Goldwater of Arizona. The author of the 1960 book *The Conscience of a Conservative,* Goldwater led a new, aggressive, and growing conservative movement. Impatient with Eisenhower's brand of moderate Republicanism, Goldwater rejected the whole New Deal liberal order along with any Republicans who compromised with it. The "Goldwaterites" were anti–big government, anti-taxation, anti–Social Security, anti-union, anti–foreign aid, anti–disarmament, and anti–federal aid to education. In the name of states' rights, they were also anti–civil rights. "The federal Constitution does not require the States to maintain racially mixed schools," Goldwater had written in *The Conscience of a Conservative,* in which he also questioned the Supreme Court's reasoning in *Brown v. Board of Education.* The problem of race relations, he wrote, "is best handled by the people directly concerned."[52]

In June 1964, Goldwater was one of the six Republican senators who voted against the Civil Rights Act. Though he claimed to be opposed to discrimination and segregation, he assailed the bill's ban on discrimination in public accommodations and employment, asserting that there was no constitutional basis for such regulations and that the bill posed a "grave threat to the essence of our basic system of government." The following month, at the Republican National Convention in San Francisco, the Goldwater steamroller turned back the demands of party moderates for a robust plank on civil rights, instead squeezing that burning issue into a section entitled "Faith in the Individual." Though the platform supported the implementation of the Civil Rights Act of 1964, it stated that the elimination of discrimination was, at bottom, "a matter of heart, conscience, and education." The platform stood for freedom and individual responsibility, rejecting what it claimed was the Democrats' "subservience to central power" in the name of "benevolence."[53]

Thus began the Republicans' "southern strategy." "We're not going to get the Negro vote as a bloc in 1964 and 1968," Goldwater had predicted in 1961, "so we ought to go hunting where the ducks are." The "ducks" were southern voters and politicians—like South Carolina's Strom Thurmond. After voting against the 1964 Civil Rights Act, Thurmond announced that he was again abandoning the Democratic Party, this time for Goldwater and the GOP. "The party of our fathers is dead," he sighed. Having realigned himself, Thurmond was eager to realign the two parties and suggested that liberal Republican senators like Jacob Javits of New York and Clifford Case of New Jersey "move over" to the Democrats so that the GOP could become, in his words, "the true, great conservative party."[54]

Though foreseen by FDR, a marriage of Republicans and segregationists like Thurmond had once seemed improbable. "It is doubtful," historian Richard Hofstadter had written in 1949, "that either liberals or conservatives in the Republican party would welcome into the fold an element that would forfeit the hope of recovering so many northern Negro votes." But in 1964, the Republican Party did exactly that—and continued its advance on the South.[55]

Helping Goldwater were two men. One was Alabama's Democratic governor George Wallace, a fierce, demagogic defender of segregation. Running in the Democratic primaries for president against Johnson in 1964, Wallace's highlighting of the racial issue as well as his attacks on invasive liberal government, "permissive" judges, and welfare recipients resonated not only with southern conservatives but also with middle- and working-class Americans in the North. His tactic of linking his racist message with other antigovernment and class resentments contributed to the reshaping of the political landscape. While refusing to support Johnson and declining to endorse Goldwater, Wallace boasted that Republican leaders got his message to "conservatize" their principles.[56]

Goldwater's other helper and ally was a Hollywood actor, former Democrat, and former General Electric spokesman, Ronald Reagan. A few days before the November 1964 election, in a nationally televised speech entitled "A Time for Choosing," Reagan injected a thrilling dose of adrenalin into the conservative movement. Borrowing words from FDR, he reminded Americans that they had a "rendezvous with destiny" and proceeded to ridicule the "schemes of the do-gooders," denounce the "immorality and discrimination of the progressive tax," scorn liberals who asked Americans to "trade our freedom for the soup kitchen of the welfare state," and heap praise on "individual freedom consistent with law and order."[57]

For his part, Johnson, hoping to hold onto the South, campaigned as a southerner—but one who would not appeal to people's prejudice and who believed, as he told a New Orleans crowd, that prosperity and opportunity "must know no color line." Discarding his prepared text at that Louisiana rally, he told the story of an ailing southern senator who yearned to give one final progressive speech back home in which listeners would *not* hear the stock mantra of *"Nigra, Nigra, Nigra!"* Johnson was no enemy of the South, he underscored to southern audiences. "I know the burdens that the South has borne," he declared at a rally in Augusta that fall. "I know the ordeals that have tried the South through all these years. I want to see those burdens lifted off the South." Like Roosevelt and Truman before him, Johnson longed to end both the poverty and isolation of the South.[58]

Though Johnson won a stunning victory in 1964—garnering an astounding 486 electoral votes to Goldwater's 52—his remarkable courage on civil rights cost him in the South. Goldwater carried, in addition to his own state of Arizona, Mississippi, Alabama, South Carolina, Louisiana, and Georgia. He had succeeded in reaching a new generation of young, socially conservative voters with no ties to the New Deal or to FDR. Johnson held the rest of the South and even won back Virginia, Florida, and Tennessee, states that had gone Republican in 1960. But some of his majorities—unlike Goldwater's—were disturbingly small. As LBJ had foreseen, a backlash against his championing of civil rights was shattering southern bonds of loyalty to the Democratic Party.[59]

As southern conservatives began to find more comfortable political lodgings in the GOP, the Democratic Party became the decidedly liberal party that Roosevelt had so hopefully envisioned. A two-party South was finally emerging, offering an escape route not only for conservative Democrats but also for liberal ones, who would no longer need to equivocate on the issue of race.

In the next election in 1968, the GOP continued its quest for dominance in the southern states where Goldwater's "ducks" lived. Richard Nixon, the party's candidate, mastered the "southern strategy." He sought to appeal to the South while not offending the North. His approach? Nothing so foolhardy as to openly raise the specter of race. Instead he blended the old code words of "states' rights" and "limited government" with new ones that were soothing music to southern ears. He opposed the "forced busing" of children to achieve racial integration in public schools and advocated "strict construction" of the Constitution to rein in judges who would impose racial equality from the bench. Nixon proved skillful at harvesting the smoldering resentments of what he called "the silent majority" against liberal elites, noisy protesters, and "special interests" like the civil rights movement and antipoverty organizations.[60]

At the Republican Party's Miami convention in 1968, Nixon made a memorably artful speech. Without disavowing civil rights, he played to fears about a breakdown of "law and order"—another Nixon code word—in America's cities, the site of recent riots, protests, and rising crime rates, especially in black neighborhoods. His tactic was to emphasize the primacy of security from domestic upheaval. "Let those who have the responsibility to enforce our laws," he said, "be dedicated to the great principle of civil rights. *But* let them also recognize that the first civil right of every American is to be free from domestic violence."

Momentum was on the Republican side. A host of factors in 1968 spurred southern voters toward the GOP: fear of the consequences of the 1965 Voting Rights Act that guaranteed a greater political role for blacks; the appeal of Republican promises of smaller government with lower taxes and less spending; greater prosperity in the wake of industrial growth in the Sunbelt; the increasing migration of northern Republicans to the South; and the tripling of the number of native white southern voters who identified themselves as Independents (36 percent in 1968 compared to 12 percent in 1952).[61]

Another helpful factor for the future of the GOP was none other than Alabama's segregationist governor George Wallace, who ran for president in 1968 on the American Independent Party ticket. In addition to carrying the states of Alabama, Georgia, Louisiana, Mississippi, and Arkansas, Wallace made a good showing in other southern states and won about ten million votes nationwide. Especially in the South but elsewhere, too, Wallace's third party served as a useful way station for at least some disaffected Democrats, allowing them to break from their party without immediately turning to the GOP. But perhaps even more important for the future of realignment, he trumpeted the South as the prime guardian of the nation's values and virtues.[62]

Nixon captured the rest of the South, except for Texas, the only southern state that remained faithful to the Democrats and their candidate, Vice President Hubert Humphrey of Minnesota. For the first time, less than half of southern white men now identified as Democrats. Southerners' disaffection with their ancestral party had become a political reality, and, at least in future presidential elections, the GOP would be able count on the South as a key part of its base.[63]

While Republicans capitalized on their conservative message, the Democrats decided to stand up for progressive principles—with dubious results. After 1968, liberals achieved what southerners had long accused them of doing—they seized control of the party machinery in the name of a "new politics," cast out the old, and, in 1972, nominated for president one of their own, South Dakota senator George McGovern. But in only one state of the union would McGovern be victorious: Massachusetts. So successful was Nixon in cultivating his "silent majority" that he swept all of the South—the first Republican to do so—and received 79 percent of southern white ballots. "Who needs Manhattan," Nixon's political strategist Kevin Phillips observed, "when we can get the electoral votes of eleven southern states?"[64]

After the Democrats digested the extent of their candidate's defeat, it was time for them to regroup and rethink—and recover from that devastating repudiation at the polls. Would they continue to desouthernize the party or try to resouthernize it? Commenting on the 1972 election, in which he had won the Democratic primaries in Florida,

Michigan, and Maryland, George Wallace offered his opinion that from now on, the Democratic Party "is going to be controlled by people who feel like the people of Alabama feel."[65]

As "old" politicians reasserted themselves, they looked once again to the South for a comeback. Their nominee was a political outsider, former Georgia governor Jimmy Carter. Southerners had little doubt that this Southern Baptist and successful peanut farmer from the sleepy village of Plains was one of them. In the beginning of his 1975 autobiography *Why Not the Best?* Carter presented himself as a "Southerner and an American," mentioning "Southerner" first. Campaigning in the South, he strove to regain lost ground among whites. "Come January," he drawled, "we are going to have a President in the White House who doesn't speak with an accent!" Taking a cue from George Wallace, he criticized Washington's liberal elites and voiced pointed reservations about busing, abortion, and big government. Indeed, throwing his support to Carter was Wallace himself. In the rest of the nation, Americans saw in Carter a new kind of white southerner—a moderate and an idealist who could transcend the racial conflicts of the past. In the November election, that centrist appeal won him points in the South and was crucial to his narrow victory over incumbent Gerald Ford. Carter carried the entire South with the exception of Virginia.[66]

Was it true, as a headline in the *Washington Post* had announced, that the "Prodigal South" had returned to its traditional home in the Democratic Party? Not exactly. Carter received overwhelming support from southern blacks but finished behind Ford among white southerners.[67]

While Jimmy Carter was fashioning himself as a new kind of Democrat, Ronald Reagan was brilliantly presenting himself as a new kind of Republican—not an isolationist of the 1930s, not a country-club stuffed shirt defending the interests of big business, not a vitriolic McCarthyite, not a hard-edged ideologue like Goldwater, not a fellow traveler of white supremacists, but a sunny Californian. He spoke easily to the concerns of average Americans, put a genial face on conservatism, and expertly channeled the energy and the ideas of the conservative movement into the GOP.

A committed political activist and adept strategist, Reagan unified the disparate threads of conservatism. He possessed a winning talent, wrote James MacGregor Burns, for talking "order and stability to the traditionalists, individual liberty to the libertarians, anti-regulation to the free-marketers, and anti-elitism to the populists." Millions of Reagan followers, including disaffected blue-collar Democrats, poured into the GOP, pushing out eastern liberals and moderates. Under Reagan's leadership, the Republican Party was broadened, strengthened, and reshaped. And especially in the South, Reagan forged a wide base by combining states' rights, economic conservatism, and traditional Christian social values. While he avoided all overt talk about race, he appeared to condone southern racism by kicking off his campaign—and preaching about "restoring to state and local governments the powers that properly belong to them"—in the village of Philadelphia, Mississippi (population five thousand), where civil rights workers Andrew Goodman, James Cheney, and Michael Schwerner were killed in 1964.[68]

As Reagan vigorously campaigned around the country in the fall of 1980, Jimmy Carter could not escape from the problems of his presidency, ranging from runaway inflation to a botched rescue of American hostages in Iran. Many voters, moreover, had not forgotten the televised speech in July 1979 in which he presumptuously scolded Americans for their "self-indulgence," belaboring what he diagnosed as "growing doubt about the meaning of our own lives." A week before the election, appearing on CBS's *60 Minutes,* the president awarded himself a C for domestic policy and "maybe a B" for leadership. When voting returns were tallied, Reagan swept the country, including the South. The vote in the Electoral College was a lopsided 489 to 49. The support the South had given to Carter in 1976 proved to have been ephemeral: now the only southern state the president carried was his home state of Georgia.[69]

As president, Reagan infused the conservative principles of small government and rugged individualism with such a homey, reassuring tone that increases in economic inequality and racial discrimination during his presidency mattered little to his supporters. In the next election in 1984, although registered Democrats still far outnumbered Republicans in the South, many of them voted for Reagan, their ranks boosted by young white southerners who now identified as Republicans. On election night, the map of the nation was red all over: the president again carried the South as well as the rest of the nation, leaving only the blue islands of Minnesota and Washington, D.C., to his Democratic opponent, Minnesota senator Walter Mondale. One political scientist who studied the South remarked that Reagan proved to be more of a southern president than Carter or Lyndon Johnson ever were.[70]

Optimistic, forward-looking, unthreatening, cheerfully promising a new "morning in America," a trained master of body language and timing, Reagan acted the part of a "Roosevelt of the Right" who ultimately accomplished from the right what FDR could not achieve from the left: he secured the realignment of the two political parties and helped transform the South into a competitive political arena. In 1984, though Reagan captured the entire South, more than half of the senators from the eleven states of the Confederate South were still Democrats.[71]

While an invigorated GOP believed that it was on the way to becoming the nation's new majority party and eventually the dominant party in the South, leaders of the anemic Democratic Party appeared stuck—devoid of fresh ideas and an innovative agenda, still trying to win elections and govern on the spent intellectual and political capital of FDR's New Deal and LBJ's Great Society. And just as critical, the party was still fractured, as it had been since 1968. "New" and "old" brands of liberalism vied for control of the party: it was a contest between a left-leaning McGovernite vision of economic and social justice born in the protest movements of the 1960s and a more centrist, mainstream philosophy, favored by Humphrey and his followers, stressing economic growth and defense.[72]

Which wing would come to dominate the party? And could either wing recapture the White House without the South? As population shifted to the Sunbelt, the South had boosted its clout in the House of Representatives and increased its representation in the Electoral College—at the expense of the decaying industrial Northeast. Almost half of the 270 electoral votes needed to elect a president could come from the electoral votes of the eleven southern states. The South still offered, in the words of political scientists Earl Black and Merle Black, the "greatest regional prize in modern presidential politics."[73]

Preparing for the election of 1988, many Democratic leaders, hoping to counter the country's swing to the right after Reagan's eight-year run, sought to steer their party to the center—and give it a southern accent, too. First, they selected Atlanta as the site of their 1988 convention. "Democrats are telling the South we're back in competition for its support," remarked one politico.[74] Second, they hoped to tilt the party back to the center by scheduling a March "Super Tuesday" with sixteen state primaries, thirteen of which would take place in southern or border states. They expected southern voters to select a moderate Democrat—like Senator Al Gore of Tennessee or Richard Gephardt of Missouri. It was a reasonable calculation—except that it backfired. Gephardt and Gore split the centrist vote in the South, and the party nominated liberal governor Michael Dukakis of Massachusetts and Texas Senator Lloyd Bentsen as his running mate.

Though the Republican candidate, George H. W. Bush of Texas, lacked the extraordinary personal appeal of Ronald Reagan, he wisely stuck to Reagan's script, promising to be a faithful heir, and followed the advice of his shrewd campaign manager, South Carolinian Lee Atwater. The result: Bush carried not only the entire South but most of the rest of the country, too. The vote in the Electoral College was an unsymmetrical 426 for Bush to 111 for Dukakis. Even without the charismatic Reagan leading the ticket, the GOP now controlled the South, proving that party realignment in the southern states had clearly taken hold. But in aggressively reshaping itself, had the Republican Party tilted too far to the right—and too far to the South? The GOP, a southern mayor remarked after the election, risked becoming a "new kind of Dixiecrat party—a place of refuge for whites who resent the role blacks play in the Democratic Party."[75]

In 1992, two centrist southern Democrats, Arkansas governor Bill Clinton and his running mate Senator Al Gore of Tennessee, were determined to offset Republican gains and win back some southern states. Their strategy consisted of presenting a hazy picture of where they stood politically—alternating between middle-of-the-road positions geared to southern whites and old-fashioned appeals to blacks. The plan worked. A few southern states reopened their doors to Democrats: Clinton and Gore carried their own states as well as Louisiana, Georgia, and the border states of West Virginia and Kentucky. When Clinton ran successfully for reelection in 1996, he lost Georgia but added Florida to his list.[76]

Democrats rejoiced in having finally found a popular party leader with an appealing centrist message who could win two full terms in the White House—the first Democrat to do so in half a century, since Franklin Roosevelt. But the midterm elections of 1994, in which Democrats lost control of both the House and the Senate, as well as the negative fallout from Clinton's liaison with Monica Lewinsky, portended a short-lived Democratic revival. Indeed, in 2000 and 2004, the Democratic gains of 1992 and 1996 evaporated.

The presidential contest of 2000 found two southerners battling for the White House. Al Gore lost the election to the governor of Texas, George W. Bush, the first southern Republican candidate for president in American history. It was also the first time since 1888 that a president was elected with fewer popular votes than the loser—in this case, half a million fewer. Still, every southern and border state fell into Bush's column, including Gore and Clinton's states of Tennessee and Arkansas.[77]

In 2004, Americans reelected the president over Massachusetts senator John Kerry and his running mate Senator John Edwards of North Carolina. Though Bush won with the narrowest margin for an incumbent in American history, it was still a clear victory for him and legitimized his title to the White House after the flawed election of 2000.[78]

Conservatives hailed 2004 as a landmark election, the first time since 1952 that Republicans—without Supreme Court intervention—had won decisive control of the White House as well as both chambers of Congress. "Republican hegemony in America," exulted conservative columnist Fred Barnes, "is now expected to last for years, maybe decades."[79]

Perhaps the conservatives were right. Voters' concerns about moral values and national security and trends like population growth in red states, Republican gains in some blue states, and some Latinos moving to the right all appeared to favor the GOP. The electoral map of the 2004 election showed a vast, uninterrupted ocean of red with only three small islands of blue—in New England, on the Pacific Coast, and around the Great Lakes.[80]

Had geography become destiny? Had FDR's brand of realignment overreached its goal, taking his party too far to the left and making the South forevermore red? Had the GOP become the permanent majority party of the nation? While Democrats contemplated a grim future in the minority outback, Republicans celebrated. The Democrats' belief in "a massive, untapped reservoir of blue flowing beneath the surface," crowed one conservative expert in American politics in 2005, "may now be nearing its end."[81]

End of story? But what about the endless vicissitudes of events and leadership—and prognostications made with defective crystal balls? Historic changes lay ahead.

Epilogue

IN 2008, THE DEMOCRATIC CANDIDATE, Senator Barack Obama of Illinois, son of a black Kenyan father and a white Kansan mother, campaigning with a progressive message, won the White House. If Franklin Roosevelt could have revisited Planet Earth at the beginning of the twenty-first century's second decade, he would have been pleased to see that his goals of a responsible, liberal Democratic Party and a competitive, two-party South had been achieved. And he might have thanked Lyndon Johnson, Ronald Reagan, and Barack Obama for their contributions.

Even though Obama—unlike presidential candidates Stevenson, Kennedy, Johnson, Carter, Dukakis, Clinton, Gore, and Kerry—had neither a southern running mate nor southern roots, he carried three southern states: North Carolina and Virginia, which had not voted Democratic for president since 1976, and Florida, which had done so only once. A combination of forces in those states—including the migration of African Americans back to the South and the high turnout of black and young voters—turned those red states blue.[1]

But especially helpful to Obama in the South, as well as in much of the rest of the nation, was an energized electorate, disappointed and troubled after eight years of Republican rule under George W. Bush. Just one year after the 2004 election, only 37 percent of Americans approved of President Bush's job performance, and his numbers were even lower for his handling of the war in Iraq, federal spending, and immigration. In 2006, Democrats captured the House of Representatives, the Senate, and a majority of governorships and state legislatures from the Republican Party. And by the spring of 2008, George Bush's approval rating had sunk to 28 percent. It was a virtually impossible task for the Republican candidate, Arizona senator John McCain, to distance himself sufficiently from such a deeply unpopular administration and lead a faltering party to victory. Wake County, North Carolina, which includes Raleigh, the state capital, illustrated the sea change that had taken place over the previous fifteen years. Wake County gave Bill Clinton a narrow victory in 1992, turned against him in 1996, and voted for George W. Bush in 2000 and 2004. But in 2008 it went for Obama by a whopping margin of 16 percent.[2]

The Deep South, with its preponderance of working-class rural white voters, predictably stayed in the Republican column. Whereas FDR carried Alabama for the Democrats by 74 percent in 1936 and 1940, John McCain won the state by 21 percent. For that dramatic reversal, "there's no other explanation than race," remarked one political analyst. But, during the first decade of the twenty-first century, political scientists have found that inextricably intertwined with race are a host of other factors, including economics, a passion for low taxes, evangelical religion, pro-military sentiments, and anti-unionism. And as prosperity has increased in the South, some affluent whites have also shifted to the Republican Party.[3]

Curiously, although the Democratic Party was reduced to minority status in the South—and although it was especially uncompetitive there in presidential elections—in terms simply of partisan identification and *not* voting behavior, half of southern voters still considered themselves Democrats. A Gallup poll, tracking data from 2008, found that the nation's five most politically balanced states were Texas, Mississippi, South Carolina, Alabama, and Georgia. Running close behind—though leaning Democratic—were Louisiana, Tennessee, North Carolina, Florida,

Arkansas, and Virginia. In addition, despite GOP dominance in the presidential race in the South in 2008, four southern states that year installed Democratic legislatures, four elected Democrats to the Senate, and five chose Democratic governors.[4]

And contrary to the predictions of overly optimistic Republicans in 2004, in the 2008 election, Democrats indeed discovered new reservoirs of blue. They widened their base, as several of the once deep red western states changed their colors to blue. New Mexico and Nevada cast their electoral votes for Obama, as did Colorado, which had voted for a Democratic presidential candidate only twice in the ten presidential elections since 1964. The red state of Indiana, which had voted only once for a Democrat for president since 1964, also cast its electoral votes for Obama.

In the election of 2008, Democrats won not only the presidency but control of both chambers of Congress. A reason for celebration? Not exactly. That kind of one-party rule in Washington has proved fleeting—Democrats had it in 1993 and lost it two years later; Republicans had it in 2003 and lost it in 2007.

Still, if FDR could have witnessed the 2008 election, he would have had no reason to complain about ideologically incoherent parties. But might party polarization have gone too far?

While the Democratic Party, created by slave owners and inherited by white supremacists, has become the political party of liberals and moderates, of ethnic diversity and inclusion, the Republican Party, founded by abolitionists, has recently gone the opposite way and come to resemble a rightist party dominated by its conservative southern base. In 2010 it had few of the Yankee moderates, liberal "Rockefeller Republicans" and progressives in the tradition of Theodore Roosevelt and Wendell Willkie, who had balanced its conservative wing in the past. Indeed, in some Republican circles, the name Theodore Roosevelt has itself become anathema, a toxic reminder of "big government" and "socialism."[5]

In that year, half of the Republicans in the House of Representatives and slightly less than half in the Senate were from southern states, giving the South almost as much influence in the GOP as it had in the Democratic Party early in the twentieth century. Republicans have "maxed out in the South," limiting their appeal in the rest of the country, wrote political scientist Merle Black. "Might as well designate 'Dixie' as the official party anthem for next month's Republican National Convention," a Miami columnist had remarked in 1996. For how much longer, one Republican commentator wondered, would southerners continue to "wag the Republican dog?"[6]

Pushing the party even further to the right are Republican and conservative activists who insist that the GOP remain absolutely faithful to hard-core conservative political tenets. More focused on ideological purity than on winning elections, they purged the Republican Party of moderates by meddling—FDR-style—in party primaries and pitting conservative candidates against established middle-of-the-road politicians, people like Pennsylvania's Senator Arlen Specter, Utah's Senator Robert Bennett, Florida's Governor Charlie Crist, and others.[7]

Republicans, however, are not alone in seeking to impose ideological orthodoxy on their party. Left-leaning Democrats successfully defeated Connecticut's centrist senator Joseph Lieberman in the party primary in 2006, only to see Lieberman exit the Democratic Party and win the November election as an Independent.

Franklin Roosevelt's impulse for creating two ideologically coherent and responsible parties is by no means dead in the twenty-first century— on the contrary, it may be even stronger. Having complained at the Jackson Day dinner in 1939 about a "Democratic Tweedledum and a Republican Tweedledee" and having warned a few months later against "a Republican Tweedledum and a Democratic Tweedle-dummer," Roosevelt would surely have been pleased to see a polarized political landscape inhabited by parties with mostly coherent ideological messages.[8]

*   *   *

Still, significant problems remain. Democratic and Republican senators and representatives passionately defend the principles of their parties—just what FDR had in mind. But have bipartisanship and compromise become things of the past?

Years ago, bipartisan support for important legislation was not a hard sell. When the Senate passed Franklin Roosevelt's Social Security Act in 1935, sixteen Republicans voted with the Democratic majority and only five voted nay (four Republicans and eight Democrats abstained). Thirty years later, half of the Republicans in Congress signed on to President Lyndon B. Johnson's Medicare Act. And when Congress sought to enact Civil Rights legislation in 1964, Senator Everett Dirksen of Illinois, the GOP minority leader, worked alongside majority leader Mike Mansfield of Montana to overcome a filibuster by southern Democrats.[9]

But these days, few vestiges linger of that bipartisan spirit. "Today, Democrats and Republicans live in different universes, both intellectually and morally," wrote *New York Times* columnist Paul Krugman in March 2010, lamenting the impossibility of any cooperation between the two parties.[10] This is the downside to party realignment and polarization, for in the American system of checks and balances, some measure of cooperation between the parties may sometimes be necessary. If one party has control of the White House and House of Representatives and also has a filibuster-proof majority in the Senate, there may well be no need for help from the minority party to pass important bills. But at other times, when a majority party in the Senate cannot muster enough votes to end a filibuster or when it cannot impose discipline on its own members, the absence of cooperation between the two parties can be a cause of fatal deadlock.

And yet, even when gestures of bipartisanship come to the rescue, they may come at a price of such crippling compromises that little is actually accomplished. The best remedy in those situations may be to await the next election in the hope that one party will secure solid control of all branches of government, transcend checks, balances, veto traps and filibusters, bring the nation a step closer to resembling majoritarian British parliamentary democracy—and permit the majority to govern effectively and energetically in accord with its popular mandate.

Party polarization may have its pros and cons, and Americans can debate whether conflict between the parties has grown too intense or whether party conflict and healthy criticism are essential in an open democracy. But there is little reason to debate party discipline.

Just as Franklin Roosevelt recognized, only if politicians toe their parties' lines is effective government possible. And yet, his greatest failure was his ambivalent party leadership. And that is the challenge. A majority party in a nation as large and diverse as the United States will inevitably be broad and inclusive, making it difficult to achieve that discipline and unity. In 2010, Democratic Party leaders struggled to hold together social liberals, fiscal conservatives, midwestern moderates, southern centrists, and coastal progressives. During President Obama's first year in office, Democrats in Congress divided on an economic stimulus package and especially on crucial health care legislation. Democratic centrists like Nebraska's Ben Nelson, Arkansas's Blanche Lincoln, and Louisiana's Mary Landrieu extracted severe concessions from the party's liberal leadership. Voters' enthusiasm for the Democratic Party waned in 2010 precisely because Democrats accomplished relatively little during the first year and a half of the Obama administration, feuding among themselves instead of uniting to pass key bills.

Which takes us back to Franklin Roosevelt. Yes, any majority party must keep the doors to its tent wide open; and yes, a majority party must accept certain internal tensions.[11] But without British-style party discipline and a strong party leadership system, even a president whose party has a majority in both chambers of Congress will find it difficult to lead and carry out his or her agenda. And an activist, courageous president—one who is deeply committed to his program and who is temperamentally comfortable, as was Roosevelt, with conflict—may once again find himself tempted to put on political boxing gloves and jump into the arena with dissidents and obstructionists from his own party.

Franklin Roosevelt's political struggle in 1938 was two-pronged: first, to neutralize the obstructionist coalition of Republicans and conservative Democrats by expelling from the Democratic Party a few outspoken and defiant conservatives and replacing them with liberals, and second, to oversee the transformation of the Democratic Party into a stoutly liberal party and the GOP into the nation's conservative party. The end result, in addition to the paramount goal of rescuing and reenergizing the New Deal, was to be the injection of dynamic, meaningful two-party competition into the nation and especially into the politically life-less South.

The *real* underlying problem, however, was not—and is not—one of parties, party discipline, or party realignment. The basic problem is making government work. And the major obstacle to energetic, dynamic government is our horse-and-buggy political system itself, bequeathed to twenty-first-century Americans by the Framers, those elitist, self-protective, eighteenth-century gentlemen who feared energy in government as well as popular power and majority rule.

Ideally the solution to stalled, ineffective government would be certain constitutional changes that would make our system more majoritarian—and therefore more democratic, more energetic, more accountable, and more capable of responding to the critical wants and needs of the people: an end to the Electoral College, weighted in favor of the small states; a Senate based on population instead of the present grossly unrepresentative system; and simultaneous elections and identical term lengths for president, representatives, and senators, replacing the majority-crushing staggered elections we now have and eliminating the distractions of midterm elections. Such a new electoral timetable would encourage voters to think more in terms of electing a responsible party team to office and would permit the expression of a loud national majority voice. And, of course, there should be an end to minority-empowering filibuster rules. But short of those extremely unlikely constitutional reforms and rule changes, only a disciplined and unified majority party and a president who is a strong party leader can overcome checks, balances, and our antimajoritarian political system.

Indeed, after President Roosevelt tried unsuccessfully to alter the makeup of the Supreme Court in 1937, he realized that it was pointless to struggle further for constitutional change. Instead he decided to fight for a more unified and accountable Democratic Party. And, as we have seen, in order to reach that end, he came up with the idea of the purge—his attempt, in one brief electoral season, to reshape the political landscape by creating a solid liberal majority party that could outmaneuver the Framers' majority-pulverizing constitutional blueprint.

But there would be no quick fix to the problem. On the contrary, the path to the realignment of American political parties, strewn with threats, manifestos, walkouts, third parties, compromises, reconciliations, Supreme Court decisions, and demographic changes, has been complex, tortured, and long. It would take seventy years to resolve the tangled problems to which FDR devoted one frantic, memorable summer.[12]

And even after those seven politically tumultuous decades, the political realignment that eventually took hold may shift again. In 1964, after Goldwater's defeat, the future seemed sunny for Democrats—just as in 1972, McGovern's gigantic loss augured well for Republicans.

One lesson from 1938, 1948, 1968, 1980, and 2008 is that in an open, two-party democracy there is no such thing as a stable, stationary political landscape. American political parties—despite continued efforts at ideological purity—still contain internal contradictions and conflicts. They are alive, kinetic, and in flux.

And the other final and crucial lesson of 1938 and 2010 is that without strong political parties, robust party leadership and British-style party discipline, even a president with a powerful mandate for change cannot overcome an antiquated eighteenth-century political system and lead the nation forward. Other purges may lie ahead.[13]

Notes

1. Getting Ready to Fight

1. *New York Times*, April 3, 1938, "Dutch Is Up: FDR vs. Congress."
2. *New York Times*, April 1, 1938, "See Election Move in Roosevelt Note."
3. James MacGregor Burns and Susan Dunn, *The Three Roosevelts: Patrician Leaders Who Transformed America* (New York: Atlantic Monthly Press, 2001), 372.
4. Roosevelt, Speech before the Democratic National Convention, June 27, 1936.
5. Clyde P. Weed, "What Happened to the Republicans in the 1930s?" *Polity*, 22, 1, Autumn 1989, 21.
6. Samuel Rosenman, *Working with Roosevelt* (New York: Harper, 1952), 137.
7. "Critical election of 1936": See Bernard Sternsher, "The New Deal Party System: A Reappraisal," *Journal of Interdisciplinary History*, 15, 1, Summer 1984, 53–81. "durable shift of party strength": V. O. Key, Jr., "A Theory of Critical Elections," *Journal of Politics*, 17, 1, February 1955, 8.
8. Madison to unknown, 1833, in *Writings of James Madison*, ed. Gaillard Hunt, 9:520–528. See also Robert Dahl, *How Democratic Is the American Constitution?* (New Haven: Yale University Press, 2001), 36–37.
9. James MacGregor Burns, *Roosevelt: The Lion and the Fox* (New York: Harcourt, Brace, 1956), 287.
10. Glass, Byrd, Tydings, and Gore abstained from voting on the Social Security Act of 1935.
11. Press Conference, August 16, 1938, in *The Public Papers and Addresses of Franklin D. Roosevelt*, ed. Samuel Rosenman (New York: Macmillan, 1938–1950) (hereafter *PPA*), 7:489.

12. "I expected the punishment": *Washington Post,* August 11, 1938, "Corrigan's Reception Here." "My compass went wrong": *Hartford Courant,* July 19, 1938, "Pilots Aged $900 Plane Across Sea."

13. "Wilson called for": *New York Times,* April 3, 1938, "Dutch Is Up." See also *PPA,* 1938, Notes, 7:182–192. "I hope the Democratic party": FDR to James Byrnes, July 26, 1937, in *F.D.R.: His Personal Letters, 1928–1945,* ed. Elliott Roosevelt, 3 vols. (New York: Duell, Sloan and Pearce, 1947–50), 1:696. Interestingly, while FDR sought to link the Democratic Party to a spirit of cooperation and common purpose between the executive and legislative branches, political scientist Sidney Milkis points out that Brownlow, the plan's architect, dismissed that notion. The underlying objective of the proposal, Brownlow wrote, was "not to unify executive and legislature but to unify governmental policy and administration"—in other words, simply to strengthen presidential government. See Sidney M. Milkis, "E. E. Schattschneider, the New Deal, and the Rejection of the Responsible Party Doctrine," in *PS: Political Science and Politics,* 25, 2, June 1992, 183–184. Milkis makes the interesting argument that "the New Deal was based on a party strategy to replace traditional party politics with executive administration."

14. "more efficient and business-like": *New York Times,* March 31, 1938, "Strikes at Foes." "Hoover's approval": *New York Times,* March 27, 1938, "Tactics of Executive Peril Reorganization." "dictator bill": 1938, *PPA,* Notes, 7:191. See also Kenneth S. Davis, *FDR: Into the Storm, 1937–1940* (New York: Random House, 1993), 35.

15. "totalitarian regimes": *New York Times,* April 1, 1938, "See Election Move in Roosevelt Note." "one-man rule": quoted in Richard Polenberg, *Reorganizing Roosevelt's Government* (Cambridge, Mass.: Harvard University Press, 1966), 126.

16. "dressed up as Paul Revere": *New York Times,* April 8, 1938, "Vote Is 191 to 160, Paul Reveres on Hand." "defend their liberties": Harold Ickes, *The Secret Diary of Harold L. Ickes: The Inside Struggle, 1936–1939,* 3 vols. (New York: Simon and Schuster, 1954), 2:354.

17. "certain form of *hysteria*": Polenberg, *Reorganizing Roosevelt's Government,* 127, note. Italics added. "330,000 telegrams": *New York Times,* March 29, 1938, "Wide Power Given." See also *Time,* April 18, 1938, "The Congress."

18. "Power of Dictator": *New York Times,* March 11, 1933, "Roosevelt Gets Power of Dictator. "duplication, waste, disorder": *New York Times,* March 27, 1938, "Tactics of Executive Peril Reorganization."

19. "might have had a dictator": FDR to Joseph P. Kennedy, in Michael R. Beschloss, *Kennedy and Roosevelt: The Uneasy Alliance* (New York: Norton, 1980). "stupid and ridiculous": "Reorganization of Executive Branch," 1938, *PPA,* Editor's Notes, 7:192. "Thank the Lord": FDR to Wilbur Cross, September 4, 1937, in

FDR: His Personal Letters, 1:711. "500 airplanes": Burns, *Roosevelt: The Lion and the Fox*, 355.

20. "Gallup in April 1938": *Atlanta Constitution*, April 8, 1938, "America Speaks." "63 percent of Americans": *Atlanta Constitution*, February 6, 1938, "Survey Shows New Deal Democrats Hold Lead in Party."

21. *New York Times*, March 29, 1938, "Wide Power Given." See also *Time*, April 4, 1938, "The Congress: Ninth-inning Rally."

22. "the vote was close": *New York Times*, March 29, 1938, "Wide Power Given." "Senator Robert Wagner": Joseph J. Huthmacher, *Senator Robert F. Wagner and the Rise of Urban Liberalism* (New York: Athenaeum, 1968), 244. "unrelenting pressure": Polenberg, *Reorganizing Roosevelt's Government*, 135.

23. "If this thing doesn't go through": Farley, quoted in Polenberg, *Reorganizing Roosevelt's Government*, 162. See also *Chicago Daily Tribune*, April 9, 1938, "Kill Dictator Bill." "major catastrophe": Ickes, *Secret Diary of Harold Ickes*, 2:354.

24. *Time*, April 18, 1938, "The Congress."

25. *The New York Times*, April 2, 1938, "House Rebels at Speed on Reorganization Bill." See also *New York Times*, April 9, 1938, "Bill Recommitted."

26. "boos, laughter": *New York Times*, April 1, 1938, "Two Hours of Uproar." "lethal blow": *Time*, April 18, 1938, "The Congress." "no longer the leader of his country": *New York Times*, April 9, 1938, "Bill Recommitted."

27. "roar of spiteful cheers": *Atlanta Constitution*, April 9, 1938, "Chamber Refuses Vote of Confidence in Chief Executive." "Here's our leader!": Polenberg, *Reorganizing Roosevelt's Government*, 166.

28. "Roosevelt's stunning defeat": *Chicago Daily Tribune*, April 9, 1938, "Kill Dictator Bill." "stock market soared": *New York Times*, April 10, 1938, "Along Wall Street." "anti-Roosevelt": quoted in Polenberg, *Reorganizing Roosevelt's Government*, 170.

29. Ickes, *Secret Diary of Harold Ickes*, April 10, 1938, 2:356–358.

30. "no occasion for personal recrimination": Davis, *FDR: Into the Storm*, 223. "hit him with words": Ickes, *Secret Diary of Harold Ickes*, April 10, 1938, 2:358.

31. Burns and Dunn, *Three Roosevelts*, 296.

32. Address on Constitution Day, September 17, 1937, *PPA*, 6:363.

33. Burns, *Roosevelt: The Lion and the Fox*, 294.

34. "frightful proposition": *Newsweek*, February 13, 1937, 7–9. "utterly destitute": *New York Times*, March 30, 1937, "Virginian Is Bitter." "move against racial segregation": *Congressional Record*, 75th Congress, 1st Session, Appendix, 661. "implacable antagonism": quoted in Polenberg, *Reorganizing Roosevelt's Government*, 126, note.

35. "usually liberal senators": Burns, *Roosevelt: The Lion and the Fox*, 298. See also *New York Times*, August 23, 1937, "Congress Regains Sway." "temptation to a

President": *New York Times*, August 8, 1937, "The Liberal Who Fights New Deal Liberalism." "road to an American dictatorship": *Hartford Courant*, July 14, 1937, "Court Bill Seen Dead."

36. E. David Cronon, "A Southern Progressive Looks at the New Deal," *Journal of Southern History*, 24, 2, May 1958, 169.

37. *Atlanta Constitution*, April 11, 1937, "Gridiron Club Roasts Court Plan."

38. *Time*, November 15, 1937.

39. James MacGregor Burns, *The Deadlock of Democracy: Four-Party Politics in America* (Englewood Cliffs, N.J.: Prentice-Hall, 1963), 170.

40. Burns, *Roosevelt: The Lion and the Fox*, 348.

41. "five women": Elizabeth Gasque of South Carolina, Caroline O'Day of New York, Nan Honeyman of Oregon, Virginia Jenckes of Indiana, and Mary Norton of New Jersey. "smooth the way for the passage": *New York Times*, June 26, 1937, "Congress Guests of President."

42. "pristine shoes": Burns and Dunn, *Three Roosevelts*, 229. "With Roosevelt, you could never forget": Samuel I. Rosenman, "Reminiscences," 1960, Oral History Research Office, Columbia University, Interviews conducted by J. N. Perlstein, 222.

43. *New York Times*, June 28, 1937, "Outing Promises Gain in Good-Will."

44. "out the window": *Chicago Daily Tribune*, July 23, 1937, "Packing Measure Is Sent to Doom in Committee." "most humiliating defeats": *New York Times*, July 23, 1938, "A Full Surrender." "emasculated Court bill": HR 2260, signed on August 26, 1937. See Davis, *FDR: Into the Storm*, 96.

45. *PPA*, 1938, Notes, 7:xxxii.

46. "I found him fuming": James A. Farley, *Jim Farley's Story: The Roosevelt Years* (New York: Whittlesey House, 1948), 95. "completely humiliated": Rosenman, "Reminiscences," 1960, Oral History Research Office, Columbia University, interview 4, side 1, July 27, 1959, 154. "I've got them on the run—never get angry at me": Farley, *Jim Farley's Story*, 95–96.

47. Josephus Daniels to Roosevelt, April 5, 1935, in Cronon, "Southern Progressive Looks at New Deal," 173.

48. "shenanigans": Samuel I. Rosenman, *Working with Roosevelt* (New York: Harper, 1952), 176. "tricked the voters": *Time*, September 12, 1938, "The Janizariat."

49. "Hatred glowed": Farley, *Jim Farley's Story*, 120. "took no pains": George Creel, *Rebel at Large: Recollections of Fifty Crowded Years* (New York: Putnam, 1947), 295.

50. *New York Times*, April 3, 1938, "Dutch Is Up: FDR vs. Congress."

51. Thomas L. Stokes, *Chip off My Shoulder* (Princeton: Princeton University Press, 1940), 463.

52. Address at Democratic Victory Dinner, Washington, D.C., March 4, 1937, in *PPA*, 6:114.

53. "Capacity for vindictiveness": Jonathan Alter, *The Defining Moment: FDR's Hundred Days and the Triumph of Hope* (New York: Simon and Schuster, 2006), 235. "streak of vindictiveness": Frances Perkins, Oral History, Columbia University Libraries, pt. 7, sess. 1, p. 315. "weak and vacillating": James Farley, *Behind the Ballots: The Personal History of a Politician* (New York: Harcourt, Brace, 1938), 344–345.

54. Alter, *Defining Moment*, 233–34.

55. Press Conference, April 8, 1938, in *PPA*, 7:194, 196.

56. Press Conference, April 8, 1938, in *PPA*, 7:198.

57. Press Conference, April 21, 1938, in *PPA*, 7:278.

58. *Chicago Daily Tribune*, October 4, 1936. See also *Chicago Daily Tribune*, August 20, 1937 and August 30, 1937. Even Al Smith, the former governor of New York and 1928 Democratic presidential candidate, defected. Though these men and others quit the party of their own accord, the *Tribune* maintained that Roosevelt had expelled them in a bloodless version of "the communist purge in Russia, when Dictator Stalin similarly disposed of the Trotskyites."

59. Cronon, "Southern Progressive Looks at New Deal," 175.

60. "Roosevelt must either fight": Paul Anderson, "Roosevelt Must Fight!" *New Republic*, April 16, 1938. "take up the executive reorganization bill again": *New York Times*, May 17, 1938, "President Insists on Reorganization."

61. "ending the stormy session": *New York Times*, June 19, 1938, "Session Ends." "wedding": *New York Times*, June 19, 1938, "Roosevelts' Youngest Son Weds."

62. Joshua Lee to FDR, June 22, 1938, Roosevelt Papers, Franklin Delano Roosevelt Library, Hyde Park, N.Y. (FDRL), PPF 1820.

63. "Nazi contender": *Atlanta Constitution*, June 23, 1938, "Louis Strikes Like Tornado." "Schmeling unpredictable": *Los Angeles Times*, June 19, 1938, "The Sports Parade."

64. "pressure from Farley": *Hartford Courant*, October 19, 1936, "Joe Louis Almost GOP Campaigner." "for FDR's opponent": *New York Times*, November 5, 1940, "Joe Louis Speaks 4 Times." See also *Washington Post*, November 5, 1940, "Welles and Joe Louis Wind Up Hot Maryland Election." For rumor of Louis selling his support, see *Atlanta Constitution*, November 5, 1940, "Says Louis Peddled His Vote." "Stick to your boxing": *Chicago Defender*, November 9, 1940, "What the People Say."

65. *New York Times*, June 24, 1938, "Schmeling in Hospital."

66. "honked their horns": *Chicago Defender*, June 25, 1938, "Louis Beats Schmeling." "I always feel sorry": Eleanor Roosevelt, "My Day," *Atlanta Constitution*, June 25, 1938.

67. "Corcoran": Frances Perkins, Oral History, Columbia University Libraries, pt. 7, sess. 1, p. 311. "liked to crack jokes": Elliott Roosevelt and James Brough, *A Rendezvous with Destiny* (New York: Putnam, 1975), 92; Robert H. Jackson, *That Man: An Insider's Portrait of Franklin D. Roosevelt*, ed. John Q. Barrett (New York: Oxford University Press, 2003), 34. "closely-knit duo": Samuel I. Rosenman, "Reminiscences," July 27, 1959, interview 4, side 1, 124.

68. *New York Times*, May 27, 1938, "New Deal 'Purge' to Have Next Test in Iowa Primary."

69. "There has got to be a fight": John Morton Blum, ed., *From the Morgenthau Diaries: Years of Crisis, 1928–1938* (Boston: Houghton Mifflin, 1959), 329. "Stanley High": Stanley High, "Whose Party Is It?" *Saturday Evening Post*, February 6, 1937. "White House strenuously denied": Walter Lippmann, "Today and Tomorrow," *Los Angeles Times*, June 30, 1937. See also *Chicago Daily Tribune*, February 6, 1937, "The Good Neighborly Purge." "let the cat out of the bag": *Hartford Courant*, June 29, 1937, "Today and Tomorrow," by Walter Lippmann.

70. "nominations are entirely": Farley, *Jim Farley's Story*, 121. "nothing to say publicly": *New York Times*, May 18, 1938, "Roosevelt Firm in Saying Nothing."

71. "The American public": *Atlanta Constitution*, June 25, 1938, "Roosevelt to Carry War into Primaries." "sweltering evening": *New York Times*, June 26, 1938, "87° on 8th Day of Wave."

72. "Alsop heard an aggressive commander": *Atlanta Constitution*, July 4, 1938, "The Capital Parade," by Joseph Alsop and Robert Kintner. "old magic": *New York Herald Tribune*, June 25, 1938, editorial.

73. Fireside Chat on Party Primaries, June 24, 1938, in *PPA*, 7:398–400.

74. Rosenman, interview by James Perlstein, July 27, 1959, Carmel, New York, 154.

75. Burns, *Roosevelt: The Lion and the Fox*, 271. Italics added.

76. Frances Perkins, *The Roosevelt I Knew* (New York: Viking, 1946), 125. See also Ronald C. Schurin, "The President as Disciplinarian: Wilson, Roosevelt, and Congressional Primaries," *Presidential Studies Quarterly*, 28, 2, Spring 1998, 409–421.

77. *New York Times*, September 3, 1938, "Roosevelt Scorns Party Lines."

78. *New York Times*, June 26, 1938, editorial comment on the President's "Fireside Chat."

79. *Atlanta Constitution*, June 1, 1938, "Fair Enough," by Westbrook Pegler.

80. "It's too dangerous": *Christian Science Monitor*, June 27, 1938, "The Wide Horizon." "Democratic voters had a right to know": *Washington Post*, August 21, 1938, "President Enters Elections in Fine Fettle."

81. "was all strong food": Rosenman, *Working with Roosevelt*, 177. "aching for a show down": *Washington Post*, August 21, 1938, "President Enters Elections in Fine Fettle," by Ernest Lindley.

82. "Their attempt to pack the Court": *New York Times*, June 8, 1938, "FDR Dissatisfied with Gillette's Victory in Iowa." "*plain declaration of war*": Bailey to Byrd, June 27, 1938, in William E. Leuchtenburg, *The White House Looks South: Franklin D. Roosevelt, Harry S. Truman, Lyndon B. Johnson* (Baton Rouge: Louisiana State University Press, 2005), 128. "Even South Carolina's James Byrnes": David Robertson, *Sly and Able: A Political Biography of James F. Byrnes* (New York: Norton, 1994), 270. "purgees must fight": *Los Angeles Times*, June 30, 1937, "The Party Purge."

83. "only ten years as majority party": 46th Congress, 1879–81; 53rd Congress, 1893–95; 63rd Congress, 1913–15; 64th Congress, 1915–17; 65th Congress, 1917–19. "not to take sides": Farley, *Behind the Ballots*, 358–59. "dirty party-splitting work": Farley, *Jim Farley's Story*, 183. "not please everybody": Farley, *Behind the Ballots*, 358–59.

84. "To Jim Farley": Ickes, *Secret Diary of Harold Ickes*, 2:391. "pure politics": Farley, quoted in *Washington Post*, August 21, 1937, "Court Foes' Defeat Is Asked by Guffey."

85. "spineless jellyfish"; "The man who starts out": Farley, *Behind the Ballots*, 363, 375. "non-participation": Farley, *Behind the Ballots*, 357. "I wondered if Alaska": Farley, *Jim Farley's Story*, 141.

2. The Nonpartisan Leader

1. James MacGregor Burns, *Roosevelt: The Lion and the Fox* (New York: Harcourt, Brace, 1956), 133.

2. Frank Freidel, *F.D.R. and the South* (Baton Rouge: Louisiana State University Press, 1965), 41.

3. Burns, *Roosevelt: The Lion and the Fox*, 144.

4. "excessively cautious": *Hartford Courant*, January 8, 1932, "Today and Tomorrow." See also *Hartford Courant*, February 11, 1932, "Today and Tomorrow." "real first choice": *Los Angeles Times*, June 29, 1932, "Today and Tomorrow," by Walter Lippmann. "Lippmann confidently predicted": *Hartford Courant*, September 20, 1935, "Outstanding Thinkers Express Opinion." See also *Los Angeles Times*, July 3, 1935, Walter Lippmann, "Today and Tomorrow."

5. Machiavelli, *The Prince* (1514), chap. 18.

6. FDR to Bernard Baruch, December 19, 1931, in *FDR: His Personal Letters, 1928–1945*, ed. Elliott Roosevelt, 3 vols. (New York: Duell, Sloan and Pearce, 1947–50), 1:244. Italics added.

7. James MacGregor Burns and Susan Dunn, *The Three Roosevelts: Patrician Leaders Who Transformed America* (New York: Atlantic Monthly Press, 2001), 316.

8. "uneducated worm": FDR to Josephus Daniels, September 28, 1940 in *FDR: His Personal Letters*, 2:1068. "an All-Wise Press hopped all over him": FDR to Arthur Krock, July 3, 1931, in *FDR: His Personal Letters*, 1:204–205.

9. "clouded the issues": see Merle Fainsod, "Consolidating Party Control," *American Political Science Review*, 42, 2, April 1948, 316–326. "hazy political message": Rexford Tugwell, *Roosevelt's Revolution: The First Year, A Personal Perspective* (New York: Macmillan, 1977), 13. "forlorn Americans": Wagner, quoted in Arthur M. Schlesinger, Jr., *The Age of Roosevelt: The Crisis of the Old Order* (Boston: Houghton Mifflin, 1957), 1:240. "Nothing drastic": Tugwell, *Roosevelt's Revolution*, 13.

10. Kenneth S. Davis, *FDR: The New York Years, 1928–1933* (New York: Random House, 1979), 294–295. See also Burns, *Roosevelt: The Lion and the Fox*, 133.

11. "criticize, cry down, or defame": James Farley, *Behind the Ballots: The Personal History of a Politician* (New York: Harcourt, Brace, 1938), 115. "sixth sense": Edward J. Flynn, *You're the Boss* (New York: Viking, 1947), 122.

12. Kenneth Davis, *FDR: The New York Years*, 325. See also Burns and Dunn, *Three Roosevelts*, 234.

13. "Never before in modern history": Davis, *FDR: The New York Years*, 334. "liberal thoughts, of planned action": Burns, *Roosevelt: The Lion and the Fox*, 139.

14. "campaign speech that October in Atlanta": October 24, 1932, GeorgiaInfo, http://georgiainfo.galileo.usg.edu/FDRspeeches/FDRspeech32-2.htm. "bread with the beer": *New York Times*, July 21, 1940, "Third Term?"

15. "collection of proposals": Burns, *Roosevelt: The Lion and the Fox*, 143. "Take a method and try it": Davis, *FDR: The New York Years*, 294.

16. Schlesinger, *Age of Roosevelt: The Crisis of the Old Order*, 242. See also Hoover, Press Conference, December 9, 1932, in *The State Papers and Other Public Writings of Herbert Hoover*, ed. William S. Myers (Garden City, N.J.: Doubleday, 1934), 1:460. See also Press Conference, May 22, 1932, in *ibid.*, 2:195–196.

17. "protected by scores of police": *Washington Post*, October 23, 1932, "Detroit Reds Delay Hoover on Arrival." "frivolous promises": *New York Times*, October 23, 1932, "Sharp Speech in Detroit." "solemn defeatist": Frances Perkins, *The Roosevelt I Knew* (New York: Viking, 1946), 115.

18. Marriner Eccles, *Beckoning Frontiers: Public and Personal Recollections*, ed. Sidney Hyman (New York: Knopf, 1951), 97, 95.

19. *New York Times*, September 11, 1932, "Roosevelt's View of the Big Job," by Anne O'Hare McCormick.

20. "epic struggle of ideas": Rexford Tugwell, "The Protagonists: Roosevelt and Hoover," *Antioch Review*, 13, 4, Winter 1953, 442. "contradictory"; "lavish way": Tugwell, *Roosevelt's Revolution*, 4.

21. Farley, *Behind the Ballots,* 188.

22. "The only principle in the cabinet's make-up": Burns, *Roosevelt: The Lion and the Fox,* 150. "On the whole Mr. Roosevelt has chosen well": *Los Angeles Times,* February 28, 1933, "Today and Tomorrow" by Lippmann.

23. "reassured Senator Pat Harrison": William Coker, "Pat Harrison: Strategy for Victory," *Journal of Mississippi History,* 28, 1966, 267–285. See also Freidel, *F.D.R. and the South,* 39. "I think we've got a great president": Freidel, *F.D.R. and the South,* 40.

24. "He was courtesy itself": Perkins, *Roosevelt I Knew,* 113. "declare to the world": Burns, *Roosevelt: The Lion and the Fox,* 348.

25. *New York Times,* August 15, 1937, "An Unchanging Roosevelt."

26. Davis, *FDR: The New York Years,* 407.

27. "we'll have eight years": Tugwell, *Democratic Roosevelt,* 412. "perfect system of government": FDR, *On Our Way* (New York: John Day, 1934), 248–249.

28. James MacGregor Burns, *The Deadlock of Democracy: Four Party Politics in America* (Englewood Cliffs, N.J.: Prentice-Hall, 1963), 157. Earlier in his political career, FDR had been more committed to strengthening and liberalizing the Democratic Party. The Democratic Party, he said in 1919, "is and must be a progressive Democracy." In 1924, after the defeat of the lackluster conservative Democrat John W. Davis for president, Roosevelt again underscored the need to make the party a "stronger and more militant organization nationally" so that it could rightly claim to be *"the* Progressive Party of the country." But these were only words—no deeds followed them, no party building, no organizing at the grass roots. (See Davis, *FDR: The New York Years,* 292; FDR to Key Pittman, December 4, 1924, quoted in Sidney Milkis, "Franklin D. Roosevelt and the Transcendence of Partisan Politics," *Political Science Quarterly,* 100, Autumn 1985, 479–504.)

29. "men and women of *all parties"*: Burns, *Deadlock of Democracy,* 157, 159. "displayed a greater freedom": Roosevelt, Fireside Chat, June 28, 1934, *The Public Papers and Addresses of Franklin D. Roosevelt,* ed. Samuel Rosenman (New York: Macmillan, 1938–50) *(PPA),* 2:372.

30. "We must be loyal": Radio Address to Young Democratic Clubs of America, August 24, 1935, in *PPA,* 4:234. "Democrat of convenience": Tugwell, *Democratic Roosevelt,* 413.

31. Langdon W. Post to FDR, September 23, 1933, Franklin Delano Roosevelt Library, Hyde Park, N.Y. (FDRL), OF 300, box 27; Elmendorf Carr to FDR, September 24, 1933, FDRL.

32. "(1) say nothing, (2) do nothing": Burns, *Roosevelt: The Lion and the Fox,* 201. "In Minnesota, *hands off"*: Burns, *Roosevelt: The Lion and the Fox,* 202.

33. "magnificently justified exception": Burns, *Roosevelt: The Lion and the Fox,* 281. "Pittman of Nevada": FDR to Pittman, 25 August 1934, quoted in Burns,

Roosevelt: The Lion and the Fox, 376. See also Sidney Milkis, "Presidents and Party Purges," in *Presidents and Their Parties,* ed. Robert Harmel (New York: Praeger, 1984), 157–158. "utterly dangerous effort": James T. Patterson, *Congressional Conservatism and the New Deal: The Growth of the Conservative Coalition in Congress* (Lexington: University of Kentucky Press, 1967), 13.

34. "my dear old friend": FDR to Carter Glass, April 15, 1929, and FDR to Glass, October 29, 1934, in *FDR: His Personal Letters,* 1:49, 1:428. "lord of Virginia politics": Raymond Clapper, "Roosevelt Tries the Primaries," in *Current History,* 49, October 1938, 16.

35. Stanley High, "Whose Party Is It?" *Saturday Evening Post,* February 6, 1937, 37.

36. "I am heartened": *New York Times,* August 11, 1936, "Text of Roosevelt Letter to Labor." See also *New York Times,* August 16, 1936, "Labor Takes First Step toward Political Party." "I do not believe that the President himself mentioned": See High, "Whose Party Is it?" 37.

37. "enduring liberal majority": See Sidney Milkis, *The President and the Parties: The Transformation of the American Party System since the New Deal* (New York: Oxford University Press, 1993). "common good transcended political parties": *New York Times,* September 3, 1938, "Roosevelt Scorns Party Lines."

38. Introduction, *PPA,* 7:xxviii.

39. Julius Turner, *Party and Constituency: Pressures on Congress* (Baltimore: Johns Hopkins University Press, 1951), 36. See also Patterson, *Congressional Conservatism,* 250.

40. Madison, *Federalist* No. 51.

41. "sprawling holding company": Burns, *Roosevelt: The Lion and the Fox,* 378–379.

42. Robert E. Jenner, *FDR's Republicans: Domestic Political Realignment and American Foreign Policy* (Lanham, Md.: Rowman and Littlefield, 2010), 70. In addition to the politicians listed, Henry Cabot Lodge of Massachusetts and New Jersey's William Barbour were also GOP progressives.

43. "square deal": Republican Platform 1940, in *History of American Presidential Elections,* ed. Arthur M. Schlesinger, Jr. (New York: Chelsea House, 1971), 4:2963. "wave the flag and shout": *Atlanta Constitution,* July 7, 1938, "Landon Blames Slump on F.D.R."

44. E. E. Schattschneider, *The Semisovereign People: A Realist's View of Democracy in America* (New York: Holt, Rinehart and Winston, 1960), 76.

45. Stanley High, "Whose Party Is It?" *Saturday Evening Post,* February 6, 1937, 10.

46. Democrats had a majority in the Senate in 1879–81, 1893–95, and 1913–19. In the House they had a majority for twenty-two years, in 1875–81, 1883–89, 1891–95, and 1911–17.

47. "old foes": David Brady and Joseph Stewart, Jr., "Congressional Party Realignment and Transformations of Public Policy in Three Realignment Eras,"

American Journal of Political Science, 26, 2, May 1982, 354–355. "three-syllable word": Perkins, *Roosevelt I Knew*, 113.

48. William E. Leuchtenburg, *The White House Looks South: Franklin D. Roosevelt, Harry S. Truman, Lyndon B. Johnson* (Baton Rouge: Louisiana State University Press, 2005), 78.

49. Burns, *Roosevelt: The Soldier of Freedom* (New York: Harcourt Brace Jovanovich, 1970), 37.

50. "programs to discriminate": Ira Katznelson, *When Affirmative Action Was White: An Untold History of Racial Inequality in Twentieth-Century America* (New York: Norton, 2005). "protected the white civilization": *Atlanta Constitution*, January 11, 1938, "Lynch Bill Foes Cry Party Split."

51. "No man in Washington": Leuchtenburg, *White House Looks South*, 80. "hundreds of millions of dollars": "Pat Harrison and the New Deal," C. O'Neal Gregory, M.A. thesis, University of Mississippi, 1960, quoted in James T. Patterson, "The Failure of Party Realignment in the South, 1937–1939," *Journal of Politics*, 27, 3, August 1965, 611. See also Dewey Grantham, *The Life and Death of the Solid South: A Political History* (Lexington: University of Kentucky Press, 1988), 105ff. "the road to hell": Freidel, *F.D.R. and the South*, 51.

52. James L. Sundquist, *Dynamics of the Party System: Alignment and Realignment of Political Parties in the United States* (Washington: Brookings Institution, 1973), 245ff.

53. "wholly out of character": Samuel I. Rosenman, "Reminiscences," Oral History, Columbia University, Interview 4, Side 1, July 27, 1959, 155. "make many compromises": Samuel I. Rosenman, Oral History, Truman Library, Independence, Missouri, 1968 and 1969, recorded by Jerry Hess, 54.

54. R. G. Tugwell, "The Compromising Roosevelt," *Western Political Quarterly*, 6, 2, June 1953, 341.

3. Favorite Son of the South

1. "Franklin Roosevelt Comes Home": quoted in Jennifer Fox, "Hail to the Chief: Presidential Visits to Atlanta," *Atlanta History*, 36, 3, 1992, 42. "my State of Georgia": William E. Leuchtenburg, *The White House Looks South: Franklin D. Roosevelt, Harry S. Truman, Lyndon B. Johnson* (Baton Rouge: Louisiana State University Press, 2005), 33–34, 30.

2. Leuchtenburg, *White House Looks South*, 33.

3. "exercised in the pool": Cleburne Gregory, "Franklin Roosevelt Will Swim to Health," *Atlanta Journal*, October 26, 1924, in *F.D.R., Columnist: The Uncollected Columns of Franklin D. Roosevelt*, ed. Donald Scott Carmichael (Chicago: Pellegrini and Cudahy, 1947), 11–12. "I do wish you were down here": FDR to

Henry Morgenthau, April 24, 1929, in *F.D.R.: His Personal Letters, 1928–1945*, ed. Elliott Roosevelt, 3 vols. (New York: Duell, Sloan and Pearce, 1947–50), 1:51. "You would love": Leuchtenburg, *White House Looks South*, 30.

4. Cleborne Gregory, "Franklin Roosevelt Will Swim to Health," *Atlanta Journal*, October 26, 1924, 12.

5. "I ate them all": *Macon Daily Telegraph*, May 2, 1925, in *F.D.R., Columnist*, 61. "wouldn't have been good: "Confidential Memorandum Regarding Dinner at White House Monday Evening, May 17, 1937," quoted in Leuchtenburg, *White House Looks South*, 427 note. "glorious symbol": FDR to Marvin McIntyre, December 8, 1938, in *FDR: His Personal Letters*, 2:839.

6. Address at Barnesville, Georgia, August 11, 1938, in *The Public Papers and Addresses of Franklin D. Roosevelt*, ed. Samuel Rosenman (New York, Macmillan, 1938–50), (*PPA*), 7:463.

7. Remarks to State Superintendents of Education at the White House, December 11, 1935, in *PPA*, 4:499.

8. George Tindall, "Southern Mythology," in *The South and the Sectional Image*, ed. Dewey Grantham (New York: Harper and Row, 1967), 14.

9. *F.D.R., Columnist*, 11–12. See also Leuchtenburg, *White House Looks South*, 32.

10. *F.D.R., Columnist*, April 18, 1925, 33.

11. "I must not get mixed up": *F.D.R., Columnist*, April 16, 1925, 30. "no interest in toppling": Leuchtenburg, *White House Looks South*, 37–38. "You people can mix it up": *F.D.R., Columnist*, April 16, 1925, 30.

12. *F.D.R., Columnist*, April 18, 1925, 35.

13. *Chicago Tribune*, September 5, 1976, "From Redneck to Chic."

14. "generals without an army": George Brown Tindall, *The Emergence of the New South, 1913–1945* (Baton Rouge: Louisiana State University Press, 1967), 633. Other southern liberals, however, found the opposite to be true: "Georgia liberals today are unorganized because no army is effective without an acknowledged leader," wrote one man to an Atlanta weekly newspaper. (Letter to editor, George Homstead, January 7, 1939, Franklin Delano Roosevelt Library, Hyde Park, N.Y. (FDRL), OF 300, box 15.) "populists sought to free": Alan Brinkley, "The New Deal and Southern Politics," in *The New Deal and the South*, ed. James C. Cobb (Jackson: University Press of Mississippi, 1984), 110–111; William A. Link, *The Paradox of Southern Progressivism, 1880–1930* (Chapel Hill: University of North Carolina Press, 1992), passim.

15. Clarence Cason, *90 Degrees in the Shade* (1935; reprint, Tuscaloosa: University of Alabama Press, 2001).

16. Thomas L. Stokes, *Chip off My Shoulder* (Princeton: Princeton University Press, 1940), 512.

17. "The older I grow": E. David Cronon, "A Southern Progressive Looks at the New Deal," *Journal of Southern History*, 24, 2, May 1958, 152. "Roosevelt Southern Clubs": Club literature, FDRL, OF 300, box 15. See also G. W. Jones, Treasurer, February 13, 1932, "The Original Roosevelt Man," FDRL, OF 300, box 15.

18. "patrician background": Leuchtenburg, *White House Looks South*, 37. "Glass had touted Roosevelt": Frank Freidel, *F.D.R. and the South* (Baton Rouge: Louisiana State University Press, 1965), 24. "Holding fast to sound Jeffersonian principles": Glass, November 1, 1932, in Rixey Smith and Norman Beasley, *Carter Glass* (New York: Longmans, Green, 1939), 319.

19. "I give you my word": Leuchtenburg, *White House Looks South*, 39. "Georgia's joy": Leuchtenburg, *White House Looks South*, 41.

20. Dewey Grantham, *The Democratic South* (Athens: University of Georgia Press, 1963), 70.

21. "With the help of FERA": Eliot Wigginton, "The Mountains: A Different Mix of Politics," in *The Prevailing South: Life and Politics in a Changing Culture*, ed. Dudley Clendinen (Atlanta: Longstreet Press, 1988), 156–157. "first to come to our rescue": Mrs. Lamar Rutherford Lipscomb, Atlanta, to FDR, February 1937, FDRL, OF 300, box 15.

22. "The people of Georgia will not turn away": *Atlanta Constitution*, July 11, 1938, in FDRL, OF 300, box 15. "80 percent of the people": Joe Starnes to Marvin McIntyre, December 1, 1935, FDRL, OF 300-Alabama, 1933–37.

23. "mid-Hudson home district": Roosevelt carried his village of Hyde Park but never the township of Hyde Park and not Dutchess County. "Roosevelt was the Democratic Party": Leuchtenburg, *White House Looks South*, 121.

24. Ferrol Sams, Jr., "God as Elector: Religion and the Vote," in Clendinen, *Prevailing South*, 50. See also Leuchtenburg, *White House Looks South*, 42–43.

25. "some southern politicians": for example, George of Georgia, Smith and James Byrnes of South Carolina, and Pat Harrison of Mississippi, and others. "many New Deal policies": George Brown Tindall, *The Disruption of the Solid South* (Athens: University of Georgia Press, 1972), 30.

26. Stokes, *Chip off My Shoulder*, 527, 530.

27. "Wages and Hours Bill": see Jonathan Grossman, "Fair Labor Standards Act of 1938: Maximum Struggle for a Minimum Wage," *Monthly Labor Review*, 101, 6, June 1978, 22–30. "higher wages would also improve productivity": Ben Bernanke, *Essays on the Great Depression* (Princeton: Princeton University Press, 2000), 252. See also Grossman, "Fair Labor Standards Act of 1938."

28. Arthur M. Schlesinger, Jr., ed., *History of American Presidential Elections* (New York: Chelsea House, 1971), 3:2859.

29. FDR to Edward House, June 16, 1937, in *FDR: His Personal Letters*, 1:689.

30. U.S. Department of Labor, Bureau of Labor Statistics, Record of the Discussion before the U.S. Congress on the FLSA of 1938, I (Washington, D.C.: Government Printing Office, 1938), 20–21.

31. "fatal blow": *New York Times*, August 8, 1937, "Wage-and-Hour Bill Creates a Sectional Rift." See also *Atlanta Constitution*, December 11, 1937, "Cox Says Pay Bill Would Put South in 'Strait-Jacket.'" "The whole bill is determined to check": *New York Times*, July 31, 1937, "Southerners Rake Wage Bill as Evil to Whole Nation."

32. *New York Times*, July 31, 1937, "Southerners Rake Wage Bill as Evil." See also *Atlanta Constitution*, December 11, 1937, "Cox Says Pay Bill Would Put South in 'Strait-Jacket.'"

33. "has gone off the deep end": Harold Ickes, *The Secret Diary of Harold L. Ickes: The Inside Struggle, 1936–1939.* (New York: Simon and Schuster, 1954), July 31, 1937, 2:182. "You cannot prescribe": Leuchtenburg, *White House Looks South*, 128.

34. "some labor leaders feared": James MacGregor Burns, *Congress on Trial: The Legislative Process and the Administrative State* (New York: Harper, 1949), 71. "Southerners on his committee": Burns, *Congress on Trial*, 57.

35. "three western Democrats": *Atlanta Constitution*, September 26, 1937, "Democratic Voters Oppose Administration 'Purge' in New Poll." "I believe that the twenty-seven million": *New York Times*, August 21, 1937, "Guffey Reads Out Court Bill Foes." See also *Washington Post*, August 21, 1937, "Court Foes' Defeat Is Asked by Guffey." "You said vigorously": FDR to Guffey, August 21, 1937, FDRL, PPF 451. See also James T. Patterson, "The Failure of Party Realignment in the South, 1937–1939," *Journal of Politics*, 27, 3, August 1965, 604.

36. *New York Times*, August 15, 1937, "An Unchanging Roosevelt Drives On," by Anne O'Hare McCormick.

37. Address at Roanoke Island, N.C., August 18, 1937, in *PPA*, 6:332.

38. "crackdown was imminent": *Saturday Evening Post*, February 6, 1937, "Whose Party Is It?" by Stanley High. See also *Los Angeles Times*, June 30, 1937, "Today and Tomorrow" by Walter Lippmann. "obstructing popular rule": *Newsweek*, August 28, 1937. "reprisals against the opposition": *Chicago Daily Tribune*, August 30, 1937, "Senators See Roosevelt Trip as Vengeance."

39. *Atlanta Constitution*, September 26, 1937, "Democratic Voters Oppose Administration 'Purge' in New Poll."

40. *New York Times*, September 26, 1937, "Roosevelt Views Yellowstone Park."

41. "pilot train": *Christian Science Monitor*, September 30, 1937, "When a President Goes Traveling."

42. *Washington Post*, September 26, 1937, "West Puzzles on Real Aim of Roosevelt Visit." See also *New York Times*, September 26, 1937, "Roosevelt Views Yellowstone Park."

43. Remarks at Cheyenne, Wyoming, September 24, 1937, in *PPA*, 6:382.

44. "mostly avoided controversial subjects": *New York Times*, October 5, 1937, "Third-term Talk Growing in West." See also Address at St. Paul, Minnesota, October 4, 1937, in *PPA*, 6:403. "greeted each other effusively": *New York Times*, September 28, 1937, "President Tells of His 'Planning' for Better Nation." "bigger objectives": *New York Times*, September 28, 1937, "Text of the President's Speech Delivered at Boise." See also *Hartford Courant*, September 28, 1937, " 'Petty' Issues Put Aside by Roosevelt."

45. "slammed the president as a would-be American dictator": *Washington Post*, September 26, 1937, "West Puzzles on Real Aim of Roosevelt Visit." "sneaking off to California": *Hartford Courant*, September 27, 1937, "Wheeler-Roosevelt Split Seen to be Permanent."

46. "drove furiously from Chicago": *Washington Post*, September 26, 1937, "West Puzzles as Roosevelt Hides Trip's Real Purpose." See also *New York Times*, September 25, 1937, "Roosevelt Shuns a Court Reprisal." "unwanted guest": *Christian Science Monitor*, September 25, 1937, "President Puts New Deal Again on the Counter." "lip service": Informal Remarks in Casper, Wyoming, September 24, 1937, in *PPA*, 6:384. "crossed Nebraska in the middle of the night": *New York Times*, October 3, 1937, "West Ponders Effect of Roosevelt's Tour." See also Kenneth Davis, *FDR: Into the Storm* (New York: Random House, 1993), 118.

47. *Atlanta Constitution*, September 26, 1937, "U.S. Senators Wheeler, Burke, O'Mahoney Are Upheld in Polls."

48. "tackling the problems of the day": Remarks at Casper, Wyoming, September 24, 1937, in *PPA*, 1937, 6:384. "I feel that I regain my strength": Informal Remarks at Boise, Idaho, September 27, 1937, in *PPA*, 6:387. "told me I was lucky": *Los Angeles Times*, September 28, 1937, "Itinerant Rides Roosevelt Train."

49. "returned to the Wages and Hours bill": President Calls Congress into Extraordinary Session, October 12, 1937, in *PPA*, 6:428. See also Message to the Extraordinary Session, November 15, 1937, in *PPA*, 6:46. "investigated Hawaii's application for statehood": *New York Times*, October 13, 1937, "Members Are Divided on Need for Session."

50. "stock market sank": Kenneth Roose, "The Recession of 1937–1938," *Journal of Political Economy*, 56, 3, June 1948, 239–248. "headed for another depression": James MacGregor Burns, *Roosevelt: The Lion and the Fox* (New York: Harcourt, Brace, 1956), 320. "hailed prospect of balanced budget": FDR to Garner, July 7, 1937, in *FDR: His Personal Letters*, 1:693.

51. "jaw visibly swollen": Robert H. Jackson, *That Man: An Insider's Portrait of Franklin D. Roosevelt*, ed. John Q. Barrett (New York: Oxford University Press, 2003), 138. "on rough seas": Davis, *FDR: Into the Storm*, 150. "the holiday mood": Jackson, *That Man*, 140ff. "boiled owl": FDR to Eleanor Roosevelt, Novem-

ber 30, 1937, in *FDR: His Personal Letters,* 1:730. "cruise was cut short": *New York Times,* December 4, 1937, "Roosevelt Cruise is Cut by Two Days."

52. "swapped everything": See Burns, *Congress on Trial.* "recommit it to committee": *Atlanta Constitution,* December 18, 1937, "House Shelves Roosevelt Wage-Hour Bill." "133 Democrats": James T. Patterson, *Congressional Conservatism and the New Deal: The Growth of the Conservative Coalition in Congress* (Lexington: University of Kentucky Press, 1967), 196. "triumphant roar of applause": *Atlanta Constitution,* December 18, 1937, "House Shelves Roosevelt Wage-Hour Bill." "pure selfishness": Burns, *Congress on Trial,* 79.

53. "goose egg affair": *Atlanta Constitution,* December 22, 1937, "Congress Quits without Passing Single Must Bill." "fighting like a cornered lion": Diary entry, November 8, 1937 in John Morton Blum, ed., *From the Morgenthau Diaries: Years of Crisis: 1928–1938* (Boston: Houghton, Mifflin, 1959), 394.

4. Southern Insurgents

1. *Hartford Courant,* December 4, 1937, "Douglas Gives Secret Recovery Program." See also *New York Herald Tribune,* December 4, 1937. James T. Patterson, *Congressional Conservatism and the New Deal: The Growth of the Conservative Coalition in Congress* (Lexington: University of Kentucky Press, 1967), 201.

2. "illegal and contrary to public policy"; "take the initiative away": Patterson, *Congressional Conservatism and the New Deal,* 137, 201. "fight against party's liberal platform": *New Republic,* June 22, 1938.

3. "I feel that we should stand by": Bailey to Stacy Brewer, May 11, 1935, quoted in Patterson, *Congressional Conservatism and the New Deal,* 28. "Bailey boasted": Bailey to Earl Godbey, November 11, 1936, quoted in Patterson, "The Failure of Party Realignment in the South, 1937–1939," *Journal of Politics,* 27, 3, August 1965, 611. "prepared to act the part of fox": Bailey to Stacy Brewer, May 11, 1935, quoted in Patterson, *Congressional Conservatism and the New Deal,* 28.

4. "leasing out their party": *New York Times,* May 1, 1938, "Party Chiefs Confused." "We will return": Bailey quoted in *Raleigh News and Observer,* July 8, 1934, quoted in George Tindall, *The Emergence of the New South, 1913–1945* (Baton Rouge: Louisiana State University Press, 1967), 612.

5. "party changing before their eyes": Rexford Tugwell, *The Democratic Roosevelt* (Garden City, N.Y.: Doubleday, 1957), 418. See also James L. Sundquist, *Dynamics of the Party Sytem: Alignment and Realignment of Political Parties in the United States* (Washington: Brookings Institution, 1973), 245ff. "Children are supposed to look after": Ronald L. Heinemann, *Harry Byrd of Virginia* (Charlottesville: University Press of Virginia, 1996), 155. "adding-machine mentality": Ronald L. Heinemann, *Depression and New Deal in Virginia* (Charlottesville: University Press of Virginia, 1983), 179. See also Jordan Schwartz, *The New Dealers: Power*

Politics in the Age of Roosevelt (New York: Knopf, 1993), 321; Jason Smith, *Building New Deal Liberalism* (Cambridge: Cambridge University Press, 2006), 116–117; Allan Michie, *Dixie Demagogues* (New York: Vanguard Press, 1939).

6. "black voters had shifted": Nancy J. Weiss, *Farewell to the Party of Lincoln: Black Politics in the Age of FDR* (Princeton: Princeton University Press, 1983), passim. "negro party": Alan Brinkley, "The New Deal and Southern Politics," in *The New Deal and the South,* ed. James C. Cobb (Jackson: University Press of Mississippi, 1984), 115. "theatrical exit": *New York Times,* June 26, 1936, "Smith of South Carolina Walks Out Again." "photos circulated of Eleanor Roosevelt": Tyndall, *Emergence of the New South,* 617.

7. "Vandenberg extended an invitation": Patterson, "Failure of Party Realignment in the South," 605. "Vandenberg offered to support a conservative": *Washington Post,* September 19, 1937, "Events of Week May Unite All Conservatives." "liquidation": *New York Times,* June 2, 1936, "Coalition Advised by Herald Tribune."

8. "absolved southerners": *Fayette-Chronicle,* September 28, 1937, quoted in Leuchtenburg, *White House Looks South,* 127. "take a walk": *Nation,* July 10, 1937.

9. "no conditions": *New York Herald Tribune,* June 3, 1938, quoted in Patterson, *Congressional Conservatism and the New Deal,* 256. "I am unable to see much difference": James MacGregor Burns and Susan Dunn, *The Three Roosevelts: Patrician Leaders Who Transformed America* (New York: Atlantic Monthly Press, 2001), 381.

10. "nothing to gain by disrupting": Sundquist, *Dynamics of the Party System,* 246. "cordially disliked": Patterson, "Failure of Party Realignment in the South," 616.

11. "the balance of power": Alexander P. Lamis, *The Two-Party South* (New York: Oxford University Press, 1984), 8–11. See also Vincent P. de Santis, "Republican Efforts to 'Crack' the Democratic South," *Review of Politics,* 14, 2, April 1952, 262. "the worst thing that could happen": Richard Hofstadter, "From Calhoun to the Dixiecrats," *Social Research,* 16, 1949, 140. See also Paul Lewinson, *Race, Class, and Party: A History of Negro Suffrage and White Politics in the South* (New York: Oxford University Press, 1932), 74.

12. "neither you nor I desire to be a party": Bailey to Clarence Shuping, August 31, 1935, quoted in Patterson, "The Failure of Party Realignment in the South," 610. "very preservation": Freidel, *F.D.R. and the South,* 80.

13. *Atlanta Constitution,* January 12, 1938, "Warning from the South."

14. "inertia": Lamis, *Two-Party South,* 34. "not a half-way Democrat": Patterson, *Congressional Conservatism and the New Deal,* 254. Still, there were limits to southerners' patience with the Democratic Party. Glass began to wonder if he

and his southern colleagues would continue to cast their electoral votes for the Democratic presidential candidate or if they would "have spirit and courage enough to face the new Reconstruction era that northern so-called Democrats are menacing us with." "Administration of my Party": Bailey to D. J. B. Cranill, May 22, 1935, quoted in Patterson, *Congressional Conservatism and the New Deal,* 27.

15. "have come into the house": Bailey to E. Worth Higgins, August 16, 1939, quoted in Patterson, "Failure of Party Realignment in the South," 613. "We'll not let anybody": *Atlanta Constitution,* January 13, 1938, "Democrats Split on Lynching Bill."

16. *New York Times,* June 26, 1936, "Smith of Carolina Walks Out Again."

17. *Nation,* July 10, 1937.

18. *New York Times,* October 1, 1937, "Party Bolt Plea Derided by Farley."

19. "magic of spending": *New York Times,* April 5, 1936, "Hoover Attacks Charges He Left Heritage of Ruin." "day of reckoning": *New York Times,* December 8, 1937, "Role of New Deal in Slump Debated"; *New York Times,* December 9, 1937, "Mr. Douglas' Views."

20. *New York Times,* December 16, 1937, "10 Points Drafted." See also *Newsweek,* December 27, 1937, "Congress Revolt Wins, and a Revolution Loses."

21. "reduced public expenditures": Patterson, *Congressional Conservatism and the New Deal,* 205. "thirty to forty": *New York Times,* December 16, 1937, "10 Points Drafted."

22. "leaked to the syndicated columnist": Patterson, *Congressional Conservatism and the New Deal,* 209. "scorned in much of the press": *Atlanta Constitution,* December 15, 1937, "The Capital Parade," by Joseph Alsop and Robert Kintner. See also Patterson, *Congressional Conservatism and the New Deal,* 204. "Democrats ran for cover": *New York Times,* December 17, 1937, "Congressmen Shun 'Coalition' Move: Democrats Balk at Appearing to Be Rebels." See also *New York Times,* December 17 1937, "Coalition Manifesto." "Gerry denied": *New York Times,* December 19, 1937, "In the Nation." "patriotically dramatic": Patterson, *Congressional Conservatism and the New Deal,* 209. "Anyone who signs that thing": *Newsweek,* December 27, 1937, 12. See also *New York Times,* December 19, 1937, "Barren Session Waning," by Arthur Krock.

23. "father of this waif": *Congressional Record,* 75th Congress, 2nd Session, p. 1935, quoted in Patterson, *Congressional Conservatism and the New Deal,* 204. "paternity": *Congressional Record,* 75th Congress, 2nd Session, p. 1935, quoted in Patterson, *Congressional Conservatism and the New Deal,* 204.

24. *New York Times,* December 21, 1937, "Senate Democrats Praise 'Manifesto.'"

25. "Liberty League": *Congressional Record,* 75th Congress, 2nd Session, November 15, 1937–December 21, 1937. "conciliatory spin on the document": *New York*

Times, December 17, 1937, "Congressmen Shun 'Coalition' Move." "wise and necessary"; "Stand up": *New York Times*, December 21, 1937, "Senate Democrats Praise Manifesto."

26. John Robert Moore, "Senator Josiah W. Bailey and the 'Conservative Manifesto' of 1937," *Journal of Southern History*, 31, 1, February 1965, 36.

27. "enemies he has made": *New York Times*, June 27, 1936, "Drama in Night Session." "There are good evidences here": Bailey to Julian Miller, December 20, 1937, quoted in Moore, "Senator Josiah W. Bailey and the 'Conservative Manifesto.'"

28. "other New Deal critics": *Philadelphia Inquirer*, December 21, 1937. "platform of some party in the future": *Atlanta Constitution*, December 17, 1937, "Publicity Upsets Secret Program of Bloc in Senate." "businesses also printed": Moore, "Senator Josiah W. Bailey and the Conservative 'Manifesto,'" 38.

29. *New York Times*, December 16, 1937, "10 Points Drafted."

30. Radio Address, November 4, 1938, in PPA, 7:586. See also Burns, *Roosevelt: The Lion and the Fox*, 365.

31. Kenneth Davis, *FDR: Into the Storm* (New York: Random House, 1993), 244. When the son of the famous architect Frank Lloyd Wright huffed to *Life* that Roosevelt had dared to infringe on the "integrity and the dignity" of the architectural profession, the architect of the New Deal shot back. "By the way," Roosevelt said, "did Thomas Jefferson have a license when he drew the sketches for Monticello, the University of Virginia and a number of other rather satisfactory architectural productions?" (*New York Times*, June 14, 2001, "A Pied-a-Terre Designed by a President.") Roosevelt identified with Jefferson; both men were amateur architects, champions of average Americans, and foes of the nation's economic elite. And they were both believers in perpetual change. "The earth belongs to the living," Jefferson had written to James Madison, explaining that each generation had the right to make new laws for itself and govern the way it pleased (Jefferson to Madison, September 6, 1789, in Susan Dunn, *Something That Will Surprise the World: The Essential Writings of the Founding Fathers* (New York: Basic Books, 2006), 284–288).

5. The Partisan Leader Takes His First Steps

1. Harold Ickes, *The Secret Diary of Harold Ickes* (New York: Simon and Schuster, 1953–1954), 2:182.

2. Annual Message, January 3, 1938, in *The Public Papers and Addresses of Franklin D. Roosevelt*, ed. Samuel Rosenman (New York: Macmillan, 1938–50) (PPA), 7:3–13.

3. "Roosevelt exited": Ickes, *Secret Diary of Harold Ickes*, 2:288. See also *Atlanta Constitution*, January 4, 1938, "State House Lauds Message of F.D.R." "that's telling 'em": *Atlanta Constitution*, January 4, 1938, "Roosevelt Told 'Em."

4. Ickes, *Secret Diary of Harold Ickes*, 2:288.

5. "eccentrically attired": Clarence Caston, *90 Degrees in the Shade* (1935; reprint, Tuscaloosa: University of Alabama Press, 2001), 82. "spewing out hatred": *Chicago Daily Tribune*, September 30, 1937, "Find Heflin on U.S. Payroll." "Roman candidate": George Tindall, *The Emergence of the New South, 1913–1945* (Baton Rouge: Louisiana State University Press, 1967), 245. "walkout": *Atlanta Constitution*, September 14, 1937, "Voice of Heflin Booms."

6. "praising the president": *Los Angeles Times*, October 27, 1933, "Comeback Bee Stings Heflin"; *Atlanta Constitution*, February 6, 1936, "Roosevelt Lauded." "once forcibly ejected": *Chicago Daily Tribune*, September 30, 1937, "Find Heflin on U.S. Payroll."

7. "Hill was lukewarm": *Washington Post*, November 8, 1937, "Alabama Race." "broad swath of Alabamans": *Washington Post*, December 23, 1937, "The South on Wages." "meeting with Hill": *Washington Post*, December 6, 1937, "May Have Bone in Jaw Scraped." "Hill trounced Heflin": *New York Times*, January 5 1938, "Hill, New Dealer, Swamps Heflin." See also *Washington Post*, January 5, 1938, "Rep. Hill Leading Heflin"; *Time*, 17 January 1938.

8. "conspicuously absented": *New York Times*, January 9, 1938, "Seeks Good of All" and "Bailey Likes Jackson." "the Jackson I know": *Washington Post*, January 9, 1938, "Sen. Bailey Shuns Jackson Dinner."

9. *New York Times*, January 9, 1938, "Seeks Good of All."

10. "In 1904"; "slough off": Jackson Day Address, January 8, 1938, in *PPA*, 7:37–45.

11. "old law partner": *New York Times*, March 25, 1938, "Roosevelt Tours Warm Springs." "town center that was reconstructed": *Atlanta Constitution*, April 7, 1936, "150 Are Known Dead"; *New York Times*, March 23, 1938, "Roosevelt Leaves for Warm Springs Visit"; B. M. Sigmon, "The Gainesville Tornado," *American Journal of Nursing*, 37, 2, February 1937, 131.

12. *Atlanta Constitution*, March 24, 1938, "Chief Executive Hits Selfishness, 'Feudal System.'"

13. "greatest leader"; "cheers and whistles": *Atlanta Constitution*, March 24, 1938, "Roosevelt Revives Wage Fight."

14. "You were not content"; "minds are cast in the 1938 mold": Address at Gainesville, March 23, 1938, in PPA, 7:164–169.

15. David Nolan Thomas, "Roosevelt vs. George: The Presidential Purge Campaign of 1938," M.A. thesis, University of North Carolina, 1953. See also *Atlanta Constitution*, March 24, 1938, "Roosevelt Revives Fight."

16. "irritation that president had presumed": *New York Times*, March 27, 1938, "Presidential Ire Aroused of Late"; *Time*, April 4, 1938. "I exulted": Thomas L. Stokes, *Chip off My Shoulder* (Princeton: Princeton University Press, 1940), 529.

17. Bayer Aspirin: *Atlanta Constitution*, March 24, 1938, ad, 8.

18. Samuel I. Rosenman, *Working with Roosevelt* (New York: Harper, 1952), 173.

19. Fireside Chat, April 14, 1938, in *PPA*, 1938, 7:242.

20. *New York Times*, April 7, 1938, "U.S. Recognizes Anschluss."

21. "German octopus": See Henry Wolfe, *The German Octopus* (New York: Doubleday, 1938). "peace at any price": FDR to Joseph Tumulty, December 23, 1937 in *FDR: His Personal Letters, 1928–1945*, ed. Elliott Roosevelt, 3 vols. (New York: Duell, Sloan and Pearce 1950), 1:736. See also FDR to Endicott Peabody, October 16, 1937, in *FDR: His Personal Letters*, 1:717. "breeding far more serious trouble": FDR to John Cudahy, April 16, 1938 in *FDR: His Personal Letters*, 2:776.

22. ("cripple any president"): Kenneth Davis, *FDR: Into the Storm* (New York: Random House, 1993), 189.

23. "209 nays to 188 yeas": *Christian Science Monitor*, January 10, 1938, "House Blocks Vote of People." "standing invitation": *Washington Post*, January 3, 1938, "Big Navy, Boycott of Japan Tydings' Peace Prescription."

24. "against Hitler's anti-Semitic policies": Caroline Keith, *"For Hell and a Brown Mule": The Biography of Millard E. Tydings* (Lanham, Md.: Madison Books, 1991), 97. "among the staunchest supporters": James MacGregor Burns, *Roosevelt: The Soldier of Freedom* (New York: Harcourt Brace Jovanovich, 1970), 40. "striking back": In the spring of 1938, those foes even included his own vice president. Jack Garner, it was reported in April, three days after the president's fireside chat, was in open rebellion against Roosevelt. In the early years of FDR's administration, Garner used to remind recalcitrant Democrats that FDR was "the leader of your party, so he's your guy." But the president had begun to move too fast for Garner's taste. The secretary of labor, Frances Perkins, reported hearing Garner say, "Mr. President, you know you've got to let the cattle graze." The vice president could not stomach Roosevelt's Court bill, Wages and Hours bill, and proposals for more relief spending. Not only was Roosevelt no longer his guy, Garner, according to Harold Ickes, was "sticking his knife into the President's back."

25. *New York Times*, April 29, 1938, "Gov. Phil Keynoter."

26. "failed capitalism": *New York Times*, June 5, 1938, "New Party Forced, Says La Follette." "coddling": *New York Times*, May 24, 1938, "Slow Progress of the N.P.P." "opposed military preparedness": *New York Times*, April 25, 1938, "La Follette Warns of Arms Program."

27. *New York Times*, June 5, 1938, "New Party Forced, Says La Follette."

28. "darkly shadowed": *Life*, May 9, 1938, 9. "symbol of their inalienable rights": *New York Times*, April 30, 1938, "Explains Liberal Emblem." His painful explanations didn't allay people's suspicion and scorn. Even the Wisconsin *Capital Times*, a newspaper that had been friendly to La Follette, editorialized that the cause of liberalism would be better served if liberals followed one leader "and

that is Roosevelt." "spoke admiringly": Phil La Follette, interview by Max Lerner, *Nation*, May 14, 1938.

29. *New York Times*, May 2, 1938, "Hoover Scans 'New Party.'" See also *New York Times*, April 30, 1938, "Opinion in Capital on 3d Party Varies."

30. *New York Times*, May 6, 1938, "La Follette Move Decried by Ickes."

31. "third party threat": FDR to Josephus Daniels, November 14, 1938, in *FDR: His Personal Letters*, 2:827. "joked about the grotesque Nazi resonances": FDR to William Phillips, May 18, 1938, in *FDR: His Personal Letters*, 2:785.

32. *New York Times*, May 14, 1938, "President Invites La Follette on Cruise, Amid Rumors of Strained Relations."

33. *New York Times*, May 15, 1938, "La Follette on Roosevelt Trip."

34. Ickes, *Secret Diary of Harold Ickes*, 2:395.

35. "party imploded": *Los Angeles Times*, May 16, 1938, "The Political Bandwagon." "Any sound political realignment": Philip La Follette to Edwin Hadfield, October 7, 1937, quoted in Donald McCoy, "The National Progressives of America, 1938," *Mississippi Valley Historical Review*, 44, 1, June 1957, 78.

36. Press Conference, April 21, 1938, in *PPA*, 7:264.

37. Lindsay Warren to Steve Early, April 29, 1938, Franklin Delano Roosevelt Library (FDRL), OF 300, box 27.

38. *New York Times*, May 1, 1938, "Party Chiefs Confused."

39. "deep ideological rift:": V. O. Key, *Southern Politics and the Nation* (New York: Knopf, 1949), 82. "I want to make the state liberal": Claude Denson Pepper, *Pepper: Eyewitness to a Century* (New York: Harcourt Brace Jovanovich, 1987), 66.

40. "do some fighting": *Time*, May 2, 1938. "filibustered": Pepper, *Pepper*, 66. "man who was trying to help you": *Time*, May 2, 1938.

41. "Don't you think": Memorandum for the President from James Roosevelt, James Roosevelt Papers, FDRL, box 52. "check for ten thousand dollars": James MacGregor Burns, *Congress on Trial: The Legislative Process and the Administrative State* (New York: Harper, 1949), 81. "asked Jimmy to endorse Pepper": Pepper, *Pepper*, 71. "stopped in Palm Beach": Pepper, *Pepper*, 70. "From the bottom of my heart": Claude Pepper to James Roosevelt, February 7, 1938, James Roosevelt Papers, FDRL, box 52.

42. "best wisecrack": *Time*, May 2, 1938. "fared much better": *New York Times*, February 13, 1938, "James Roosevelt Arouses Floridians."

43. FDR to Arthur Murray, May 13, 1938, in *FDR: His Personal Letters*, 2:781. See also *New York Times*, May 5, 1938, "New Deal Backers Hail Florida Vote."

44. "Jimmy Roosevelt guessed": *New York Times*, May 5, 1938, "New Deal Backers Hail Florida Vote." "stampede": Frances Perkins, *The Roosevelt I Knew* (New York: Viking, 1946), 263. "no longer oppose the wage bill": *New York Times*, May 8, 1938, "Decide to Abandon Fight on Wage Bill."

45. "Despite these compromises": *Chicago Daily Tribune*, June 15, 1938, "Pass Wage Act." See also Andrew J. Seltzer, "The Political Economy of the Fair Labor Standards Act of 1938," *Journal of Political Economy*, 103, 6, December 1995, 1302–1342. "opened the door": *New York Times*, June 15, 1938, "Wage Bill Passed by House."

46. "calamity-howling executive": Fireside Chat, June 24, 1938, in *PPA*, 7:392. "most vital social legislation": Davis, *FDR: Into the Storm*, 241. "increase in their pay": Bureau of Labor Statistics Report, *New York Times*, May 17, 1938, "President Insists on Reorganization." "historic feat": *New York Times*, June 17, 1938, "In the Nation."

47. *Wall Street Journal*, June 8, 1938, "The Iowa Primaries."

48. "denied him admission to House floor": *Washington Post*, June 7, 1938, "Results in Iowa." "Wearin was known": John E. Hopper, "The Purge: Franklin D. Roosevelt and the 1938 Democratic Nominations," Ph.D. diss., University of Chicago, 1966, 73. See also *Time*, June 23, 1938, "Pumps and Polls"; *Newsweek*, June 6, 1938, "Hopkins Intervention in Iowa." "voted against AAA, the NIRA": *Washington Post*, May 31, 1938, "Harrington Off to Aid Gillette."

49. Jerry Harrington, "Senator Guy Gillette Foils the Execution Committee," *Palimpsest*, 62, 1981, 176.

50. "political whip"; "puppet": Harrington, "Senator Guy Gillette Foils the Execution Committee," 177. "If Mr. Hopkins lived in Iowa": *Des Moines Register*, May 25, 1938, quoted in Hopper, "Purge," 82.

51. "playing politics with human misery": *Chicago Daily Tribune*, May 26, 1938, "Political Use of WPA Billions." "trading WPA jobs": *Washington Post*, May 26, 1938, "Senate Storm Breaks Over Hopkins Role"; *Atlanta Constitution*, April 26, 1938, "Loaded WPA Rolls Charged in Florida." "politics oozed": *Los Angeles Times*, May 27, 1938, "Holt and Copeland Link WPA Funds to Politics."

52. "Senate rejected Hatch's proposal": *Washington Post*, June 3, 1938, "Hatch Asks a 'Cleanup.'"

53. "political termites": Harrington, "Senator Guy Gillette Foils the Execution Committee," 177. "statements of neutrality": *Chicago Daily Tribune*, May 26, 1938, "Senators Lash Political use of WPA Billions." "prostitute the basic principles": Harrington, "Senator Guy Gillette Foils the Execution Committee," 179. "absentee ballot": *New York Times*, June 4, 1938, "Herring Favors Gillette." "monetary assistance": David Robertson, *Sly and Able: A Political Biography of James F. Byrnes* (New York: Norton, 1994), 270.

54. "say nothing publicly": *New York Times*, June 1, 1938, "Roosevelt to Bar Primary Comment"; *New York Times*, June 5, 1938, "Gillette Favored to Defeat 'Purge.'" "public telegram": *Washington Post*, June 4, 1938, "Roosevelt Son Backs Wearin." "silent and neutral": *New York Times*, May 28, 1938, "Gillette Rushes

Into Iowa Battle." "keep your mouth shut": Edwin Watson, Ross McIntyre, Steve Early to Harry Hopkins, May 31, 1938, FDRL, File 4096. Personal Papers. See also Hopper, "Purge," 83. "he came up pitifully short": *New York Times,* June 7, 1938, "Gillette Winning in Iowa."

55. "vindication for democracy": *New York Times,* June 8, 1938, "FDR Satisfied with Gillette's Victory in Iowa." "would not seek another term": *New York Times,* June 17, 1938, "Wearin Not to Run for House."

56. *New York Times,* June 12, 1938, "Last Days of Congress Dominated by Politics." See also Ronald C. Schurin, "The President as Disciplinarian: Wilson, Roosevelt, and Congressional Primaries," *Presidential Studies Quarterly,* 28, 2, Spring 1998, 409–421.

57. *Chicago Daily Tribune,* June 1, 1938, "Wheeler Warns Party of Peril."

58. James MacGregor Burns, *The Crosswinds of Freedom* (New York: Knopf, 1989), 109.

59. *Atlanta Constitution,* June 13, 1938, "Roosevelt and Gillette Shed Coats at Chummy Meal in White House."

60. *Newsweek,* June 27, 1938, "Congress Ends Seesaw Session."

6. Rolling Westward

1. *New York Times,* July 10, 1938, "Campaign Tour."

2. *Atlanta Constitution,* July 11, 1938, "Capital Parade," by Joseph Alsop. See also *Time,* July 18, 1938; *Christian Science Monitor,* July 8, 1938, "President's Purge."

3. *Chicago Daily Tribune,* July 9, 1938, "President Aids 'Dear Alben.'"

4. "Cavalry captain": Address at Marietta, Ohio, July 8, 1938, in *The Public Papers and Addresses of Franklin D. Roosevelt,* ed. Samuel Rosenman (New York, Macmillan: 1938–50) (*PPA*), 7:430. "Bulkley's bill": *Christian Science Monitor,* July 8, 1938, "President's Purge."

5. James MacGregor Burns and Susan Dunn, *The Three Roosevelts: Patrician Leaders Who Transformed America* (New York: Atlantic Monthly Press, 2001), 377.

6. "a few people fainted": *Atlanta Constitution,* July 9, 1938, "Roosevelt Backs Barkley." "pushed to get near": *Atlanta Constitution,* July 11, 1938, "Capital Parade."

7. *Atlanta Constitution,* July 19, 1938, "Roosevelt's Popularity Increases."

8. "president tried to dissuade Chandler": J. B. Shannon, "Presidential Politics in the South: 1938, I," *Journal of Politics,* 1, 2, May 1939, 160. "Barkley had helped Happy": Alben Barkley, *That Reminds Me* (New York: Doubleday, 1954), 164. "I wish they could both win": James Farley, *Jim Farley's Story* (New York: Whittlesey House, 1948), 125 and 134.

9. Marvin McIntyre, Memo to FDR, March 7, 1938, in *F.D.R.: His Personal Letters, 1928–1945,* ed. Elliott Roosevelt (New York: Duell, Sloan and Pearce, 1947–50), 2:765.

10. Address at Covington, Kentucky, July 8, 1938, in *PPA*, 7:432–439.

11. John E. Hopper, "The Purge: Franklin D. Roosevelt and the 1938 Democratic Nominations," Ph.D. diss., University of Chicago, 1966, 102; *New York Times*, July 1, 1938, "Hopkins Punishes 2 on Kentucky WPA."

12. "plopped himself down": Barkley, *That Reminds Me*, 166. "Roosevelt enjoyed imitating": Barkley, *That Reminds Me*, 166. See also Sean Savage, *Roosevelt the Party Leader* (Lexington: University of Kentucky Press, 1991), 140; Harold Ickes, *The Secret Diary of Harold Ickes*, 2 vols. (New York: Simon and Schuster, 1954), 2:342.

13. "appearance in Kentucky": Farley, *Jim Farley's Story: The Roosevelt Years*, 134. "nicknames of people": *Time*, August 1, 1938.

14. "You can't do that to me": *Time*, August 1, 1938. "Please, God": Allan Michie, *Dixie Demagogues* (New York: Vanguard, 1939), 207. "successful introduction of legislation": *Louisville Courier-Journal*, February 15, 1938, quoted in Hopper, "Purge," 109.

15. "yes man": *Washington Post*, August 4, 1938, "Barkley Admits He Is 'Yes Man.'" "Liberty League backed Chandler": *Louisville Times*, August 2, 1938. See also Shannon, "Presidential Politics in the South: 1938, I," 164.

16. Barkley, *That Reminds Me*, 164.

17. "president listened": *Los Angeles Times*, July 10, 1938, "Roosevelt Makes Plea for Liberal Policies." See also *New York Times*, July 10, 1938, "Names Two Senators." "restrained and tepid pat": *New York Times*, July 10, 1938, "Roosevelt Calls on Voters in Oklahoma and Arkansas."

18. *Chicago Daily Tribune*, July 10, 1938, "President Hits Thomas' Foes."

19. *New York Times*, July 31, 1932, "Arkansas Awaits Huey Long's Visit." See also *Washington Post*, September 25, 1932, "From a Senator's Diary."

20. *Hartford Courant*, July 10, 1938, "Roosevelt Goes to Aid of Thomas."

21. "appealed to the White House": Josh Lee to FDR, June 22, 1938, Franklin Delano Roosevelt Library, Hyde Park, N.Y. (FDRL), Personal Papers, N. 1820. See also Hopper, "Purge," 122. "Not only did Harold Ickes": Hopper, "Purge," 123.

22. Farley, *Jim Farley's Story*, 124.

23. "most serious of our home-grown": *New Republic*, July 13, 1938, "The President's Son," 279. "popular proposal in Oklahoma": Hopper, "Purge," 120.

24. "conservative positions": *Chicago Daily Tribune*, July 10, 1938, "President Hits Thomas' Foes." "made old Dr. Townsend look": Hopper, "Purge," 120.

25. *Chicago Daily Tribune*, July 10, 1938, "President Hits Thomas' Foes."

26. *Los Angeles Times*, July 10, 1938, "Roosevelt Makes Plea for Liberal Candidates."

27. *Los Angeles Times*, July 1, 1938, "Political Purge Opinion Shown."

28. "As my boys would say": *New York Times,* July 10, 1938, "Names 2 Senators." "Your visit was most timely": Elmer Thomas to FDR, July 13, 1938, Democratic National Committee, FDRL, box 56. See also Hopper, "Purge," 125.

29. Frank Freidel, *F.D.R. and the South* (Baton Rouge: Louisiana State University Press, 1965), 101.

30. "Elliott's hilltop ranch": Patrick Hughes, "West Texas Swing: Roosevelt Purge in Land of the Lone Star," *West Texas Historical Association Yearbook,* 75, 1999, 41–51. "In times of emergency": *Christian Science Monitor,* July 11, 1938, "President Sees Rich Crops along Rim of 'Dust Bowl.' "

31. *Christian Science Monitor,* July 11, 1938, "President Sees Rich Crops."

32. *Los Angeles Times,* July 12, 1938, "Nation's Chiefs Exchange Wires."

33. "cattle and cotton": *Los Angeles Times,* July 11, 1938, "Texans Hear President Rap Cheap Labor." "I am proud": *Los Angeles Times,* July 11, 1938, "Texans Hear President Rap Cheap Labor."

34. *New York Times,* July 12, 1938, "President Hails 5 Texans." See also Frank H. Smyrl, "Tom Connally and the New Deal," Ph.D. diss., University of Oklahoma, 1968, 229.

35. " 'cool' toward the senator": *New York Times,* July 12, 1938, "President Hails 5 Texans." "calculated gesture": "I was asked to join the President's train," Connally later recalled. "When we got to Wichita Falls, the home of Allred, the train stopped. Elliott Roosevelt, the President's son, came to the car where I was sitting. 'Dad wants you to come out on the back platform with him, Senator,' he said. When I reached the back platform, Roosevelt . . . announced to the crowd with a big flourish and in a sarcastic tone of voice that he was appointing Allred to the court vacancy." Connally, in an icy rage, concluded that Roosevelt's intention was public mortification.

36. "representatives were unopposed": Joseph Manfield, Milton West, and Clyde Garrett. "quackery": Hughes, "West Texas Swing," 44.

37. *New York Times,* July 12, 1938, "President Hails 5 Texans."

38. Address at Amarillo, Texas, July 11, 1938, in *PPA,* 7:449–450.

39. "life of a hobo": J. T. Salter, ed., *The American Politician* (Chapel Hill: University of North Carolina Press, 1938), 157. "one of the most conservative districts in Texas": *New York Times,* July 26, 1938, "Maverick Defeat Held Garner Trend." "managed to alienate the American Federation of Labor": *Newsweek,* August 1, 1938, "Primary Upsets." "brother of his police chief": *New Republic,* August 3, 1938, "Bad News from Texas."

40. "write the prescription": *Louisville Courier-Journal,* August 1, 1938, "Washington Merry-Go-Round," by Drew Pearson. See also Hopper, "Purge," 129. "approved funds for an airfield": FDR to James Roosevelt, n. d.; James Roosevelt

to Daniel Bell, May 2, 1938, James Roosevelt Papers, FDRL, file 25. "strong letter of support": Ickes, *Secret Diary of Harold Ickes*, 2:421.

41. George Brown Tindall, *The Emergence of the New South, 1913–1945* (Baton Rouge: Louisiana State University Press, 1967), 622.

42. "annual look-see": Informal Remarks at Grand Junction, Colorado, July 12, 1938, in *PPA*, 7:456. "no chance to beat him": Ickes, *Secret Diary of Harold Ickes*, 2:421.

43. "made no reference": *Time*, July 25, 1938. "That river isn't just the problem": Remarks at Pueblo, Colorado, July 12, 1938, in *PPA*, 7:453.

44. "no opposition in the Democratic primary": *Chicago Daily Tribune*, July 14, 1938, "Nevada Senator Has Chilly Ride with Roosevelt." "off-hand remark": *Hartford Courant*, July 14, 1938, "Oklahoma Win Hailed by New Deal."

45. "considered himself a socialist: Hopper, "Purge," 135. "Little man": *Hartford Courant*, July 14, 1938, "Oklahoma Win Hailed by New Deal." "wisecracks": Hopper, "Purge," 134. "never will be wrong": *New York Times*, May 27, 1938, "New Deal 'Purge' to Have Next Test in Iowa." "Brother Hilliard": *Time*, September 19, 1938, "Fledgling's Fall."

46. "unable to come up with a better opponent": Hopper, "Purge," 135. "personal victory": *New York Times*, July 14, 1938, "Roosevelt Silent as Both Candidates in Nevada Join Him." See also *Hartford Courant*, July 14, 1938, "Oklahoma Win Hailed by New Deal."

47. *Atlanta Constitution*, July 14, 1938, "Crowd Interrupts FDR to Applaud His Foe, McCarran." See also *Hartford Courant*, July 14, 1938, "Oklahoma Win Hailed by New Deal."

48. "trout for lunch": *Hartford Courant*, July 14, 1938, "Oklahoma Win Hailed by New Deal." "took center stage": *New York Times*, July 17, 1938, "The Roosevelt 'Purge' Fails to Materialize." "rally for himself": Farley, *Jim Farley's Story*, 124.

49. *Washington Post*, August 18, 1938, "The Inner Conflict," by Mark Sullivan.

50. *New York Times*, April 17, 1938, "Missouri Sees Clark Sweep."

51. "Democratic Party would refuse": *Hartford Courant*, July 19, 1937, "Rift Widening among Democrats." "Van Nuys threatened": *New York Times*, February 17, 1938, "Court Bill's Foes Rally to Van Nuys." "group of senators": *Chicago Daily Tribune*, June 15, 1938, "U.S. Senators Aid Van Nuys." "Van Nuys Thistle and the New Deal Rose": *Hartford Courant*, July 7, 1938, "Acceptance of Van Nuys Convenient." See also *Wall Street Journal*, July 7, 1938, "Why Indiana Democratic Machine Abandoned 'Purge.'"

52. The president had discussed possible challengers to Lonergan with Homer Cummings, his attorney general also from Connecticut. But Lonergan felt the pressure and, at the last minute, headed off an attack by announcing on the radio that he supported FDR's "noble aims" and stood "with the President."

53. *Washington Post*, September 30, 1937, "Politics and People."

54. Robert Sims, "James P. Pope, Senator from Idaho," *Idaho Yesterdays*, 15, 10, 1971, 9–15.

55. "Roosevelt showered the senator": Marian McKenna, *Borah* (Ann Arbor: University of Michigan Press, 1961), 343. "hydro-electric power and irrigation project": *Hartford Courant*, August 1, 1938, "Hull Lauds Senator Pope." See also *Christian Science Monitor*, August 11, 1938, "New Deal Seeks to Discount Defeat of Pope."

56. "Farley put aside his negative feelings": *New York Times*, August 11, 1938, "Pope, New Dealer, Defeated in Idaho." "Hull's support": *Hartford Courant*, August 1, 1938, "Hull Lauds Senator Pope." See also *Christian Science Monitor*, August 11, 1938, "New Deal Seeks to Discount Defeat of Pope." "thwart those sincere": Sims, "James P. Pope, Senator from Idaho," 14.

57. Sims, "James P. Pope, Senator from Idaho," 15.

58. "morally and completely violated": 478th Press Conference, Hyde Park, August 23, 1938, in *PPA*, 7:499–501. "Pope traveled to Hyde Park": *New York Times*, August 30, 1938, "Senator Pope Undecided." "vetoed Pope's idea": *New York Times*, August 31, 1938, "Pope Decides Not to Run."

59. *New York Times*, July 17, 1938, "Roosevelt, on the Road."

60. Address at Treasure Island, San Francisco, July 14, 1938, in *PPA*, 7:456–458.

61. Ickes, *Secret Diary of Harold Ickes*, 2:342.

62. "lunatic fringe": *New Republic*, September 14, 1938, "Is the Country Conservative?" "highly popular with voters": *New York Times*, September 1, 1938, "M'Adoo Defeated."

63. "not so sugary": Farley, *Jim Farley's Story*, 134. See also FDR to William McAdoo, March 16, 1938, Personal Papers File, FDRL, 308. See also Hopper, "Purge," 146. "short-cut to Utopia"; "cruel delusion": *New York Times*, September 1, 1938, "M'Adoo Defeated."

64. *Los Angeles Times*, July 17, 1938, "President Cheered by Thousands."

65. *New York Times*, July 17, 1938, "Roosevelt 'Hopes M'Adoo will win.'" See also *Time*, July 25, 1938.

66. "headline": *Los Angeles Times*, July 17, 1938, "Re-election of M'Adoo Urged." "McAdoo autocracy": *Los Angeles Times*, July 17, 1938, "Re-election of M'Adoo Urged."

67. *Los Angeles Times*, July 17, 1938, "President Cheered by Thousands."

68. "Please stop and chat": *Los Angeles Times*, July 17, 1938, "President Cheered by Thousands." "we like you but": *Los Angeles Times*, July 17, 1938, "Re-election of M'Adoo Urged." See also *New York Times*, July 17, 1938, "Roosevelt 'Hopes M'Adoo Will Win.'"

69. *New York Times*, July 17, 1938, "Roosevelt on the Road Still 'Packs Them In.'"

70. *New York Times,* July 17, 1938, "Roosevelt on the Road, Still 'Packs Them In.'"

71. *"Houston* newly scrubbed": *Christian Science Monitor,* July 8, 1938, "Cruiser Is Converted into Presidential Yacht." "I take it you have a screamingly funny time": FDR to Marvin McIntyre, August 1, 1938, in *FDR: His Personal Letters,* 2:800.

72. "We all feel the atmosphere": *New York Times,* July 27, 1938, "Chamberlain Finds War Peril Eased." "derisive taunts": *Washington Post,* July 27, 1938, "Chamberlain Denies Policy Pushes Czechs to Surrender." "sell helium to Germany": *New York Times,* July 19, 1938, "Rosendahl Favors Reich Helium Plea." See also Ickes, *Secret Diary of Harold Ickes,* 2:427.

73. "'Pa' Watson": Elliott Roosevelt and James Brough, *A Rendezvous with Destiny* (New York: Putnam, 1975), 91. "38-pound yellow tail": *New York Times,* August 5, 1938, "Roosevelt Meets Panama President." "I got tired": *New York Times,* August 11, 1938, "Move Is a Surprise." "Rooseveltia Frankliniana": in *PPA,* Note 7:432. "Schmittsonian": Remarks in Hyde Park, August 27, 1938, in *PPA,* 7:503.

74. "occasionally they picnicked": *Washington Post,* August 3, 1938, "Roosevelt Signs Bird Refuge Bills." "sent ashore food": *Hartford Courant,* July 28, 1938, "Roosevelt Finds Fish Biting Well." "Roosevelt Loafs": *Atlanta Constitution,* July 18, 1938, "Roosevelt Loafs in Cool Breezes." "grand cruise": Remarks in Hyde Park, August 27, 1938, in *PPA,* 7:504.

75. *New York Times,* August 10, 1938, "Roosevelt Lands."

76. *New York Times,* August 10, 1938. "Roosevelt Lands." See also *Hartford Courant,* August 10, 1938 [untitled].

77. Thomas won 45 percent of the vote, compared to 21 percent for Marland and under 40 percent for Gomer Smith.

78. "Walter George is my friend": editorial, FDRL, OF 300, box 15. "photograph of Farley": *Atlanta Constitution,* June 1, 1938, "The Capital Parade."

79. *Atlanta Constitution,* June 22, 1938, "George Victory Predicted."

80. *Los Angeles Times,* August 11, 1938, "Ally Backed by Roosevelt."

81. Farley, *Jim Farley's Story,* 141.

7. Marching through Georgia

1. *Atlanta Constitution,* August 12, 1938, "Gathered to Hear the Speech of President Roosevelt at Barnesville."

2. "pine and peaches"; "Mama is that him?": *Atlanta Constitution,* August 12, 1938, "Crowd Cared Not for Rates."

3. *New York Times,* August 10, 1938, "Roosevelt Found Holding the South."

4. *Atlanta Constitution,* August 12, 1938, "Crowd Cared Not for Rates."

5. "little New Deal": George Brown Tindall, *The Emergence of the New South, 1913–1945* (Baton Rouge: Louisiana State University Press, 1967), 618. "greatest

human lover": James Fleissner, "August 11, 1938: A Day in the Life of Senator Walter F. George," *Journal of Southern Legal History*, 9, 2001, 55–101.

6. *Atlanta Constitution*, August 12, 1938, "Side Features of Memorable Roosevelt Visit."

7. D. C. Brown, *Electricity for Rural America* (Westport, Conn.: Greenwood Press, 1980), 32.

8. Davis L. Carlton, ed., *Confronting Southern Poverty in the Great Depression* (Boston: St. Martin's Press, 1996), 14–15.

9. Paul Mertz, *New Deal Policy and Southern Rural Poverty* (Baton Rouge: Louisiana State University Press, 1978), 221–252.

10. *New York Times*, August 28, 1938, "'White Supremacy' Issue Revived."

11. *Atlanta Constitution*, August 12, 1938, "Crowd Cared Not for Rates."

12. *New York Times*, August 28, 1937, "Court Bill Foes Report Hostility."

13. "oratorical contest": *New York Times*, August 21, 1938, "Four Marked for a 'Purge.'" "Miss Lucy": *New York Times*, August 18, 1938, "Personality Issue in Vote on George." "I am a Democrat": *Atlanta Constitution*, August 16, 1938, "Democratic Party Is Not One Man Party; Senator Certain He'll Win Despite 'Uneven Contest.'" "first contested primary": *Atlanta Constitution*, April 23, 1938, "Rivers to Reveal Plans."

14. "Every vote we poll": *Atlanta Constitution*, October 29, 1936, "FDR Fund Aided at Luncheon Here." "cast votes against some key administration bills": Luther Ziegler, "Senator Walter George's 1938 Campaign," *Georgia Historical Quarterly*, 43, 1959, 333. See also Brad Telfeyan, "The 1938 Georgia Democratic Senatorial Primary: The Repudiation of President Franklin D. Roosevelt's 'Purge Campaign,'" Honors thesis, History Department, Vanderbilt University, 2002.

15. "could be deceptive": Thomas G. Corcoran and Clark Foreman, "The Voting Record of Senator George in the Seventy-third, Seventy-fourth and Seventy-fifth Congress," in President's Secretary's File, Franklin Delano Roosevelt Library, Hyde Park, N.Y. (FDRL). "better New Deal voting record": Raymond Clapper, "Roosevelt Tries the Primaries," *Current History*, 19, 1938, 18–19. "I don't consider George a New Dealer": *Atlanta Constitution*, August 17, 1938, "Roosevelt Feels Little Reaction to His 'Purge' of Senator George."

16. *Atlanta Constitution*, September 2, 1938, "George Is Asked by Camp to Show Letter"; *Atlanta Constitution*, August 23, 1938, "Corcoran, Cohen Are Reds."

17. Frances Perkins, Oral History, Columbia University Libraries, pt. 7, sess. 1, pp. 311–313.

18. "I hasten to assure you": George to FDR, June 27, 1938, FDRL, PSF 151. See also William E. Leuchtenburg, *The White House Looks South: Franklin D. Roosevelt, Harry S. Truman, Lyndon B. Johnson* (Baton Rouge: Louisiana State

University Press, 2005), 92. "welcome and support any program": *Atlanta Constitution*, July 10, 1938, "Solid South Split over F.D.R. Study."

19. June 29, FDRL, PSF 151.

20. "I think you're foolish": James Farley, *Jim Farley's Story: The Roosevelt Years* (New York: Whittlesey House, 1948), 122, 133–34. "happened to be in Atlanta": Farley, *Jim Farley's Story*, 128–129. See also David Nolan Thomas, "Roosevelt vs. George," Master's Thesis, University of North Carolina, 1955, 34. "15 minutes before the deadline": Clapper, "Roosevelt Tries the Primaries," 18. See also *New York Times*, June 5, 1938, "Two New Dealers Seek Georgia Seat."

21. "wild man": V. O. Key, *Southern Politics* (New York: Knopf, 1949), 115. "red suspenders": *Atlanta Constitution*, September 14, 1938, "Talmadge Closes Race at Forsyth." See also *New York Times*, September 16, 1938, "Majority Piled up for George." "This man is darkness": Leuchtenburg, *White House Looks South*, 125.

22. "uncouth red-neck": Key, *Southern Politics*, 116. "racket": George Wolfskill and John Hudson, *All but the People: Franklin D. Roosevelt and His Critics, 1933–1939* (New York: Macmillan, 1969), 14. "can't walk around": Leuchtenburg, *White House Looks South*, 125. "loafers and bums": FDRL, OF 300, box 15. "Nigger, nigger": Leuchtenburg, *White House Looks South*, 124. "starved social services": Tindall, *Emergence of the New South*, 616. "mean as cat shit": Leuchtenburg, *White House Looks South*, 125. See also James Cobb, "Not Gone, but Forgotten: Eugene Talmadge and the 1938 Purge Campaign," *Georgia Historical Quarterly*, 59, 1975, 197–209.

23. *Atlanta Constitution*, August 12, 1938, "FDR Opens War against George."

24. "support of the ultra-right-wing Liberty League": *Atlanta Constitution*, August 2, 1938, "Capital Parade," by Joseph Alsop. "Senate in 1936": *New York Times*, August 16, 1936, "Talmadge Presses Fight in Georgia."

25. Editorial, *Messenger* (Walker County, Georgia), August 1938, FDRL, OF 300, box 15.

26. "There are thousands like me": Dr. J. M. McAllister, Rochelle, Georgia, to FDR, August 15, 1938, FDRL, OF 300, box 15. "We have a traitor": Reuben Garland, Attorney, Atlanta, to FDR, August 26, 1938, FDRL, OF 300, box 15. "best speech": W. G. Hollomon to FDR, August 1938, FDRL, OF 300, box 15. "I have a high regard": *Atlanta Constitution*, August 13, 1938, "Atlantans Are Divided in Opinion."

27. *Atlanta Constitution*, August 17, 1938, "Attack on Sen. George Disapproved in Georgia Poll."

28. Thomas L. Stokes, *Chip off My Shoulder* (Princeton: Princeton University Press, 1940), 497.

29. *Atlanta Constitution*, August 13, 1938, "One Word More," by Ralph McGill.

30. "reacted angrily and defensively": David L. Carlton, ed., *Confronting Southern Poverty in the Great Depression: The Report on the Economic Conditions of the South* (Boston: St. Martin's Press, 1996), 23. "Giving the South a Bad Name": *Charleston News and Courier*, August 14, 1938. See Leuchtenburg, *White House Looks South*, 110, note.

31. "historic first": *Atlanta Constitution*, August 12, 1938, "Roosevelt Opens War against George." "hate a dictatorship"; "sovereign state is to choose"; "What right": *Savannah Evening Press*, quoted in *Atlanta Constitution*, August 13, 1938, "FDR's attack on George."

32. *Atlanta Constitution*, August 13, 1938, "Opinions Divided on FDR Speech."

33. Thomas, "Roosevelt vs. George," 47–48, 37.

34. "misinformed": *Atlanta Constitution*, August 16, 1938, "Senator Certain He'll Win Despite 'Uneven Contest.'" "avoided discussing his voting record": *Atlanta Constitution*, August 13, 1938, "Coming Georgia Primary." "great and good man": *New York Times*, September 18, 1938, "New Deal's Delay Costly in Georgia." "I serve notice": *Washington Post*, August 16, 1938, "George Calls Roosevelt Attack a 'Second Sherman's March.'"

35. "brass band played"; "Imagine Tom Watson": *Atlanta Constitution*, August 21, 1938, "Human Liberties Are Endangered by F.D.R.—George."

36. Bertram Wyatt-Brown, "The Sound and the Fury," in *C. Vann Woodward: A Southern Historian and His Critics*, ed. John H. Roper (Athens: University of Georgia Press, 1997), 49.

37. C. Vann Woodward, "The South in Search of a Philosophy," Phi Beta Kappa Address, University of Florida, 1938 (Gainesville: University of Florida, 1938), 12.

38. C. Vann Woodward, *Thinking Back: The Perils of Writing History* (Baton Rouge: Louisiana State University Press, 1986), 32.

39. "Atlanta businessmen chose George": *New York Times*, August 18, 1938, "Personality Issue in Vote on George." "my predecessor": *Atlanta Constitution*, August 23, 1938, "Corcoran, Cohen Are Reds—George." "book for the 1930s": Woodward, *Thinking Back*, 42. "statue of Watson": *Atlanta Constitution*, December 4, 1932, "Tribute Is Paid Tom Watson."

40. *Atlanta Constitution*, August 23, 1938, "George Calls Him Red."

41. "You may be sure": *Atlanta Constitution*, August 18, 1938, "One Word More," by Ralph McGill. "jackasses": *Atlanta Constitution*, July 7, 1938, "One Word More" by Ralph McGill. "whipping boys": Key, *Southern Politics*, 118.

42. "negotiating with Huey Long": Tindall, *Emergence of the New South*, 615. "communistic, free-spending": Brinkley, "The New Deal and Southern Politics," in *The New Deal and the South*, ed. James Cobb (Jackson: University Press of Mississippi, 1984), 111.

43. "orgy of exploitation": *Atlanta Constitution*, July 24, 1938, "Talmadge Claims Solution of Relief." "five billion dollars they have set aside": *Atlanta Constitution*, May 20, 1938, "Talmadge Opens Senate Campaign." "Ah'll make America": *Atlanta Constitution*, August 12, 1938, "Capital Parade," by Joseph Alsop and Robert Kintner. "I'm for Gene Talmadge": *New York Times*, August 17, 1938, "Speech by George Wins Public Favor."

44. Press Conference, April 21, 1938, in *The Public Papers and Addresses of Franklin D. Roosevelt*, ed. Samuel Rosenman (New York: Macmillan, 1938–50), 7:263–265.

45. *Atlanta Constitution*, August 12, 1938, "Capital Parade," by Joseph Alsop and Robert Kintner.

46. Clapper, "Roosevelt Tries the Primaries," 18.

47. Thomas Camp, interview, (Lawrence Camp's son), March 26, 1952, in David Nolan Thomas, "Roosevelt vs. George," 35. See also *New York Times*, June 15, 1938, "In the Nation" by Arthur Krock.

48. "I'm neutral": *Atlanta Constitution*, August 11, 1938, "Capital Parade." See also Luther Ziegler, "Senator Walter George's 1938 Campaign," *Georgia Historical Quarterly*, 43, 1959, 333–352. "Georgia Marches On with Roosevelt": D. N. Thomas, "Roosevelt vs. George," 64. See also *Atlanta Constitution*, August 17, 1938, "One Word More." "in accord with the president's objectives": *New York Herald Tribune*, August 12, 1938, quoted in Hopper, "Purge," 174. "$53 million in WPA funds": *New York Times*, September 11, 1938, "53,000,000 Grant Stirs Georgians." See also *New York Times*, September 22, 1938, "Bridges in Politics."

49. "uphold the hands": *Atlanta Constitution*, August 28, 1938, "Chief Executive Is Not Dictating." "humanitarian program": *Atlanta Constitution*, July 22, 1938, "Camp Reiterates George Anti-FDR." "father of free rural mail": *Atlanta Constitution*, August 28, 1938, "Tom Watson Recognized as Father of R. F. D."

50. "worth as much as the northern workers": *Atlanta Constitution*, September 2, 1938, "George Is Asked by Camp to Show 'Letter' to F.D.R." "attempted no dictatorship": *Atlanta Constitution*, August 21, 1938, "Record of George, 'Vested Interests,' Assailed by Camp."

51. "Rivers a member of Ku Klux Klan": *New York Times*, June 1, 1938, "Farley Seen in Growing Rebellion." "Talmadge relished lambasting Eleanor": *Atlanta Constitution*, August 11, 1938, "Capital Parade." "George spoke for only one hour": *Atlanta Constitution*, September 2, 1938, "George Is Asked by Camp to Show 'Letter' to FDR." "none other than Clark Foreman": Clapper, "Roosevelt Tries the Primaries," 18. See also Harry Ashmore, *Civil Rights and Wrongs* (New York: Pantheon, 1994), 25.

52. Cason, *90 Degrees in the Shade* (1935; reprint, Tuscaloosa: University of Alabama Press, 2001), 12–13.

53. "voters who had paid the poll tax": *Atlanta Constitution*, August 25, 1938, "One Word More." "first returns": J. B. Shannon, "Presidential Politics in the South: 1938, II," *Journal of Politics*, 1, 3, August 1939, 285.

54. "none other than Tom Watson": C. Vann Woodward, *Tom Watson: Agrarian Rebel* (New York: Macmillan, 1938), 392. See also *New York Times*, August 16, 1938, "Talmadge Presses Fight in Georgia." See also Louis T. Rigdon, *Georgia's County Unit System* (Decatur, Ga.: Selective Books, 1961), 24–26. "Supreme Court": *Baker v. Carr* (1962) and *Reynolds v. Sims* (1964). "momentous political decisions": Jimmy Carter, *Turning Point: A Candidate, a State, and a Nation Come of Age* (New York: Crown, 1992).

55. "carried Warm Springs": *Atlanta Constitution*, September 16, 1938, "Rivers and George Are Renominated." "refused to concede": *Atlanta Constitution*, September 17, 1938, "Complete Text of Talmadge Radio Speech." "urged Republicans to cross over": *New York Times*, August 21, 1938, "Camp Says George Had Republican Aid." See also *Atlanta Constitution*, August 22, 1938, "Candidates Slate Busiest Schedule."

56. "elated, pink-faced": *Atlanta Constitution*, September 16, 1938, "No Statement from President on George Vote." "There must be differences": *Atlanta Constitution*, September 16, 1938, "George Welcomed by Large Crowd."

57. *Time*, September 26, 1938, "Primaries."

58. "George beat his only opponent": *New York Times*, November 9, 1938, "Summaries of Results of Yesterday's Polling." "only about 55,000": *New York Times*, November 9, 1938, "Summaries of Results of Yesterday's Polling."

59. *Atlanta Constitution*, December 30, 1938 , "Party 'Love Feast' Presages Success of Jackson Dinners."

60. November 26, 1938, in *FDR: His Personal Letters, 1928–1945*, ed. Elliott Roosevelt (New York: Duell, Sloane, and Pearce, 1947–50), 2:830.

61. Farley, *Jim Farley's Story*, 196.

62. "Wheeler of Montana, attacked": *New York Times*, March 1, 1941, "Wheeler Asserts Aid Bill Seeks War."

63. "do what the American people want done": *New York Times*, January 28, 1941, "George Urges Changes." "foolish spectacle": *New York Times*, March 1, 1941, "Wheeler Asserts Aid Bill Seeks War." "13 Democratic senators": *Chicago Daily Tribune*, October 28, 1939, "Final Senate Test."

64. *New York Times*, March 13, 1955, "Senator George—Monumental, Determined," by William S. White.

8. "Cotton Ed"

1. *Charleston News and Courier*, July 30, 1938, quoted in Daniel W. Hollis, "Cotton Ed Smith: Showman or Statesman?" *South Carolina Historical Magazine*, 71,

1970, 252. See also Allan Michie, *Dixie Demagogues* (New York: Vanguard Press, 1939), 266.

2. Beverly Smith, "FDR, Here I Come," *American Magazine*, 195, 1, January 1939, 146.

3. "grew up during the Reconstruction": J. B. Shannon, "Presidential Politics in the South: 1938, II," *Journal of Politics*, 1, 3, August 1939, 286. "short-lived Southern Cotton Association": Theodore Soloutos, "The Southern Cotton Association, 1905–1908," *Journal of Southern History*, 13, 4, November 1948, 492–510. "My sweetheart": Robert McCormick, "He's for Cotton," *Collier's*, 101, 17, April 23, 1938, 48.

4. "price of cotton rose": McCormick, "He's for Cotton," 52. "for prohibition and against women's suffrage": Smith, "FDR, Here I Come," 147.

5. "conscientious objector": Hollis, "Cotton Ed Smith," 247. "didn't fully comprehend what we were trying to do": John Hutson, Oral History Project, NXCP88-A54, Columbia University, 129. "sabotage": Smith, "FDR, Here I Come," 20. See also McCormick, "He's for Cotton."

6. "Smith rebelled"; "Yankee plot": *Time*, August 29, 1938; *Charleston News and Courier*, July 31, 1937, quoted in Hollis, "Cotton Ed Smith," 250. "about the year 1999": Smith, "FDR, Here I Come," 147.

7. Michie, *Dixie Demagogues*, 277.

8. "important reforms": John Huss, *Senator for the South: A Biography of Olin D. Johnston* (Garden City, N.Y.: Doubleday, 1961). "announced his candidacy": *New York Times*, May 17, 1938, "Gov. Johnston Will Run in South Carolina." "refused to confirm Johnston's claim": *New York Times*, May 18, 1938, "Roosevelt Firm in Saying Nothing."

9. "What is this, a conspiracy?"; "I'm going to beat you": *Washington Post*, May 18, 1938, "On Capitol Hill." "head massage"; "When I get ready": *Chicago Daily Tribune*, May 18, 1938, "Cotton Ed Gives Senate Diners a Taste of Fire."

10. "ancient soil of his home state": Smith, "FDR, Here I Come," 21. "humbly deferred": McCormick, "He's for Cotton," 52. "political fluke": James Byrnes to FDR, May 19, 1938. Byrnes forwards a letter to FDR from Hugh Haynsworth, Sumter, S.C., May 7, 1938, quoted in *Charlotte Observer*, clipping in Franklin Delano Roosevelt Library (FDRL), OF 200, box 30. "Pro–New Deal South Carolina Democrats also explained": May 18, 1938, F. Bull, Department Adjutant, VFW, Sumter, S.C., to FDR, FDRL, OF 300, box 30. "tried to dissuade Roosevelt": David Robertson, *Sly and Able: A Political Biography of James F. Byrnes* (New York: Norton, 1994), 274–275.

11. Marvin McIntyre to Steve Early, July 30, 1938; Steve Early to Marvin McIntyre, July 30, 1938, Democratic National Committee MSS, FDRL, box 61. See also Marvin McIntyre to Steve Early, July 29, 1938, FDR MSS, FDRL, OF 5224; Olin

Johnston to FDR, July 19, 1938; McIntyre to Johnston, July 19, 1938; McIntyre to Johnston, July 29, 1938, all in FDR MSS, FDRL, Personal Papers File 2361. See also John E. Hopper, "The Purge: Franklin D. Roosevelt and the 1938 Democratic Nominations," Ph.D. diss., University of Chicago, 1966, 185–186.

12. James F. Byrnes, *All in One Lifetime* (New York: Harper, 1958), 101–104.

13. *Atlanta Constitution*, July 31, 1937, "Southern Senators Revolt against Pay-Hour Bill."

14. FDR to Harold Ickes, August 17, 1938, in *FDR: His Personal Letters, 1928–1945*, ed. Elliott Roosevelt, 3 vols. (New York: Duell, Sloan and Pearce, 1947–50), 2:803.

15. "110 degrees": Smith, "FDR, Here I Come," 145. "three candidates toured": *Washington Post*, August 28, 1938, "Two States, California and South Carolina."

16. Michie, *Dixie Demagogues*, 283.

17. William E. Leuchtenburg, *The White House Looks South: Franklin D. Roosevelt, Harry S. Truman, Lyndon B. Johnson* (Baton Rouge: Louisiana State University Press, 2005), 99, 100.

18. "Old Sleepy": Hollis, "Cotton Ed Smith," 250. "43 percent": V. O. Key, *Southern Politics in State and Nation* (New York: Knopf, 1949), 131. "permit a big buck Nigger": *New York Times*, August 23, 1938, "Negro Issue Raised at South." See also James MacGregor Burns, *Roosevelt: The Lion and the Fox* (New York: Harcourt, Brace, 1956), 364.

19. "peal of joy": *Columbia State*, August 28, 1938, quoted in Hollis, "Cotton Ed Smith," 254. "Every red-blooded white man": *New York Times*, August 23, 1938, "Negro Issue Raised in South."

20. *Charleston News and Courier*, July 30, 1938, in Hollis, "Cotton Ed Smith," 252.

21. "pulled out of race": *Hartford Courant*, August 29, 1938, "President Sees Issue in Carolina." "vilify and abuse": *Washington Post*, August 30, 1938, "Withdrawn Candidate Brands Johnston False Liberal." "polls still placed Smith ahead": *New York Times*, August 29, 1938, "Smith Lead Seen in South Carolina."

22. *Hartford Courant*, August 29, 1938, "President Sees Issue in Carolina."

23. *Atlanta Constitution*, August 29 1938, "Capital Parade," by Joseph Alsop and Robert Kintner.

24. *New York Times*, August 29, 1938, "Roosevelt Draws E. D. Smith's Fire."

25. "repudiation of the New Deal": *Atlanta Constitution*, September 1, 1938, "Not a Repudiation." "Well, you beat me": Byrnes, *All in One Lifetime*, 104.

26. "We conquered in '76": *Columbia State*, August 31, 1938, quoted in Hollis, "Cotton Ed Smith," 254. "It takes a long time": Michie, *Dixie Demagogues*, 285. "I am sure you are rejoicing": Josiah Morse to Samuel Mitchell, August 31, 1938, quoted in George Brown Tindall, *The Emergence of the New South, 1913–1945* (Baton Rouge: Louisiana State University Press, 1967), 629.

27. "Downey won by 100,000": *New York Times,* September 1, 1938, "M'Adoo Defeated." "Downey was a true liberal": *New York Times,* September 3, 1938, "Roosevelt Scorns Party Lines." "California had 'every right'": Roosevelt to Downey, September 2, 1938, quoted in Hopper, "Purge," 150. "hearty support": *New York Times,* September 4, 1938, "Downey Discloses Greeting by Farley."

28. "three hours": *New York Times,* October 1, 1938, "Cotton Senators Wait Hours." "This isn't a democracy": *Chicago Daily Tribune,* October 1, 1938, "Cotton Ed Smith Spouts Anger." See also *Christian Science Monitor,* October 1, 1938, "Smith Is Angered."

29. "Downey proposed a ban": Roosevelt to Downey, September 2, 1938, in *FDR: His Personal Letters,* 2:808. "shrewd and persistent propaganda": *Atlanta Constitution,* October 23, 1939, "Britain Luring U.S., Says Borah." "voted to repeal": *Hartford Courant,* October 1, 1939, "South Now Seen Solidly Backing Administration Embargo Repeal Drive." "exceptions": *Hartford Courant,* October 27, 1939, "Repealers Win." "keep out of European wars": *Hartford Courant,* September 16, 1939, "Lindbergh for Neutrality." "stick to the air": *Atlanta Constitution,* October 23, 1939, "Cotton Ed Ready to Vote for Repeal."

30. "green light": *New York Times,* May 16, 1940, "More Third Term Votes." "remained neutral": *Atlanta Constitution,* July 27, 1940, "Willkie Clubs Springing Up." "go fishing": *New York Times,* November 5, 1940, "'Cotton Ed' Smith to 'Go Fishing.'"

9. The Maryland Shore

1. "Take Tydings' hide off": Harold Ickes, *The Secret Diary of Harold Ickes,* 3 vols. (New York: Simon and Schuster, 1954), 2:95. "jumped on the purge bandwagon": *Washington Post,* August 26, 1938, "Farley Urges Roosevelt to Go to Maryland."

2. "opposed nearly every New Deal measure": *New York Times,* July 29, 1938, "Tydings Favored in Maryland Race." "against the TVA": *New York Times,* May 4, 1933, "Shoals Bill Voted." Only three Democrats voted against the TVA. "voting only 'present'": *Washington Post,* September 1, 1938, "I'll Lick Whole Damn Crowd." Unlike her boss, Frances Perkins did not hold a negative view of Tydings: "I had had a number of run-ins with Millard Tydings, but I wouldn't even so have said he was a bad Senator. . . . I would never have thought of Tydings as a man who was an enemy of the people. He just differed with you on something or other. He was a little arrogant about it, but that was all." Frances Perkins, Oral History, Columbia University Libraries, pt. 7, sess. 1, p. 313. "running on hot air": Caroline Keith, *"For Hell and a Brown Mule": The Biography of Senator Millard E. Tydings* (Lanham, Md.: Madison Books, 1991),

203, 295, 307. "bone and sinew": *Washington Post*, July 24, 1938, "Supported 'Bone and Sinew' of New Deal, Tydings Claims." See also *New York Times*, September 13, 1938, "Tydings Leading Lewis."

3. "delivered newspapers": Keith, *"For Hell and a Brown Mule": The Biography of Senator Millard E. Tydings*, 123ff. "married an heiress and socialite": James T. Patterson, *Congressional Conservatism and the New Deal* (Lexington: University of Kentucky Press, 1967), 25. "bloated aristocrat": Keith, *"For Hell and a Brown Mule,"* 352–53.

4. "Farley had never forgotten": *Newsweek*, September 5, 1938. "Roosevelt killed it": Keith, *"For Hell and a Brown Mule,"* 344.

5. *New Republic*, September 28, 1938, "Washington Notes."

6. "president of the University of Maryland": *New York Times*, April 26, 1938, "Roosevelt Linked in Maryland Fight." "farm in Maryland": Ickes, *Secret Diary of Harold Ickes*, 2:282.

7. *New Republic*, June 29, 1938.

8. *Washington Post*, September 1, 1938, "Communists Give Lewis an Unwelcome Pat on the Back."

9. "I'm no enemy": Keith, *"For Hell and a Brown Mule,"* 333. "Tydings appealed to unorganized farmers": *New York Times*, September 8, 1938, "Lewis Tradition."

10. "I'm going to lick": *Washington Post*, September 1, 1938, "I'll Lick Whole Damn Crowd." "Republicans attending his rallies": *Washington Post*, September 1, 1938, "Tydings People Fear GOP Kiss." "Let him call a spade a spade": *Washington Post*, August 18, 1938, "Tydings to Win Despite Purge."

11. "campaign funds": David Robertson, *Sly and Able: A Political Biography of James F. Byrnes* (New York: Norton, 1994), 270. "puppet of Mr. Roosevelt": Keith, *"For Hell and a Brown Mule,"* 331. "willing to sacrifice his last drop": Thomas Stokes, *Chip off My Shoulder* (Princeton: Princeton University Press, 1940), 501–502. "Lewis spoke at only a few events": *Washington Post*, September 1, 1938, "I'll Lick Whole Damn Crowd."

12. "Will you call Breck Long": FDR to Marvin McIntyre, August 23, 1938, in *FDR: His Personal Letters*, 2:805. "guts to fight": Josephus Daniels to FDR, September 3, 1938, quoted in E. David Cronon, "A Southern Progressive Looks at the New Deal," *Journal of Southern History*, 24, 2, May 1958, 175. See also Daniels to FDR, August 22, 1938, Democratic National Committee MSS, Franklin Delano Roosevelt Library (FDRL), box 36. "mobilized the postmistress": Maude Toulson, September 12, 1938, Democratic National Committee MSS, FDRL, box 26. See also U.S. Senate, Investigation of Senatorial Campaign Expenditures and Use of Governmental Funds, 1:31–32, 2:103–104. "investigations of Toulson": *Los Angeles Times*, September 9, 1938, "Postmistress Ruled Political Act Violator." See also *New York Times*, September 7, 1938, "Tydings Charges Vote 'Coercion.'"

13. "legislative fathers": *Los Angeles Times*, August 16, 1938, "President, in Broad-cast, Praises Foe of Tydings." "shirt sleeves": *New York Times*, August 17, 1938, "Roosevelt Urges Defeat of O'Connor and Tydings." "betrayed the New Deal": Press Conference, August 17, 1938, in *The Public Papers and Addresses of Franklin D. Roosevelt*, ed. Samuel Rosenman (New York: Macmillan, 1938–50) (*PPA*), 7:489.

14. *New York Times*, August 29, 1938, "Roosevelt Asks Support for E. D. Smith's Opponent."

15. *Washington Post*, September 6, 1938, "Eastern Shore Hears President."

16. "When Roosevelt arrived in Denton": *New York Times*, September 6, 1938, "Maryland Cordial to Roosevelt." "huge signs": *Washington Post*, September 6, 1938, "Eastern Shore Hears President."

17. "tossing his head": *Washington Post*, September 6, 1938, "Eastern Shore Hears President." "the nation cannot stand": Address at Denton, Maryland, September 5, 1938, in *PPA*, 7:515.

18. James Farley, *Jim Farley's Story* (New York: Whittlesey House, 1948), 144.

19. "I hope as a square dealer": *New York Times*, July 29, 1938, "Tydings Favored in Maryland Race." "I am confident": Keith, *"For Hell and a Brown Mule,"* 340. "not permit her star": *New York Times*, August 22, 1938, "Senator Tydings's Appeal." "lift to the masthead": *Christian Science Monitor*, September 1, 1938, "Tydings Campaign."

20. "move toward 'dictatorship'": *Washington Post*, August 20, 1938, "Legion Chief for Maryland Blasts Purge." "Mussolini and Hitler 'rolled into one'": *Washington Post*, editorial, quoted in Keith, *"For Hell and a Brown Mule,"* 341. "issue is not one of liberals against conservatives": *Chicago Daily Tribune*, September 1, 1938, "The Coat Tail Rips Again."

21. *New York Times*, September 22, 1938, "Bridges in Politics."

22. "voters bought Tydings' argument": *New York Times*, September 4, 1938, "Independent Maryland Confronts Roosevelt." "60,000 black voters": *New York Times*, September 4, 1938, "Independent Maryland Confronts Roosevelt."

23. Farley, *Jim Farley's Story*, 145.

24. *New York Times*, November 1, 1938, "Legislators Make Plea on Palestine."

25. "Bob says": Farley, *Jim Farley's Story*, 204. "I don't care for hell and a brown mule": *Washington Post*, September 23, 1939, "Pro-embargo Group Roils Sen. Tydings." "I would rather have it": *New York Times*, August 29, 1940, "Action in the Senate;" *New York Times*, August 20, 1940, "Tydings Speaks Up for Conscription."

26. "consolidate the Navy and War Departments": *New York Times*, June 26, 1949, "Group Urges Speed on Arms Unity Bill." "Tydings would agree": *Washington Post*, July 24, 1938, "Supported 'Bone and Sinew.'"

27. *New York Times*, July 21, 1950, "Tydings Charges M'Carthy Perjured Himself."

28. Harold Ickes, "McCarthy Strips Himself," *New Republic*, 123, 6, August 7, 1950, 17.

29. "whimpering lap dog": *New York Times*, February 10, 1961, "Millard Tydings, Ex-senator, Dies." "today Tydings tried to notify": *New York Times*, July 21, 1950, "Tydings Charges M'Carthy Perjured Himself." "faked composite photograph"; "so alarmed was Ickes": Keith, *"For Hell and a Brown Mule,"* 97.

30. *New York Times*, August 21, 1954, "Editorial Views on the Communist Bill."

31. *Washington Post*, February 25, 1953, "'Young Bob' 58 and Sick, Ends Life with Pistol."

10. New York Streets

1. *New York Times*, October 22, 1938, "O'Connor Charges Coercion to Mayor."

2. *New York Times*, August 9, 1938, "O'Connor, Fighting 'Purge,' Asks Aid."

3. "one of the highest ranking Democrats": *New Republic*, August 24, 1938, "Big Jim as Saviour." "public trough": *New York Times*, September 17, 1938, "Fay Charges Slur."

4. Sidney Kingsley, "Dead End" (New York: Random House, 1936), 12–13. See also Sidney Kingsley, "It Often Pays to Take a Walk along the East River," *New York Times*, November 10, 1935. The 1937 movie version of "Dead End" starred Humphrey Bogart and the "Dead End Kids"; a dozen sequels with the "kids" followed.

5. "O'Connor was virtually a stranger": William O'Donnell to James Roosevelt, August 10, 1938, Franklin Delano Roosevelt Library (FDRL), OF 300, box 26. "home in wealthy Bayport": *New York Times*, September 6, 1938, "O'Connor to Halt Drive till Friday." See also *Washington Post*, September 18, 1938, "O'Connor's Rival Given New Boost."

6. "Mr. President, have you anything to say"; "tell the people just that": Press Conference, August 17, 1938, in *The Public Papers and Addresses of Franklin D. Roosevelt*, ed. Samuel Rosenman (New York: Macmillan, 1938–50) (*PPA*), 7:487–489. "Let's have it out": *Washington Post*, August 21, 1938, "President's Purge Campaign Sets State Election Stakes High."

7. "sweet": *New Republic*, October 5, 1938, "Ninth Inning Rally." "note of caution": James T. Patterson, *Congressional Conservatism and the New Deal* (Lexington: University of Kentucky Press, 1967), 278 note.

8. *New York Times*, September 15, 1934, "M'Goldrick's Vote Blow to Tammany."

9. "backing of various labor organizations": John E. Hopper, "The Purge: Franklin D. Roosevelt and the 1938 Democratic Nominations," Ph.D. diss., University of Chicago, 1966. "Flynn to go to bat": Edward J. Flynn, *You're the Boss*

(New York: Viking Press, 1947), 150. "cancelled a meeting": *New York Herald Tribune*, September 18, 1938.

10. "Fay's campaign manager": Richard Polenberg, "Franklin Roosevelt and the Purge of John O'Connor," *New York History*, 49, 1968, 318. "I served in Congress with him": *New York Times*, August 21, 1938, "President Agrees Labor Act Needs Change."

11. "Fay relished the challenge": *New York Times*, August 21, 1938, "President Agrees Labor Act." "shameless knifing": *New York Times*, September 15, 1938, "O'Connor Urges Rebuke to Purge." Fay also unearthed more personal grounds for attack: while Fay was fighting in France, O'Connor had remained at home, serving on a draft board. "O'Connor calls himself a patriot," jeered pro-Fay veterans groups. And Fay also ridiculed O'Connor for living on a Long Island estate miles away from his teeming district. "Are the people of the Sixteenth": *New York Times*, September 17, 1938, "Fay Charges Slur." "You Can't Pitch": *New York Times*, September 15, 1938, "O'Connor Urges Rebuke to Purge." "do the most damage": *New York Times*, September 12, 1938, "Fay Assails Barton."

12. "called for O'Connor's defeat": *New York Times*, September 20, 1938, "'Purge' of O'Connor Up for Vote Today." "fake 'Communist petitions'": *New York Times*, September 14, 1938, "O'Connor and Fay Speed Up Campaign."

13. Polenberg, "Franklin Roosevelt and the Purge of John O'Connor," 306–308.

14. *New York Times*, September 18, 1938, "Moley Denounces 'Purge' of O'Connor."

15. "September 12 issue": *New Republic*, November 2, 1938, "Father Coughlin: Anti-Semite." "Protocols": *Social Justice*, September 12, 1938.

16. *New York Times*, September 9, 1938, "Fish Urges Party to Name O'Connor."

17. "endorsements": *New York Herald Tribune*, September 19, 1938. "blessing of Republican moderates": *New York Times*, September 14, 1938, "O'Connor and Fay Speed Up Campaign." "hard-line conservative Republicans": *Hartford Courant*, August 29, 1938, "President Sees Issue in Carolina." "liberalize their party's image"; "promised to administer them more efficiently": Polenberg, "Franklin Roosevelt and the Purge of John O'Connor," 314.

18. "executive dictatorship": *New York Times*, September 16, 1938, "Failure of 'Purge' Hailed by Dulles." "selling out": *New York Times*, September 20, 1938, "O'Connor Assails Roosevelt on War."

19. *New York Times*, August 9, 1938, "O'Connor, Fighting 'Purge,' Asks Aid."

20. "crucial distinction": *New York Times*, August 9, 1938, "O'Connor, Fighting 'Purge,' Asks Aid." "old-line Tory Republicanism": James MacGregor Burns, *Roosevelt: The Lion and the Fox* (New York: Harcourt, Brace, 1956), 365.

21. "willing to plunge the nation into war": *New York Times*, September 20, 1938, "O'Connor Assails Roosevelt on War." "equivalent to accusing the President":

New York Times, September 21, 1938, "O'Connor and His Rivals Cast Votes Early."

22. "hurricane of 1938": Charles F. Brooks, "Hurricanes into New England," *Geographical Review,* 29, 1, January 1939, 119. "State Liquor Authority": *New York Times,* September 20, 1938, " 'Purge' of O'Connor up for Vote Today."

23. "margin might have been small": *New York Times,* September 22, 1938, "Vote in 16th." "I have never had such a lift": Kenneth Davis, *FDR: Into the Storm, 1937–1940* (New York: Random House, 1993), 295.

24. *New Republic,* October 19, 1938, "After the 'Purge' at Home."

25. *New York Times,* September 23, 1938, "O'Connor May Give Plans."

26. "Hoover did not 'play politics' ": *New York Times,* October 22, 1938, "O'Connor Charges Coercion to Mayor." "shoulder to shoulder": *New York Times,* September 22, 1938, "Vote in 16th Blow to Party Leaders." "Orson Welles's radio show": *Washington Post,* November 1, 1938, "Martian Invasion by Radio"; *New York Times,* October 31, 1938, "Radio Listeners in Panic."

27. "Krock bought into O'Connor's bizarre scenario": *New York Times,* September 22, 1938, "In the Nation." "did not and cannot": *New York Times,* November 5, 1938, "Deny Backing O'Connor."

28. *New York Times,* October 20, 1939, "Asks Stand of O'Connor."

29. "misleading and deceiving": *New York Times,* November 2, 1938, "O'Connor Tells Court He Is Still a Democrat." O'Connor was served three times with papers and threw them in the gutter. "won the first round": *New York Times,* November 29, 1938, "O'Connor Loses Vote Suit." "not use words from other party labels": *New York Times,* November 5, 1938, "O'Connor Loses Party Label Row."

30. *New York Times,* November 9, 1938, "O'Connor Is Loser."

31. "not through with politics": *New York Times,* December 2, 1938, "O'Connor in Washington." "tried to recruit": *Washington Post,* July 10, 1940, " 'Purgee' Rallies 500 Former Congressmen." "primaries": *New York Times,* September 18, 1940, "Leibowitz Wins."

32. Burton Boxerman, "Adolph Joachim Sabath in Congress," *Journal of the Illinois State Historical Society,* 66, Winter 1973, 431.

33. James A. Farley, *Jim Farley's Story: The Roosevelt Years* (New York: Whittlesey House, 1948), 149.

34. Frances Perkins, Oral History, Columbia University Libraries, pt. 7, sess. 1, p. 319.

11. The Dynamics of the Purge

1. *Atlanta Constitution,* November 9, 1938, "President Sits Up for Vote Returns."

2. Also on the Democratic ticket were Herbert Lehman for governor, Robert Wagner for the Senate, and the senator's son Bob Jr. for the state Assembly.

"It's a secret ballot": *Chicago Daily Tribune,* November 9, 1938, "President Has Nothing to Say about Election." "watch chain at home": *Washington Post,* November 9, 1938, "Roosevelt, Minus Lucky Chain."

3. "listened to the election returns": *Atlanta Constitution,* November 9, 1938, "President Sits Up for Vote Returns." "Times Square": *New York Times,* November 9, 1938, "Crowds in Rain Get Election Returns."

4. "not too rash": *Hartford Courant,* November 10, 1938, "Today and Tomorrow." "happy elephant": Milton Plesur, "The Republican Congressional Comeback of 1938," *Review of Politics,* 24, 1, October 1962, 525.

5. *Washington Post,* November 12, 1938, "GOP to Ask WPA Inquiry."

6. *Hartford Courant,* November 10, 1938, "Roosevelt's Band Wagon Breaks Down."

7. "Frankly, our officeholders": FDR to Herbert Pell, November 12, 1938, in *F.D.R.: His Personal Letters,* ed. Elliott Roosevelt (New York: Duell, Sloan and Pearce, 1947–50), 2:826. "we will have less trouble": FDR to Josephus Daniels, November 14, 1938, in *FDR: His Personal Letters,* 2:827.

8. *Atlanta Constitution,* December 18, 1938, "'Purgin' Time Down South.'"

9. *New York Times,* January 8, 1939, "Warns of '40 Vote." See also *Chicago Daily Tribune,* January 8, 1938, "Here Is Menu." See also *Washington Post,* January 8, 1939, "Liberals Should Unite."

10. Address at Jackson Day Dinner, January 7, 1939, in *The Public Papers and Addresses of Franklin D. Roosevelt,* ed. Samuel Rosenman (New York: Macmillan, 1938–50), *(PPA),* 8:62–67.

11. Stephen Early to R. K. Wadlow, July 30, 1940, in *FDR: His Personal Letters,* 2:1049–1050. Italics added.

12. Glass to Charles Stoll, January 9, 1939; Bailey to George Warner, March 25, 1939, both quoted in James T. Patterson, "Eating Humble Pie: A Note on Roosevelt, Congress, and Neutrality Revision in 1939," *Historian,* 31, 3, May 1969, 407–408. On May 15, 1940, Glass wrote that "Germany should be wiped off the map and our disgraceful Neutrality Act . . . expunged from the federal statue books." Glass to Wallace Tiffany, May 15, 1940, quoted in J. Garry Clifford and Samuel R. Spencer, Jr., *The First Peacetime Draft* (Lawrence: University Press of Kansas, 1986), 10.

13. "very conciliatory attitude": James T. Patterson, "The Failure of Party Realignment in the South," *Journal of Politics,* 27, 3, August 1965, 615. The president and he "are on fairly good terms," Bailey said a few months later. "He understands me and I understand him, and I really believe the man is inclined to lean away from the extreme left." "new circumstances": Frances Perkins, *The Roosevelt I Knew* (New York: Viking, 1946), 5–6.

14. "courted Tom Connally": James Byrnes, *All in One Lifetime* (New York: Harper, 1958), 108–116. "Byrd one of the two most conservative Democrats": Byrd and

Tydings voted against the relief bill of March 1935, voted against the Wagner Act, abstained from voting on Social Security, and voted against court reform, and against executive reorganization. "cajoled Mississippi's Senator"; "mollified Harry Byrd": Patterson, "Eating Humble Pie," 409, 411.

15. "Well, it took a war": *New York Times*, September 29, 1939, "Roosevelt and Glass Reconciled by War." "great victory": FDR to George Norris, July 21, 1940, in *FDR: His Personal Letters*, 2:1046. Immediately after the Democratic convention at which he received the party's nomination to run for a third term, Roosevelt commented on the clout the anti–New Deal wing of the party still wielded. "I was frankly, amazed by the terrific drive which was put on by the old-line conservatives," he wrote to Senator George Norris. "That whole crowd was greatly heartened by the 1938 elections and thought that this would give them a fighting chance to put the control of the Democratic Party back where it was in 1920, 1924, and 1928." But the liberal, New Deal contingent had fought back—and won. "That is why I feel that, from a purely political point of view, a great victory was won in Chicago," he told Norris. At least in terms of the liberals' final triumph at the 1940 convention, Roosevelt seemed to believe that the purge had not been a total failure and that it helped isolate and marginalize southern Democrats, who played a small part at the convention. But along with New York's John O'Connor, the only southern Democrat to endorse Willkie was Cotton Ed Smith of South Carolina, and Willkie was advised to make no campaign appearances in the South. FDR to George Norris, July 21, 1940, in *FDR: His Personal Letters*, 2:1046. See Steve Neal, *Dark Horse: A Biography of Wendell Willkie* (New York: Doubleday, 1984), 129. "Glass is appointed in 1941": Patterson, "Eating Humble Pie," 409, 411. See also Rorin M. Platt, "The Triumph of Interventionism: Virginia's Political Elite and Aid to Britain, 1939–1941," *Virginia Magazine of History and Biography*, 100, 3, July 1992, 346. See also Alvin Hall, "Politics and Patronage: Virginia's Senators and the Roosevelt Purges of 1938," *Virginia Magazine of History and Biography*, 82, 1974, 339–346.

16. "milk and honey": Sidney Milkis, "Franklin D. Roosevelt and the Transcendence of Partisan Politics," *Political Science Quarterly*, 100, 3, Autumn 1985, 497. See also Barry D. Karl, *Executive Reorganization and Reform in the New Deal* (Cambridge, Mass.: Harvard University Press, 1963). "You know, I'm getting suspicious": James Farley, *Jim Farley's Story* (New York: Whittlesey House, 1948), 204.

17. "1940 Democratic Party platform": In June 1940, Wheeler threatened to break with the Democratic Party "if it is going to be a war party" (*New York Times*, June 13, 1940, "Wheeler Makes a Threat to Bolt"). "could not win over Democratic isolationist hold-outs": *New York Times*, July 15, 1940, "Wheeler Demands a Ban on War."

18. "opposed court-packing": *New York Times,* July 12, 1938, "President Hails 5 Texans." See also Frank H. Smyrl, "Tom Connally and the New Deal," Ph.D. diss., University of Oklahoma, 1968, 229. "two and a half hours": *New York Times,* October 5, 1939, "Connally Assails Embargo." See also Tom Connally, *My Name Is Tom Connally* (New York: Crowell, 1954), 227–229; Patterson, "The Failure of Party Realignment in the South," 616. "southern Democrats would be 'voting right'": Edwin Watson, memo of phone conversation with Josiah Bailey, August 27, 1940, Franklin Delano Roosevelt Library (FDRL), OF 1413. "I am advocating": John Robert Moore, "Senator Josiah W. Bailey and the 'Conservative Manifesto' of 1937," *Journal of Southern History,* 31, 1, February 1965, 180–181, 186.

19. "in mortal peril"; "not moving fast enough": Glass to Elizabeth Barker, May 24, 1940, and Glass to Walter Batterson, July 21, 1941, quoted in Platt, "Triumph of Interventionism," 346 and 348. About the rabid isolationist Charles Lindbergh, Glass wrote, "The truth is if Lindbergh has ever done anything for this country except to fly across the Atlantic ocean, I do not know what it is. Yet he seems to be making some sort of impression with a class of emotional people." Platt, "Triumph of Interventionism," 350–351. "strongest support": Rexford Tugwell, *The Democratic Roosevelt* (Garden City, N.Y.: Doubleday, 1957), 476. "September 1940": report on Gallup poll, *New York Times,* September 22, 1940, "Sentiment to Aid Britain Is Growing." "rubber stamps": October 27, 1939, Patterson, "Failure of Party Realignment," 616.

20. "favor action against Nazi and Japanese expansion": George Brown Tindall, *The Emergence of the New South, 1913–1945* (Baton Rouge: Louisiana State University Press, 1967), 687. See also Francis Simkins, *History of the South* (New York: Knopf, 1965), 565. "cultural and blood ties": Alexander DeConde, "The South and Isolationism," *Journal of Southern History,* 24, 3, August 1958, 343. "military tradition": Tindall, *Emergence of the New South,* 687. "chivalry, honor, and dueling": James M. McPherson, "The Historian Who Saw through America," *New York Review of Books,* December 4, 2008, 45. "indifference to violence": Virginius Dabney, "The South Looks Abroad," *Foreign Affairs,* 19, October 1940, 178. See also Wayne S. Cole, "America First and the South," *Journal of Southern History,* 22, 1, February 1956, 44.

21. "virile leadership": Glass to Barbara Brown, May 16, 1941, quoted in Platt, "Triumph of Interventionism," 349. "America First": Wayne Cole, *America First: The Battle against Intervention* (Madison: University of Wisconsin Press, 1953), 31; James Schneider, *Should America Go to War?* (Chapel Hill: University of North Carolina Press, 1988), 124. See also Cole, "America First and the South," 41–46.

22. *Time,* February 17, 1941, 75–80. See also Tindall, *Emergence of the New South,* 694–701.

23. "vigorous support": *Los Angeles Times,* March 2, 1941, "Poll Shows Sectional Stand on Lend-Lease Measure." A Gallup poll in June 1940 revealed that 82 percent of southerners anticipated a German attack on the United States should Britain and France be defeated by Germany, compared to only 65 percent in New England and the mid-Atlantic states (*New York Times,* June 2, 1940, "War Here Is Seen If Germany Wins"). "Burke": Burke was one of the few senators who felt that the United States should enter the war in Europe rather than let France and England be defeated by Germany. "universal conscription": *New York Times,* August 11, 1940, "Glass Calls Draft 'Democratic Way.'" "fellow southerners": *New York Times,* August 25, 1940, "Senate's Dallying on Draft Continues." See also *New York Times,* August 8, 1940, "Test Vote." "amended the Selective Service bill": Kenneth Davis, *FDR: Into the Storm* (New York: Random House, 1993), 612. "limiting profits for war materiel": *New York Times,* August 29, 1940, "Final Vote 58 to 31."

24. "point-man in the Senate": David Robertson, *Sly and Able: A Political Biography of James F. Byrnes* (New York: Norton, 1994), 296–297. "one of the few senators": *New York Times,* March 28, 1937, "Court Reform Splits Southern Senate Bloc." See also Tindall, *Emergence of the New South,* 691.

25. Patterson, "Failure of Party Realignment in the South," 616.

26. Thomas Stokes, *Chip off My Shoulder* (Princeton: Princeton University Press, 1940), 486.

27. "conciliate his party and not coerce it": See Harold J. Laski, *The American Presidency* (New York: Harper, 1940), 63. "humble pie": James T. Patterson, "Eating Humble Pie: A Note on Roosevelt, Congress, and Neutrality Revision in 1939," *Historian,* 31, 3, May 1969.

28. Sidney M. Milkis, "E. E. Schattschneider, the New Deal, and the Rejection of the Responsible Party Doctrine," *PS: Political Science and Politics,* 25, 2, June 1992, 181.

29. "clout of political machines": James MacGregor Burns, *The Crosswinds of Freedom* (New York: Knopf, 1989), 117. Sam Rosenman concluded: "Strong as the President's personal appeal and logic were, they were outweighed by the long personal relationships that these Congressmen had developed over the years with their constituents, by the entrenched political machinery which operated in favor of the Congressmen in office." See also Sidney Milkis, "Presidential Leadership and Party Responsibility," in *Presidents and Their Parties: Leadership or Neglect?* ed. Robert Harmel (New York: Praeger, 1984), 151–175. "great masses of warm-hearted people": Robert H. Jackson, *That Man: An Insider's Portrait of Franklin D. Roosevelt,* ed. John Q. Barrett (New York: Oxford University Press, 2003), 57.

30. "September 1938 Gallup poll": *Washington Post*, September 18, 1938, "President Backed by 55.2% in Survey." "I knew from the beginning": James A. Farley, *Jim Farley's Story* (New York: Whittlesey House, 1948), 146–147.

31. Harold Ickes, *The Secret Diary of Harold L. Ickes*, 3 vols. (New York: Simon and Schuster, 1954), September 18, 1938, 2:472.

32. Samuel I. Rosenman, "Reminiscences," Oral History, Columbia University, Interview 4, Side 1, 27 July 1959, 158. Nor did many voters care, Rosenman added, that their senators or representatives betrayed the party platform. "The fact is," said Rosenman, "that Senator George of Georgia, for example . . . could have been elected senator from Georgia whether we'd had a platform or didn't. . . . And while theoretically in running for the US Senate he was running on the national platform, this was only a theory. I'm sure that the people of Georgia, if they had ever read the platform—particularly some of the planks—would never realize that they were voting for a man who would have to vote for some of these things. They would have been considerably astonished to learn that Sen. George was bound by the national platform. So I think that the basis of the purge, while philosophically and theoretically true—it was never accepted in practice."

33. Rosenman, "Reminiscences," Interview 4, Side 1, July 27, 1959.

34. Rosenman, "Reminiscences," Interview 4, Side 1, July 27, 1959. See also Samuel Rosenman, *Working with Roosevelt* (New York: Harper, 1952), 176.

35. James MacGregor Burns, *The Deadlock of Democracy* (Englewood Cliffs, N.J.: Prentice-Hall, 1963), 157.

36. "If there is a good liberal": *New York Times*, September 3, 1938, "Roosevelt Scorns Party Lines." "greeted with incredulity": *Chicago Daily Tribune*, September 3, 1938, "Roosevelt Statement Stirs Up Hornets' Nest." "Pick those who are known": Radio Address on Electing Liberals, November 4, 1938, *PPA*, 7:584–593.

37. Some Political Advice to the Convention of Young Democratic Clubs of America, August 8, 1939, *PPA*, 8:437.

38. "three Republican leaders": Senate minority leader Charles McNary of Oregon, Senator Warren Austin of Vermont, and Republican House leader Joseph Martin of Massachusetts. "Why Charlie": Address at Jackson Day Dinner, January 8, 1940, *PPA*, 9:27.

39. Address at Jackson Day Dinner, January 8, 1940, *PPA*, 9:28.

40. Davis, *FDR: Into the Storm*, 601.

41. *Atlanta Constitution*, September 28, 1940, "F.D.R. Junior Gives Father's Talk at Miami."

42. "charm, magnetism": See James MacGregor Burns, *Leadership* (New York:

Harper and Row, 1978), 375. "line of retreat": James MacGregor Burns, *Roosevelt: The Lion and the Fox* (New York: Harcourt, Brace, 1956), 380.

43. "that spring, he learned": Donald B. Johnson, *The Republican Party and Wendell Willkie* (Urbana: University of Illinois Press, 1960). "We ought to have two real parties": Samuel Rosenman, *Working with Roosevelt* (New York: Harper, 1952), 463–464.

44. "dictatorial complex": *Washington Post,* October 31, 1940, "Republican Nominee Predicts." "warmonger": *Atlanta Constitution,* November 1, 1940, "Capital Parade."

45. "January meeting": *New York Times,* January 20, 1941, " 'Delightful' Visit Says Willkie." "he is a very good fellow": Perkins, *Roosevelt I Knew,* 119. "Willkie reported back": *New York Times,* February 12, 1942, "Reports on Talks." "Lindbergh": *New York Times,* September 12, 1941, "Lindbergh Sees a 'Plot' for War." Jews, according to Lindbergh, posed a danger to America "in their large ownership and influence in our motion pictures, our press, our radio, and our government." The senators who attacked "Jewish Hollywood" were Burton Wheeler of Montana and Gerald Nye of North Dakota. "The motion picture industry": *New York Times,* September 12, 1941, "Flynn Says Films Bar Peace Side."

46. "Roosevelt hoped to join forces with Willkie": The idea that Willkie would lead internationalist "Conscience Republicans" to form a progressive union with New Deal Democrats was perspicaciously suggested by Arthur Schlesinger, Jr., in the *Nation,* "Can Wilkie Save His Party?" December 6, 1941, 561–564. Sam Rosenman suggested to FDR in 1944 that the Democrats needed "a good liberal businessman" like Willkie as their vice presidential candidate, "a refreshing innovation." Samuel Rosenman, Oral History, Truman Library, 1968 and 1969, recorded by Jerry Hess, 20.

47. Rosenman, *Working with Roosevelt,* 465–466.

48. "wholly off the record": FDR to Willkie, July 13, 1944, in *FDR: His Personal Letters,* 2:1520. "visitor or a dinner guest: Rosenman, *Working with Roosevelt,* 469. "The interesting thing": FDR to Willkie, August 21, 1944, in *FDR: His Personal Letters,* 2:1531–1532.

49. Willkie to FDR, draft, July 20, 1944, Willkie Manuscripts, Lilly Library, Indiana University. The letter was drafted but never mailed.

50. "Citizens of Negro Blood": Wendell L. Willkie, "Citizens of Negro Blood," *Collier's,* 114, October 7, 1944, 11, 47, 49. "cowardice": Wendell L. Willkie, "Cowardice at Chicago," *Collier's,* September 16, 1944, 11.

12. From the Purge to Realignment

1. *New York Times,* January 22, 1938, "Move to Displace Anti-lynching Bill"; George Rable, "The South and the Politics of Antilynching Legislation, 1920–1940," *Journal of Southern History,* 51, 2, May 1985, 217. See also David Brady and Joseph Stewart, Jr., "Congressional Party Realignment and Transformations of Public Policy in Three Realignment Eras," *American Journal of Political Science,* 26, 2, May 1982, 356.

2. Sidney Milkis, "The New Deal: The Decline of Parties and the Administrative State," Ph.D. diss., University of Pennsylvania, 1981, 89. "We will always have a white man's party in the South," Bailey said in a speech to young Democrats. "We will not permit Northern Democrats to frame a race policy or any social policy for us, no more than we would permit Northern Republicans to do so." See *Washington Post,* September 18, 1938, "Enemies of New Deal in South Now United."

3. "National Recovery Administration": Harvard Sitkoff, "The Impact of the New Deal on Black Southerners," in *The New Deal and the South,* ed. James C. Cobb (Jackson: University Press of Mississippi, 1984), 120. "criticizing poll taxes": William E. Leuchtenburg, *The White House Looks South: Franklin D. Roosevelt, Harry S. Truman, Lyndon B. Johnson* (Baton Rouge: Louisiana State University Press, 2005), 65. "At no time and in no manner": Frank Freidel, *F.D.R. and the South* (Baton Rouge: Louisiana State University Press, 1965), 98. "efforts which the southern people have made": Leuchtenburg, *White House Looks South,* 116. "molasses compassion": Michael Beschloss, "Lyndon Johnson on the Record," *Texas Monthly,* December 2001, 115.

4. "no forgotten men": Address at Howard University, Washington, D.C., quoted in *Chicago Daily Tribune,* October 27, 1936, "President Joins in Dedication." "executive order": Freidel, *F.D.R. and the South,* 97. See Harvard Sitkoff, "The Impact of the New Deal on Black Southerners," in Cobb, *New Deal and the South,* 129. In 1943, southern congressmen held half the Democratic seats and sixteen of thirty-six chairmanships in the Senate and twenty-two chairmanships of forty-six committees in the House. "great champion of the common people": *Chicago Defender,* November 9, 1940, "The Way of All Things," by John Sengstacke.

5. "expected party realignment": See James L. Sundquist, *Dynamics of the Party System: Alignment and Realignment of Political Parties in the United States* (Washington: Brookings Institution, 1973), 310–331. "race—later accompanied by other": Byron E. Shafer and Richard Johnston, *The End of Southern Exceptionalism: Class, Race, and Partisan Change in the Postwar South* (Cambridge, Mass.: Harvard University Press, 2006).

6. Roy Wilkins, "The Future of the Negro Voter in the United States," *Journal of Negro Education*, 26, 3, Summer 1957, 424. In 1946, Mississippi senator Theodore Bilbo would urge every "red-blooded Anglo-Saxon man in Mississippi to resort to any means" to bar blacks from voting in the Democratic primary. *New York Times*, June 23, 1946, "Bilbo Urges Mississippi Men."

7. "We believe that racial and religious minorities": Democratic Platform, in *History of American Presidential Elections*, ed. Arthur M. Schlesinger, Jr., 4 vols. (New York: Chelsea House, 1971), 4:3041. "splinter": *Chicago Daily Tribune*, July 22, 1944, "Cite Variations on Main Planks."

8. "Republican platform": *Chicago Daily Tribune*, July 22, 1944, "Cite Variations on Main Planks." "platform of this convention": *Chicago Defender*, July 1, 1944, "Lily White Domination Charged." Two years later, in 1946, Senate Republicans would hold hearings on whether to deny a seat to Mississippi's white supremacist senator, Theodore Bilbo, for urging whites in his state to use any means to prevent blacks from going to the polls. "The time to see the nigger," the Mississippi Democrat had said, "is the night before election." Bilbo died before any judgment was rendered. (*New York Times*, November 1, 1946, "Bilbo Faces Inquiry"; *New York Times*, October 18, 1946, "Assert Negro Vote Will Swing to GOP"; *New York Times*, November 18, 1946, "'Bilboism' on Trial.")

9. J. B. Shannon, "Presidential Politics in the South," *Journal of Politics*, 10, 3, August 1948, 482.

10. "too shocked": *New York Times*, April 13, 1945, "Shock, Disbelief Echo in Congress." "world tragedy": *New York Times*, April 13, 1945, "Byrnes Calls Loss a Tragedy to World."

11. "friendly to the South"; "like a Virginian": Leuchtenburg, *White House Looks South*, 161–162. "civil rights"; "Cold War rivalry": Barton J. Bernstein, "The Ambiguous Legacy: The Truman Administration and Civil Rights," in *Politics and Policies of the Truman Administration*, ed. Barton J. Bernstein (Chicago: Quadrangle Books, 1970), 272, 280. "be just to its people": Bernstein, "Ambiguous Legacy," 286, 279. The petition, "A Statement on the Denial of Human Rights in the United States of America and an Appeal to the United Nations for Redress," was presented in preliminary form to the United Nations on January 27, 1947.

12. The Truman administration filed a brief with the Supreme Court, asserting that the separate but equal rule in schools and other public facilities was a contradiction in terms, an argument that the Warren Court would accept two years later in its *Brown v. Board of Education* decision.

13. "too tame and halfhearted": Bernstein, "Ambiguous Legacy," 274; William C. Berman, *The Politics of Civil Rights in the Truman Administration* (Columbus: Ohio State University Press, 1970), 238–239. "There is no real difference":

Henry A. Wallace, "Why a Third Party in 1948?" *Annals of the American Academy of Political and Social Science,* 259, September 1948, 10. Italics added.

14. "chieftain of the National Democratic party": Leuchtenburg, *White House Looks South,* 178. "senators filibustered": Monroe Billington, "Civil Rights, President Truman and the South," *Journal of Negro History,* 58, 2, April 1973, 127–139; *New York Times,* March 7, 1948, "Southerners Plan Senate Filibuster." "aimed to wreck the South": *Washington Post,* January 21, 1948, "Miss. Governor Sees Democratic Bolt Possible." See also *New Orleans Times-Picayune,* January 21, 1948.

15. "There will continue to be segregation": *Birmingham News,* May 9, 1948, quoted in V. O. Key, *Southern Politics in State and Nation* (New York: Knopf, 1949), 334 note. "All the laws of Washington": Key, *Southern Politics in State and Nation,* 149, 333. "Strom fathered a daughter": *New York Times,* December 18, 2003, "Senator Strom Thurmond's Not-so-secret Black Daughter"; *New York Times,* December 23, 2003, "Senator Strom Thurmond's Deception Ravaged Two Lives."

16. "Truman sought to avoid": Bernstein, "Ambiguous Legacy," 287. "get out of the shadow": George Brown Tindall, *The Disruption of the Solid South* (Athens: University of Georgia Press, 1972), 36. "If we are defeated here today": Earl Black and Merle Black, *The Vital South: How Presidents Are Elected* (Cambridge, Mass.: Harvard University Press, 1992), 97.

17. *Hartford Courant,* July 15, 1948, "Matter of Fact," by Joseph and Stewart Alsop.

18. Key, *Southern Politics in State and Nation,* 335.

19. Key, *Southern Politics in State and Nation,* 335; *New York Times,* July 18, 1948, "Southerners Name Thurmond to Lead Anti-Truman Fight."

20. "the Dixiecrats": Key, *Southern Politics in State and Nation,* 329. An earlier version of the Dixiecrats dates from 1937, when anti–New Deal Democrats in several states organized independent parties called "Jeffersonian Democrats" and "Constitutional Democrats of Texas." "racial integrity": *New York Times,* July 18, 1948, "Southerners Name Thurmond to Lead Anti-Truman Fight." "I thought it was a very good thing": Samuel Rosenman, Oral History, recorded by Jerry Hess, Harry S. Truman Library, www.trumanlibrary.org/oralhist/rosenmn.htm

21. Key, *Southern Politics in State and Nation,* 336.

22. "reason and debate": Richard Kirkendall, "The Election of 1948," in Schlesinger, *History of American Presidential Elections,* 4:3127–3128. "lain in limbo": *New York Times,* October 30, 1948, "President Renews Civil Rights Plea."

23. "South still remained solid": Earl Black and Merle Black, *Divided America: The Ferocious Power Struggle in American Politics* (New York: Simon and Schuster, 2007), 74. "esoteric cult": Key, *Southern Politics in State and Nation,* 19, 277.

24. "I don't want the Dixiecrat vote": *Washington Post*, December 3, 1948, "Truman Says He'll Retain Same Cabinet." "anomalous position": Richard Hofstadter, "From Calhoun to Dixiecrats," *Social Research*, 16, June 1949, 150.

25. Adlai Stevenson, "My Faith in Democratic Capitalism," *Fortune*, October 1955, 127.

26. "I greatly deplore": *New York Times*, March 17, 1948, "Only 3 Seek Senate as Truman Backers." "support for the Dixiecrats": *Christian Science Monitor*, September 13, 1948, "Republican Hopes Take On New Glow." *New York Times*, July 27, 1952, "Sparkman for Vice President." "director of the National Negro Council": *New York Times*, July 27, 1952, "Two Negro Leaders Criticize Sparkman."

27. "sledge hammer approach": Stevenson to John S. Battle, August 27, 1952, quoted in James R. Sweeney, "Revolt in Virginia: Harry Byrd and the 1952 Presidential Election," *Virginia Magazine of History and Biography*, 86, 2, April 1978, 189–190. "curse word"; "true Democrat": Leuchtenburg, *White House Looks South*, 220–221.

28. "woo back southern voters": *Washington Post*, September 5, 1952, "Adlai Told He'd Better Court South." "so many kinfolk": *New York Times*, October 12, 1952, "Stevenson Assails Party 'Apostates.'" "distant cousin": *New York Times*, September 3, 1952, "Filibuster Fight." "prejudices he deplored"; "contemptible": *New York Times*, September 21, 1952, "Governor Cheered." See also Stuart Brown, "Civil Rights and National Leadership: Eisenhower and Stevenson in the 1950s," *Ethics*, 70, 2, January 1960, 124.

29. "Republican moderates": *New York Times*, August 4, 1952, "16 G.O.P. Leaders Tie F.E.P.C. to Party."

30. *New York Times*, September 3, 1952, "Eisenhower Hailed in Tour of the South."

31. "Campaigning South": *New York Times*, September 3, 1952, "Eisenhower Hailed in Tour of the South." "whatever the color": *New York Times*, September 4, 1952, "Eisenhower Urges South to Protect Rights of Negroes." "do not believe we can cure all the evils": *New York Times*, August 4, 1952, "16 G.O.P. Leaders Tie F.E.P.C. to Party." "eyes shifted to Harlem": *New York Times*, September 7, 1952, "Eisenhower Stirs Georgia Disfavor." "friend of the South": *New York Times*, September 3, 1952, "Eisenhower Hailed in Tour of the South."

32. "which direction to take": *Washington Post*, August 30, 1952, "Adlai Given Promises of Negro Vote." Mary McLeod Bethune, the administrator of Negro affairs in the National Youth Administration under FDR, went further: convinced that Sparkman's "heart is sound," on the basis of little evidence, she put him in the same category with liberal southerners like Hugo Black, Estes Kefauver, and Lyndon Johnson. *Chicago Defender*, October 25, 1952, "Mrs. Be-

thune Tells Why." "former Dixiecrats like Fielding Wright": *New York Times,* August 24, 1952, "South Democratic but Not Too 'Solid.'" "toward the right": *New York Times,* October 12, 1952, "Stevenson Assails Party 'Apostates'"; *New York Times,* September 19, 1952, "Byrnes Will Vote for Eisenhower"; *New York Times,* September 10, 1952, "Texas Democrats Back Eisenhower."

33. "lever to start building": *New York Times,* November 6, 1952, "How Solid the South?" "40 percent of the districts": Shafer and Johnston, *End of Southern Exceptionalism,* 167.

34. *Washington Post,* December 14, 1952, "Rip Van GOP Awakens."

35. *New York Times,* November 16, 1952, "Strong, Southern Wing."

36. "tour of the southern states": *Washington Post,* April 29, 1953, "Democratic Chief Seeks to Tighten Ties in the South." "olive branch": *New York Times,* May 1, 1953, "Mitchell in Plea for Unity in South."

37. *Los Angeles Times,* May 11, 1957, "One-party South Thing of Past, President Says." See also Cornelius Cotter, "Eisenhower as Party Leader," *Political Science Quarterly,* 98, 2, Summer 1983, 255–283.

38. "desegregation cases": Robyn Ladino, *Desegregating Texas Schools* (Austin: University of Texas Press, 1997). "I do not believe": Leuchtenburg, *White House Looks South,* 415.

39. "gradualist": *Chicago Defender,* February 18, 1956, "Our Opinions." "exploit for political ends": *Chicago Daily Tribune,* February 13, 1956, "Decries Integration as Issue." "opposing cuts": *New York Times,* February 12, 1956, "Democrats Are Fearful of the Civil Rights Issue."

40. "urged a plank acceptable to South": *New York Times,* August 13, 1956, "Humphrey Urges Patience on Bias." "erstwhile liberal": *Chicago Defender,* August 4, 1956, "Same Old Shell Game."

41. "no new ground, political or philosophical": *New York Times,* September 9, 1956, "On the Road with the New Stevenson." "Wright": *New York Times,* August 24, 1952, "South Democratic but Not Too 'Solid.'" "unwise and suicidal": *New York Times,* June 19, 1956, "George Calls Bolt by South 'Suicidal.'" "If the South does not present a solid front": *New York Times,* July 12, 1956, "South's Leaders Meet Tomorrow." See also *New York Times,* July 27, 1956, "South's Democrats to Plan Solid Front."

42. "no trace": *New York Times,* August 4, 1956, "Rosenman Hails Harriman's Stand." See also *New York Times,* April 1, 1956, "Democrats' Divisions Now Taking Spotlight," by Arthur Krock; *New York Times,* August 4, 1956, "Stevenson Irked by Rival's Speech." "Stevenson won't carry any more states": *New York Times,* August 15, 1956, "Stevenson Victory Now Held Sure." "Tagged as the candidate of the South": *New York Times,* July 29, 1956, "Stevenson's Vote Now Put at 404." "greater percentage": *Washington Post,* November 10, 1956,

"Eisenhower-Nixon Ticket Made Gains among Negro Voters in All Sections." "Now both the Democrats and the Republicans": Samuel Lubell, "The Future of the Negro Voter in the United States," *Journal of Negro Education*, 26, 3, Summer 1957, 408, 413–414.

43. *New York Times*, August 5, 1956, "America's 'Four-party' System," by James MacGregor Burns.

44. *Washington Post*, November 18, 1958, "Rights Plank Splits Democratic Leaders."

45. James MacGregor Burns, *The Crosswinds of Freedom* (New York: Vintage, 1989), 323–324.

46. Leuchtenburg, *White House Looks South*, 269.

47. "congenial": *New York Times*, September 7, 1960, "Democrats Face a Setback in South." "rights of racial minorities": *New York Times*, February 14, 1956, "Text of Nixon's Address"; *New York Times*, November 1, 1956, "Nixon Says G.O.P. Aids Civil Rights." "choice for Southerners": *New York Times*, November 9, 1960, "Kennedy Scores Heavily in South."

48. Leuchtenburg, *White House Looks South*, 269.

49. John F. Kennedy, Address, June 11, 1963, *New York Times*, June 12, 1963, "Transcript of the President's Address."

50. *New York Times*, November 28, 1963, "A Time for Action."

51. "work against equal rights": C. Vann Woodward, "Look Away, Look Away," *Journal of Southern History*, 59, 1993, 489. "heal the wounds": interview of LBJ by William S. White, quoted in Leuchtenburg, *White House Looks South*, 374.

52. Barry M. Goldwater, *The Conscience of a Conservative* (Shepherdsville, Ky.: Victor, 1960), 31–38.

53. "Goldwater was one of the six": *New York Times*, August 15, 1976, "The Transformation of Southern Politics." "no constitutional basis": *New York Times*, June 19, 1964, "Text of Goldwater Speech on Rights." "platform stood for freedom": Republican platform of 1964, in Schlesinger, *History of American Presidential Elections*, 4:3634, 3645.

54. "hunting where the ducks are": *Washington Post*, October 9, 1963, "Ike and Barry Agree on a Brief Platform." See also *New York Times*, November 19, 1961, "Goldwater Solicits G.O.P. Votes from Southern Segregationists." "The party of our fathers is dead": *New York Times*, September 18, 1964, "The Old Order Falling"; *New York Times*, September 17, 1964, "Thurmond Break Is Made Official." "move over": *New York Times*, September 23, 1964, "Thurmond Is Uneasy over G.O.P. Liberals."

55. Hofstadter, "From Calhoun to Dixiecrats," 150.

56. *New York Times*, July 20, 1964, "Wallace Drops Presidency Bid." Wallace's anti-government populism, wrote political scientist Joseph Lowndes, "was a mo-

ment of founding violence for the modern Right in a way the Goldwater campaign was not, because it relied on politics outside of accepted norms or institutional party channels." Joseph E. Lowndes, *From the New Deal to the New Right* (New Haven: Yale University Press, 2008), 78–80.

57. *Chicago Daily Tribune,* October 27, 1964, "TV's Reagan Speaks." See Reagan, "A Time for Choosing," October 28, 1964, Ronald Reagan Presidential Foundation, http://www.reaganfoundation.org/reagan/speeches/rendezvous.as.

58. "know no color line"; "Nigra, nigra, nigra": Leuchtenburg, *White House Looks South,* 321. "I know the ordeals": *New York Times,* October 23, 1964, "Johnson, in South, Decries 'Radical' Goldwater Ideas." See also Leuchtenburg, *White House Looks South,* 377.

59. "young, socially conservative voters": John Petrocik, "Realignment: New Party Coalitions and the Nationalization of the South," *Journal of Politics,* 49, 2, May 1987, 362. "new generation": Paul Allen Beck, "Partisan Dealignment in the Postwar South," *American Political Science Review,* 71, 2, June 1977, 486. See also Harold W. Stanley, "Southern Partisan Changes: Dealignment, Realignment or Both?" *Journal of Politics,* 50, 1, February 1988, 84–85.

60. "old code-words": Alexander Lamis, *The Two-Party South* (New York: Oxford University Press, 1984), 26. "smoldering resentment": *New York Times,* November 23, 1975, "The Lively Politics of America's Right."

61. Beck, "Partisan Dealignment in the Postwar South," 479–484.

62. "way station": Political scientists Byron Shafer and Richard Johnston argue that in 1948 and 1968, the third parties of Thurmond and Wallace had few lasting effects and that in future elections, many of the districts they won returned to the Democratic fold. Rather than serving as a bridge to the GOP, according to the authors, they were bridges to "oblivion." Shafer and Johnston, *End of Southern Exceptionalism,* 165–170. "guardian of the nation's values": Lowndes, *From the New Deal to the New Right,* 80.

63. Merle Black, "The Transformation of the Southern Democratic Party," *Journal of Politics,* 66, 4, November 2004, 1010.

64. "79 percent": Leuchtenburg, *White House Looks South,* 396. "who needs Manhattan": quoted in Michael Lind, *Up from Conservatism* (New York: Free Press, 1996), 128. See also Garry Wills, *Nixon Agonistes* (Boston: Houghton Mifflin, 1969), 265.

65. *Hartford Courant,* November 8, 1972, "Wallace Sees Change in Party."

66. "Southerner and an American": Jimmy Carter, *Why Not the Best?* (Nashville: Broadman Press, 1975), 1. "come January": Lamis, *The Two-Party South,* 39. "cue from George Wallace": Lowndes, *From the New Deal to the New Right,* 160. "carried the entire South": Black, "Transformation of the Southern Democratic Party," 1004.

67. "Prodigal South": *Washington Post,* July 17, 1976, "Return of the Prodigal South." "finished behind Ford among white southerners": Everett Carll Ladd, "The Brittle Mandate: Electoral Dealignment and the 1980 Presidential Election," *Political Science Quarterly,* 96, 1, Spring 1981, 14; Everett Carll Ladd, "On Mandates, Realignments, and the 1984 Presidential Election," *Political Science Quarterly,* 100, 1, Spring 1985, 13.

68. "order and stability to the traditionalists": Burns, *Crosswinds of Freedom,* 628–629. "Philadelphia, Mississippi": *Washington Post,* August 11, 1980, "Chilling Words in Neshoba County," by Andrew Young. See also Lowndes, *From the New Deal to the New Right,* 160.

69. "60 Minutes": *Washington Post,* October 27, 1980, "Carter: Toll of a Clockwork Presidency." See also Burns, *Crosswinds of Freedom,* 530. "The vote": Interestingly, the southern districts that remained the most loyal to the Democrats in 1980 were the ones that had voted for George Wallace in 1968, suggesting that while Wallace's third party may have served as a bridge to the GOP for some Democrats, for others it represented—at least temporarily—a return ticket home. See Shafer and Johnston, *End of Southern Exceptionalism,* 169.

70. "outnumbered Republicans": *Christian Science Monitor,* July 27, 1984, "Reagan Plunges Into Campaign." "young white southerners": Petrocik, "Realignment: New Party Coalitions and the Nationalization of the South," 362. "more of a southern president": Merle Black, quoted in *New York Times,* October 16, 1986, "Splintering of Once-solid South."

71. Burns, *Crosswinds of Freedom,* 628–629, 636.

72. See Bruce Miroff, "From Friends to Foes: George McGovern, Hubert Humphrey, and the Fracture in American Liberalism," paper presented at conference "Rethinking Liberalism," March 20, 2009, Boston University.

73. "South had boosted its clout": Florida gained four seats after the 1980 census, Texas three, and Tennessee one. "increased its representation": *Washington Post,* April 7, 1981, "17 House Seats." "greatest regional prize": Black and Black, *Divided America,* xiv.

74. Richard Moe, Mondale's former chief of staff, quoted in *New York Times,* February 15, 1987, "Taking a Stand for Dixie's 1988 Vote."

75. "realignment": *New York Times,* October 30, 1988, "South, Key for the Democrats." The election was the "supreme test of realignment," commented a Republican pollster. "Reagan gave the Republicans a shot in the arm, but they were on their own this time." "new kind of Dixiecrat party": *New York Times,* April 5, 1989, "The Capital," by R. W. Apple.

76. James MacGregor Burns and Georgia Sorenson, *Dead Center: Clinton-Gore Leadership* (New York: Scribner's, 1999), 67–69. Clinton's criticism of the wel-

fare system during his campaign, interpreted by some as a coded message to white voters, convinced some observers that he was playing "divisive racial politics." On the other hand, because he had the votes of the vast majority of blacks, he did not need to win a majority of the white vote.

77. "first southern Republican candidate": Shafer and Johnston, *End of Southern Exceptionalism,* 199. "fewer popular votes": Gerald Pomper, "The Presidential Election," in *The Election of 2000: Reports and Interpretations,* ed. Pomper (New York: Chatham House, 2001), 125.

78. James Ceaser and Andrew Busch, *Red over Blue: The 2004 Elections and American Politics* (Lanham, Md.: Rowman and Littlefield, 2005), 6.

79. "landmark election": Ceaser and Busch, *Red over Blue,* 19–21. "Fred Barnes": *Weekly Standard,* November 22, 2004, "Realignment, Now More Than Ever."

80. Four of the six New England states voted for Gerald Ford in 1976, but all six voted for John Kerry.

81. Ceaser and Busch, *Red over Blue,* 12.

Epilogue

1. "high turnout": See *New York Times,* November 6, 2008, "Obama Makes Historic Inroads in South." Obama picked up 42 percent of the white vote in Florida, 39 percent in Virginia, and 35 percent in North Carolina. See also Ronald Walters, "The Black Vote Stopping the Republican Realignment," *Phylon,* 49, 3–4, Autumn-Winter 2001, 219–228.

2. Gallup poll 2005: www.gallup.com/poll/19891/Bush-Approval-37.aspx. Gallup poll 2008: www.gallup.com/poll/106426/Bush-Job-Approval-28-Lowest-Administration.aspx. "Wake County": *New York Times,* November 5, 2008, "Obama Makes Historic Inroads in South."

3. McCain in the South: McCain won by 9 percent in South Carolina, 11 percent in Texas, 13 percent in Mississippi, 15 percent in Tennessee, 19 percent in Louisiana, 20 percent in Arkansas, and 21 percent in Alabama. The vote in Alabama was 1,264,879 votes to 811,764. "there's no other explanation": *New York Times,* November 11, 2008, "For South, a Waning Hold on National Politics." Other analysts contend that factors other than race play a role. Byron E. Shafer and Richard Johnson, *The End of Southern Exceptionalism: Class, Race, and Partisan Change in the Postwar South* (Cambridge, Mass.: Harvard University Press, 2006). Shafer and Johnston see the partisan realignment of the South as having been based on economics rather than race, but the attempt to completely disentangle race and economics underestimates considerable evidence of the power of race in southern politics, at least from the 1960s through 1980s. "affluent whites": Mark D. Brewer and Jeffrey Stonecash, "Class, Race Issues, and

Declining White Support for the Democratic Party in the South," *Political Behavior,* 23, 2, June 2001, 131.

4. Gallup poll: *New York Times,* January 29, 2009, "The Opinionator: Where Did All The Republicans Go?" See also Gallup poll: www.gallup.com/poll/114016/State-States-Political-Party-Affiliation.aspx. There were thirty-five states with significant pluralities of adults identifying themselves as Democrats and only five states—Utah, Idaho, Wyoming, Nebraska, and Alaska—in which a plurality of adults identified as Republicans. The most competitive region in recent presidential elections (that is, the region with the closest races) has been the Midwest, especially Ohio, Michigan, Wisconsin, Minnesota, Iowa, and, in 2008, Indiana. The governors' mansions in the West and Midwest also told an interesting story of shifting political winds. In 2009, one could journey from the Canadian border to Mexico though Montana, Wyoming, Colorado, Arizona, and New Mexico, with detours into the midwestern states of Kansas and Oklahoma, and not pass through a single state with a Republican governor. In addition, in 2009, more than half of the congressional delegations from Arizona, Nevada, and Colorado and all of the New Mexico delegation were Democrats—and both of Montana's senators as well as Colorado's were Democrats. "2008 vote in southern states:" See *New York Times,* November 6, 2008, "Obama Makes Historic Inroads in South."

5. "ethnic diversity and inclusion": See Merle Black, "The Transformation of the Southern Democratic Party," *Journal of Politics,* 66, 4, November 2004, 1002. "name of Theodore Roosevelt:" *Washington Post,* February 21, 2010, "At CPAC, Glenn Beck Scolds Republican Party."

6. "Democratic Party early": Roger Biles, *The South and the New Deal* (Lexington: University Press of Kentucky, 1994), 151. "maxed out": *New York Times,* November 11, 2008, "For South, a Waning Hold." The "emerging Republican majority" that Kevin Phillips so perspicaciously discerned in 1970 may have deteriorated, after forty years of notable success, into the emerging Republican minority. See Kevin Phillips, *The Emerging Republican Majority* (Garden City, N.Y.: Anchor Books, 1970). "Might as well designate": William E. Leuchtenburg, *The White House Looks South* (Baton Rouge: Louisiana State University Press, 2005), 397. "wag the Republican dog": quoted in *Eye of the Storm: The South and Congress in an Era of Change,* ed. John Kuzenski, Laurence Moreland, and Robert Steed (Westport, Conn.: Praeger, 2001), 197. "Before the Republican leaders leap blithely at the political bait in the South they will want to look at the consequences," wrote *Washington Post* columnist Roscoe Drummond in December 1956, when Republicans were beginning to make their gains in the South. Would it really help the party, he asked, to create for itself a "right-of-Eisenhower southern conservative wing deeply opposed to the party's national

policies on civil rights?" For a few decades, that right-of-Eisenhower position did help the party—but by the year 2008, the consequences Drummond had warned about in 1956 had become real. "right-of-Eisenhower wing": *Washington Post*, December 8, 1956, "A GOP in Dixie?" by Roscoe Drummond.

7. "purge the Republican Party of moderates": *Washington Post*, November 1, 2009, "In a War within GOP." Others included Michigan's representative Joe Schwarz, Maryland's representative Wayne Gilchrest, and New York's newcomer Dierdre Scozzafava.

8. "Tweedledum and Tweedledummer": *Washington Post*, August 11, 1939, "Roosevelt Will Bolt."

9. "Social Security:" Social Security Online, www.ssa.gov/history/tally.html; *New York Times*, June 20, 1935, "Security Measure Passed by Senate."

10. "Krugman:" *New York Times*, March 4, 2010, "Senator Bunning's Universe."

11. "doors open:" *New York Times*, May 25, 2009, "Powell Jousts with Cheney."

12. "the path to realignment": See V. O. Key, "Secular Realignment and the Party System," *Journal of Politics*, 21, 1, May 1959, 198, 209.

13. Political scientist Sidney Milkis points out that Arthur Schlesinger, Jr., warned President John Kennedy in 1962 to avoid involvement in the 1962 congressional primaries, giving the example of FDR's failed purge. Lyndon Johnson also declined to influence intraparty politics. President Richard Nixon, however, did take sides in the New York state Republican primary in 1970, lending his support to conservative candidate James Buckley, effectively purging the moderate incumbent Charles Goodell while also stirring up a negative backlash among GOP regulars. See Milkis, "Presidential Leadership and Party Responsibility," in *Presidents and Their Parties: Leadership or Neglect,* ed. Robert Harmel (New York: Praeger, 1984), 170–171.

Acknowledgments

I AM DEEPLY GRATEFUL to many friends, colleagues, and students for their contributions to this book. James T. Patterson generously advised me on various aspects of this project. His book *Congressional Conservatism and the New Deal* inspired me with its insights into the political history of the 1930s. Bruce Miroff made invaluable suggestions about parties and realignment. Milton Djuric once again tirelessly helped me research the intricacies of New Deal politics and offered innumerable substantive and stylistic suggestions for the manuscript. Mark Stoler also gave me his perspicacious advice. Cynthia Koch and Robert Clark at the FDR Library in Hyde Park helped me navigate my way through the extensive presidential archives. And Kate Scott in the U.S. Senate Historical Office supplied key information.

My student Tyler Hull greatly aided me in Williamstown and in Hyde Park in researching various aspects of the purge. Two other Williams students, Ryan Ford and Alex Tanton, also ably assisted me in this project. Alison O'Grady, Jo-Ann Irace, Rebecca Ohm, Linda McGraw, and Wendy Sherman at the Williams College library; Robin Keller at the Faculty Secretarial Office; and Mark Connor, Terri-Lynn Hurley and Lynn Melchiori at the Williams Office of Information Technology all skillfully assisted me, often beyond the call of duty. And I am especially grateful to three Deans of Faculty at Williams College—Thomas Kohut, William Wagner, and Andrea Danyluk—and to the chair of Leadership Studies, James McAllister, for their most collegial support of my teaching and research.

I am indebted to my talented editor at Harvard University Press, Kathleen McDermott, for her many astute suggestions for the manuscript. And my agents, Ike Williams and Katherine Flynn, contributed their ideas while enthusiastically cheering me on.

And once again, my deepest appreciation and my love go to James MacGregor Burns, whose books *Roosevelt: The Lion and the Fox* and *Roosevelt: The Soldier of Freedom* continually astonished me with their brilliance and originality. Jim read and reread my manuscript, contributing his intimate knowledge of Franklin Roosevelt and sharing with me, once again, his optimism, energy, and Rooseveltian generosity of spirit.

Index